Beulah Bondi

ALSO BY AXEL NISSEN
AND FROM McFARLAND

---

*Agnes Moorehead on Radio, Stage and Television* (2017)

*Accustomed to Her Face: Thirty-Five Character
Actresses of Golden Age Hollywood* (2016)

*Mothers, Mammies and Old Maids: Twenty-Five
Character Actresses of Golden Age Hollywood* (2012)

*Actresses of a Certain Character: Forty Familiar Hollywood
Faces from the Thirties to the Fifties* (2006; paperback 2011)

# Beulah Bondi

*A Life on Stage and Screen*

AXEL NISSEN

McFarland & Company, Inc., Publishers
*Jefferson, North Carolina*

Library of Congress Cataloguing-in-Publication Data

Names: Nissen, Axel, author.
Title: Beulah Bondi : a life on stage and screen / Axel Nissen.
Description: Jefferson, North Carolina : McFarland & Company, Inc.,
Publishers, 2021 | Includes bibliographical references and index.
Identifiers: LCCN 2021015837 | ISBN 9781476681887 (paperback : acid free paper) ∞
ISBN 9781476642598 (ebook)
Subjects: LCSH: Bondi, Beulah, 1892-1981. | Motion picture actors and actresses—
United States—Biography. | BISAC: PERFORMING ARTS / Film /
History & Criticism | PERFORMING ARTS / Theater / History & Criticism
Classification: LCC PN2287.B48555 N57 2021 | DDC 791.4302/8092 [B]—dc23
LC record available at https://lccn.loc.gov/2021015837

British Library cataloguing data are available

ISBN (print) 978-1-4766-8188-7
ISBN (ebook) 978-1-4766-4259-8

Front cover image: Beulah Bondi in *The Furies* (1950)

Printed in the United States of America

*McFarland & Company, Inc., Publishers
Box 611, Jefferson, North Carolina 28640
www.mcfarlandpub.com*

To Liv Nissen
*You and me against the world*

# Table of Contents

# Preface

"The fortunate person is the one who has something he or she wants to do and is able to do it. I'm really happiest when I'm acting."[1]

Beulah Bondi (1889–1981) lived a long life, full of meaning, creative activity, harmony, and joy. There is much to be learned from such a life. My chief purpose as Bondi's first biographer has been to establish the facts of that life and then to give a shape to the telling of those facts that makes her experience and achievements meaningful for others. When writing about a subject that has not been extensively treated before, there is a thrilling sense of discovery at every turn, but there are also myriad less interesting facts and incidents that are whirled up by the biographer's time machine. They must surface, but need not show. The trick is to find the story that matters.

Assuming that most of my readers come to this book out of a love for Hollywood in its so-called Golden Age or, possibly, out of a love for the American theater, I have given emphasis to Bondi's career over her private life and to her career on the stage and the screen over her work in other media. I am confident that the importance of her film work overshadows everything else she achieved, but I have also chosen to dwell on her stage career, both for its intrinsic interest and for the reflected light it sheds on her work in film. There are both continuities and contrasts between these two, partially overlapping, career paths, which are mutually illuminating and reflective of the era Bondi was active in.

Beulah Bondi had different dreams than most of the girls she grew up with in Indiana at the turn of the last century. Her life would follow a different path. Part of this story is how she struggled to find that path; how a young girl from an upper middle-class family in a small, quiet college town managed to make it in a profession that was still not quite respectable and became one of the most admired actresses of her day. Though she was not a movie star in the usual sense and her name was never a household word, she gained a respect and recognition both within the entertainment industry and with audiences, that many movie stars might envy her. Like Agnes Moorehead, Beulah Bondi was that anomaly in the movie business: the star character actress.

Bondi had an uncanny ability to be in the right place at the right time, but she had a lot to make up for. Her professional acting career did not begin until she was 30 years old. All that went before had been a long preparation, lovingly presided over by her mother, Eva Marble Bondy, who guided and trained her and remained till the end the most important person in her daughter's life. Bondi recalled that her mother "believed in

1

raising and expanding consciousness—in letting go of the past, planning for the future, and living in the now."[2] I have often found with actresses of a certain period and generation, even those who marry, that their bond with their mother remains primary in their life.

Bondi was a rich woman with what many actors lack: a keen business sense. She was a tough-as-nails negotiator, who had the guts and the insight to turn down Samuel Goldwyn's offer of a seven-year contract after only one film, and never looked back. So, unlike so many contract players, who were put into anything and everything, Bondi handpicked every role. She was so cautious and protective of her own artistic reputation, that she even scorned the hegira for an actor after the advent of television—the recurring role in a series—because she could not know how the character would develop. She could have been Grandma Walton, but preferred to play a featured role in two episodes of *The Waltons* instead.[3] The second of these proved her final performance and garnered her an Emmy in 1977.

Bondi was Victorian in some ways and modern in others. She was prim and proper, rather than prudish. She was spiritual, rather than conventionally religious. She was always looking to learn from life, both to improve her craft and to broaden her horizons. According to a 1938 feature article: "Miss Bondi believes that to be successful in character work on stage or screen, a player must like and understand every class of people and must have no racial or social prejudices."[4] She said in 1977, when she was 88, on the subject of modern films: "I go to films to learn. Good acting, good writing, good directing, all the technical parts is what I learn from. I'm not squeamish; it's just I don't yearn for the other."[5] She stopped acting in movies in 1963 mainly due to the lack of congenial material. As always, her timing was impeccable.

Like most women of her generation, especially actresses, Bondi did not tell her age (at least not her correct one) and she did not socialize on the set. "Working with different stars," she said, "I've enjoyed each and every one, and have always had this great empathy and feeling for them. But I couldn't socialize with them…. Between scenes I have to be by myself. That way the character stays with me. I knew the stars as the characters they played."[6] With this in mind, and considering that she died nearly 40 years ago, I have not expended any great energy in seeking living witnesses to her life. Her glory days in the 1930s have all but passed out of living memory.

I have done extensive genealogical research into Bondi's family background, which is unusual and captivating, and I have also sought to recreate parts of her social circle in detail. Stars do not live their lives surrounded by other stars, no matter what the papers and the columnists might want us to believe; nor do character actors live their lives surrounded by stars or other character actors. They live their lives largely as ordinary people do, surrounded by ordinary people. In Bondi's case, she kept half a dozen of her youthful friendships from her Indiana hometown her entire life, in addition to a much more eclectic and changeable circle of friends in Los Angeles, New York, and elsewhere.

Beulah Bondi will surprise you, as she did me. Who knew that she had once been a kindergarten teacher? That was in Vernal, Utah, when she was in her mid–20s. Who knew that she starred in the first American opera ever written by a Native American? That was back in 1913, six years before the start of her professional acting career. Who knew that she could ride a horse and did her own riding in *Lone Star* with Clark Gable, when she was 62? Admittedly, she fell off the horse. Who knew that she was still driving and could read a menu without glasses in her late 80s?[7] Who could imagine that venerable, genteel, spiritual Beulah Bondi made the best daiquiris her friend, the veteran wine columnist Robert Balzer, ever tasted? He once walked in on her "at work at her blender" and discovered that her secret was a single lime Lifesaver.[8]

I have not uncovered any scandals or deep secrets in Bondi's life. I was not expecting to. Partially, this is because her work was her life for a large part of that life. Though she had many close friends and strong ties to her family, her private life was in most ways uneventful. She suffered, of course, the ups and downs, the small disappointments and the large griefs, that all people experience. Maybe she even felt a passion towards some individual at some point. Maybe the feeling was mutual. It is hard to know at this late date. As far as her private life is concerned, I concentrate on what I *do* know, namely that—beyond her work, her friends, her many hobbies and interests—her overriding passion was to be a good daughter. Abram and Eva Bondy gave her a start in life in the quiet, idyllic college town of Valparaiso, Indiana, that anyone might envy her. She never ceased to be grateful for that gift.

Bondi did have one well-kept secret, though it was hardly the stuff of gossip columns. She was at least half Jewish. I say "at least," because I am uncertain about her mother's ethnic background. I do know that Eva Marble Bondy was a Presbyterian and, while the possibility of a Jewish Presbyterian cannot be ruled out, it does not seem the most likely combination. That means that Bondi was probably the result of what used to be called a "mixed" marriage. I had a theory that this marriage might have caused the rift I had sensed in the Bondy clan. It turns out, there was another cause for that.

Bondi chose to keep her Jewish heritage a secret, I suspect, out of a reasonable fear that, if revealed, it might have a detrimental effect on her career. She knew that an identifiably Jewish actress would never have been vaunted as "Everybody's Mother," as read the heading of a feature article on Bondi in January 1947, where she was also identified as the "Typical American Mother" and "the personification of motherhood to casting directors just as she is to movie fans." For, the article assures us, "the movie mother must be acceptable to each movie goer as his own idea of 'mother.'" A Jewish character actress, then, would never have been cast five times as James Stewart's mother or, for that matter, three times as Lionel Barrymore's wife. As things were, the writer assures his readers, "when Jimmy Stewart winds an arm around her [Bondi's] shoulders and looks at her affectionately and says with a lilt of love in his voice, 'Hiya, Mom,' ... the audience accepts the 'relationship' with complete satisfaction."[9]

Had Bondi allowed herself to be identified as the daughter of a second-generation Jewish immigrant with parents whose first language was Yiddish, she might easily have ended up with Ann Brody's jobs, rather than her own high-profile career. Who was Ann Brody, you ask? Well, that is exactly the point. How many major Jewish character actresses can you name? There was Florence Bates, but she changed her surname from Jacoby to Bates. Bondi only changed the final letter of hers.

Not only did Bondi avoid direct identification with an ethnic minority, she also studiously avoided any film role with an ethnic slant. This had not been the case during her stage career. As we shall see, she played both Native American and African American characters in stock in the 1920s. We might wish she had not. Yet once she came to Hollywood, she never again took an ethnic role. She quickly learned that in films ethnic meant marginal. Bondi also assiduously avoided servant roles on the big screen. If you played a maid, you ran the risk of being treated like one.

All things considered, Beulah Bondi had an enviable life. She is a good example of what happiness can come with finding your rightful place in the world, of finding out what you like to do most and doing it as much and as often as possible. As you might expect, what Bondi liked to do most was to act. But not only that. She also loved to travel. At an age when many settle comfortably into their rocking chairs or recliners, she was jet-setting around to the four corners of the globe. She traveled around the world twice. She went to Africa four times.[10] She celebrated Tito's 80th birthday with the Serbian leader in Belgrade. She climbed Mt. Sinai "to the very peak, riding horses and camels and whatever I could."[11] She loved Hawaii and deserts. She collected elephants and made jam. Her comfortable Spanish Colonial home in Whitley Heights, where she lived for 40 years, was filled with art works from around the world, rather than Hollywood memorabilia.[12]

Bondi's friends were connoisseurs, artists, intellectuals, and other truth seekers and a tight-knit group of women she had grown up with in Valparaiso. She had an affinity for painters and counted well-known mid-century artists like Joseph Cummings Chase, Robert Lee Eskridge, Alfredo Ramos Martinez, Juanita Vitousek, and Robert Strong Woodward among her personal friends. According to Richard Lamparski, "she was never part of the Hollywood scene": "She was more interested in good books, metaphysics, and world politics than in Hollywood."[13] Bondi was not distracted for a moment by the glitz and glamor of Tinseltown. She sought no influence, she sought no favors, she sought no hue and cry beyond the respect and recognition of her peers and the love of her audience. She once said: "I never cause any riots."[14] I love that. That is vintage Bondi: Insightful, wry, never self-pitying. What she wanted was "to be able to gain an inner response from an audience." "An actress who gives a great performance," she said, "makes a gathering of people feel at one with her emotionally."[15]

While few industry players and movie folk gathered at her home, some young actors, like her *Track of the Cat* co-star Tab Hunter, came under her wing. He never forgot her and wrote in his 2005 memoir: "When she spoke to you, you knew she was speaking from her soul."[16] Others also testified to Bondi's strong, charismatic presence. Here is one such encounter described in 1937: "Professionally speaking, I have held hands with quite a few stellar lights. Holding Bondi's hand, momentarily, was entirely different. I have never felt such harmonious vibrations come from any other player. Right away we chimed."[17] Though Bondi had an iron constitution and might well have lived to be a 100, she was accident-prone. That would ultimately be her undoing in her 92nd year.

There are thousands of books about movie stars, but there is only one book about Beulah Bondi. It is an awesome responsibility to write the story of someone's life. All the more, when that story is being told in book-length form for the first time. Yet at the end of the intriguing and engaging process writing this biography has been, I am most aware of a feeling of gratitude: Gratitude that I was able to tell this story and gratitude to the remarkable woman who lived it. I have dedicated this book to another remarkable woman: my mother Liv.

*Note*: A few abbreviations are used throughout the text to indicate the source of material. BBP refers to the Beulah Bondi Papers, Margaret Herrick Library, Academy of Motion Picture Arts and Sciences; NYPL refers to the Beulah Bondi clipping file, Billy Rose Theatre Division, New York Public Library for the Performing Arts; WCFTR refers to the Beulah Bondi clipping file, Wisconsin Center for Film and Theater Research.

# 1

# Valparaiso, Indiana
## *Early Life and Career*

"What we are today is the result of all our yesterdays."[1]

"I was born with women's lib."[2]

You can take the girl out of Valparaiso, but you cannot take Valparaiso out of the girl. There is a sense in which this story begins and ends with Valparaiso, Indiana, the place that shaped Beulah Bondi's identity and values more than any other, though she was neither born nor buried there, and moved away for good when she was in her mid–30s. Even so, she kept coming back, both in a spiritual and in a literal sense. She kept coming back even after her family ties with the town were sundered by the death of her parents and her Uncle Lou, who had instigated the family's move there and would be the last Bondy to remain. She would come back for flying visits whenever she could on her journeys between the coasts, between New York and Los Angeles. She would come back to be honored by her community as the most famous person of her day that Valparaiso had produced.

But Bondi's story does not begin in Valparaiso, it begins in Geisa, Germany, and in Rising Sun, Indiana. At least part of it does. The question of where an individual's story begins is an intriguing and complex one. How far back do you go? I am prepared to go back to Bondi's grandparents, to the grandfathers she never knew, Gabriel Bondy and Jonathan Marble; and to two long-lived grandmothers, Mary Rosenblatt Bondy and Melissa Fisher Marble, that Bondi grew up with. Mary came from Geisa. Melissa came from Rising Sun.

Geisa is a quiet, picturesque old town in the Ulster Valley in the present-day province of Thuringia and lies squarely in the middle of Germany. Before reunification, it had the distinction of being the westernmost municipality in East Germany. Back when Bondi's paternal grandmother Mary Rosenblatt lived there in the mid–nineteenth century, the town was part of the Grand Duchy of Saxe-Weimar-Eisensach (Saxony) and was a predominantly Catholic area. Mary was Jewish and had Yiddish as her first language.[3] There is a well-preserved Jewish cemetery on the outskirts of Geisa, where Bondi's ancestors lie buried. Two disastrous fires in 1858 and 1883 destroyed most of the town Mary grew up in.[4]

Mary was born on July 25, 1825, the daughter of Meyer and Miriam Rosenblatt.[5] She immigrated to the United States in 1842, when she was 17 years old.[6] She had an older brother, Elias M. Rosenblatt, who also immigrated, but that was 20 years later. Mary met and married Gabriel Bondy around 1850. Gabriel had immigrated from Bohemia, which today forms a large part of the Czech Republic.[7] His first language was also Yiddish.[8] There is some conflicting evidence about when he was born, but he was probably 20 years older than Mary.[9] They were married for 35 years and had four children who lived to maturity and three who died young.[10] Sarah, who would be known as Estelle, was born in Philadelphia in 1851; Louis was born in Philadelphia in 1852; Abram, who was also known as Abraham or Adolph, was born in Port Huron, Michigan, in 1856; and Rachel, who would be known as Rose, was born in Philadelphia in 1862.[11] Abram was Beulah Bondi's father.

Gabriel Bondy is variously described in the census as a capmaker (1850), clothing merchant (1860), dealer in dry goods (1870), and retired merchant (1885).[12] Gabriel and Mary initially lived in Philadelphia, before moving to Port Huron in the mid–1850s. They were living in Port Huron when the census was taken in 1860 and were wealthy enough to have a live-in maid. The family's property was valued at $900 and their personal estate at $1,500.[13] Port Huron lies at the southernmost end of Lake Huron on the border with Canada. This is where Bondi's father was born on September 9, 1856.[14]

By 1870, the Bondys had relocated to Davenport, Iowa, the largest of the Quad Cities on the Mississippi River, which separates eastern Iowa from Illinois. By this time, Gabriel was in the dry goods business, a business his eldest son Louis would also enter. Eighteen-year-old Louis had left home, but three of the Bondys' children were still living at home: Estelle, who was 19; Abram, who was 14; and Rose, who was 8. The value of the family's real estate had risen to $21,500 and their personal effects were valued at $400.[15]

Fast forward 15 years. In the 1885 Iowa State Census, we find Gabriel Bondy living alone at 402 W. 5th St. in Davenport. A bartender, his wife, and daughter are living in the same building, which is no longer standing on the corner of N. Ripley St. in the Hamburg Historic District. The Scott County sheriff's office, jail, and courthouse are directly across 5th St. from the parking lot where Gabriel's house once stood, with a slender single track of railway line running parallel to the street. Gabriel Bondy was 80 years old according to the census, which makes his year of birth 1805. He is listed as a "Retired Merchant" and as being married.[16]

Gabriel died the evening of Thursday, November 26, 1885. Ironically, due to a couple of news items in the local press, we have more details about his death than we do about his life. On November 29, the *Quad-City Times* carried the following article on the front page:

> Mr. G. Bondy, a longtime resident of this city [Davenport], died in Mercy Hospital Thursday evening last. He had been sick alone in his home corner of Fifth and Ripley streets several days—and was conveyed to the hospital when he was past recovery. His age was eighty years. He was quite well off at one time. A son lives in Valparaiso, Ind., and Mrs. L. Flexner, of this city, is his daughter. The funeral announcement is given elsewhere.[17]

The funeral announcement was on the last page of this four-page newspaper and there was a full report of the funeral in paper the following day. Gabriel was buried from his home at 10 a.m. on the first Sunday after his death. The *Davenport Democrat* relates:

> The late Mr. Bondy was a descendant of a great Jewish family known for centuries as rabbis, physicians and bankers. The deceased was a great Hebrew scholar, an earnest adherent to the old school and very orthodox. According to the directions he was attended to in the most

particulars according to the ancient Jewish customs. His son and daughter were present. The services were conducted by Rev. Isaac Fall at the home and at the grave. The officers and the members of the congregation and their ladies and many other Israelites paid their respects accompanying the remains to their resting place. In the evening a special prayer meeting was held to enable Mr. L.D. Bondy the son, who leaves the city, to recite the prayer for the dead according to the Jewish faith.[18]

There are several things to note about both news articles relating to Gabriel's death and burial. First and foremost, his widow Mary is not mentioned in either of them, nor are his two youngest children, Abram and Rose. The son mentioned here is Louis D. Bondy, who was 33, single, and had lived in Valparaiso, Indiana, since the 1870s. The daughter being referred to is Estelle Bondy, who had married Leopold Flexner in Davenport on April 17, 1872. Leopold was born in 1836 and emigrated from Vienna in 1866. He had trained as an architect in Europe, but was "at the head of a flourishing sash, door and blind business at Front and Perry streets" in Davenport. The couple lived in that city for many years and raised five children there at 319 E. 11th St., before moving to Portland, Oregon, in 1908.[19]

So where was Mary Bondy? She was living with Louis, the very son who in late November 1885 traveled 200 miles westward from his home in Valparaiso to make sure his father received a proper Jewish burial, while his mother stayed behind. In 1880, 24-year-old Abram and 18-year-old Rose, still unmarried, were also living with their older brother and their mother in Valparaiso. The most interesting thing, though, in the 1880 census, which is the source of this information, is that under the heading "Civil Condition," where the choices are "Single," "Married," or "Widowed. Divorced," Mary is listed as widowed.[20]

Based on the totality of this information, there is no other conclusion to draw than that sometime in the 1870s Gabriel and Mary Bondy went their separate ways. Gabriel considered himself married until he died, and legally he was; while Mary may have been passing herself off as a widow in her new home town. She lived in Valparaiso for more than 20 years with her eldest son Louis, who never married and who became the head of the extended Bondy family on his father's death. There was a perception in Valparaiso, which is expressed in Louis's 1937 obituary, that "when a young man his father died, and he became the sole support of his mother and brother and sister."[21] This was true up to a point, only Louis was 33 when his father died and, as we have seen, he had become the support of his mother and two younger siblings before that.

In 1900, Mary and Louis were living on the corner of Lafayette and Jefferson, just two blocks south west of Bondi's childhood home on N. Washington St. in Valparaiso, so Bondi would have known her German-born grandmother well.[22] Bondi was nearly 18 when Mary Rosenblatt Bondy died on March 19, 1907, at the age of 81. She passed away while visiting her daughter Rose Hirschman in Milwaukee and she lies buried with the Hirschmans in Greenwood Cemetery.[23]

Rising Sun, Indiana, is a pleasant and prosperous-looking community in Randolph township, directly on the Ohio River, and looks across the river to the northernmost tip of Kentucky. These days, Cincinnati is only 45 minutes away by car. This small town has been the county seat in Ohio county since it was created in 1844 and centers around the Greek Revival courthouse from 1845, completed the year Beulah Bondi's maternal grandmother, Melissa Fisher, married here for the first time. It is "the oldest continuously operating county courthouse in Indiana."[24] The population of Rising Sun was 1,674 in 1850.

Practically the entire town was designated a national historic district in 2006 with 322 contributing buildings and two contributing sites.[25] Still vibrant and tenanted, Main St. terminates on its southern end in a picturesque pavilion on the river. The First United Church of Christ in red brick is an interesting example of the Gothic Revival style with a touch of Second Empire in its mansard-roofed bell tower. Though sometimes marred by homeowners' predilection for vinyl siding and standing seam metal roofs, Rising Sun contains many fine examples of nineteenth-century domestic architecture, particularly on North and South High Street, which remains the town's premier residential street. Maybe Melissa lived in one of these old houses, either as a young girl or a married woman. Unfortunately, the U.S. census for 1830, 1840, and 1850 does not contain address information.

Melissa Fisher was born in Rising Sun in April 1829, 13 years after the town was registered.[26] She was the youngest of the eight children of Jacob Fisher, a farmer born in Pennsylvania in 1787, and his wife Susanna Hawk (aka Hock), born in Pennsylvania in 1791.[27] Melissa had just turned 16, when she married Daniel Clark on May 1, 1845.[28] On March 19, 1846, she gave birth to her first child, Wilson Daniel Clark. Her husband Daniel died sometime in the late 1840s, after only a few years of marriage. A widow before she was 20, Melissa went on to marry Jonathan W. Marble on June 27, 1849.[29] Jonathan was Beulah Bondi's maternal grandfather, though she never knew him. He was born in Pennsylvania in 1811 and was 18 years older than Melissa.[30]

This was the second marriage for Jonathan as well. He had married Eleanor Clark in 1833 in what was then Dearborn county, and the couple had two daughters.[31] Only Sarah, known as "Sallie," born in 1839, survived. She was part of the Marble household for the first dozen years of Jonathan and Melissa's marriage until she wed a well-to-do Hendricks county, Indiana farmer, William H. Hughes (aka Hughs), in 1862. Sallie spent her married life on a farm in Lincoln township, which is 130 miles south of Valparaiso, and raised seven children there. She died in 1894, when she was 55 and her niece Beulah was five. Sallie Hughes and her husband are buried in Brownsburg Cemetery.[32] Melissa's son Wilson Clark was also part of the Marble family, until he married Margaret Scott in the late 1870s. Wilson was a brick layer and he and his family lived in Sheridan, Indiana, until his death from consumption in 1895 at 49. He and his wife are buried in Crown View Cemetery in Sheridan.[33]

In the census, Jonathan Marble is variously identified as a cabinet maker (1850), farmer (1860), and "laborer furniture" (1870).[34] He died sometime in the 1870s. During the years of his and Melissa's marriage, they lived first in Rising Sun and then, by 1860, on a farm in Carroll township near Danville, Illinois, which is about 200 miles to the north west from Rising Sun, beyond Indianapolis. Jonathan and Melissa had their first child, Olive, in Rising Sun in June 1851.[35] Their second child was also a daughter, Eva Susanna Marble, born after their move to the farm in Carroll township on January 19, 1860, and raised in the nearby town of Danville.[36] She was partly named for Melissa's mother Susanna, who died in Rising Sun in December 1860 and is buried in Union Cemetery, where several Fishers and Marbles lie buried. Jacob Fisher died in 1865.[37] Eva Susanna Marble was Beulah Bondi's mother. Fifty-six years after her own birth and her grandmother's death, Eva dedicated a privately printed edition of her poems to "the memory of Susanna Fisher, a pioneer mother of Indiana, and her daughter Melissa, born in Ohio County, 1829."[38]

Eva's older sister Olive married Henry D. Pollock in Danville in 1877, when she was

26. Henry had just turned 27 and was a farmer's son from Attica, Indiana.[39] After living on a farm in Logan township, Indiana, where their eldest son Edward was born in 1878; and in Emporia, Kansas, the Pollocks ultimately settled in 1883 in Hartford, Kansas, which is a small town in Elmendaro township.[40] Today Hartford has an abandoned, melancholy air. A few nineteenth-century commercial buildings survive on the one block of Commercial St., which used to be called Main St. and which constituted the "business district" of this small community in its heyday. One of these two-story brick buildings, boarded up and abandoned now, may have been Henry and Olive Pollock's drug store.

A tragedy occurred in the Pollock family on the night of Saturday, June 28, 1890. Because he "had been suffering for some time with insomnia, cause by pain produced by disease of the kidneys," Henry took a dose of chloroform that night by saturating a handkerchief and putting it over his face. As the *Hartford News* wrote the next day, Henry "inhaled enough of the drug to close his eyes in that sleep from which none awaken on this earth." Olive found him dead about one o'clock at night. In his obituary in the *Hartford Call*, we can read further about the uncle Bondi never knew: "Henry Pollock had not an enemy on the face of the globe, and today, as we sit in our sanctum writing this article, every business house and workshop in the city is closed in respect to him that was so recently with us, and carried sunshine wherever he went by his kind and pleasing manners."[41] Abram Bondy visited his in-laws the Pollocks in Hartford only six weeks before Henry died.[42]

Compared with her sister Eva, Olive had a hard life. Left a widow at 39 with three children under the age of 13 to provide for, she remarried in 1894. Her second husband was John Martin Coffelt, a "prosperous farmer" and widower eight years her junior, whose wife Lizzie had died in 1892 leaving two sons.[43] Coffelt had lived in Hartford for four years, though he owned a farm 30 miles away near Americus, north of Emporia. The bride was described on this occasion in the local paper as "well and favorably known in this city and vicinity" and as "an estimable lady."[44]

The Coffelts were married for 16 years, but the marriage was not a success. In a telling gesture, the census enumerator who visited Olive and her family during the Kansas state census in 1905 has erased the line with information he had started to fill in on her husband. Clearly, they had separated. John sued Olive for divorce on April 20, 1910, on the grounds of extreme cruelty, gross neglect, and desertion and got his divorce in August that year.[45]

Divorce was still uncommon in 1910 and it was even more uncommon for a husband to divorce his wife. It must have been deeply embarrassing for Olive, her children, and her aged mother Melissa to have her domestic travails trumpeted abroad in her local newspaper. Undoubtedly, her husband intended it to be. Olive was the first person on the Marble side of the family to be divorced, though Bondi had a first cousin on the Bondy side, coincidentally also called Olive, who had been involved in a divorce some years before this that was even more acrimonious, because it involved the custody of a child. After her divorce, Aunt Olive reverted to her original married name of Pollock. John M. Coffelt remarried in 1912 and died in 1917 in Caney, Kansas.[46]

While Bondi would not have known her half-uncle Wilson and half-aunt Sallie, and seen little, if anything, of her Aunt Olive, she knew Grandma Marble as well as Grandma Bondy. Bondi's maternal grandmother Melissa Fisher Clark Marble lived a long life and made her home successively with her two married daughters. In 1900, she was living with Eva and her family in Valparaiso.[47] By 1910, she had moved in with Olive and Olive's children William and Helen at 2408 Chestnut Ave. in Kansas City, Missouri.[48] She died there of "a stroke of paralysis" in her 86th year on April 29, 1914, and was buried with her son-in-law Henry in the Pollock plot in Hartford Cemetery. We can read in the *Hartford Times*, that "the remains were accompanied here by the daughters of the deceased, Mesdames Coffelt, of Kansas City, and A.O. Bondy, of Valparaiso, Ind., and two grandchildren, Miss Helen and William Pollock."[49]

Olive Pollock would join her mother and first husband in Hartford Cemetery five years later. Though she was living in Iola, Kansas, at the time, Olive died in Detroit, Michigan, on March 14, 1919, after a gall stone operation.[50] Her unmarried daughter Helen lived and worked in Detroit as a nurse.[51] Olive Marble Pollock was 67 when she died.

In 1880, with her father dead and her three older siblings all having left home to start their own families, we find 20-year-old Eva Marble and her 51-year-old mother Melissa boarding on Franklin St. in Danville with a German-born cigar manufacturer and his large family.[52] Neither of them was working. That same year, Abram Bondy turned 24 and was living with his mother, older brother Louis, and younger sister Rose in Valparaiso. He is listed in the census as "Clerk in store," probably his older brother's dry goods store on E. Main St.[53] Young Abram had bigger goals in life than working for his brother, though. He would make his living as a traveling salesman for the Van Dyke Knitting Co., a company based in Milwaukee, which was "the largest underwear manufacturer in the West."[54] He worked for that company for 30 years: all through Bondi's childhood and coming of age.[55] It must have put his nearest and dearest in a delicate position, so to speak, when asked what their husband and father did for a living. In public records from these years, Abram is described as a salesman (1882), a traveling salesman (1893), a commercial traveler in knit goods (1900), a salesman (1902), a commercial traveler (1905), and a "Commercial Trav. Underwear" (1910).[56] So Abram was the Willy Loman of his day, though he did not come to such a tragic end. Nor did he "fall in love with long distance," like Tom Wingfield's father in *The Glass Menagerie*.

It would have spurred Abram on to even greater business efforts, that he met and fell in love with Eva Marble sometime in the early 1880s. Jew and Presbyterian, salesman and budding poet, second-generation immigrant and practically a D.A.R., they were an unlikely couple. It must have been a love match. On August 1, 1882, they were married in Cassopolis, Michigan. Neither the bride nor the groom had any family connection with this small community, which lies in Cass county in the southwest corner of the state, not far from the Indiana state line, and only numbered 912 inhabitants in 1880. Cassopolis was the county seat, though, and as such had a county courthouse where the marriage would be registered. The ceremony was performed by a local minister with his wife and daughter as witnesses. "Adolph" was 25 and resident in Chicago, Eva was 22 and living in Danville.[57] I have not found any newspaper accounts of the wedding. To me, it looks as if they eloped.

In this connection, it is also interesting to note that Eva Bondy gave birth to two children in the 19 months and three weeks between her wedding day and March 1884. It is just possible she was not pregnant when they got married, but it must have happened very soon after. Their first child, a boy, died in infancy.[58] Their son Raymond was born in Chicago on March 22, 1884.[59] Thus by the time Gabriel Bondy died in late November 1885, Abram Bondy had married and fathered a living son that Gabriel probably never saw. Raymond would be the last Bondy. When he died in 1959, the family name died with him.

Gabriel's youngest daughter Rose also married before his death and gave birth to a daughter, Leola, in 1883, who would be her only child. Her husband Jacob L. Hirschman was 18 years her senior; had emigrated from Bavaria at the age of nine; and had been associated with the *Detroit Free Press*, where he had begun his career as a cub reporter in the late 1860s.[60]

Rose and Jacob were married December 20, 1882, in the parlors of the Tremont House in Chicago.[61] Two newspaper accounts of the wedding provide us with a unique window on the Bondy family at this time. According to the *Chicago Tribune*, "The ceremony was conducted in accordance with the forms of the Reformed Jewish Church, the Rev. Dr. Hirsch officiating. Only the immediate friends and relatives of the couple were present."[62] These guests included the bride's mother Mary Bondy; her brother Louis Bondy, who also acted as groomsman; her brother Abram Bondy and his wife Eva; and her maternal uncle, Elias M. Rosenblatt. We do not find the bride's father Gabriel Bondy, nor her sister Estelle and brother-in-law Leopold Flexner among the guests listed in the Chicago *Inter Ocean*.[63]

Rose was living in Valparaiso at the time of her wedding and Jacob in Chicago, but the Hirschmans would spend most of their 47-year marriage in Milwaukee, where they moved in 1885 and where Jacob worked for the *Milwaukee Herold*, a German-language daily newspaper, for 39 years, until he retired in 1924.[64] Their daughter Leola Hirschman Sure (1883–1941) had the distinction of being only the second woman elected to the University of Wisconsin board of regents and married a doctor late in life.[65]

Estelle and Rose married within the Jewish faith. It would not have improved the family dynamic that Abram did not. I used to think that the rift in the family might have been due to Abram and Eva's marriage in 1882. I had to revise that theory in light of my discovery that Gabriel and Mary Bondy separated before 1880. The family conflict clearly stemmed from that momentous event, which would have divided loyalties and led, indirectly at least, to the removal of Mary Bondy and three of her children to Valparaiso, 200 miles away from her husband Gabriel, her daughter Estelle, and Estelle's large family.

It may have been an attempt at rapprochement, when in October 1898, 13 years after Gabriel Bondy's death, Estelle Bondy Flexner left Davenport to "make an extended visit with her mother" in Valparaiso.[66] Bondi was nine years old and this was probably the only opportunity she had to know her Aunt Estelle. Estelle died in Portland, Oregon, in 1917 at the age of 66, while her niece was performing with the Chicago Little Theatre.[67] Uncle Leopold died in San Jose, where he was living with his daughter Olive, in 1923 at the age of 87.[68] The estrangement between the Flexners, on the one hand, and the Bondys and Hirschmans, on the other, carried into the next generation and culminated in a sensational legal conflict over Louis Bondy's estate in the early 1940s. More of that later.

Little Beulah was the last of Gabriel and Mary Bondy's eight grandchildren to be born and the only one born after Gabriel's death. She was also the youngest cousin on the Marble side. Not counting Sallie Hughes's and Wilson Clark's children, Bondi had nine first cousins in all. Because only her aunts had children, they were not Bondys and Marbles, but Flexners, Pollocks, and one Hirschman. I have looked into their lives, because it tells us something about where Bondi came from and what kind of life she might have had if fate had willed it otherwise. A remarkable fact is that, with one exception, all her cousins worked for a living. Even in the late nineteenth and early twentieth century, the women worked; and even one of the two married women cousins worked. Another fact is that they produced few offspring of their own in the next generation. These nine cousins and Bondi's brother only had five children in total. Finally, Bondi's extended family was geographically spread. I have calculated that in 1920, Beulah, Raymond and the rest lived in eight different states of the union from Oregon and California to New York; by 1930, they were living in six different states and the Philippines; and by 1940, six different states. The descendants of Gabriel and Mary Bondy and Jonathan and Melissa Marble enacted their own twentieth-century diaspora.

Estelle and Leopold's five children were Vivian, Cora, Olive, Jefferson, and Aimee Flexner. Vivian and Aimee were the first to move to Portland, where they worked as stenographers and court reporters all their lives. Vivian Flexner (1875–1962), the first-born Bondy grandchild, never married.[69] For decades, Aimee Flexner (1884–1943) lived in what used to be called a "Boston marriage" with another woman, Carolyn H. Rich (1887–1960), which lasted till Aimee's death.[70] Cora Flexner (1887–1959) married Carl A. Rhode (1878–1957) in 1900. They lived in Chicago and later in Portland. Cora worked as a stenographer, mercantile clerk, and executive in the U.S. military and Carl mainly as a private investigator.[71] Jefferson E. Flexner (b. 1882) was a civil engineer and later photographer with his own studio and married Blanche Wolf from a socially prominent Jewish family in Louisville, Kentucky, in 1907. He was the first of Bondi's cousins to die. That was in 1924 at the home of his sister Cora in Chicago. He was 41.[72] Finally, the most interesting of the group, Olive Flexner (b. 1880), trained as a teacher, but did not work as one, preferring to make a career of marriage. She was married and divorced three times, until it finally stuck on the fourth attempt in 1930. That may only have been because she was left a widow six years later. Her last husband, Harold Morgan Power, was from a wealthy Placer county, California family. Like her three sisters, Olive Flexner Fearing Baxter Francis Power ended up living in Portland. She died there in 1972 at the age of 92, beating her cousin Beulah as the longest-lived Bondy by a few months.[73]

Olive was unique, too, in that she was the only one of the Flexners to have a child, and not just any child. Her son Kenneth Flexner Fearing, born in 1902, was a well-known proletarian poet and pulp fiction writer, whose most famous novel was *The Big Clock* from 1946. It was made into a film at Paramount in 1948 starring Ray Milland, Charles Laughton, and Maureen O'Sullivan and directed by O'Sullivan's husband John Farrow. It has not hitherto been known that Bondi had a cousin with a connection to the film industry. Kenneth Fearing died in 1961.

On the Marble side, Aunt Olive and Uncle Henry Pollock had three children: Edward Davis Pollock (1878–1934), Helen M. Pollock (b. 1885), and William Wiley Pollock (1888–1968). Edward worked all his life as a mail clerk, Helen was single and worked as a bookkeeper and later as a nurse, and William worked in various clerical positions. Next to Olive Flexner, William Pollock was Bondi's most peripatetic cousin, living in five different states. He was the only one of her cousins to end up living in Los Angeles. Only Edward had children of his own, with his wife Bertha Allee Pollock: Thelma, George, and Christine Pollock, Bondi's first cousins once removed.[74]

Bondi had the satisfaction, if we can call it that, of outliving them all, including the inimitable Olive Flexner, by nearly a decade. She was the youngest cousin, after all. My impression is that Bondi was not close to any of these first cousins, whom were all older than her, whom she did not grow up with, and whose lives followed such different paths from her own. On the other hand, she had a strong bond with her brother Raymond until his death in 1959. Raymond Bondy graduated from Valparaiso College in August 1903 and went to study dentistry in Chicago sometime after that.[75] He graduated from Chicago Dental College on May 26, 1908.[76] That same spring, when he turned 22, he married Sarah W. Cary, known as Sallie, who had been born and raised in Benton Harbor, Michigan. Sallie Cary was born on September 16, 1887, to Woodbridge George Cary and Fanny Bel Toles Cary, and was the only one of their three children to live to maturity.[77] Sallie's parents were divorced, which was unusual and not a little scandalous at this time. Sallie was close to her mother, who supported herself as a music teacher, and there were frequent visits back and forth in the coming years, also separately involving her father, and Raymond's parents in Valparaiso.[78] Sallie Cary was a champion sailor, like her father, "one of the last of the Great Lakes sailors," and her grandfather William M. Cary, who was a sea captain.[79]

After their wedding, the young couple settled in the village of Avon in Fulton county, Illinois, 200 miles southwest of Chicago, where Raymond set up his own dental practice.[80] Their only child, Elizabeth Beulah Bondy, who would be known as Betty, was born there on November 19, 1910.[81] By 1916, Raymond and his family were living at 6413 Harper Ave., next to Jackson Park, in the Woodlawn section of Chicago.[82] By 1927, the year their daughter turned 17, they had moved to 7705 Yates Ave. on Chicago's South Shore.[83] About a year after Betty married in April 1932, Raymond and Sallie divorced.[84] Sallie soon married Detroit advertising executive John Harold "Hal" Ressler, who was 12 years her junior, and moved to his native city. Sallie Cary Ressler died in 1967.[85]

Raymond Bondy was highly successful in his career as a dentist. He was able to retire and move to Florida at the age of 56 and remarried there the same year, that is in 1940. After Raymond's death, his daughter Betty and her family were Bondi's closest living relatives. Betty Bondy Robinson (Markert) had a daughter, also called Elizabeth, in 1935 and died five months shy of her 100th birthday in 2009.[86]

Valparaiso, Indiana, was established as Portersville in 1836 and from the beginning was the county seat of Porter county. It was renamed Valparaiso in 1837 after Valparaiso, Chile, where the man who gave the county its name, Commodore David Porter, fought an important battle in the War of 1812. As we have seen, Abram Bondy had had a family connection with this quiet Indiana college town since the late 1870s. Sometime between 1889 and 1892, he returned to Valparaiso and settled there for good. This time he brought his family, which in addition to his wife Eva and son Raymond, now also consisted of a baby girl. Beulah Bondi was born in Chicago on May 3, 1889.[87] During her lifetime, she was frequently thought to have been born in 1892, or even later than that. I have seen Bondi's birth record and there is no doubt about her date of birth. According to her friend and neighbor Allegra Nesbit: "She always said, 'It's good to keep them guessing.'"[88]

Valparaiso at the turn of the last century was just about the ideal place for a thoughtful, creative young woman from the upper-middle classes to grow up. Close and easily accessible by train to the larger vistas of Chicago, yet with none of the big city's social problems and iniquities, Valparaiso offered a safe and sheltered place for a girl to come of age, especially when her father was hard-working, devoted, and dependable; her mother was one of the most energetic, forward-looking, and respected community organizers and club women in the district; and the family home was located on Valparaiso's most prestigious and attractive residential street.

With a population of 5,000 in 1890, not long before the Bondy family moved there;

it would grow modestly to 6,500 in 1920, the year Bondi made her first, unsuccessful attempt to launch her New York stage career. Bondi lived in Valparaiso till she was in her mid–30s and moved to New York City, having finally gotten a foothold in the theater there. I have noted that in 1902, the year Bondi turned 13, Valparaiso had two daily newspapers, two lunch counters, two restaurants, three banks, seven churches, and 20 saloons. There were also three weekly newspapers and one monthly.[89]

Though the atmosphere of downtown Valparaiso and the residential neighborhood surrounding N. Washington St. is relatively unchanged since Bondi's youth, most of the buildings directly associated with her childhood have been torn down. These include her home, her school, and her church. Throughout her childhood and youth, the family lived in a relatively small but comfortable wooden house at 203 N. Washington St. It was no. 35 in the mid–1880s and no. 47 before the street renumbering of 1902.[90] The Bondys were not the first occupants of the house. It may have been built by Brigadier General Isaac C.B. Suman (1831–1911), who had commanded the 9th Indiana Volunteer Infantry during the Civil War and who lived in the house while he was postmaster of Valparaiso in the mid–1880s. He later became mayor.[91]

A relatively plain example of the Queen Anne style of the period and cubical in form, the Bondy house was characterized by a steeply pitched, hip roof; a two-story bay window topped by a front-facing gable on the right-hand side of the asymmetrical facade and a small, square tower with a steeple roof to the left. In the place of the typical Queen

This postcard shows the 200 block of N. Washington St. in Valparaiso, Indiana, in about 1900. Until she moved away permanently in the mid–1920s, this was the center of Bondi's world. The house where she grew up is second from left. It was torn down in 1968 to make way for an annex to nearby Trinity Lutheran Church, after having served as a parsonage. Bondi's "little sister" Allegra Nesbit lived in the first house on the left, an Italianate structure that was razed to make way for a new church building in 1951. The white house beyond the Bondy residence is still standing.

Anne porch, there was an unusual quarter-circular canopy over the front entrance, which was echoed by a quarter-circular set of steps below leading up to the entrance. There was also a bay window on the southern side of the house, which was probably the dining room.

The Bondys lived at 203 N. Washington St. for more than 30 years. In the 1920s, when both their children had left home for good, Abram and Eva moved to an apartment in a four-unit building they owned at 254 S. Valparaiso St., close to the old college campus, which would be their final home together.[92] In 1944, the Bondy home on N. Washington St. became the parsonage of the Trinity Lutheran Church. It was torn down in 1968 to make way for the nondescript, flat-roofed, one-and-one-half story educational wing of the church that occupies the site to this day.[93] The neighboring Vincent-Nesbit house, where Bondi's friend and "little sister" Allegra Nesbit was born in 1900, was the first sanctuary of the Trinity Lutheran Church. It was razed in one day on January 1, 1952, after the completion of the new church building behind it.[94] This means that only one original building survives on this side of Bondi's block: the large Italianate house on the corner of Erie St., where the Gardner family once lived. Ethelyn Gardner (Farrand) (1884–1952) was Bondi's friend and the granddaughter of Joseph Gardner, the founder of the Farmers' National Bank, later the Farmers' State Bank.

Bondi attended the 1st Ward Public School, which was named Columbia School after Christopher Columbus. Its name also alluded to the Columbian Exposition in Chicago in 1893, the year the school was completed. It was housed in an impressive Richardsonian

Bondi's elementary school was called Columbia School after Christopher Columbus and was housed for 72 years in this attractive Richardsonian Romanesque building in red brick and rusticated grey stone from 1893. It was demolished in 1965 and an apartment building now stands on the southeast corner of Indiana Ave. and Locust St. The white frame house in the background is still standing. Unfortunately, though Valparaiso, Indiana, still has many beautiful old buildings, Bondi's home, school, and church were all razed long ago.

Romanesque building in brick and rusticated stone at 500 Indiana Ave., which was then called Mechanic St.[95] Unfortunately, the school was demolished March 1, 1965, after 72 years of continuous use and an ugly apartment building called the Columbia Apartments built on the site.[96]

Bondy and her mother attended the First Presbyterian Church on the southwest corner of Franklin and Jefferson streets. One of the many unadorned, charmless, and utilitarian churches of this sect that are scattered across America, with multiple pointed gables and large Gothic-arched windows, this exemplar of the plain Presbyterian style was built in 1881.[97] It did not help the aesthetics of the building, that the square tower was structurally unsound and had to be lowered in 1949. The church was razed in 1974. This is a fate it shares with a lamentably high percentage of the original church buildings in the town that was known in the late nineteenth century as "the City of Churches." Despite building permission for a three-story office block back in 1975, the site of the First Presbyterian Church remains a parking lot. As we shall see, there is an extent to which the Beulah Bondi tour of Valparaiso, sadly, is a tour of parking lots.

Fortunately, there are some public buildings in Valparaiso associated with Bondi's life that are still standing. First and foremost among these is the Grand Army of the Republic Memorial Hall, better known as the Memorial Opera House, at 104 Indiana Ave., which I shall have more to say about later. The club house of the Valparaiso Woman's Club, which was such an important part of Bondi's mother's life, still stands down the street from where Bondi grew up, on the northeast corner of Washington and Jefferson. Eva Bondy was instrumental in the purchase of the building from the Elks in 1924 and worked tirelessly to pay off the debt. It had been built in 1906 as a clinic and home by Dr. David J. Loring.

Bondi's friend Gertrude Polk lived in a two-story Italianate house across the street from the Loring clinic on the northwest corner of Washington and Jefferson, where there is now a parking lot.[98] She was born in 1886, the daughter Caleb C. Polk, "founder of the Polk school of piano tuning," which was located on the southeast corner of Washington and Indiana.[99] Gertrude grew into a dancer, who trained with Ruth St. Denis and performed with the St. Denis troupe, including in Europe. She also did dramatic readings from operas with her brother accompanying her on the piano. Gertrude was the only one of Bondi's Valparaiso friends with a professional connection to the arts. She moved to California in 1918 and spent most of her adult life in Santa Barbara, where she died in 1970.[100] Like Bondi, she never married.

In the northerly direction from the house she grew up in, we find other addresses on N. Washington St. with Bondi connections. On the right-hand side of the block between Erie and Institute, before we get to the Heritage Evangelical Lutheran Church (formerly the German Lutheran Church), stood the capacious Queen Anne home of the Lowenstines, the most prominent Jewish family in Valparaiso. Jacob Lowenstine first opened his store in 1885 on the ground floor of a building owned by Bondi's Uncle Louis on W. Main St (now Lincolnway). Later, Lowenstine's department store was a Valparaiso institution for decades at what is now 57 Franklin St., on the east side of the courthouse square. The historic building burned down in February 1996 and was replaced by a modern structure.

Jacob and his wife Goldie had five children. Growing up, Bondi was friends with their youngest daughter Irene, who was just a few months older than her. In 1915, Irene married Henry George Frank and moved to Waterloo, Iowa. Bondi, who was studying at Valparaiso University, was present at the wedding and several of the festivities leading up to it.[101] Irene's husband was co-owner of Frank Bros., who advertised themselves as "Waterloo's oldest and largest clothiers."[102]

The site of the Lowenstine house is now a playground for the Central Elementary School. This school building stands on the site of the building from 1904, where, under normal circumstances, Bondi would have attended high school. As we shall see, after elementary school she went elsewhere for her secondary education. This may partly have been because Valparaiso High School was being completely rebuilt in 1903–4, when she was due to start there.

The bungalow from 1952 at 402 N. Washington St. stands on the site of the former Windle residence. Bondi's close friend Marie Windle lived in this large, imposing Queen Anne style home on the corner of Walnut St. for many years, until the house was destroyed in a fire in 1950 in which Marie and her family narrowly escaped with their lives.[103] Marie was born in Benton county, Indiana in November 1893, making her the youngest member of Bondi's group of close, lifelong friends. Marie's father, George Deming Timmons (1867–1918), was a "Valpo" professor of chemistry for 30 years and dean of the college of pharmacy for 25 years and the family lived in a typical I-house at 458 Greenwich St. on the corner of Freeman, which still stands across the street from the old college campus.[104]

Marie's mother, Mary Alice "Minnie" Sayers Timmons died, probably in childbirth, when Marie was ten. On August 20, 1918, Marie was married to William Garland Windle, Jr. (1895–1942), who was in the grocery business with his father.[105] The Windle grocery was located in the two-story, Italianate building that once bore their name and that still stands on the southeast corner of Lincolnway and Franklin.

In addition to sharing the old Windle home with William's mother, Catherine Unruh Windle, the couple also lived for a time one block up at 602 N. Washington St., an Italianate carriage house from the 1870s they had converted into a home in 1925 and which is still standing.[106] Marie Timmons Windle was found dead in a Rochelle, Illinois, motel room on October 25, 1958, making her the first of the group to pass away. She and her sister and two friends were visiting her stepmother Cecelia Higley Timmons.[107]

The palatial Georgian Colonial, 8,000 square foot home at 410 N. Washington St. with seven bedrooms and six baths was built by Mandel and Daisy Lowenstine in 1929.[108] Mandel was Irene's older brother. He was an industrialist born in 1882, who co-founded two major companies and became one of Valparaiso's richest men. He was also one of the most eligible bachelors in town, until he married a saleslady he met in a dress shop in Chicago in 1922.[109] Daisy Temple was the youngest of the seven children of a Sparta, Illinois, farmer.[110] She became part of Bondi's inner circle of friends in Valparaiso till the end of her life. The Lowenstines' home was valued at $50,000 in 1930 and at $20,600 in 1940, property values having declined significantly in the 1930s. The mansion was staffed with a live-in butler and housekeeper.[111]

The Colonial Revival home from 1925 at 703 N. Washington St. was for many years the home of Bondi's close friend Floy Brownell and her husband Walter, until they died in the early 1970s.[112] Floy Binyon was born in 1891 and raised at Cedar Lake in Lake county, Indiana, the youngest of the six surviving children of a prosperous farmer and hotelkeeper.[113] Her parents were the proprietors of Binyon's Cedar Lake Hotel, which was located just south of the Cedar Creek estuary. Floy married her Lowell High School sweetheart Walter Ezra Brownell in 1912, when they were both 21.[114] The Brownells moved to Valparaiso after their wedding. Walter worked 47 years for the McGill Manufacturing Co., where he was vice president in charge of sales and treasurer. He opened a travel agency in 1957, which was later run by his son.[115] The Brownells' daughter Beryl Ann Brownell was editor of the Woman's Department of the *Gary Post Tribune* for many years. While nearly all Bondi's close friends were fellow Presbyterians, the Brownells were Christian Science.[116]

Bondi's lifelong friend Cora Louise Banister, who was known as Louise, was born in Valparaiso in December 1885, the daughter of Alfred and Octavia (Hawkins) Banister, and grew up at 154 W. Jefferson St., just two blocks from Bondi's home.[117] This house, too, is now part of the "Beulah Bondi Parking Lot Tour." Louise's father was co-proprietor of a hardware store on the corner of Napoleon and Lincolnway, where City Hall now stands, until he went into the grocery business in 1922.[118] Louise was a graduate of the department of music at Valparaiso University, and was a charter member of the Iota Chapter of Tri Kappa, when it was organized in 1903.[119]

Louise Banister married C.L. Bartholomew on October 17, 1912.[120] Charles LeRoy Bartholomew was born near Cooks Corners, Indiana, in 1877. He graduated from the Chicago Dental School in 1899 and worked as a dentist in Morocco, Indiana; Valparaiso, and Chicago until 1923, when he returned to Valparaiso to enter the undertaking business with his father. After five years as the city building inspector (1929–34), he was elected Republican mayor of Valparaiso in 1934 and served two four-year terms from 1935 till 1942. Mr. Bartholomew received a record vote when he was reelected in 1938, which still held at his death in 1960. His obituary described him as "one of the most popular mayors in the history of Valparaiso."[121]

Louise Bartholomew lived most of her married life in two modest homes next door to each other and still standing at 508 Napoleon St. and 155 Walnut St.[122] She and her husband adopted a boy, Charles Robert Bartholomew (1921–2007), who would take over the family undertaking business, which is still operating at 102 Monroe St. Louise Banister Bartholomew died unexpectedly at her home on Walnut St. in 1972.[123]

In addition to Marie Timmons Windle, Bondi had another close friend who was the daughter of a college professor. Ada Roessler grew up with her younger sister Louise in a rambling, towered, and gabled Queen Anne style house that once stood at 601 E. Lincolnway, on the corner of College Ave.[124] Ada was born in Valparaiso on May 22, 1888, making her one year older than Bondi.[125] Ada's father, Professor John Edward Roessler (1859–1941), taught German and mathematics at Valparaiso University for 30 years and was acting president for a year starting in April 1921.[126] Her mother Anna Harbour Roessler (1863–1946) was also an instructor at the university.[127] Bondi once said she had based her character Martha Morgan in *Vivacious Lady*, "the wife of a domineering straight-laced college professor," on a woman in her home town.[128] I suspect this was Mrs. Roessler.

Ada Roessler was introduced to President Theodore Roosevelt in Washington in 1906 by her congressman. When hearing she was traveling to Germany with a friend, he told them: "It is well to go abroad, ladies, but never, under any circumstances, forget that you are Americans."[129] Like Bondi, Ada was a graduate of Valparaiso University and a member of the Kappa Kappa Kappa sorority and the Presbyterian Church.[130]

At the age of 23, Louise was the first of Bondi's close friends to marry. This event took place in the parlor of her home on June 1, 1911.[131] The groom was Joseph Spencer Bartholomew, a 33-year-old attorney and son of a pioneer Valparaiso attorney and Porter county judge.[132] Joseph's first wife, Melissa Autumn Lee, had died suddenly of "heart trouble" in 1904 at the age of 26.[133] The Bartholomews lived at 701 E. Lincolnway (corner of Greenwich) from at least 1918 till 1940.[134] As a widow, Ada lived at 252 Haas St. and worked at Windle Home Furnishings and the Brownell Travel Agency. Ada Roessler Bartholomew was the last of Bondi's circle to die, save Bondi herself, in Indianapolis in 1979, where she had lived for five years to be close to her daughter.[135]

Bondi's Valparaiso inner circle, then, consisted of Ada Bartholomew, Louise Bartholomew, Marie Windle, Floy Brownell, and Daisy Lowenstine. In their background and experience, they were a remarkably cohesive group, being nearly all college-educated and members of the Tri Kappa sorority, upper-middle class, married with children, and Presbyterian. Particularly the high educational level of the women, at a time when few women went to college, must have been unusual for a peer group of this kind. The exception in most ways was Daisy Temple Lowenstine, but, as we have seen, she was a late arrival to the group.

Louise, Marie, and Floy lived within a 0.3-mile radius of each other on or near N. Washington St. their entire adult lives. After she became a widow, Ada moved into this charmed circle and a small house on the corner of Haas and Napoleon streets. As we have seen, Daisy also lived on N. Washington St. for many years, midway between Floy and Marie. In 1955, not long before Mandel Lowenstine's death, the couple moved to a modernist high-rise apartment building at 1000 N. Lake Shore Dr. in Chicago. Daisy was still living there when she died in 1977.[136]

EVA MARBLE BONDY

Bondi's mother Eva Marble Bondy in later life. Bondi used this portrait as a frontispiece to the handsome volume of her mother's poems she had printed in 1962 under the title *Worldkins*. Eva Bondy was a multi-talented, nurturing, and wise woman, who exerted a stronger influence on her daughter than any other individual. By no means a stereotypical stage mom, she nevertheless subtly steered her daughter towards the highly fulfilling acting career she would enjoy for 60 years. A strong mother-daughter bond is one I have often found in the lives of the 100 Hollywood character actresses I have studied.

When Bondi in later years spoke of her childhood in Valparaiso, her recollections nearly always involved her mother. Eva Marble Bondy was a formidable woman, who had mastered everything from domestic economy to giving talks on esoteric topics like "English Artists of the World War."[137] She also had a local reputation as the published author of better than average poems like "What Is a Kiss?," "Despair," "Temptation," "Leave All for Love," and "The Universal Lover," all much less risqué than these titles suggest. The earliest of her poems I have found in print was "Bide a Wee," a love poem with a bird motif published in the Chicago *Inter Ocean* in 1896.[138] It was not included in *Worldkins*, the book of

her mother's poems Bondi published in 1962. Her daughter gave the most fitting description of Eva Bondy's poetry in the preface to *Worldkins*: "She was a vivid, progressive spirit
and her poems express her deep-rooted appreciation of life in all its forms—and her universal love for mankind."[139]

During her more than 40 years in Valparaiso, Eva Bondy was a force to be reckoned with in the intellectual and cultural life of the city. A charter member of the Valparaiso Woman's Club when it was founded as the Harriet Beecher Stowe Reading Circle
in 1895, Eva Bondy was President-Elect in 1901.[140] In 1913, after having help reorganize
and write a new constitution, she became president of the Tenth District of the organization of American women's clubs.[141] She was also interested in politics, particularly as they
involved women's rights. In 1915, she was elected chairman of the Porter County Franchise League.[142] Eva Bondy was also a member of the Indiana Press Club.[143] She worked
part-time as a "frequently-called substitute at Valparaiso University's Dramatic department."[144] This was back in the 1890s, when the institution was called the Indiana Normal
School and Business Institute. Eva Bondy's occupation is listed as "teacher" in the census
for 1900.[145]

Eva was curious about everything that was new and exciting and was once described
in her hometown newspaper as being "ever ready with encouragement for things original."[146] So we are not surprised to read in the same newspaper, that she "made us all want
to take an airplane ride by her description of the one she and Miss Lee enjoyed recently":
"She made it sound so easy, pleasant, and full of happy rather than startling sensations
that we felt her poem 'Lifted Wings' must have fittingly described it."[147] This was in 1928!
In a *Vidette-Messenger* "Woman's Club" column in 1932, Eva Bondy was referred to as
"one of the city's most beloved and talented women."[148]

Despite all her achievements, the question is if her best efforts were not put into raising her two children. Progressive and innovative in her child-rearing practices, Bondi
recalled how "At home, … they would play games of identity, determining scents and
tastes. Their mother would blindfold them, then dip toothpicks into various condiments
and pass tiny wads of cotton scented with herbs under their noses. Prizes were awarded
too for the largest number of correct answers."[149] Her mother "indirectly encouraged her
'acting' from the age of about four."[150] Eva had a clear perception of her daughter's talents and nurtured those talents, but she was far from being a stage mom. "She was a very
wise mother, who developed my senses when I was a child—now tell me exactly what you
hear, she'd ask, as we drove through the woods—so by the time I reached adolescence it
was easy for me to express myself in public."[151]

Part of the early training Bondi received from her mother was in the then influential Delsarte acting technique, "a highly stylized manner of elocution that assigned a definite, classic gesture to every emotion."[152] Bondi explains further: "Delsarte was a sort of
mime, an imitation…. She would suggest a word like sympathy and I would go into a pos-
ture denoting sympathy or happiness and my face would light up and I would be express-
ing happiness. She would just say a word or two…. I was inspired to go through these
gestures."[153]

One of her mother's old friends once mistook Bondi in one of her old lady roles for
Eva. She told Bondi backstage after the show, that she and Eva had both wanted to be
actresses when they were young.[154] For a woman of Eva Bondy's background and generation, though, going on the stage was not something one did. Bondi recognized that, being
born nearly three decades after her mother, she had had opportunities that her mother

had not had: "I would say that I'm doing the thing my mother would have loved to do had it been considered fit and proper."[155]

Towards the end of her long life, Bondi said in an interview: "My mother was ahead of her time, and she had a great influence on me.... She had a seeking mind. Services at our Presbyterian church did not answer all her questions and she went into deep metaphysics and Eastern philosophies. She made me feel the most important aim in life was to raise your consciousness."[156] It is not possible to overestimate the importance of Eva Bondy to her only daughter. Though Bondi had to live 40 years without her mother's presence in her life, the influence of her ideas and values never abated.

In addition to her birth family, her grandmothers, and "the girls," Beulah Bondi also grew up in close proximity to her "Uncle Lou." Among her parents' siblings, he was the one she was closest to. In his younger years, Louis D. Bondy was a slender, thoughtful-looking man with his dark hair parted on the side and a walrus moustache that was a little too big for his narrow face.[157] He was born in December 1852 and grew up like his siblings in Philadelphia and Port Huron, Michigan. He left home in 1870, the year he turned 18, and went to Chicago, determined to make his fortune in the mercantile field. According to legend, he got his start when Mr. Field of Marshall Field & Co. started him in business with a credit of $5,000.[158] As we have seen, by 1880 he was making his home with his mother and his two younger siblings Abram and Rose in Valparaiso, Indiana. His decision to settle there would have wide-ranging consequences not just for himself, but for the rest of the Bondy family.

L.D. Bondy, as he was known publicly, was a pioneering merchant in Valparaiso and would become a major property owner there. His dry goods store was located on the ground floor of the elaborately Italianate three-story red brick office building on the northwest corner of Main St. (now Lincolnway) and Franklin St., which was known as the L.D. Bondy block. In 2018, it underwent a major renovation that brought it back to its former glory. The building Bondi most associated with her uncle is now 23 E. Lincolnway. At the end of his life, he lived in an apartment there on the second floor. That was where he was discovered semi-comatose and close to death in 1937, in a scenario that strangely echoed his own father's lonely demise in Davenport 52 years earlier.

Before his sad end, though, Louis Bondy had an unusually active and useful life as a leading citizen and prime mover in Valparaiso. First and foremost, he was a canny businessman and amassed more money than any member of the Bondy family until his niece Beulah came along. His motto as a dry goods merchant was "to meet all competition prices and then deduct five percent."[159] From dry goods, Bondy expanded into real estate. He was known as "Valparaiso's ideal landlord": "always acquiring property and making extensive improvements on it."[160] On August 16, 1918, he was appointed city clerk by Mayor P.L. Sisson, when the incumbent joined the army.[161]

Uncle Lou was a lifelong bachelor, an uncommon choice at the time, but the avoidance of marriage appears to have been a strong inclination in him. Most revealing in this regard is an article that appeared in the *Lake County Times* on July 27, 1916, the year he turned 64. It contained Louis's refutation of a story that had appeared in his hometown newspaper the previous evening "to the effect that on July 20 he and Miss Rachel Finkelstein, a prominent social worker of Gary, were married." Bondy believed he was "the victim of a practical joke from some of his friends, who know that he is one of the most confirmed bachelors in the middle west." The paper added that "he was taking the matter goodnaturedly." Bondy took the "accusation" seriously enough, though, to present an alibi for the date in question, which he said he had spent at Flint Lake in the company of four men, which he then named. He added that he did not really need an alibi. "I know that I would never do anything like that," he concluded.[162] I have found no record of any woman called Rachel Finkelstein in or near Gary, Indiana, in print sources or public documents from the period, so she is probably made up.

So Louis Bondy never married, lived with his mother until she died, was "a skilled and accomplished pianist"[163]; had an interest in the arts, which he shared with his niece Beulah; and enjoyed male company in one of those fraternal orders that were so integral to early twentieth-century American life and that Sinclair Lewis satirized in *Babbitt*. You see, besides his extended family and his business, the most important element in Louis Bondy's life was the Benevolent and Protective Order of Elks (BPOE). He had been a charter member and organizer of the Valparaiso Lodge of Elks, No. 500 in 1899 and their second Exalted Ruler.[164] Indeed, the Elks Temple on the corner of Lincolnway and Lafayette was his true home. When Louis D. Bondy died, the Elks took charge of the funeral.[165] No one recited the Kaddish for him.

The only direct connection the Bondy family had with the theater was that Louis had once owned the Grand Opera House on Main St., the first public space in Valparaiso when it opened as the Fiske Opera House in 1874. The building still stands at what is now 162 W. Lincolnway and serves as the Valparaiso Chamber of Commerce. The Grand Opera House, which should not be confused with the Memorial Opera House from 1893 on Indiana Ave., does not figure in Bondi's recollections of her childhood.

The Memorial Opera House, though, would play a significant role in Bondi's life and career. It was there, in 1896, that she made her stage debut at the age of seven. The details of the story are somewhat different in Bondi's retellings late in life and in other, independent sources. In one version, Bondi had to step in on short notice in the cast of a touring company, when the child slated to play the title role fell ill. According to another source, the play was performed by the Valparaiso Dramatic Club, formed in 1892, when the professional troupe that was to entertain at the Memorial Opera House during Porter County Fair Week "failed to make an appearance as scheduled one night." The play itself has never been in question, though. It was a dramatization of Frances Hodgson Burnett's classic children's book *Little Lord Fauntleroy*.

Bondi was given only a week to learn the title role: "Forty-seven pages of fullscap!" In another version of the story, there were only seven pages. At any rate, the headline in the *Vidette-Messenger* the next day read: "A new star shines—a small one, but a bright one."[166]

Three delightful studio portraits of Bondi in her Little Lord Fauntleroy costume survive. On the back of a copy of one of them, that Bondi owned herself, we find written by hand: "Memorial Opera House Valparaiso—Ind. B.B. as Little Lord Fauntleroy age—7 yrs—1896."[167] Bondi also performed in or directed a few amateur productions at the Memorial Opera House in the 1910s. In 1976, when she returned to the site of her first performance 80 years after the event, she said: "Someday I'll come back and act…. Until then, I'll be here in spirit—and probably haunt you all."[168]

While Bondi's primary education was commonplace, her secondary schooling was unusual for a young woman of her generation and background. Bondi attended no less than three different high schools, but not, it seems, the one that was only a stone's throw from her house. Valparaiso High School was then located on the block bounded by Washington, Institute, Franklin, and Erie streets, the current site of Central Elementary School. It is possible Bondi may have started her secondary education there, but in either 1903 or 1905, depending on the source, her parents enrolled her at the Frances Shimer Academy of the University of Chicago (also known as Frances Shimer Academy for Girls), a preparatory school located in Mount Carroll, Illinois, about 175 miles west of Valparaiso.[169] The only reason I can imagine why loving parents would send their daughter away to school would be that they felt she was not being sufficiently challenged by the local schools; that they wanted her to have a wider experience and to be stimulated by encounters with pupils and teachers from different places and with different backgrounds.

Undertaken in 1853 by Frances Wood Shimer and Cindarella Gregory, Shimer College has had such a turbulent history that the phoenix has become its symbol. One of its unique characteristics throughout its existence has been a high degree of student involvement in the running of the school

**Bondi is recognizable in her debut role as Cedric Errol (aka Little Lord Fauntleroy) in a local production at the Memorial Opera House in her hometown of Valparaiso, Indiana, in 1896. She was seven. Her mother coached her, costumed her, curled her hair, and gently pushed her towards the stage. Beulah found that she rather enjoyed performing.**

and a particularly strong music and arts program, which would have appealed to Eva Bondy and her daughter. A July 1906 advertisement for the school reads:

> FOR GIRLS. Preparatory and Junior College courses. A highly interesting, practical study of Domestic Science. A separate building for this work and music. Music directed by Emil Liebling. The equipment of the school as a school and a home—its new buildings, the location, sanitary conditions, ample shaded grounds, fresh air and pure water offer conditions which are perfectly adjusted to the development of health and a broad, fine womanhood.[170]

By the time Bondi attended Shimer, Frances Shimer, who had had sole charge and ownership of the school since 1870, was no longer a presence there. In ill health, she retired from active involvement and moved to Florida in 1896 and died in 1901.

The major event of Bondi's Shimer years was not related to learning, though it had consequences for her educational career. In the early hours of February 9, 1906, a disastrous fire broke out, destroying a recently built dormitory called South Hall. Poor water pressure hindered the local fire department in doing their job effectively. There were 60 students enrolled at the time. Fortunately, none of them were injured in the fire. The material losses amounted to $50,000. The trustees immediately decided to rebuild in the hope that the new building would be ready for occupancy before commencement in June. The school was also determined that there would no interruption in teaching. Classes would be held in local churches when necessary.[171]

Despite these assurances, it was probably due to the disruption of the fire that Bondi's parents decided to send her to another boarding school; a French-language school no less, in Montreal. The boarding school was called Le Pensionnat du Saint-Nom-de-Marie (PSNM) and had been built by the order of the Sisters of the Holy Name of Jesus and Mary (SNJM). The order had been founded in 1843 and was dedicated to the education of children, particularly girls and young women.

Le Pensionnat was the flagship among the several schools built by the order and to this day is housed in a monumental Neoclassical style, grey stone building, reminiscent of Les Invalides in Paris, at the northwestern base of Mont-Royal and adjacent to the University of Montreal in the Outremont section of the city.[172] The Porter County courthouse pales in comparison with this massive structure. The school had taken two years to build and had opened in the fall of 1905, not long before Bondi's arrival.[173]

From her time in Montreal in the spring of 1906, we have a unique series of four letters to her parents in Bondi's characteristically backward sloping handwriting. They are the earliest letters from her hand that I have seen and give us a unique insight into her character and personality at close to 17 years of age. Also, though the letters are undated, the mention in one of them of the death of a girl from her neighborhood, Bessie Parks, makes it possible to determine when Bondi was in Montreal. Parks died on March 7, 1906, at age 15.[174] After saying that a certain Mr. Blumberg, who is often mentioned in the letters, "will bring my corset covers this afternoon," Bondi writes that she has received a letter from her friend Florence in Valparaiso: "I was so surprised to hear about Bessie Parks. What did she die from?"[175]

To be able to give her parents a full and forthright account of her extracurricular activities, which included going to theater, Bondi had to circumvent the nuns' surveillance of the incoming and outgoing mails by having a friend post her letters or having them come and go via Mr. Blumberg. She also had to warn her parents: "Don't mention the matinee in any letter that comes thro' the nuns."[176] She was not without artistic stimulation, though, at the school and sang and played the piano at several "entertainments."

The nun who taught her music was "so dear": "I love her more every time I'm with her. She is beautiful and her music is so soleful [sic].... One of the French girls is so jealous of me she can hardly see—because Sister Immanence[?] pays a little attention to me. The other evening after French she walked to the music room door with me and threw me a kiss so sweet I wanted to throw my arms around her, but had to be content to throw one back and say—Bonne nuit, ma soeur. Good night, sister.'" She adds with her characteristic exultation: "O! mother you have no idea how happy I am about your poems. I breathe for you every day and I know 'success' is *yours*."[177] Another letter mentions a pupil she has befriended: "Last night she put her arm around me and said—you know I like you so very much."[178]

Bondi's Montreal sojourn appears to have been a brief one. She returned to Shimer in the fall of 1906 and completed her studies there in June 1907, according to multiple, reliable accounts.[179] For example, in an article in a local Illinois newspaper from 1949, we can read: "Miss Bondi was graduated in 1907 from Shimer." Then the sentence takes an unexpected turn: "and is reputed to have some romantic memories of at least two or three young men of that day, now veteran Mount Carroll businessmen."[180] *At least* two or three! Back in the day, it behooved an unmarried woman to have some stories of lost love up her sleeve and Bondi's most persistent one related to her years at Shimer. In an 1956 interview with her friend and ally, columnist Harold Heffernan, she let slip that she had met and fallen in love with a young man when she was 18, but decided to sacrifice "the one romantic love of her life" to pursue her dream of an acting career.[181] In an interview with columnist Cobey Black the following year, she stated "I quite deliberately chose a career" and added that she did not believe that marriage and a career "go hand in hand" for women. When asked if she had any regrets about this decision, she responded vigorously: "O mercy, no. I've really had a magical life. I was never really in love but once—and I didn't marry him. I have many wonderful friends."[182]

On a visit to Mount Carroll in 1976, which was probably her last and where she participated in a three-day Beulah Bondi film festival, she was more specific about her long ago paramour: "on a ride downtown she pointed out a house where her first beau had lived and attempted to figure out which grocery store they used to meet behind."[183] It is worth adding that "downtown" in Mount Carroll consists of only two intersecting commercial streets, Main and Market, which lie about eight blocks from the Shimer campus.

Bondi retained ties to Shimer throughout her life and was a member of the alumnae association.[184] Hathaway Hall from 1904 and Dearborn Hall from 1905, which housed the music department, were not affected by the fire and are still standing as remnants of the school Bondi attended. Shimer College was forced to leave its Mount Carroll campus in 1978. Today the Neoclassical brick buildings with their arched sash windows, multiple dormers and gables, and grey stone details present a melancholy vision of dereliction and abandonment. There are fewer people living in Mount Carroll now, than when Bondi was a pupil there.

When she left Shimer for good, Bondi was 18 years of age. Surprisingly, though, that was not the end of her secondary education. In the issue of the *Chicago Tribune* for June 23, 1909, we can read that she was among the graduates from Hyde Park High School that year.[185] It is mystery why Bondi did not graduate from high school until she was 20 years old, two years after she left Shimer. Despite all the energy and money expended on her formal education, Bondi summed up her school career as follows: "I wasn't really a good student. I got just passing grades."[186]

One of my more surprising discoveries about Bondi's early life was that she spent more than a year as a kindergarten teacher in Vernal, Utah, in 1912 and 1913. I knew that her friend Margaret Hamilton had trained and worked for some time as a kindergarten teacher in her native Cleveland, but I had no idea that Bondi also had a background in pre-school education. In the long term, though, her cultural activities in Vernal would leave a more lasting mark on her life than her stint as a teacher.

Vernal lies in the Ashley Valley and is the county seat and largest city in Uintah county, right up in the northeast corner of the state. This is desert country. Bondi would have discovered her love of deserts here, which would stay with her all her days. The population in 1910 was 836 and has risen to about 10,500 today. Vernal is unique in Utah in not having been settled by Mormons.

There are few buildings left in Vernal dating back to Bondi's time. Even the famous bank building, which was sent through the parcel post "one brick at a time," dates from 1916 to 1917. Thus I was amazed to discover that the hip-roofed, one-story red brick building of the Wilcox Academy, where Bondi taught her kindergarten classes, is still standing at 65 E. 100 N., not far from the town's epicenter at Main St. and Vernal Ave. Wilcox Academy was a missionary school run by the Kingsbury Congregational Church. Today the building is used as a community center.

The first evidence of Bondi's time in Vernal is a news item in the *Vernal Express* to the effect that she had played a French maid in a playlet called *The Mystery* at the Congregational Church the first weekend in March 1912, "before a crowded house."[187] On May 24, 1912, we can read the following under the heading "Wilcox Kindergarten": "Miss Beulah Bondy will continue her work with the Primary and Kindergarten children for six weeks, beginning June 3."[188]

From the several news items in the *Vernal Express* that mention Bondi, it is clear that she participated actively in the social and cultural life of this small, rural community. She did more performing during her year or so in Vernal, than in the preceding 23. In late June 1912, she even performed in what the newspaper referred to as "vaudeville" in the brand new Orpheus Hall, which stood on the corner of S. Vernal Ave. and 100 S St. until it was razed in 1965. The paper assured its readers that "those who have seen the rehearsals say it will be more than 'a laugh a minute' the whole evening." Her partner in this endeavor was a man called A.F. Young.[189]

The high point, though, of Bondi's dramatic career in Vernal was playing Winona, the "chieftain's daughter," the lead role in *The Sun Dance Opera* at Orpheus Hall on February 20–22, 1913.[190] This full-scale opera is of great historical interest, as the first such work co-authored by a Native American. It was composed by local teacher and musician, William F. Hanson (1887–1969), in collaboration with the Yankton Dakota Sioux writer and musician Gertrude Simmons Bonnin (aka Zitkala-Ša; 1876–1938). Bonnin lived with her husband on a ranch near Whiterocks, about 30 miles west of Vernal and near the Uintah and Ouray Reservation, where they both worked with the Ute people.[191] Hanson and Bonnin had been working together on the opera since first meeting in June 1912.[192]

The *Sun Dance Opera* told "the story of the return of the sun from its death during the winter, of the kindliness of its light and warmth as it falls on the earth, of the plants and the trees that spring forth and grow under its rays, and of the whole world rejoicing in the sunshine."[193] Another news article described the opera as consisting of "twenty three solos, duets, trios, quartettes, choruses and dialogues characterizing the Indian in his own life unmolested by the races."[194] In its detailed review, the *Vernal Express* described how, after an eight-minute overture, "the curtain went up showing a scene near the foot hills with Winona, impersonated by Miss Bondy, singing her love song." The paper continues: "Miss Bondy has a rich, full, well rounded though not a voluminous voice, which is under perfect control at all times. Her dramatic ability is unquestioned and throughout the evening she won merited applause."[195]

Winona's lover Ohiya was played by the dashingly handsome, 32-year-old owner and editor of the *Vernal Express*, Ashley Bartlett, a Mormon who had fathered seven children in ten years and still found time to act. Bartlett later buried his acting ambitions and ended up as a sexton in Vernal Memorial Park cemetery, where he took up permanent residence in 1979, four months shy of his 100th birthday. Bartlett had 51 grandchildren and 111 great-grandchildren at his death.[196]

In addition to the white cast in the named, principal roles, members of the local Ute tribe participated in the dance numbers. The climax was the sun dance in the last act. The local reviewer predicted that "this opera … will win its way into fame."[197] Another newspaper reported at the time: "When the 'Sun Dance' was sung in Vernal, Indians and whites drove in from 40 miles to hear it; and having heard it, they pronounced it a triumph."[198] Indeed, the opera was such a success, a third performance had to be added on Saturday, February 22.[199]

It is remarkable and hitherto unknown fact that Bondi's life and that of one of the most important early Native American voices in English would be linked in this way. Personally, having taught Zitkala-Ša's autobiographical sketches and her short story "The Soft-Hearted Sioux" for years in my American literature courses, I am struck by this incredible coincidence, which brings together my two major research interests during the past 30 years: American literature and Hollywood character actresses.

In the spring of 1913, Bondi's mother joined her in Vernal. The two of them gave a dramatic recital at the Uintah Academy together with William F. Hanson. The *Vernal Express* wrote: "Both Mrs. Bondy and her daughter showed wonderful versatility of talent, including humor, pathos, serio-comic character, tragedy."[200] While in Vernal, Eva Bondy would collaborate with Hanson in writing several songs, that were "sung in concerts and recitals in towns and cities in Utah" and three of which were later published.[201] They were also included in *Worldkins*.

Bondi kept in touch with at least one of her pupils from Vernal. Edythe Mary Neal, the daughter of Charles J. Neal, manager of the Uintah Telephone Co., and his wife Essie, was born in Vernal in 1909 and thus was only three or four when Bondi taught her.[202] Edythe grew into a talented lyric soprano, who performed with the Los Angeles Philharmonic with Leopold Stokowski and worked as a high school teacher in Salt Lake City. She stayed with Bondi in Hollywood for ten days in July 1945. Edythe Neal married the following year and died in 1996.[203]

If nothing else, her sojourn in Vernal made it clear to Bondi that her future was not in teaching. When she returned home, she began to attend classes at Valparaiso University. On August 13, 1914, she graduated with a degree in elocution.[204] She received an MA in oratory from Valparaiso in 1916.[205]

Founded in 1859 as the Valparaiso Male and Female Academy, one of the first co-educational institutions in the United States, by 1914 Valparaiso University was one of the largest universities in the United States with 29 departments, 209 instructors, and over 5,000 students.[206] It was so affordable despite the high quality of the education it offered, that in Bondi's day it was known as the "Poor Man's Harvard."

Sadly, there is nothing left of the campus Bondi knew and the old college buildings "on the hill." The only exception is the building known as Heritage Hall, built in 1875 as a residence hall for men, which stands at the southern end of College Ave., at the heart of what was the original college campus and is now known as the West Campus or Old Campus area. During Bondi's years at the university, it was used as a dormitory and dining room and as a barracks for soldiers during World War I. Extensively remodeled in 2010, it now serves as the university's law clinic.

Arguably, the most important event during Bondi's college years was social rather than academic. Bondi joined a sorority at this time with special links to her home state. The Kappa Kappa Kappa sorority, also known as "Tri Kappa," is unique in being found only in Indiana. The sorority was founded in 1901 and by 1917 had grown to 1,800 members; "the purpose of the organization then as now to bring the members more closely together in an unselfish relationship."[207] Charity towards fellow members soon extended to charity in general: "Fund-raising for local projects was a central mission of Kappa from its inception."[208]

Through her membership in Tri Kappa, Bondi solidified existing friendships and formed new ones that would last throughout her life. I have discovered that practically all her closest and lifelong friends from Valparaiso were "Kappas." Louise Banister (Bartholomew) and Gertrude Polk were charter members of the Iota chapter, based in Valparaiso, which they all belonged to and which was formed in 1903.[209] Bondi herself, Ada Roessler (Bartholomew), Marie Timmons (Windle), Irene Lowenstine (Frank), Allegra Nesbit, and another close friend called Margaret Rowell joined somewhat later, in Bondi's case before 1914. She was president of the Iota chapter in 1914–15.[210]

While she was still living in the area, Bondi was a regular attendant at the sorority's annual luncheons, which started in 1915 and which during the first years were held in February at the Hammond Country Club.[211] In mid–April 1921, Bondi attended the Tri Kappa biennial convention at the Claypool Hotel in Indianapolis.[212] She had just begun a season with Gregory Kelly's stock company at English's Theatre in Indianapolis, which marked her return to the stage after an absence of more than a year.

After so many years of schooling, the question of what she was going to do with it all must have been pressing by the time she completed her Master's degree in 1916. She was 27 years old. As far as any specific career was concerned, she seems to have ruled out the obvious choice, which was teaching. She had acted regularly but not often in amateur productions and given recitals and dramatic readings. Yet in terms of progress, little had happened since her year in Vernal, Utah, that had been so rich in artistic rewards and where she had had a paying job as well. Arguably, there had even been a falling off in artistic activity since her return to Valparaiso in 1913, though she did participate in some student productions.

On June 30, 1914, for example, she had a leading role in a production of Madeleine Lucette Ryley's *An American Citizen* at the Memorial Opera House, where she had debuted as Little Lord Fauntleroy 18 years earlier. The *Valparaiso Times* assured its readers that "everything is in readiness for a most enjoyable evening," though the writer of this news item seemed more concerned with the weather and that there would be "no long waits between the acts." One of Bondi's professors, Rollo Anson Tallcott, was also in the cast.[213] The four-act comedy had starred Nat Goodwin and Maxine Elliott on Broadway in 1897. On February 16, 1916, Bondi played the female lead Agatha Posket in Arthur Wing Pinero's 1885 farce *The Magistrate*, also at the Memorial Opera House.[214]

Despite these regular, if infrequent, stage appearances, Bondi insisted that, for the longest time, she had no idea of making acting her profession. In an early feature article from 1926, she recalled that she "went in for reading and was a feature amateur actress in my home town at a tender age," but "had no definite desire to begin a professional career." In 1950, she repeated that she "had no very early ambitions for a stage career." She added that "in college she did become very conscious of diction" and ended up with a "Master's in oratory." In a lengthy interview with Frank Aversano in 1979, she emphasized her lack of youthful ambition yet again: "I don't think I ever had any thought really of going into the theatre or becoming an actress. I think I just enjoyed it. I don't know whether it was ego or what it was, but I was at complete ease and I loved performing … at an early age."[215]

There was more to it, though, than a lack of a clear vocation early in life. In the article from 1950, we can read that "both her parents were not pleased at first when she decided to go on the stage."[216] 26 years later, Aversano was also left with the impression that both her parents were against her becoming a professional actor.[217] From what we know of Eva Bondy's temperament, youthful ambitions, and nurturing of her daughter's talents, it seems clear the parental opposition to Bondi pursuing acting as a career chiefly came from her father. Abram Bondy is a shadowy figure in the narrative of Bondi's life compared to her mother, but the few letters to her parents we have from her hand make it clear that she loved both of them with a passion. Revealingly, when her father does put in a rare appearance in Bondi's recollections, it is usually in connection with his concern about her wanting to become an actress. It was not that he was adamantly or violently opposed; there was no overt patriarchal prohibition. With a loving daughter such as Beulah, such brutal methods were not necessary. It was more a quiet planting of seeds of doubt, more a refusal even to discuss seriously the possibility that she might go on the stage as a living. Such a "silver cord" was often identified with the maternal influence in a child's life back then, but in Bondi's case I am sure it was felt even more strongly in her relationship with her father.

Both Bondi's parents loved the theater, so Mr. Bondy's opposition was not so much to the stage in general as to the stage as his daughter's place of work: "whenever she took her parents to the theater to prove all actors weren't trash, her father would say of an actor like, say, Grant Mitchell, 'Well, he's playing a gentleman, you understand.'"[218] Little could they know then, that Bondi would make her Broadway debut in 1925 in a play with Grant Mitchell in the lead.

By 1916, the year she turned 27, she finally knew what she wanted to do with her life. Yet the path forward to a professional career as an actress was anything but clear. She was a respectable woman of the upper-middle classes, who had lived a sheltered life and who had had no experience of the rough and tumble of the professional theater. She was better educated than practically any actress of her generation, but she had no professional contacts and no non-amateur acting experience. How was she to make the decisive step and actually earn her living as an actress with the potential pitfalls and risks that might entail? How was she to overcome her father's soft-spoken but adamant opposition to acting as a career?

The deciding factor turned out to be gaining admission to an idealistic, non-commercial, professional and educational theatrical arena, which would propel her towards an acting career without burning her bridges to her old life of respectability and privilege. This new arena, this new world that she entered in the fall of 1916, was the world of Maurice Browne and the Chicago Little Theatre.

Frederick Maurice Browne was born in Reading, England in 1881 and came to the United States in 1910 to be reunited with his soon-to-be wife Ellen Van Volkenburg, an American he had met in Europe.[219] Public school educated and variously talented, Browne had lived an adventurous life as a published poet, soldier in the Boer War, world traveler, failed educator, and popular lecturer prior to settling in Van Volkenburg's hometown Chicago. He and "Nellie Van," as he called his wife, founded the Chicago Little Theatre there, which opened in November 1912, and spearheaded the artistic movement which borrowed its name and would be known as the Little Theatre Movement.

The Chicago Little Theatre was an art theater modeled on the Abbey Theatre in Dublin and was meant to be an alternative to the commercial theater and the star system. It was the Abbey's Lady Gregory who advised them not to hire professional actors: "Engage and train, as we of the Abbey have done, amateurs: shopgirls, school-teachers, counter-jumpers; cut-throat thieves rather than professionals. And prepare to have your hearts broken."[220] The Little Theatre's emphasis was on Greek classical dramas and modern classics by Ibsen, Shaw, Strindberg, Synge, Wilde, and Yeats. *The Trojan Women* by Euripides would become the company's signature play. There were also important differences in staging from the commercial theater, with more emphasis on innovation and experimentation in lighting, scenery, and music.

Browne was the artistic director of the company and Van Volkenburg the leading actress. They produced the plays together. In addition, Van Volkenburg pioneered the presentation of puppets and puppetry at the theater. The Little Theatre was also unique in being "perhaps the first English-speaking public theatre to base our activities on subscription membership." The membership fees gave them a working capital, though the subscription system led to the misconception that the theater was open to members only.[221]

The theater was located on the fourth floor of the Chicago Arts Building (aka the Studebaker Building) at 410 S. Michigan Ave., a beautiful 10-story Richardsonian Romanesque office building facing Grant Park, completed in 1885 and extensively renovated in 1898, where a 91-seat theater was purpose built. As Browne wrote in his memoirs: "we thought, poor innocents—a small theatre would cost less than a large one; therefore ours was to be a *little theatre*."[222]

Bondi recalled in a 1953 interview, that she had been doing courses at the Columbia School of Oratory in Chicago, when "the professional Chicago Little Theater accepted her as a trainee."[223] Without her parents' knowledge, Bondi had auditioned for Browne and for May Donnally Kelso (1855–1938), "a middle-aged stern-looking woman dressed in black," 62 at the time, who taught voice at the Little Theatre School and "had the power of imparting to others the beauty of her spirit and as much of her empirical knowledge as we were capable of receiving."[224] With her solid background in elocution and oratory, Bondi impressed May Kelso.

Bondi recalled in 1950, that they were accepting ten pupils and there were 250 applicants: "She was told to go home and learn an act from a Galsworthy play, a scene from Medea and several other assorted roles and return a week later." When Browne asked her "Why do you want to be an actor?," she responded: "I don't know that I do, and I don't know that I can act, but I'll never know unless I have the chance."[225]

On October 16, 1916, Maurice Brown wrote a letter to Bondi addressed to N. Washington St., which she kept all her life. He had received a favorable report on her from Mrs. Kelso, he wrote, which confirmed his own judgment. He continued: "I shall be glad to take you as a member of the Little Theatre. If you decide to come, I would recommend that you come as soon as possible so as not to miss any more of the work than is absolutely necessary."[226] Classes had started October 9.[227]

Uncle Louis lent her $450 for the school fees with the words: "Well, we'll say nothing about it and here is your four hundred and fifty dollars, and when you become a great actress you can repay me."[228] The tuition was $250, so the rest of the money must have been for living expenses.[229] There was still her father to be won over. He finally gave his seal of approval, Bondi recalled in 1979, when she invited him and her mother to a "beautiful Sunday program" followed by tea "without telling them any of the things that had gone before": "they met Mr. and Mrs. Browne and got the feeling of the whole Little Theatre and after the tea, when we went home, I said, 'Would you object if I became part of that unit?' and my father said, 'I couldn't imagine anything lovelier.'" In a slightly different version of the story, he relented by saying: "You'll need more money now."[230]

When Bondi arrived on the scene in October 1916, the Chicago Little Theatre had existed for four years and was embarking on its fifth season, which would be its final full season. The burgeoning and bold formative period was over. Bondi had missed out on landmark productions of *The Trojan Women* by Euripedes, *The Stronger* and *Creditors* by August Strindberg, *On Baile's Strand* and *The Shadowy Water* by William Butler Yeats, and *Anatol* by Arthur Schnitzler. Browne himself admitted that by this point "the glory had departed."[231] The theater was embroiled in a lengthy, acrimonious rent dispute with the landlord of the Fine Arts Building, which would be the beginning of the end, though the company lasted another year. On December 12, 1916, a headline in the *Chicago Tribune* read: "Little Theatre Near End? Directors Predict Demise Unless Financial Bolster Is Soon Secured."[232] Calls for financial assistance would be numerous in the coming year.

Bondi would initially not have been aware of all the turmoil. Her focus would have been not on what she had missed, but on what she had gained. Even though the Little Theatre was on its last legs, she was able to be part of this pioneering theater company for a little over a year and benefited broadly from the experience. The Little Theatre had the advantage for Bondi of being a stage company and an acting school in one. It was also "the centre and focus of Chicago's eager mental life," with a stream of celebrated artists and intellectuals enjoying the performances and gathering socially in the famous tea room afterward.[233]

Bondi looked back on the experience with unalloyed joy and gratitude. At the end of her life, she recalled that they had "wonderful training from nine-thirty in the morning to one thirty a.m. because as amateurs we had our own special dancing and diction classes."[234] The dance instructor was Mary Wood Hinman. There was also instruction in graphic art, Dalcroze eurhythmics, and music.[235]

An important part of the school experience was that "the amateurs had to put on a production of their own with costumes, scenery and direction from a member of the senior company."[236] The student production Bondi was part of was a dramatization by Marguerite Merington of *Cranford*, a classic novel of nineteenth-century English village life by Elizabeth Gaskell, which had been published in 1853. *Cranford*, novel or play, was not exactly the type of vehicle the Little Theatre normally went in for. I can imagine one reason for the choice was that, apart from Peter Jenkyns, and the dog Carlo, all the remaining nine characters were female. Browne recalled in his memoirs, that nearly all the aspirants wanting to be part of the company were women.[237] Then again, maybe the students were allowed to choose the play themselves.

*Cranford* was first performed as part of "a holiday program of seven performances" starting December 26, 1916. Bondi's hometown newspaper, the *Vidette-Messenger of Porter County*, informed its readers that she had "the leading role."[238] She was cast as the timorous spinster Miss Matilda Jenkyns, whose home and tea shop provide the setting for the play.[239]

Bondi was 27 playing 57 (or thereabouts). In playing "Miss Matty," Bondi's was set on her path as a character actress. Portraying women much older than her years would be her specialty for decades.

All the work both on stage and off was undertaken by the students, who doubled as actors and crew. In addition to her role, Bondi was responsible for "Draperies" and "Properties."[240] The only male, apart from the dog, involved in this entire enterprise was actor Jack Martin. Browne and Van Volkenburg were doing George Bernard Shaw's *Mrs. Warren's Profession* at the time and were not involved in this production, which was directed by Loretto Coffield Clarke. Woman directors would be very uncommon in Bondi's future stage and film experience.

Maurice Browne attended a performance and gave the actors his notes. Bondi recalled in 1950: "One of my most poignant memories was the occasion when I played 'Mathilde Brown' [*sic*].... Mr. Browne with program in hand commended each person in turn. I was last and by the time he reached me I had decided that I would never make an actress and had better go back to Valparaiso and get married. 'But what my director said changed all that,' said Beulah. 'I know you now by the process of elimination,' he told me, 'your characterization was so fine.'" Her eyes filled with tears as she spoke.[241] In a 1957 interview, Bondi added: "That was my first moment of hope. I've never been so thrilled. Being a very shy person, I've had the success of shy people who express themselves by finding something to hide behind."[242]

Browne had little to say of Bondi in his remarkably frank autobiography *Too Late to Lament*, published in 1955, the year he died age 73, though he did indirectly compliment her in his praise of the veteran Irish character actress Sara Allgood: "Sara Allgood at her prime was, with the possible exceptions in years to come of Beulah Bondi and Nellie Van, the finest character-actress whom I have seen."[243]

*Cranford* was even reviewed by the *Chicago Evening Post*. Bondi kept a clipping of the review, where we can read that the production was "apt and engaging," that some of young students "represent old age with facile characterization," and that they were "giving an extremely happy account of themselves in 'Cranford' and are also reflecting credit upon Mr. Browne." The critic concluded that "the performance is better than some I have seen given in the Little Theater by the senior company."[244]

*Cranford* was also presented intermittently in January and February 1917 and Bondi's father saw it then.[245] Bondi may also have appeared in the production of John Millington Synge's *Deirdre of the Sorrows* in February 1917.[246]

The entry of the United States into World War I in early April 1917 sounded the death knell for the Chicago Little Theatre, which had struggled financially from day one. Maurice Browne and the theater had declared bankruptcy on February 24, 1917.[247] An endowment of $10,000 had been raised, but the backers failed to live up to their promises. The subscribers and other audience members had fallen away.[248] After a long-running rent dispute with the owners of the Fine Arts Building, they finally had to give up their beloved "fourth-floor back" theater in the summer of 1917 and put their props and sets in storage.[249] In their last (half) season, they gave only 20 performances: nine in Chicago and 11 out of town.[250] The company's final production was Euripedes' *Medea* in Gilbert Murray's translation at the Central Music Hall in Chicago and on tour. Bondi played a member of the chorus of Corinthian women.[251] Though she had not been there at the beginning, she was with them till the bitter end. After the performance on December 1, 1917, the Chicago Little Theatre was history.[252]

# 2

# From Stock to Stock-in-Trade
## *1919–1924*

"It's too bad there aren't more stock companies today for young people."[1]

No other individual meant more to the development of Bondi's professional acting career than Stuart Walker. We have seen that her mother inspired her and trained her from an early age, gave her the best possible foundation in the basics of public speaking and acting, but there were limits to what Eva Bondy could do for her daughter in advancing her career professionally. For that purpose, Bondi needed a person with a solid footing in the world of the theater. After World War I, few people had a more central position in the American theater, particularly in the Midwest, than actor, director, playwright, and producer Stuart Walker.

Stuart Armstrong Walker was born in Augusta, Kentucky, on March 4, 1880, making him nine years Bondi's senior.[2] He had begun his theatrical career as an actor and served his apprenticeship with legendary producer David Belasco, making his stage debut in 1909. He was also associated with the equally legendary Jessie Bonstelle, before becoming known in 1915 as the producer-director of an independent repertory company called the Portmanteau Theatre. From this time until he went to Hollywood in 1930, Stuart Walker was one of the most important stage producers in the United States, working particularly to bring quality repertory theater to the Midwest and to nurture new talent. His motto was "America's best plays—America's best actors."[3]

Actors have always been dependent on producers who are willing to take a chance on them, particularly at the start of their careers. Walker was famous for his willingness to sponsor unknown beginners and allow them to learn on the job. A number of actors who would go on to successful careers got their start with him. As Walker's biographer records: "He became their mentor, parent, father-confessor, advisor and controlling agent. He expected unquestioned loyalty from his company members."[4] In 1929, the *Cincinnati Enquirer* offered one statistic. "At the beginning of this year, 45 players trained by Stuart Walker were playing on Broadway, 15 of whom were playing leads, one of whom was starred, and two of whom were featured."[5] Bondi was one of the two featured Walker alumni on Broadway that season. In January 1929, she had opened in her career-altering role as Emma Jones in Elmer Rice's *Street Scene*.

Walker kept Bondi continuously employed for months and years on end between 1919 and 1930. On the basis alone of being the one who gave her more work than any other individual employer, he exerted a lasting influence. That is not to suggest that Bondi did not finally outgrow her mentor, which she did, or that she would not have had a career without him. She might well have. But as my friend, producer Paul Gregory once told me when I asked him if he or Orson Welles had done more for Agnes Moorehead: You always owe the most to the person who gives you your start. Walker was to Bondi what Welles would be to Moorehead 20 years later.

Beyond the question of employment, which is no small matter for an actor in a highly competitive field, Walker's influence was also felt in the force of his brilliant, mercurial, and stimulating personality. He was a hard taskmaster and he had buckets of experience and insight to pass on to a receptive and talented woman like Bondi. Some of the things Walker taught her were preserved in interviews down through the years. For example, Bondi never forget an incident involving Walker and a young actor "pouting over his part" and threatening to walk out. "Walker held up a glass of water, stuck his little finger therein, held his wet finger up. 'You see this drop of water here?' he asked the rebel. 'Yes? Now do you see the glass of water and how little that drop is missed?'"[6]

Among other things, Walker taught Bondi that power on the stage could also reside in repose: "Quiet poise, my dear, is much more eloquent than words. And when movement is necessary make it count. Unnecessary gestures not only are amateurish but confusing."[7]

In her last interview, two months before she died, Bondi recalled her first season with Walker in 1919: "Mr. Walker was very severe that first summer in Indianapolis.... He told me years later, he knew I had talent, and that the theater was a hard life. He was either going to make me or break me; he was very hard on me, but would always give me a pat on the back when I did things right.... He put a good tough hide on me so I could not be hurt or disappointed. By his preparing me, I never have felt in any way timid or apprehensive when I meet a new producer or director. I can meet them on an equal footing."[8]

For Bondi, it all started back in 1917, when Maurice Browne put in a word for her with Walker, whose new stock company was based at the Shubert-Murat Theatre in Indianapolis. Bondi was granted an interview with the then 37-year-old Walker, who "assured her that she had a future on the stage and would soon hear from him." Two years passed and no word from Walker. Bondi kept her hand in by directing and acting in amateur productions and appearing in one-woman shows for clubs and societies. She also sent Walker a short note three times a year to remind him of her existence.

In May 1919, she was on her way to play Sonya, the aged mother, in a student production of *The Flickering Flame* at DuPauw University in Gary, Indiana, when she discovered, while changing trains in Indianapolis, that her trunk had been lost or delayed. Forced to stay overnight to find the trunk, Bondi attended a production of Walker's company at the Murat that evening. During the interval she sent in a note to Walker, but only to say she was enjoying the play. As she recalled in 1953: "The great man sent for me, interviewed me again backstage, and at last actually engaged me as a professional."[9] Clearly, Bondi was in the right place at the right time. Walker's third season in Indianapolis had begun on May 5 with Edward Childs Carpenter's *The Cinderella Man*.[10] On June 2, 1919, Beulah Bondi made her professional stage debut at the Murat Theatre in Indianapolis as Mrs. Tompkins in the Stuart Walker stock company's production of Jerome K. Jerome's drama *The Passing of the Third Floor Back*. She was 30 years old.

*The Passing of the Third Floor Back* was a modern-day morality play from 1908 about "how the traveler who stops for lodging in the sordid London boarding-house touches the slumbering better half to life in each of his fellow lodgers, and leaves the place and its inmates and atmosphere transformed at the end of his brief sojourn."[11] It may have created a vogue for dramas using boarding houses as a microcosm of the world, which included *The Lodger* (1917) by Horace Annesley Vachell and *39 East* (1919) by Rachel Crothers. It certainly was a forerunner of other mystical and supernatural plays, like Sutton Vane's *Outward Bound* (1924) and Alberto Casella's *Death Takes a Holiday* (1929), that tried to go beyond realism to explore the human condition and the connections between life and the afterlife.

The best female roles in the play were the landlady Mrs. Sharpe (Beatrice Maude), the maid Stasia (Lael Davis), and the spinster Miss Kite (Elizabeth Patterson), but Mrs. Tompkins, who hopes her daughter Vivian (Margaret Mower) will make an advantageous marriage to save the family from penury and disgrace, was not a bad beginning for a novice. It was the first of a long series of dissatisfied wives and bad mothers Bondi would play during her career on the stage and screen, culminating in the 1950s with her role as Ma Bridges in William A. Wellmann's visually stunning western melodrama *Track of the Cat* and Mrs. Crane in Samuel Raphaelson's *Hilda Crane*, her penultimate role on Broadway. In *The Passing of the Third Floor Back*, Mrs. Tompkins's big scene, if you can call it that, was her nostalgic exchange with the Stranger (George Gaul) about their ostensibly shared youth. Bondi was "noticed" for the first time in a professional production when the *Indianapolis Star* listed among those who "deserve particular mention and praise": "Beulah Bondy as the shrewish wife who remembers the romance of her youth."[12]

As her husband, Major Tompkins, Bondi had Aldrich Bowker, a 44-year-old character actor from Ashby, Massachusetts. For the next ten years, "Bowkie" would be her most "significant other" in the company, paired with her as her husband or in other roles both comic and dramatic in nearly 40 Stuart Walker productions. Nearly completely bald, jowly, and paunchy, with beetling, dark eyebrows, Bowker was best known for playing Grandpa Martin Vanderhof as a replacement on Broadway and in the Chicago company of *You Can't Take It with You*. He had a brief but intense film career, mainly at Warner Bros., between 1939 and 1942, but never acted with Bondi on the big screen. Ill health forced him to retire and he died in Los Angeles of arteriosclerosis in 1947, as Bondi was aboard ship bound for her first trip to Hawaii.[13]

The work week in the Stuart Walker stock company was rigorous to say the least. The company members ate, drank, and breathed theater almost uninterruptedly Monday to Saturday and only on Sundays did they have any time off. Each week there was a new play, which would open on Monday night and run every evening through to Saturday. In addition, there were matinees on Wednesday, Thursday, and Saturday. As if that was not enough: during the daytime they were also engaged in learning their lines, blocking, and rehearsing next week's play. According to JoAnn Yeoman, Walker "had his method of rehearsing down to a science." The actors were fortunate, though, in that Walker paid them for rehearsals, which was not required by Equity until 1926.[14] Stock would be Bondi's most important learning arena. She said in 1937, that she considered it "the only training for an actor," adding: "I just wonder how young people will ever do without it."[15]

In addition to Mrs. Tompkins, the six other identifiable roles Bondi played in Indianapolis that summer show the breadth and variety in the types of parts she performed early in her career. Between early June and the company's final performance of the season on August 30, 1919, Bondi gained new, vital experience playing (in chronological order): a conventional, upper-class, British mother in a costume drama; an unconventional, middle-class mother in a contemporary drama; an old deaf aunt in a light comedy bordering on farce; an elderly Irish American landlady in a melodrama; a young performer in vaudeville in a comedy; and a rich, American dowager in a comedy. Only the second to last of these characters was anywhere close to her own age.

I will have more to say about Arnold Bennett and Edward Knoblock's family saga *Milestones* when we get to 1930, as Bondi appeared in this drama on Broadway that year. In 1919, she played the shipbuilder protagonist John Read's mother, Mrs. Rhead. Mrs. Rhead is nearly 60 and only appears in the first act, set in her drawing room in 1860. She is yet another bad mother, in that she wants her daughter Gertrude to make the sensible choice in a husband, rather than following her heart. Mrs. Rhead is conservative and does not realize the world is changing. She makes lace and reads Dickens. For this costume drama, Bondi was decked out in widow's weeds with a little lace cap on her head.[16] There was not much to the role and Bondi was not mentioned in the reviews. The showy character part was her independent-minded daughter, Gertrude Rhead, played by Elizabeth Patterson, who was 15 years older than Bondi. Bondi was already becoming accustomed to playing elderly women, a major component both of her stage and film careers.

Dutch-English Rudolf Besier's *Don* from 1909 was the play of the week starting July 7, 1919. Besier is best known as the author of *The Barretts of Wimpole Street* from 1930. *Don* was only his second play and is subtitled "A Comedy in Three Acts." Yet *Don* is not a comedy in any conventional sense (apart from the fact that it ends happily), but is instead a tense and gripping drama about a young, handsome idealist, Stephen "Don" Bonington, who imagines it is his duty to save a female friend, Elizabeth Thompsett, from an unhappy marriage. The play represents with startling economy the rapidly accelerating chain of events that ensues when Don (George Gaul) brings Elizabeth (Margaret Mower) to safety in his parents' home on the same weekend that his fiancée Ann and her parents, General and Mrs. Sinclair, are visiting. Ann Sinclair (Beatrice Maude) has nicknamed Stephen "Don," not after Don Juan, but after Don Quixote and there is no small degree of Ibsen's idealist Brand in him as well. According to Ann, he "doesn't seem to understand the little amenities of life."[17]

The play is not without its humorous aspects, despite the seriousness of what develops into a life-and-death conflict between Stephen and Mrs. Thompsett's working-class, fanatically religious husband Albert (George Sommes). This expert situation comedy element occurs particularly in the first act and as a result of the hero's utter obliviousness to, or sheer disregard for, how his behavior—coming between a husband and wife, running away with her on the very weekend he is supposed to be entertaining his future in-laws, spending a night alone with her in a hotel—will look from the point of view of conventional morality. That morality is represented by his parents, Canon Paul Bonington (Edgar Stehli) and Evelyn Bonington (Elizabeth Patterson), and by his prospective father-in-law, General Bertram Sinclair (Aldrich Bowker).

The only one capable of seeing the seriocomic aspects of the situation is the general's wife, Ann's mother, and Stephen's potential mother-in-law, Ella Sinclair (Beulah Bondi), who is described in the stage directions as "a handsome, masterful, well-preserved, humorous woman of the world."[18] This was the best role Bondi played during her first season on the stage, just as, from a modern-day perspective at least, *Don* was the most interesting play she performed during that season. The uniqueness of the play was recognized even back in 1919. The *Indianapolis News* called it "one of the last decade's none too numerous plays of literary distinction."[19] The *Indianapolis Star*'s review opened with: "No more delightful comedy than 'Don' has been presented by the Stuart Walker players in their three seasons in Indianapolis." Further down, we read: "It seemed to the audience to be something new." And even further down: "Beulah Bondy is very clever as Mrs. Sinclair."[20]

In Frank Craven's light comedy *Too Many Cooks*, which had been a hit on Broadway in 1914, Bondi had the relatively minor role of elderly Aunt Louise and "tottered about the stage."[21] As she recalled in 1932, she only had two lines in her one scene, where she and many other members of the interfering Cook family come to look at the home of the young newlywed leads. To distinguish her from the other relatives, Bondi decided to make her Aunt Louise deaf and to carry an ear trumpet: "Then during the scene, though I had no lines, I could listen through the ear trumpet and speak my two lines in the high voice of a deaf woman and do the little things deaf people do."[22] The newlyweds were played by recently married and recently arrived, rising stars Gregory Kelly and Ruth Gordon, who would show up in Bondi's life again in not too long.

The part that really got Bondi noticed by the press, though, was the folksy, Hibernian landlady Mrs. Halloran in Willard Mack's popular melodrama *Kick In* from 1914. This production opened on July 28, in the thirteenth week of the season. *Kick In* was one of the few good old-fashioned crime and suspense melodramas in Bondi's stock repertoire. It has something of the same feeling as the roughly contemporaneous *Kindling* in its focus on poor honest folk trying not to be tarnished by their contact with the seamy side of life; and in the happy ending, where justice prevails, good is rewarded, and evil punished. *Kick In* had a morphine addict prominent among the characters, the heroine's ne'er-do-well brother Charley, here played by Gregory Kelly, while *Kindling* could only proffer a thinly veiled pimp.

Mrs. Halloran is prevalent in Act II, less so in Act III, and also gets a look-in at the police station in Act IV. This is a landlady role far above the average in visibility and importance, being much more than a door-opener or comic relief character. While the *Indianapolis Star* simply listed Bondi at the end of their review among "others in the cast," the *Indianapolis News* wrote: "Beulah Bondy does a nice bit in the part of Mrs. Halloran, an Irish landlady. It is done in just the right spirit and without caricature."[23] Beyond brief mentions in reviews, Bondi finally got her own news item in the *Indianapolis News* on July 31, after two months with the company, giving readers some of her background.[24] In their "Notes of the Stage" the following day, the *Indianapolis Star* wrote: "Miss Bondy has received far too little recognition of her skill both as a comedienne and as a make-up artist. Her performance in the current 'Kick In' is a particularly fine one, and both her make-up and brogue fit to perfection the type of good old Irish landlady that is known as 'Mother.'"[25] It is worth adding that the closest Bondi ever came to playing a landlady on film was the fantasy sequence in *It's a Wonderful Life*, which shows what might have happened to James Stewart's family and friends had he never been born.

Bondi had the chance to support Stuart Walker for the second and final time the following week, when the company played James Montgomery's hit comedy *Nothing but the Truth* from the 1916–17 season on Broadway. The first time had been in her second week, when the company reprised one of its most popular productions from the 1918 stock season in Indianapolis, Edward Sheldon's *Romance*, and Bondi played a minor role as a guest at a reception in the first act.[26] Since then Walker had been too busy directing to perform himself, but Gregory Kelly's arrival meant Walker could share the directing duties with him.[27] Despite a good premise about what happens when a man bets $10,000 he can tell "nothing but the truth" for 24 hours, Montgomery's comedy was trite, tedious, and unsophisticated. Walker played the truth teller Bob Bennett. Bondi was cast in her most unlikely role of the season, given her previous parts as older women, as a "'tough' vaudeville queen."[28] She and Ruth Gordon played sisters and fellow vaudevillians Mabel and Sabel, who get mixed up in the action, albeit fairly extraneously. Mabel (Gordon) was the better part, with Sabel (Bondi) basically just an adjunct to Mabel. The *Indianapolis Star* wrote: "The two chorus girls … are filled with idiotic optimism, Miss Gordon covering herself with glory as 'an innocent girl.' It too obvious that 'rough stuff' has not been the forte of Miss Gordan and Miss Bondy."[29]

Bondi's first chance to create a character in a brand-new play came at the end of the season. *Piccadilly Jim* was written by P.G. Wodehouse and Guy Bolton and was based on the former's comic novel of the same name from 1917. Bondi played Eugenia Crocker, an unmistakable dowager of the type that would dominate the stage in the 1920s and the screen in the 1930s. Mrs. Crocker's second, beleaguered husband Bingley Crocker (Edgar Stehli) is a former character actor in a modest way with one ne'er-do-well son, James Crocker (Gregory Kelly), the "Piccadilly Jim" of the title and the darling of the papers with his scandals and numerous "contretemps." The elder Crockers met crossing the Atlantic to New York and were married by the time they arrived. Mrs. Crocker is passionately Anglophile and plans to stay on in London indefinitely, where she hopes to become a force in society. Her fondest dream is that her husband will be knighted, so she can impress her sister and rival, Nesta Pett (Elizabeth Patterson), who had once accused Mr. Crocker of being a gold-digger, leading to the sisters' estrangement. According to the novel, "This was a woman who, like her sister Nesta, had been able all her life to accomplish more with a glance than other women with recrimination and threat."[30]

Indianapolis responded with enthusiasm to the play. The *Indianapolis News* wrote: "'Piccadilly Jim' has a better chance along Broadway than any of Mr. Walker's first productions since 'Seventeen.'" Eugenia and Bingley Crocker were only seen in the opening and finale of the piece. Despite his positive overall impression, the reviewer felt impelled to point out that the prologue "arouses expectations that are not fulfilled. Every theatergoer will expect to meet the stepmother [Mrs. Crocker] and father of Piccadilly Jim later in the play and be somewhat disappointed when they do not show up before the finale."[31]

The last performance of *Piccadilly Jim* on August 30 marked the end of the Stuart Walker season at the Murat. The play was taken on a brief tour to Wilkes-Barre, Pennsylvania; Wilmington, Delaware; Hartford, Connecticut; and Washington, D.C., in December 1919 with Bondi still in the role of Mrs. Crocker. Critics there wrote that "'Piccadilly Jim' is destined to enjoy a long and successful career," that the play "proved to be a pleasing bit of amusement without at all ruining William Shakespeare's claim to immortality as a dramatist," and that "none of the roles of the piece make deep demands on the histrionism of the players, who are all of experience and ability."[32] Despite the hopeful predictions, *Piccadilly Jim* never made it to Broadway.

When the season at the Murat was over and it became clear that Bondi was not going into Walker's next venture, a lengthy tour of his hit play *Seventeen* starting in Detroit, the Indianapolis papers wrote that "Mr. Walker's plans for others of the company, including…. Beulah Bondy have not been disclosed."[33] Yet the *Indianapolis Star was* confident that "Beulah Bondy will eventually find herself on Broadway."[34] As a token of the genuine affection she had inspired, the Writers Club of Indianapolis hosted a farewell picnic in her honor at Garfield Park on August 27.[35] In summing up the season, which he called the "most successful" so far, and selecting the six best plays among the 18 presented by Stuart

Walker's company, the drama critic for the *Indianapolis News* selected three that Bondi contributed to: *Milestones*, *Don*, and *Too Many Cooks*.[36] Despite an auspicious beginning to her professional acting career, though, it would be two and a half years before Bondi rejoined the Stuart Walker stock company and six years until she stood on a Broadway stage.

The year of 1920 may be best described as the lost year in Bondi's adult life and acting career; "lost" both because we have little information about her doings and whereabouts this year and because she made no progress in her career. In an interview late in life, she more than suggested that her year off from acting was a result of advice from her demanding mentor Stuart Walker. In an interview in 1961, she described how her first year as a professional actress had left her "a wraith and a physical wreck." She related how she had been "singled out daily for tongue lashings, ridicule and endless repetition of the most minute stage business while the professionals sat and watched."[37] She told an audience after a showing of *Make Way for Tomorrow* in Valparaiso in 1976, that "her first director," who was "extremely cruel," once told her she "'had no more talent than on the head of a pin.'"[38]

In 1979, Frank Aversano, who interviewed Bondi extensively for an article in *American Classic Screen*, was told the same story with the line about her lack of talent attributed to Walker. Aversano also got the impression that "Mr. Walker's rather unique direction resulted in her having to take a year off from the theater."[39] When Walker's fourth season at the Shubert-Murat opened on June 1, 1920, Bondi was not a part of the company. Clearly, he had decided not to reengage her for a second season. Possibly, he was testing her resilience and staying power. In an interview in 1937, Bondi called him "one of the greatest trainers of young stage talent" and added: "He will either make you or break you."[40] Long after Walker's death, Bondi continued to defend his behavior, saying in 1961 that "it was the severest kind of discipline, but there was a purpose in it. It was to put strength in me, to toughen me."[41]

The only specific information we have about Bondi's whereabouts this year is the 1920 U.S. Census. When census enumerator Lucille Palmer called at Bondi's childhood home at 203 N. Washington St. on January 12, 1920, she found two families living there. According to the record, the owner of the house was now a 51-year-old register clerk in the post office, Harry Albery, originally from Ohio, who lived there with his wife Mamie, grown children Lola and Lester, and father-in-law George W. Wolf. We also find A.O. Bondy, now living as a renter in the house he formerly owned with his wife Eva. He is listed as being 64, born in Michigan, and his occupation is "Real Estate." The place of birth of Abram's father is given as "Prussia," which has been crossed out and replaced by "Europe"; and of his mother, "Saxony," which has been crossed out and replaced by "Germany." The mother tongue of both Abram's parents is given as "Hebrew." Eva M. Bondy is listed as being 59, born in Illinois, with both her parents born in Indiana. Under occupation is written "None."[42] Eva would turn 60 a week after the census was taken. Then, on the bottom of the following page of the census, enumerated the next day, we find "Beulah Bondy," who gives her age correctly as 30 and her occupation as "Actress."[43]

What is more interesting is that on February 24, 1920, Bondi appears in the census a second time. This time she is living in a boarding house at 814 Halsey St. in the Bedford-Stuyvesant section of Brooklyn, New York. The boarding house is a large one and has a decidedly theatrical bent, as nearly all the 45 other lodgers are actors. Bondi gives her age as 30 and her occupation as "Actress Theatre."[44] I do not recognize any of the actors' names as being people she had worked with in stock. It seems reasonable to assume that she had gone to New York of her own volition to seek work on the stage. This venture was unsuccessful, and she likely returned home to Valparaiso and lived quietly with her parents for the remainder of the year.

As we have seen, Bondi had acted with leading man Gregory Kelly and his wife Ruth Gordon during her first season with the Stuart Walker stock company in Indianapolis. Kelly became the instrument of her return to the stage in mid–April 1921, when she joined the stock company he had formed with his wife as an off-shoot of Stuart Walker's. While Walker's company was playing at the Murat as usual, Kelly and his company was installed at English's Theatre, part of a large hotel which occupied the northeast quadrant of Monument Circle in Indianapolis between 1880 and 1948.

Bondi was not continuously employed in the company this spring, as Angela Ogden was their first character woman. She worked intermittently with them from April till early June. Among the plays we know she did were *Clarence*, *A Tailor-Made Man*, *Happiness*, *Adam and Eva*, and *A Prince There Was*. In Booth Tarkington's *Clarence*, which was the first show of the Kelly-Gordon season, she played the secretary Mrs. Martyn, who only appears in Act I.[45] There was not much to her role in *A Tailor-Made Man* either, as a stereotypically snobbish and conservative dowager, though she is seen in three of the play's four acts.[46] Mrs. Stanlaw is chiefly concerned that her daughter is throwing herself in an unseemly way at the hero of this male Cinderella story by Harry James Smith, which ran for a year on Broadway in 1917–18.

Bondi had even smaller roles in her remaining plays at English's. None of these parts could compare with the many good opportunities she had been given during her first season in stock in 1919. She had taken one step back in order to begin to move forward again. Her only other stage-related activities in 1921 were directing a few amateur productions of plays like *The Boomerang* and *Miss Somebody Else*.[47] At the end of the year, she was engaged by a stock company in Toledo, Ohio, as "an additional character woman."[48] It was time to get her acting career back on track.

The year she turned 33, 1922, was arguably the busiest year of Bondi's acting career. There was certainly no single year where she played a wider range of roles. She spent the whole year acting in stock companies, starting with the Toledo Players in Toledo, Ohio; then rejoining Stuart Walker's stock company in Cincinnati between April and September, and finally returning to Toledo for the remainder of the year. She worked in stock for at least 38 weeks that year, maybe more. In sum, I have documented that she performed 30 different roles in 27 different plays. She had only played one of them, Mrs. Halloran in *Kick In*, before.

That year there was nothing she could not do and the number and variety of her roles is stunning. She played everything from stiff-necked, upper-class dowagers to whorehouse madams. Agewise, she ranged from young women to tottering old grandmothers. She played working-class slaveys and middle-class mothers; spinsters and secretaries and spinsters who were secretaries; French maids, Italian primadonnas, and kidnappers. She even sang! And then she played a role or two we might well wish she had not…

Starting in January 1922, The Toledo Players, based at the Toledo Theatre on St. Clair Street in Toledo, Ohio, was the third stock company Bondi worked for, after her first stint with Stuart Walker in 1919 and her season with Gregory Kelly in 1921. Her first production with her new company was Rachel Crothers's romantic comedy with spiritual overtones, *A Little Journey*, which had been a hit on Broadway during the 1918–19 season. John Corbin, writing in the *New York Times*, deemed it "a simple, moving story, deftly and very convincingly told."[49]

As the title suggests, the play depicts a journey, a train journey, in fact, in which a number of passengers of various ages and backgrounds are thrown together in a Pullman car with all the dramatic potentialities that such temporary propinquity can generate. Naturally, there is a love story, in this case between a high-minded young rancher with saint-like qualities and an urbane, sophisticated good-time girl from New York fallen on bad times, who, homeless and destitute after a lover has failed to marry her, is on her way to throw herself on the mercy of her brother in the West. The different plotlines come to a dramatic climax when the train is involved in a serious crash, which gives a whole new and more literal meaning to the passengers being thrown together. Today, *A Little Journey* seems tedious in its mysticism, forced spirituality, and moral earnestness: Think *Lost Horizon* meets *The Passing of the Third Floor Back* with a dash of Bret Harte's "The Luck of Roaring Camp" at the end in the form of an orphaned baby "adopted" by her fellow train passengers after her mother is killed.

Bondi in an unidentified little old lady role during her years in stock. Bondi was canny enough to recognize that her future lay in character roles and specialized in playing women much older than herself from the beginning of her career. It took some years, though, before Hollywood understood her potential in elderly woman roles. Lucy Cooper in *Make Way for Tomorrow* from 1937 was the first of many, but remained her finest effort in this vein.

Among the ensemble cast is a little old lady, a grandmother called Mrs. Bay, who is traveling with her young, pretty granddaughter Lily. Mrs. Bay may have been the most significant character Bondi played this entire year. Her interpretation of the role made a resounding hit, not just in Toledo, but when she reprised it in Cincinnati in mid–May. It cemented her "niche" as a young actress who could play old ladies convincingly. Though not her first old lady role, it was her first high-profile one, the one that really got her noticed. There is a sense, then, in which all Bondi's little old ladies can be traced back to Mrs. Bay—especially her most famous one, Lucy Cooper in *Make Way for Tomorrow*—in her mix of sweet and annoying. Furthermore, Mrs. Bay is deaf, which creates some incidental comedy. Despite her age and impairment, she is vital, energetic, and full of the joy of life. A little judgmental, yes; protective of the purity of her granddaughter and travel companion, Lily (Lael Corya), but basically good-hearted. Outspoken, as well, she comes into her own after the train wreck and calls two of the more unsympathetic characters, Mrs. Welch and Mr. Smith, "fat" on several occasions.[50] This bit of tartness in her composition is deftly done.

The critic for the *Toledo Blade* wrote: "Beulah Bondy, as the fussy but spry and determined old lady, Mrs. Bay, does a bit that is almost flawless. The part is an element in the comedy relief of the piece, but Miss Bondy makes few sacrifices of truth and realism to win laughs. In voice, gestures and mannerisms she displays complete mastery."[51] The *Cincinnati Enquirer* was no less impressed in its review of a play that, as in Toledo, had not been seen in that city before. The critic wrote specifically about Bondi: "One of the neatest bits of eccentric characterization seen on a Cincinnati stage in a long time is that provided by Miss Beulah Bondy in the role of Mrs. Bay. It would be a very passive performance but for her."[52]

Bondi also turned out three redoubtable dowagers this year; the type of older, domineering women, married or widowed, who rule the roost and dictate to society, and a type Bondi would be closely identified with, particularly during the early years of her film career. These three were Mrs. Guildford in *The Saving Grace*, Mrs. Burke-Smith in *Kindling*, and Lady Hurley in *Passers-by*. *The Saving Grace* was "an English comedy of the first water"[53] by C. Haddon Chambers, which had opened on Broadway in 1918. The play had some similarities with the later, better, and more familiar Somerset Maugham play *The Circle* (1921) in exploring what an adulterous affair ending in a scandalous marriage and ensuing social ostracism does to the married couple involved. Maybe "exploring" is saying a bit too much in the case of *The Saving Grace*. Despite the high opinion of the *New York Times*, today this comedy seems paper thin and very old-fashioned.

Mrs. Guildford was the "heavy" of the piece, "a grande dame very solidly and subtly characterized"[54] and the thoroughly unpleasant neighbor of hero and heroine Blinn and Georgina Corbett (played by Aldrich Bowker and Spring Byington). As dowagers often do, Mrs. Guildford gets a good build-up, before her grand entrance at a dinner party in Act II. She even refers to herself as a "she-bear" and "even a she-cat." It must be said in her defense, that Mrs. Guildford does thaw out somewhat and is partially mollified by the discovery that Blinn is "one of the Shropshire Corbetts."[55] It comes as no surprise that the original incumbent of the role, Charlotte Granville, was 58 when she played it, while Bondi was only 32. Audiences grew so accustomed to seeing Bondi in older parts, that when she played a woman in her 20s in *The Boomerang*, the *Toledo Blade* felt compelled to comment: "Beulah Bondi in a young girl role astonished those who recall her chiefly in eccentric character parts."[56]

*The Saving Grace* was followed at the Toledo Theatre by a melodrama in which Bondi played yet another domineering dowager. The author, Charles Kenyon, called his play *Kindling* a "comedy drama," but it had some standard melodramatic traits and the radical politics were more window-dressing than a deep social critique. The critic for the *New York Times* found it "an unusually interesting play" back in 1911, when it opened on Broadway with a 61-year-old Helen Tracy as Mrs. Burke-Smith.[57]

This dowager's arrival is also elaborately preannounced. Mrs. Burke-Smith is the owner of the building in which the poor but honest heroine, Maggie Schultz (Margaret Cusack), lives and is brought to the latter's aid by her niece, Alice (Spring Byington), Mrs. Burke-Smith's niece that is. Complications ensue when Mrs. Burke-Smith hires Maggie as a seamstress and the young woman is tempted to stray from the path of righteousness by her desire to give her unborn child a better future. Mrs. Burke-Smith has strong opinions on every imaginable subject. Like Mrs. Guildford, though, by the end of the play she has been made to see the error of her ways, which clears the way for the young couple she has power over to live happily ever after.

The local paper was fulsome in its praise of the production: "Never has the Toledo Theatre company presented anything with greater dramatic effect or finer understanding." The local paper also found that "Mrs. Burke-Smith is played—hyphen and all—with rare insight by Beulah Bondy."[58] The upstairs washerwoman neighbor, Mrs. Bates, is an amusing role, especially in her no holds barred encounter with Mrs. Burke-Smith, where Mrs. Bates calls her a "high-toned robber."[59] The part was originated by Annie Mack Berlein on Broadway in 1911–12. Annie Mack, who was born in 1850, also created the landlady Mrs. Halloran in the crime drama *Kick In* on Broadway, a role which Bondi had first played in Indianapolis in 1919 and which she reprised at the Cox Theatre in Cincinnati the first week of July 1922. The local reviewer found "the play fails to be quite convincing." More specifically: "Beulah Bondy, as the Irish landlady, Mrs. Halloran, and Lael Corya as her daughter Daisy provide the main comedy relief, and do it with the accustomed skill. Their scenes are the brightest spots of the performance."[60]

C. Haddon Chambers's *Passers-by*, "a character romance of distinguished charm," opened both in London and in New York in 1911 and was "the most successful play of the last London season" according to the *New York Times*.[61] This is a kind of precursor of Shaw's *Pygmalion* (1914) with Peter Waverton (Arthur Albertson) as a kind of Professor Higgins, who tries to have a positive influence on "passers-by," and his valet William Pine (Corbet Morris) in the place of Higgins's housekeeper Mrs. Pearce. Today the play seems like sentimental claptrap of the most tedious kind.

Bondi's role, Lady Amelia Hurley, is Peter Waverton's half-sister and a real piece of work. "An unpleasantly officious person,"[62] she is responsible for the separation of Peter and his one great love Margaret Summers (Spring Byington) back in the day when the former was governess to Lady Hurley's children. Lady Hurley occurs in Act II and III and is thoroughly unpleasant in both. As an arch villainess, there is little to this character; no depth or psychological interest. Unlike Mrs. Guildford and Mrs. Burke-Smith, Lady Hurley is unredeemably evil-minded and refuses to see the error of her ways. The *Cincinnati Enquirer* raved about the production and found that "it is in the character roles chiefly that the play makes its strongest appeal." "Beulah Bondy is excellent as Lady Hurley" and the play as a whole was "the dramatic treat of the summer season."[63]

As an extension of this discussion of Bondi's dowager roles of 1922, we can add the doting mother of all time, Mrs. Bonington in Rudolf Besier's *Don*, who is willing to sacrifice any principle to save her son Stephen "Don" Bonington from a scarlet woman or her potentially murderous husband. We recall that Bondi played Don's worldly mother-in-law Mrs. Sinclair in Indianapolis in 1919. In Cincinnati in mid–August 1922, Judith Lowry played Mrs. Sinclair and Bondi played Mrs. Bonington: "Beulah Bondy was in her own element as the poet's fussy and adoring mother—really the mother militant, ready to fight for her son no matter what was said of him."[64]

Among Bondi's inevitable spinster roles this year, we find Lizzie Roberts in *The Lottery Man*, Miss Montmorency in *Too Many Husbands*, Sadie in *The Show Shop*, and Miss Curtis in *The Charm School*. The last two were also secretaries, a not uncommon combination of roles, as few working women, on the stage at least, were married. Lizzie Roberts in Rida Johnson Young's farce *The Lottery Man* had been created on Broadway by classic comedienne Helen Lowell back in 1909. Described by the *New York Times* critic as " a poor, weak, anaemic-looking beanpole," Miss Lizzie finds herself in the unfortunate position of being lady companion to a much more substantial woman, Mrs. Peyton (Adelaide Hibbard), a "faddist," who is "addicted to 'transformations and tight lacing.'"[65] Lizzie must try out all the obesity pills and other diet remedies before her employer will risk them. Again, Bondi scored a hit with her new Toledo audience: "It is from Beulah Bondi and Adelaide Hibbard, however, that the laughs chiefly emanate. Miss Bondi is again proving her ability as a versatile character woman. Her make-up as Lizzie Roberts, an elderly, attenuated spinster of the now almost extinct 'old maid' type, is a scream, and her acting of the role decidedly clever. With her old-fashioned clothes, her dismal expression of countenance, and her woebegone voice, she closely approached burlesque, but never got 'out of character' for an instant."[66]

*Too Many Husbands* from 1919 is the play that shows most clearly that Somerset Maugham was not Oscar Wilde and never would be. This is because the striving for Wilde's lightness of touch and deft inversion of conventional values is so blatant, that a comparison becomes inevitable, a comparison that is not to Maugham's advantage. Unfortunately, there is only a single line in *Too Many Husbands* that can compare with any of the quips in *The Importance of Being Earnest* (see below). In what may best be seen as an attempt to illustrate how the World War has dealt a savage blow to the upper-classes and turned British class relations topsy-turvy, Maugham even drags in a blatantly extraneous scene where a cook interviews her prospective employer, rather than the other way around.

In *Too Many Husbands*, which was presented in the fifth week of Stuart Walker's season in Cincinnati, Bondi got a chance to play one of her more unusual roles and a highly amusing one at that. Miss Esmeralda Montmorency is unmarried and a working woman. Her line of work is being a professional "co-respondent" in divorce cases, at a time when adultery had to be proven if a couple wanted to get a divorce in the quickest and easiest way. So Miss Montmorency, who is described as "a spinster of a certain age," "might be fifty-five," and "looks rather like a hard-boiled egg,"[67] is making a good living by spending a night playing cards with the soon-to-be ex-husband in a hotel room in such a way that outwardly looks bad and is bound to incriminate him in the divorce court. Sometimes this procedure also involves the "discovery" of the ostensibly erring couple by a hired detective, as was shown in several plays and films of the 1920s and early 1930s.

Miss Montmorency only appears in one scene at the end of the play, but it is by far the funniest of them all. As the title suggests, the heroine has gotten herself into a muddle by remarrying after her first husband dies in World War I, only to discover after the war is over that the rumors of his death have been greatly exaggerated. With two living husbands, Victoria Lowndes or Cardew (Beatrice Maude) ends up deciding to divorce both of them and marry someone else. When confronted with a request to be co-respondent in both divorce cases, Miss Montmorency adamantly refuses to "misconduct" herself with both gentlemen and utters the best line in the play: "I have to think of my self-respect. One gentleman is business, but two would be debauchery."[68] The *Cincinnati Enquirer* observed that "Beulah Bondi contributes an engaging character bit in the part of Miss Montmorency."[69] Victoria's divorce lawyer, Mr. Raham, who is orchestrating the entire divorce proceedings and who brings Miss Montmorency over to meet her potential "paramours," was the debut role with the company of William H. Evarts. A former child actor best known as the original Peck's "Bad Boy," Evarts would go on to perform in 35 more plays with Bondi up until 1924, all under Stuart Walker's aegis.[70]

*The Show Shop* by James Forbes from 1914 was a classic backstage comedy and a terrific satire on the vagaries of fate and critical success in the theater. Theater manager Max Rosenbaum's secretary Sadie is a precursor of so many sharp-tongued secretaries and stenographers in later plays and films, such Miss Taylor in *Five Star Final*, Bessie Green in *Counsellor-at-Law*, and Miss Stevens in *Blessed Event*. The *Cincinnati Enquirer* found that "Beulah Bondy is delicious as the sarcastic stenographer, Sadie, in the first act."[71] The real opportunity for a character actress in this play, though, was Mrs. Dean, the stage mother of all time. She had been created by Zelda Sears on Broadway and was played by Spring Byington in Cincinnati.

The best opportunity for Bondi among these single working woman roles came with Alice Duer Miller and Robert Milton's *The Charm School* in Cincinnati in late August. It was the final production of her 16 hectic weeks and as many different roles for Stuart Walker. The "sentimental and sympathetic spinster"[72] Miss Theodosia Curtis is the best part by far in this trite, trivial, and tendentious comedy. The only interesting thing about the play as a whole is that it inverts the usual pattern by making the impact of male beauty on women its focus and leaving all the wooing and proposing to a woman. The male beauty was the hero Peter Bevans (Tom Powers) and the wooer was heroine Elise Challoner (Lael Corya).

Unlike most old maids in plays of this era, Miss Curtis gets a proposal from the hero's best friend, David Mackenzie. She accepts, though she has had a mad crush on her boss, the owner of the school, Peter Bevans ("such a privilege, such an inspiration"[73]). Starting in Act II, he inspires her to improve her style of dress and looks. In general, Miss Curtis is scatter-brained, high-strung, absent-minded, ineffectual, and devout.

Minnie Dupree had scored a huge hit in the role on Broadway, when it opened two years previously in August 1920.[74] It was made into a silent film with Kate Toncray as Miss Curtis and in 1936 as a Paramount musical called *Collegiate* with Nora Cecil in the part. Of Bondi's efforts in the role, the *Cincinnati Enquirer* wrote: "The most delicious bit of the evening, however, is furnished by Miss Beulah Bondy in a character part as Miss Curtis, the middle-aged school secretary. The charm of the new principal reaches even to her fluttering heart, and she is both lovable and pathetic in her hopeless predicament, which she faces bravely. Hers is a portrayal worthy of any stage or any company."[75]

On the stage in the 1920s, Bondi also frequently played servants, a category of roles she would never play on the big screen. The year of 1922 saw four of these portrayals: a housekeeper, a cook, and two maids. With the exception of *A Very Good Young Man*, *Mamma's Affair* was the best shared opportunity between Bondi and veteran character actress Elizabeth Patterson, who went on to a film career before Bondi and was almost as successful for nearly as long as her, even though she was 14 years older. Patterson had been part of the Walker company during Bondi's first season in Indianapolis in 1919. In mid–June 1922, she came to Cincinnati for a week to take the central role of the "sentimental hypochondriac" Grace Orrin in a comedy about Mrs. Orrin and her friend Mrs. Marchant (Julia McMahon) wanting their children Eve (Beatrice Maude) and Henry (Corbet Morris) to marry "in the expectation that the great love they bear each other will thus be perpetuated."[76] Naturally, a derailment of their dearly held plans ensues, in this case engineered by Mrs. Orrin's handsome new doctor, Brent Janson (Arthur Albertson), and his Irish-inflected housekeeper Mrs. Bundy (Bondi).

It turns out to be the downtrodden daughter Eve who requires medical attention. When Dr. Janson takes her under his care, Mrs. Bundy does her level best to splice them. Her job is not an easy one, though, as her employer is a confirmed bachelor and she utters her best line when she has reached a peak of exasperation with his lack of cooperation and self-insight: "Oh! You're not a man—you're and emotional vivisectionist!"[77] The *Cincinnati Enquirer* devoted a whole paragraph of its review to Bondi's performance as Mrs. Bundy: "Any review of the play which failed to take notice of the effective character work of Beulah Bondy, who plays the part of Mrs. Bundy, the matchmaking housekeeper of Dr. Jansen, would not be complete. Miss Bondy this week strengthens the fine opinion formed of her remarkable gifts by her performances in other plays this season."[78]

The role of Lottie in Clare Kummer's debut play *Good Gracious Annabelle* was small but sparkling and Bondi stole the show yet again in a minor role: "Quite the most outstanding piece of work is contributed by Beulah Bondy as the eccentric maid Lottie."[79] Lottie appears in the second act in the servants' hall at the hero Mr. Wimbledon's house, where the titular heroine Annabelle (Spring Byington) has been hired as a cook. Lottie is the "under cook" and not a maid, as the review suggests. The *New York Times* described the character as "a masterpiece of nonsense."[80] Her function is clearly comic relief and she keeps popping in and out. Lottie is superstitious, believes in astrology, and drinks. She serves Annabelle her breakfast in her first scene and later objects vociferously to any hanky-panky being imputed to her ministrations for a certain Mr. Murchison. "I'd just as lieve go to-day as to-morrow" is her favorite phrase and refers to her employer's tendency to fire servants frequently. She is interrogated by the house detective Wickham (John Drury), mistakenly thinking he has a romantic interest in her, and found *non compos mentis*. Lottie was created on Broadway by May Vokes, "the perpetual slavey,"[81] during the 1916–17 season. Vokes went on to create the role of the maid Lizzie Allen in *The Bat*. The Cincinnati premiere of this play on July 10, 1922, marked the 100th performance of the Stuart Walker company at the Cox Theatre.[82]

Even though Alexander Woollcott described it as a "sprightly and diverting farce"[83] when it opened on Broadway in 1919, *Wedding Bells* by Salisbury Field was another silly and tedious romantic comedy of the period with little to recommend it. Bondi played the maid Hooper, a role so small it does not appear in the abridged version in *The Best Plays of 1919–20*. Leading man Tom Powers made his Stuart Walker debut in Cincinnati in this production, while Spring Byington played the female lead. The *Cincinnati Enquirer* observed of the company three months into its summer season: "it is in light comedy that we have come to appreciate them most."[84] Of Bondi's efforts in Frederic and Fanny Hatton's satire of the Long Island "house party" *Upstairs and Down* in early October 1922, the *Toledo Blade* wrote: "Beulah Bondy as a French maid and Penelope Hubard as an Irish one, proved fascinating downstairs 'belles.'"[85]

And now I get to the roles that are so far from Bondi's silver screen image that it is hard to imagine she ever played them or *how* she played them or, in a few cases, *why* she played them. To begin with the most painful case. A line about our actress that you probably never expected to read in an advertisement is this: "Have you seen Beulah Bondi in blackface in 'Come Seven'?"[86] Yet there it is, clear as day, in an ad in the lower right-hand corner of p. 4 of the *Cincinnati Enquirer* for June 10, 1922. How could this be? Is it really possible that Beulah Bondi played a blackface role back in the day? Yes, she did. In fact, she did not just play one blackface character, she played two. The first of these was Lithia Blevins, a minor, matronly role in Octavus Roy Cohen's *Come Seven*, subtitled "A

Blackface Play in Three Acts." Cohen, a descendant of Portuguese Jews from South Carolina and a prolific author, was mainly known for his stories of African American life in the *Saturday Evening Post*, or rather his tendentious and stereotypical version of African American life; and the "Jim Hanvey" series of detective stories.

*Come Seven* was distinguished, if you can call it that, by being "the first play presented in this country in which all the characters are negroes and all the actors are white." In other words, Bondi was not the only cast member in blackface. They all were.

It is hard to imagine Bondi as a maid in films, as she is seen here in the 1920s. Bondi played a much wider range of roles on the stage than she did on the screen. While she was best known for comedy roles during her days in stock, dramatic roles would predominate during her long film career.

The reviewer for the *Cincinnati Enquirer* said of Cohen and the play after the June 4 premiere at the Cox, that "his characters are absolutely true to life."[87] The critic for the *New York Times* had taken a more skeptical view of the play's realism when it opened on Broadway on July 19, 1920: "It is distinctly a Negro comedy for white folks—that is, it concerns itself mainly with those characteristics of the negro which are most readily recognized by theater audiences. Their shiftlessness, their pompousness and their pretensions are set against a background of the proverbial crap shooting, and the result is pretty good entertainment. Probably a sociologist would find considerable fault with the delineation of the negro character, but Mr. Cohen has set out to write an amusing play, and in the main he has done it."[88]

It is an explanation, though not an excuse, that with few, if any, racially integrated theater companies in the 1920s, to the extent that one wanted to have characters of color in a play they had to be played by white actors. The alternative would have been to have no racial minority characters on the stage at all. Given plays like *Come Seven*, that may well have been a better alternative. All we can learn of Bondi's performance in *Come Seven* is that she and a fellow actress "make the most of their opportunities."[89]

We have evidence that during

her first season in Cincinnati, Bondi resided across the river at the Woodford in Covington, Kentucky.[90] A four-story, square, Italianate apartment building in pale brown brick favored by theatrical folk (Spring Byington was also staying there at the time), The Woodford still stands at 303 Greenup St., on the corner of 3rd St. in the Licking Riverside section of central Covington. Later, we know Bondi stayed at Howe's Family Hotel, which was located at 1322 E. McMillan St. in the Walnut Hills section of Cincinnati. Bondi befriended the proprietors' young daughter Frances and even got her a bit part in one of Stuart Walker's plays. Twenty years later, Frances Howe McSurely recalled in a letter to Bondi: "We were so fond of you and your mother. Your kindness to a starstruck girl will never be forgotten. I keep telling the boys that I was in a Stuart Walker production. My one and only stage experience was as a patient in a waiting room."[91]

After her season in Cincinnati ended with The Charm School in early September, Bondi went home to Valparaiso for a few days' rest, before returning to Toledo, Ohio, for the opening of the Toledo Theatre's third season on September 18.[92] Though it seems unlikely, she was given even greater opportunities to stretch herself as an actress there, than in Cincinnati. The first show at the theater on St. Clair Street was The Boomerang, a hit comedy from the 1915–16 season in New York and a play Bondi was intimately familiar with, having directed a couple of amateur productions and played a minor role in it in Cincinnati in June. The Toledo Blade noted with wonder: "Beulah Bondi in a young girl role astonished those who recall her chiefly in eccentric character parts."[93]

Eccentric, indeed, and they would get more so as the season progressed. In the second week, the Toledo Theater company revived The Great Lover from 1915, a backstage drama about the intrigues in a major opera house, which had been written by the Frederic and Fanny Hatton and Leo Ditrichstein, who also starred. Bondi was cast as the temperamental Italian prima donna Giulia Sabittini, a role created on Broadway by Beverly Sitgreaves when she was 52. The Toledo Blade found Bondi's performance "of equal excellence" as that of the leading man: "Miss Bondy has added another clever characterization to her long and steadily growing list of successes. She played it with fire and snap and verve."[94]

Bondi's role in The Great Lover, as far as I can understand, required no real singing, but Bondi did sing as Marie in Buddies, dealing with a squad of "doughboys" billeted in France right after the Armistice and described as "a comedy of quaint Brittany."[95] This was the only musical comedy she appears to have done during her years in stock. To judge from the positive response, she might well have done more. "The play offers an evening of happy surprises," the Toledo Blade wrote, "notably Beulah Bondy singing." She scored "a distinct hit" as Marie.[96]

Bondi's role in the "crook comedy" The Dummy was also a new departure, as she played lady crook and kidnapper Rose Hart.[97] After playing a French maid in Upstairs and Down and a young lady getting engaged to Neil Pratt in Too Many Cooks, it was right back to the underworld in Back Pay by bestselling author Fanny Hurst, where she played two roles: Angie Simms, "the dragged-down and hopeless keeper of a disreputable resort" and an "exhilarated French demimondaine who 'Bernhardted all over the place.'"[98] Imagine, Beulah Bondi as a whorehouse madam! It boggles the mind. And it was not the first time. Back in Cincinnati in mid–June, she had played a similarly shady lady, Lola Mulvaney, in Dodson Mitchell's drama Cornered. The reviewer felt she had been given "too little to do as the owner of the Pekin Pleasure Palace in the first act."[99]

As if that was not enough "exoticism," Bondi closed out the year in a drama called

*The Broken Wing*, where she played the Mexican servant Ouichita. When Mary Worth had created the role on Broadway, the papers noted that she gave "a very interesting portrayal of a Mexican servant" and that she acted "the small, and rather inconsequential part, of Ouichita, a Mexican servant, with more than ordinary realism."[100] This production opened at the Toledo Theatre on Christmas Day 1922 and Bondi would remain in Toledo till late February 1923, if not longer.

The year of 1923 was another busy year for Bondi, who worked extensively in stock in Toledo, Indianapolis, and Cincinnati and added several characterizations to her already ample list of stage successes. She also got a new name by the end of the year. Through a process that may have begun as a misprinting in an advertisement, she emerged in early 1924 as Beulah Bondi and Beulah Bondi she would remain for the rest of her long life.

Bondi's sojourn in Toledo, Ohio, continued until the spring of 1923. Stuart Walker began his second season at the Cox Theatre in Cincinnati on March 24, 1923. On April 15, the *Cincinnati Enquirer* wrote that Bondi and a raft of other well-known players, including Blanche Yurka, Ian Keith, and Elizabeth Patterson, were to appear with the Walker company during the summer.[101] Bondi first appeared this season in Walter Hackett's comedy *Captain Applejack* on June 18, 1923. The *Cincinnati Enquirer*'s drama and music editor, William Smith Goldenburg noted: "Beulah Bondy, who was such a favorite last season, returns to the cast this week in one of her typical characters."[102] What was new this year was that Bondi would alternate between performing some weeks at the Cox Theatre in Cincinnati and others at the Murat in Indianapolis. Before she was done working for Walker this season on September 1, she had played ten weeks in seven different plays; three of them she did both in Cincinnati and Indianapolis. Among the new roles in her repertoire this year, we find Mary Grayson in *It's a Boy!*, Wa-Wa in *Tiger Rose*, Osprey Mandelharper in *A Very Good Young Man*, Letty Douthett in *Spite Corner*, Miss Smith in *Enter Madame*, Hattie in *The First Year*, and Eustasia in *The Dover Road*. I will discuss them in chronological order, starting with two roles Bondi played in Toledo.

*It's a Boy!* from 1922 was yet another of the many "first year" comedies from the period and closely patterned on author William Anthony McGuire's hit play *Six-Cylinder Love* from the previous season. "The playwright's formula is an old one," wrote Nunnally Johnson in the *Brooklyn Daily Eagle*, "the one that consists in contrasting simple, honest and straightforward country folk with tricky, sophisticated and extravagant city men and women."[103] Predictably, the New York critics felt the copy was not as good the original. When staged in Toledo in early February 1923, the play offered Bondi yet another opportunity to play a little old lady, Mary Grayson, the hero's mother-in-law, and she scored with it. The *Toledo Blade* wrote: "Acting honors this week go to Beulah Bondy": "Miss Bondy has a chance at one of her delightful 'old lady' roles and she does wonders with it. Her makeup is amazingly perfect, and she makes one of the sweetest little old-fashioned, gray-haired mothers imaginable—gentle, fluttering, quaint, yet with a dash of real spirit now and then."[104] The role of Mary Grayson had been created by Jean Adair on Broadway in 1922.

*Tiger Rose* was a period costume melodrama of the Canadian frontier, that had been a huge hit for author Willard Mack and legendary producer David Belasco during the 1917–18 season with Lenore Ulric in the title role of "Tiger Rose" Bocio. The storyline tangentially involved two Aboriginal Canadian characters of the Siwash tribe, Mak-a-Low and his wife Wa-Wa. In the Broadway production, which ran for 384 performances, Mak-a-Low was played by an actor known as Chief Whitehawk, who we may assume was Native American, while Wa-Wa was created by Jean Ferrell. This is less radical than it sounds, as the couple are never seen on stage at the same time. In Toledo in February 1923, Bondi played Wa-Wa. Wa-Wa was a typical maid-companion role in which Bondi was given little to do but fetch and carry, act as messenger and intermediary, and heartily disapprove of her employer's "no good" love affair with Bruce Norton. This production must have brought back memories of her starring role ten years earlier in *The Sun Dance Opera* in Vernal, Utah. For several reasons, it is unthinkable that Bondi would play this type of ethnic minority role on the big screen.

If there is one of Bondi's many stock performances I would dearly loved to have seen, it is her Osprey Mandelharper in *A Very Good Young Man*, a character dismissed by the critic for the *New York Times* as a "vulgar little flirt."[105] Martin Brown's comedy

Bondi in one of her more unlikely roles as the Aboriginal Canadian maid Wa-Wa in Willard Mack's forgettable melodrama *Tiger Rose* at the Toledo Theatre in February 1923. The role was mostly monosyllabic. Bondi's expression seems to suggest: "How did I get into this?" Ten years earlier, she had starred in the production of the first American opera written by a Native American. Called *The Sun Dance Opera*, it was created by pioneering Yankton Dakota Sioux writer Zitkala-Ša (aka Gertrude Simmons Bonnin) and William F. Hanson.

had not been a hit on Broadway, but when Stuart Walker presented it at the Cox Theatre in Cincinnati for the first time on July 2, 1923, it was found to be "one of the most amusing farces that has crossed the theatrical horizon in these many moons."[106] The play deals with a "very good young man" called Leroy Gumph (Corbet Morris), whose future bride Pearl Hannigan (Jean Spurney) and mother-in-law Mrs. Hannigan (Teresa Dale) feel he needs to sow a few wild oats before he settles down. The question, of course, is if they are not tempting fate by encouraging him to live the high life for a time.

In his desperate attempt to live up to expectations, Leroy gets involved with a barely young woman of what used to be called the "maneating" variety, Osprey Mandelharper, and her matrimonially ambitious mother. According to the *Cincinnati Enquirer*, "Beulah Bondy, in the role of the kittenish Osprey Mandelharper, and Elisabeth Patterson, as her doting mother, give interpretations that are rare bits of histrionic art."[107] So popular and successful was this pairing, that a

Cincinnati playwright offered to write a vaudeville sketch for the two of them, but "both ladies prefer to remain in the legitimate."[108]

The production was repeated to equal acclaim at the Murat in Indianapolis the following week and was Bondi's season debut there. The *Indianapolis Star* wrote: "Miss Patterson is a 'riot' as Mrs. Mandelharper and Miss Bondy is equally as ludicrous and entertaining as Osprey…. The whole play is a joyous riot."[109] The rival *News* observed: "Miss Bondy, whose makeup is a triumph of the ridiculous, simpers, runs after every young man, chews gum excitedly, puts on airs, and constantly simulates gaiety, all in true Mandelharper fashion. She and Miss Patterson are splendid foils for one another." The conclusion was that "the evening was a huge success."[110] *A Very Good Young Man* was directed by Melville Burke, who would be instrumental in Bondi's Broadway debut two and a half years later.

Frank Craven's light comedy *Spite Corner* was also played in both Cincinnati and Indianapolis and followed directly on from *A Very Good Young Man* in the second half of July. Bondi played the gossip Letty Douthett in both cities, though the rest of the cast mostly differed, and had a good chance to showcase her versatility in going from a character of roughly her own age in *A Very Good Young Man* to one who was much older. *Spite Corner* was described as a "comedy of New England tempers" about a family feud between the Deans and the Lattimers, which a pair of young lovers—one from each family in classic *Romeo and Juliet* style—is determined to put behind them. The approach was comedic here, though, and the finale predictably happy and marital. The play, one of three Craven plays Bondi would do during her stock years, gave "Aldrich Bowker, Elisabeth Patterson and Beulah Bondy the opportunity to play three eccentric New Englanders," who "are well versed in acrimonious repartee" and "have on tap numerous bitter and biting sentences calculated to make the hearer quail beneath their burning truth."[111] All three received plaudits in both cities. "It is seldom that these three find such good opportunities for their cleverness," wrote the *Indianapolis News*, while the *Cincinnati Enquirer* also emphasized the significance of the three gossip roles and put a large part of the success of the play down to them.[112] Mrs. Douthett was what I would call a Nora Cecil type of role.

As we have already seen, one type of role that was part of Bondi's stage repertoire but that she never played on the screen was the secretary. In Indianapolis in the summer of 1923, Bondi play Miss Smith in Gilda Varesi and Dolly Byrne's hit from 1920, *Enter Madame*. There was not much to this secretary role, where Miss Smith is encountered briefly in Act I, somewhat more in Act II, and hardly at all in Act III, as personal assistant to the predictably temperamental prima donna Lisa Della Robbia (Spring Byington). Miss Smith is the sensible, ironical, and perpetually unfazed type of working woman that was so often portrayed by Ruth Donnelly in films. According to the critic for the *Indianapolis Star*, Bondi "adds greatly to the comic" scenes as "the prim secretary."[113]

We have already seen Bondi play a Native American "squaw" in the Western melodrama *Tiger Rose* in February 1923. If that was not enough, she added her second blackface role to her repertoire that summer, when she played the African American maid Hattie in Frank Craven's classic comedy *The First Year*. This play was a huge hit on Broadway, ran for 760 performances from 1920 to 1922 and gave its name to an entire comic subgenre about the trials and tribulations of young couples during their "first year" of marriage, also known as the "period of adjustment." Naturally, today any blackface role is an embarrassment, which we might be tempted to look aside from. When so highly respected an actress as Beulah Bondi played at least two of them, we have to pause and consider them.

As long as a theater company was not integrated as, indeed, the Stuart Walker stock company was not, the only way in which a racial minority character might appear in a play would be if a white actor played him or her. Unfortunately, these characters are often egregious racial stereotypes. It strikes me, though, that Hattie in *The First Year* is far from the worst of its kind. As far as maid roles go, it is quite an opportunity. Hattie is ubiquitous at the dinner party in Act II. There is no physical description of her in the text, beyond the fact that she is "poorly dressed," but we understand from the hero Tommy Tucker's reaction when first seeing her that she looks a mess. She has waited on table before, but "washes best, tho.'"[114] She is clumsy and breaks things.

Hattie is basically a comic maid in the comic maid tradition, that we now recognize mainly from films and associate with actresses both black and white, like Hattie McDaniel and Thelma Ritter. The humor in Hattie's case arises from her being totally unsuited to the challenge of serving at an important dinner party, just like Martha in *Big Hearted Herbert* (1934), Malena Burns in *Alice Adams* (1935), and Sadie Dugan in *A Letter to Three Wives* (1949). It is not suggested that her unsuitability is due to her race, so much as her unkempt appearance, clumsiness, and lack of experience.

The role of Hattie was created on Broadway by Leila Bennett, who was also white and got a rave review for her efforts in the *New York Times*.[115] Bennett reprised her role, still in

Seeing is believing. It is a matter of no small historical interest that even an actress of Bondi's stature and broadly humanitarian outlook played two blackface roles on the stage in the 1920s. Here she is seen as Hattie in Frank Craven's then famous comedy *The First Year*, a role she performed first at the Murat Theatre in Indianapolis in August 1923 and reprised a year later at the Cox Theatre in Cincinnati. Hattie is a character in the comic maid tradition, that would be embodied in films by actresses like Hattie McDaniel, Louise Beavers, Nydia Westman, and Thelma Ritter.

blackface, in the 1932 film version starring Janet Gaynor and Charles Farrell. The Indianapolis newspapers that summer in 1923 found it an "interesting piece of acting" when Bondi "puts on blackface to play Hattie" and wrote that she gave "an amusing and faithful picture of the emergency servant at Joplin."[116]

In addition to *A Very Good Young Man* and *Spite Corner*, A.A. Milne's supernatural and sophisticated drawing room comedy *The Dover Road* was the third play Bondi acted in both in Cincinnati and Indianapolis that summer. I call it supernatural, because there is something not just larger than life but a little uncanny about "the rich but eccentric bachelor"[117] Mr. Latimer and the way in which travelers along the Dover Road on their way to France and divorce end up as his more or less willing house guests. Often as not, this delay in the dissolution of their various marriages leads to a reappraisal of their situation and a change of heart. That is what happens to the estranged marrieds, Leonard and Eustasia, who are suddenly confronted with each other and their new partners Anne and Nicholas, at Mr. Latimer's house in the country and forced to spend an uncomfortable week together in close proximity. This play from 1921 is an interesting precursor of Noël Coward's *Private Lives*, which did not premiere in New York until 1931. Milne himself dubbed it an "absurd comedy."[118] Writing in the *New York Times*, Alexander Woollcott called it "one of the best examples of fine-textured high comedy that has come out of England in the last ten years."[119] *The Dover Road* was the first producing and directing venture on Broadway of Bondi's future friend and director Guthrie McClintic.

In Cincinnati and Indianapolis, Mr. Latimer was played by leading man and local favorite, Tom Powers. The runaway husband Leonard was played by Bondi's frequent co-star L'Estrange Millman and Ruth Hammond portrayed his new love Anne. Bondi played the wife, Eustasia, which is a good, meaty part, though she is the least visible of the four reluctant guests. Corbet Morris was her new, younger lover Nicholas. I wonder how Bondi dealt with all the play's posh, British upper-class sophistication; not to mention the required RP accent. I cannot remember her ever having a British accent on the screen, even in *The Invisible Ray*, where she played a British peeress. Indeed, Eustasia was completely out of the run of her typical characters on the big screen and shows how her years in stock gave her a richer range of roles than her film work ever would.

Bondi certainly made a good impression on the critics, as did the play. The reviewer for the *Enquirer* noted that this was the first time *The Dover Road* had been performed in Cincinnati and that "nothing more diverting has been offered by the Stuart Walker Players since their successful season at the Cox Theatre opened." He wrote further: "Beulah Bondi again is proving how versatile an actress she is by giving a superior character portrayal of the solicitous and talkative Eustasia, who drove her husband away and in a week nearly bored to death a prospective second mate."[120] The drama critic for the *Indianapolis Star* felt that "Miss Bondi comes into her own again as Eustasia. The sugar coating she gives that simpering wife is well worth sitting through the whole performance."[121] Molly Pearson created the role of Eustasia on Broadway in 1921 and Athene Seyler in London in 1922. Though she was available, there was absolutely no chance that Bondi would be cast in this role when Milne's play was filmed in 1934 as *When Sinners Meet*. Eustasia was played by Billie Burke, about as different a character actress from Bondi as can be imagined.

Bondi's final production of the season in Cincinnati was Harry James Smith's *Two Kisses*, described in a review as "a red-plush bedroom comedy," which makes it sound a lot more daring than it was. The two kisses of the title referred to the heroine's difficult choice between two competing lovers and her method for deciding whom she truly loves. In the leading role, Ruth Hammond had to see herself upstaged by her "support," as "Most of the undiluted comedy was furnished by Beulah Bondy as a designing widow not averse to a little coquetry on the side…." Both her interpretation and that of Corbet Morris were seen as "examples of really artistic buffoonery."[122]

The Stuart Walker season in Indianapolis came to a close with the final performance of *The Dover Road* on Saturday, September 1. Though she could not have known it at the time, Bondi would never act for Walker again in the place where it had all started back in 1919. A friend of a friend recalled those heady days, when she had been a stagestruck teenage girl in the audience at the Murat: "when I was a kid in Indianapolis, Beulah Bondi was a favorite actress of mine when she was with the Stuart Walker stock company there. How enriched my theatre life was made by Stuart Walker! … What heady fare for a kid of 12 to 16…. There was gossip about Stuart and his boy friends, but I am eternally grateful to that wonderful stock company for molding my theatrical taste for the best."[123]

As for the year as a whole, 1923 ended much as 1919 had done, and 1924 would as well: with an insignificant part in an insignificant play on a pre–Broadway tour, which never made it to Broadway. I say insignificant play, because in all the newspaper accounts, even the most stridently supportive, it sounds like a dud. I say insignificant part, because, despite having read dozens of news items and reviews of the play, I have only been able to determine that Bondi played the hero's "aged mother."[124] She is not mentioned in the reviews.

In an interview in 1926, Bondi recalled that the producers did not want even to consider her for the part. She was "at once dismissed with the curt remark that this was no time for joking." Clearly, producers Lewis and Gordon did not know her history of playing older parts. Not one to give up easily, Bondi came into their offices one day "made up as a woman of 55" and was "employed immediately for the role, with due apologies."[125] She was 34 at the time and her contract shows that she was being paid $100 a week.[126]

Unlike *Piccadilly Jim* in 1919 and *The Proud Princess* in 1924, which also failed to open on the Great White Way, the 1923 flop was not produced by Stuart Walker. In fact, Bondi had never worked with any of the cast members or director Lester Lonergan before. The most immediately intriguing thing about this new play by Hutcheson Boyd was the title: *The Naked Man*. Despite the title, though, there was nothing risqué about this drama. The only thing being bared was the main character's soul.

According to the *Baltimore Sun*, *The Naked Man* grew out of "the idea that there is hidden in every man the boy he used to be": "in the play there is made the experiment of bringing the boy face to face with the man he has become."[127] The man in question was a wealthy businessman and philanthropist, Vincent Armstrong, played by Walter Eddinger, hitherto best known for comedic roles, including Leroy Gumph in *A Very Good Young Man* on Broadway. Armstrong is in the process of writing his autobiography and is assisted in this process by "the childish treasures from an old trunk" that his mother has saved for him.[128] Out of the trunk, too, comes the man as a boy of nine. The day before the play opened at the Lyceum in Baltimore, the *Chicago Tribune* wrote that its author "Hutchinson [sic] Boyd, was represented in New York last week by 'The Talking Parrot,' described by the critics as the worst play ever staged there."[129]

The critical response to *The Naked Man* in December 1923 was lukewarm. The *Baltimore Evening Sun* wrote: "Mr. Boyd's idea for a play may be all right, but his execution of it is not so good."[130] The *Baltimore Sun* noted that the play begins well, but ends in "a disappointing muddle" after the author "seems to lose control of his dialogue and his situations."[131] The play underwent a number of changes during the Baltimore tryout, before being shown three days each in Hartford and New Haven, Connecticut. The only fan of the play seems to have been the critic for the *Hartford Courant*. He wrote: "the play as a whole is one that is thoroughly worth while. But it is not for the multitude…"[132] How is that for a rousing endorsement?

The *Hartford Courant* also had a few kind words for the leading actor, finding "Mr. Eddinger's playing in the real things of the characterization was extremely good."[133] This high opinion of Eddinger's acting was not pervasive. In fact, Eddinger seems to have been a major cause of the play's failure. We can read in the reviews: "His interpretation, while carefully studied, lacks conviction at times, and becomes somewhat laborious by reason of his monotonous delivery of lines"; "His method never gets beyond that of a metronome"; and "Walter Eddinger was a disappointment in the panting, monotonous delivery of his lines."[134] To make matters worse, the boy actor Charles Eaton was called "the real star of the performance."[135]

So *The Naked Man* is only significant in Bondi's life and career as the point at which she went through the transformation from Bondy to Bondi. I have discovered that it was in an advertisement for this show in the *Baltimore Sun* on December 2, 1923, that her name was spelled "Bondi" for the first time. Intentional or a printer's error? We will probably never know for certain. At any rate, the error, if that is what it was, was not corrected in any of the later ads for the show. The spelling "Bondi" appeared for the first time in regular news items on December 9 and December 12, 1923. In the former, she was referred to as "Beaulah Bondi," a not infrequent misspelling of her Christian name.[136] By early in the new year, the name change was complete and I have only found a very few instances of "Beulah Bondy" in the newspapers from 1924.

What is even more interesting than the timing are all the various reasons that have been given for the change. Bondi herself contributed to the confusion by giving different explanations down through the years. The first time the name change was discussed in the press was in 1927, when the *New York Times* suggested, wrongly, that it was just before her Broadway debut in *One of the Family* in late 1925, that she "changed the final letter of her last name," "for reasons apparently not connected with numerology." In 1944, the actress observed that Bondi "seemed at little more classy for an actress." Two years later, when visiting her brother in Florida for the first time, she said she had been advised that it would be better in billing if all the letters of her surname were "above the line." In a similar vein, Bondi's friend and former neighbor in Valparaiso, Allegra Nesbit, explained shortly after Bondi's death in 1981, that "Beulah had her last name changed from Bondy to Bondi so that all the letters of her name fit above the line on theater marquees."[137]

John Springer offered the explanation in 1963, that "a critic who saw it misprinted in a theater program thought it looked better that way." Dennis Brown got the same story when he interviewed Bondi towards the end of her life. Finally, Jordan Young, who also interviewed Bondi not long before her death, had the impression that the change was "an attempt to pacify family members who disapproved" of her pursuit of an acting career.[138] The fact that the change occurred after Bondi had been a professional actress for more than four years makes this the least plausible explanation. All in all, it seems clear what happened. Under a new management, Bondi's surname was misspelled in an ad and, liking the look of "Bondi," she decided to keep it.

Stuart Walker kept Bondi almost continuously employed throughout 1924. She was with him in Baltimore, when he inaugurated his first seasons of plays at the Academy of Music there in February and, after a month off, she returned to the Cox Theatre in Cincinnati in May and performed there till the end of November. In all, I have noted that she played 24 different roles for Walker that year, none of which she had played before, except Eustasia in *The Dover Road* and Hattie in *The First Year*. She played mothers, usually elderly ones, in *The Proud Princess* (Mrs. Johnson), *Kempy* (Ma Bence), *The Breaking Point* (Lucy Livingstone), *The Storm Bird* (Ma Tetson), *If I Were King* (Mother Villon), *Money to Burn* (Mrs. Lake), *The Hero* (Sarah Lane), *Old Heidelberg* (Frau Doerffel), and *Spanish Love* (Concepcion); upper-class dowagers in *Trelawny of the Wells* (Mrs. Trafalgar Gower) and *Lady Windemere's Fan* (Duchess of Berwick); a spinster in *The Goldfish* (Amelia Pugsley); servants in *The Importance of Being Earnest* (the governess Miss Prism), *Icebound* (the maid Hannah), and *Three Wise Fools* (the housekeeper Mrs. Saunders); and unidentified or minor roles in *The Boomerang*, *Society*, *My Lady's Dress*, *Three Roses*, *Pot Luck*, *Mary the Third*, and *The Thunderbolt*. As usual, Walker's repertoire was full of the then popular and now completely forgotten plays of the day, with the notable exception of the two Oscar Wilde comedies and Dion Boucicault's *Trelawny of the Wells*. Walker rarely revived nineteenth-century plays.

While the productions were not always treated kindly by the reviewers, Bondi usually was. As Ma Bence in *Kempy*, which she played both in Baltimore and Cincinnati, she was "The outstanding character part of the play": "A high degree of naturalism makes Miss Bondi's contribution true artistic dramatic expression."[139] The *Baltimore Sun* wrote of her performance in *The Breaking Point* by Mary Roberts Rinehart: "Beulah Bondi, as Lucy Livingstone, again serves with unusual ability in the role of an elderly, motherly woman. This is a part which is not as simple and easy as one might imagine, and it is to the actress' credit that she succeeds so remarkably well."[140]

As a hypochondriac elderly widow and mother in *The Hero*, she "brings to bear all her wonted

Bondi in an unidentified role from her days in stock in the 1920s. She worked mainly for legendary producer Stuart Walker, who preferred comedy to tragedy and plays with contemporary settings to period costume dramas. If I were to venture a guess based on what Bondi is wearing, I would say Arthur Wing Pinero's *Trelawny of the Wells*, which is set in the early 1860s. Bondi played Mrs. Trafalgar Gower in a Walker production of this play at the Cox Theatre in Cincinnati in June 1924.

cleverness to give a natural portrayal of a fidgety old lady whose sense of humor is keen and whose appetite for patent medicine is never quite satisfied."[141] In *The Goldfish*, "Beulah Bondi again is giving a delightful character study as Amelia Pugsley, matrimonially ambitious, but unsuccessful in that direction."[142] The *Cincinnati Enquirer* called Bondi's Hannah in the Pulitzer Prize-winning play *Icebound* by Owen Davis, "one of the finest bits of character acting this talented player has given."[143]

Other of Bondi's characterizations were deemed "delightful," "skillfully portrayed," and "clever."[144] Critical opinion was divided, though, on her Mrs. Lake in *Money to Burn*, another of her elderly mothers in another vapid comedy by the Nugents *père et fils*, which she performed for a week with Walker's stock company at the Victory Theatre in Dayton, Ohio. The *Dayton Daily News* thought that "Beulah Bondi was excellent as Mrs. Lake, the ambitious member of the family," but the *Dayton Herald* wrote that she "was uncertain in her part of the elderly Mrs. Lake."[145] Unfortunately, William Smith Goldenburg's dull, patronizing review of *The Importance of Being Earnest* does not give any sense of the production as a whole or of Bondi's performance as Miss Prism.[146] I can just picture, though, Zeffie Tilbury saying "Prism, where is that handbag?" and Bondi quailing at her words.

By the end of the year, Bondi was physically and mentally exhausted. Yet she soldiered on. She had a central role in Walker's new brain child *The Proud Princess*, a romantic comedy by Edward Sheldon and Dorothy Donnelly, which Walker hoped would repeat the success he had had with a dramatization of Booth Tarkington's *Seventeen* in 1918. *The Proud Princess* had its world premiere at the Academy of Music on February 11, 1924, as the opening production of Walker's first season in Baltimore and was also presented for a total of three weeks in Cincinnati in May and November 1924.

The play was described by one critic as "the old Cinderella theme over again, only in this case the Cinderella happens to be the very wealthy daughter of an oil magnate." The same reviewer wrote further: "Two of the best character creations are those of Beulah Bondi as the mother and Aldrich Bowker as the father. They appear as plain home folks who are led into the mazes of society by their ambitious daughter. The more one sees of Miss Bondi's work, the more deeply one is impressed with her sound and sincere artistry."[147] Bondi was also deemed "excellent," "splendid," and "satisfying," as the heroine's nouveau riche mother, Mrs. Johnson.[148]

Yet *The Proud Princess* was not distinguished. We can read in the reviews, that it "provides a pleasant evening's entertainment, though the piece has been fashioned along rather obvious lines"; that "it is not a brilliant play, but it might be made so"; and that "lacking native brilliance, the earnest efforts of the conscientious players raise the play above its real level."[149] Walker was undeterred by the lukewarm reception. After the play closed at the Cox on November 30, 1924, he had planned a pre–Broadway tour prior to a New York opening.

By this time, Bondi was so physically weakened, that she came down with pleurisy, an inflammation of the covering of the lungs which often leads to sharp chest pains when breathing deeply. *The Proud Princess* was also in bad shape and Walker closed the play in Cleveland in mid–December 1924. He wanted Bondi to come back to Cincinnati, but she was unwell and was also considering whether it was not time to take a new stab at New York. In a long, typewritten letter dated December 15, Walker accused her of being ungrateful and disloyal and warned: "In New York the competition is keen and bitter and unfair. People are used like props or scenery or lights. Nowadays their time of glory at best is short. The big salaries are not constant and not as big as we hear and they are not for every week in the year by a large margin. You are still young enough to bide your time and think yourself very happy to be placed for as long as you want to be and I can negotiate your cost." At the bottom of this long diatribe, Bondi has written by hand: "All this because I left—with pleurisy—and went home—collapsed Christmas Eve and was in bed three months! B.B."[150]

# 3

# Broadway Baby

## *1925–1930*

"The ingenue field is all littered up as it is, without me adding to the confusion…. There are so few young women playing old lady roles that I consider it excellent tactics to continue along my present route."[1]

By the spring of 1925, Bondi was well enough to go back on the stage, but she did not return to the fold of Stuart Walker's stock company. Despite Walker's warnings, she went once again to hammer at the gates of the New York theater and this time they opened for her. There is a mystery about Bondi's New York debut, though, which I want to lay out for you. Bondi repeatedly claimed that her first New York play was *Wild Birds*. It opened on April 9, 1925, at the Cherry Lane Theatre, which is still operating at 38 Commerce St. in Greenwich Village. Subtitled "A Tragedy in Three Acts," the play was written by a young, budding playwright with whom Bondi would be closely associated throughout her stage career, Dan Totheroh. A native of California, Totheroh was born in San Francisco in 1894. *Wild Birds* had been awarded the first prize in the University of California play contest in 1922 by judges Eugene O'Neill, Susan Glaspell, and George Jean Nathan. It had originally been staged at the University Theater at Berkeley and at the Players' Theater in San Francisco, "where it attracted police attention, but was allowed to continue after brief interference."[2]

Very much inspired by O'Neill, *Wild Birds* was a conventional and old-fashioned play in its use of coincidence, the black-and-white, stereotypical characters, and the melodramatic ending with the long-lost father arriving just minutes too late to save his daughter's life. We meet two "wilds birds"—Mazie, a 1920s flower child, and equally down-on-his-luck orphan Adam Larson—who for a brief moment know love and envision a brighter future on a barren, isolated prairie farm, before an all-encompassing darkness and disaster descend over them. Mazie was portrayed by Mildred MacLeod, who had played Bondi's daughter in the brief *The Proud Princess* tour just a few months previously.

The mystery I mentioned is that I have only found one independent, historical source linking Bondi to this production; by independent, I mean that the information cannot be traced back to the actress herself. In a brief October 23, 1925, news item, Bondi is described as one who "goes in for eccentric characters, and last season was prominently placed in 'Wild Birds.'"[3] In the 1933 edition of *Who's Who in the Theatre*, we can read that Bondi "made her first appearance in New York at Cherry Lane Theatre,

59

May, 1925 as Mrs. Slag in 'Wild Birds,'"[4] but the likely source of this information is Bondi herself.

The trouble is that the actor who opened as Mrs. Slag in *Wild Birds*, and played the role for several weeks after that, was Mina C. Gleason.[5] Gleason was born in Boston in 1858 and was actor James Gleason's mother. Am I suggesting that Bondi lied about her participation in the production? Of course not. How, then, do we explain that she claimed to have made her first New York stage appearance in a role created by another actress? The most likely explanation is that Bondi was Gleason's understudy and either stepped in for her at one or more performances or took over the role permanently. Either way, she cannot have played Mrs. Slag for long, as *Wild Birds* only ran for five weeks and closed after 44 performances in mid–May 1925.[6]

Gleason's performance was lauded by the critics, while the play met with a mixed reception. Stark Young of the *New York Times* wrote that "the play itself, when all is said and done, is one of those instances in art where much is projected but less is achieved. Motives and situations are proposed rather than created…. 'Wild Birds' has at bottom a ragged, desperate urge, an adventure into the depths of living forces, but it does not get itself expressed." He conceded, though, that "in spite of its lack of convincing pungency and sense of truth it manages pretty constantly to engage the interest and so make us think it is going to be better than it is."[7]

The *Brooklyn Standard Union*, on the other hand, thought the production was "excellent" and wrote specifically that "Mina C. Gleason did well as the wife."[8] According to the *Reading Times*, "Dan Totheroh … aims at poetic heights of tragedy and succeeds at hitting wild birds that are flying rather low." In the *New York Daily News*, Burns Mantle described *Wild Birds* as "another of those sad plays in which the burden of woe seems some way unjustified by the reactions inspired." The critic for the *Birmingham News* opined ironically that "the piece will probably not be popular because of its somber coloration. Two of the cheerful episodes are the flogging to death of a crippled boy and the leap of an expectant mother into a well." One critic went so far as to call *Wild Birds* "the world's most gloomy and sordid play."[9]

Despite the quibbles and the occasional tone of mockery, *Wild Birds* received more serious consideration than it warranted. Influential drama critic Alexander Woollcott included it on his list of the ten best new plays of the 1924–25 season, albeit in the tenth and final place.[10] Despite the editor's reservations, *Wild Birds* was also included in Burns Mantle's theatrical yearbook *The Best Plays of 1924–1925*.[11] On April 20, 1925, Doubleday, Page published *Wild Birds* as a book.[12] It was a sign of the lack of serious American drama at this time, that Totheroh's mediocre play was getting such respectful attention.

Despite the brevity of her tenure as Mrs. Slag, it was a significant role for Bondi beyond constituting her New York debut. The ill-fated heroine's foster mother, Mrs. Slag was a classic exemplar of several negative stereotypes of the era—the slattern, the farm woman, the termagant wife—that would become staples of Bondi's future film repertoire. She was also the rural counterpart to Bondi's most famous role on Broadway, the equally unsympathetic New York gossip Emma Jones in *Street Scene*. There was not much depth to this role, though. Mrs. Slag is just a pale reflection of her even more evil-minded husband John, who was played by Dodson Mitchell, 21 years Bondi's senior and the author of *Cornered*, a melodrama she had played in Cincinnati in 1922. We are not encouraged to wonder how this ill-matched couple came by their evil ways and deadly disposition.

On April 25, while she was still part of the *Wild Birds* company, Bondi signed a contract to join the celebrated Elitch Gardens Players in Denver. After five seasons as a professional actress, she was to be paid $125 per week.[13] Among the plays we know she did during her time in Denver, we find *Chicken Feed*, *Quarantine*, *Anna Christie*, *Craig's Wife*, *Hell-bent fer Heaven*, *Rollo's Wild Oat*, and *Outward Bound*, though some of these were performed when she returned to Elitch Gardens in the summer of 1926. The leading players during the 1925 season were Fredric March and his future wife Florence Eldridge. Bondi would support March in Cecil B. DeMille's *The Buccaneer* in 1937. It was likely during her time at Elitch Gardens, that she formed a lasting friendship with Denver socialite and culture maven Jean Chappell Cranmer (1886–1974).

Bondi's close friend Jean Chappell Cranmer (left) was a violinist, co-founder of the Denver Symphony Orchestra, and mother of four. Born in 1886, the daughter of powerful Denver industrialist Delos A. Chappell, she was married to millionaire stockbroker and visionary city planner George E. Cranmer. My guess is that the two women met in the mid–1920s, when Bondi spent two summers working in stock at Denver's legendary Elitch Gardens Theatre. This candid was taken in the summer of 1936, probably in the garden of Cranmer's palatial Italian Renaissance style home at 200 Cherry St., adjacent to Cranmer Park. Like practically all Bondi's contemporaries, Cranmer predeceased her, in 1974.

The end of 1925 saw Bondi's long-awaited debut on Broadway. Though she had been in *Wild Birds* earlier in the year, the Cherry Lane Theater was not an official Broadway theater. It was one of Stuart Walker's regular directors, Melville Burke, who got her the job. He told her: "Come with me, I'm starting rehearsals on a new play, and they need an old lady—I know you can do it and I'll fight your battles for you."[14] The play was a new comedy by Kenneth Webb called *One of the Family*. After three try-out performances at the New Lyric Theatre in Bridgeport, Connecticut October 19–20 and a matinee and an evening performance at Reade's Plainfield Theatre in New Jersey on October 24, Bondi made her official Broadway debut at the 49th St. Theatre on Tuesday, December 22, 1925.[15] For only 19 years, this theater stood at 235 W. 49th St., next to St. Malachy's, the Actors' Church, and across from the brand new Forrest Theatre (now the Eugene O'Neill). A hotel now occupies the site.

On the way from Bridgeport to Broadway, Richard Sterling was replaced by Grant Mitchell in the starring role of Henry Adams. In the 1920s, Mitchell was one of the classic interpreters of "the little man" and Henry Adams, despite his grandiloquent name, was the epitome of the type. Indeed, the familiar moniker was a not very subtle dig at the pretensions of the Boston Brahmin class, chiefly represented in the play by Henry's snooty spinster aunt, Priscilla Adams (Louise Closser Hale). Henry is a seemingly confirmed bachelor and the chief support of his ne'er-do-well, spendthrift, female relations, who suddenly one day comes home with a wife; a wife with the democratic surname Smith, Joyce Smith to be exact. This impulsive marital union causes an uproar in the family, which is only stilled when Henry, somewhat under the influence of an uncustomary cocktail, makes his own personal "declaration of independence," with hearty support from Joyce (Kay Johnson).

*One of the Family*, then, was a "first year" type of play, in which the challenges of early married life are given either a comic or more serious treatment. In this case the treatment was light, ultra light. Indeed, it was not a distinguished play in which to make one's debut on the Great White Way and Bondi's part as the Adams' maid Maggie was a modest one. Yet she was widely noticed, despite the limitations of the part; indeed, there is every evidence she dominated the stage whenever she put in one of her brief appearances. The *Brooklyn Times Union* wrote: "Beauluh [sic] Bondi won rounds of applause in her few lines as an atavistic and tart-tongued family servant," the *Brooklyn Daily Eagle* thought she "did well" as "the slavey of the Adams house," and the *Brooklyn Standard Union* wrote that "a very large share of the evenings honors went to Beulah Bondi, who took the part of Maggie, the Adams' old servant." Brooks Atkinson failed to mention her in his *New York Times* review.[16] Even better than the praise from a financial perspective was the fact that *One of the Family* was a hit and lasted 236 performances. It transferred to the Klaw Theatre on January 20, 1926, and finished its run at the Eltinge 42nd St. Theatre between February 8 and July 10, 1926.[17]

Maggie is in and out of all three acts of the play; disgruntled, uncooperative, uppity, and rude. She is described in the stage directions as "thin and angular": "her manner is taciturn, and her tongue is sharp." Her generally tart demeanor is illustrated by her complaint about the tea things she has set out on the dining room table that have been forgotten by the family: "All the cold things are getting hot and all the hot things are getting cold." Maggie is in the habit of singing, off key, when she is annoyed. Henry tells Joyce that "her bark is worse than her bite" and that "she's been with us so long, she thinks she runs the house." According to the bemused Joyce: "She isn't a servant—she's a retainer."[18]

Among Bondi's many maid roles from the 1920s, Maggie is most similar to the gruff, outspoken old family factotum Hannah in Owen Davis's *Icebound* (1923), though the setting and social background of the two plays are very different. Had *One of the Family* been filmed, which it was not, Maggie would have been a Margaret Hamilton sort of role. Despite her success, Bondi never played a maid on Broadway again.

Bondi stayed till the end of the run on July 10 and then went to Denver for her second season of stock at the Elitch Theatre. Stuart Walker had to do without her at the Keith Theatre in Indianapolis, where his season had started May 3, though her appearance there had been announced.[19]

Bondi was 36 when she made her Broadway debut in Kenneth Webb's unremarkable "first year" comedy *One of the Family* at the 49th St. Theatre on December 22, 1925. She made a personal hit as Maggie, a patrician Boston family's cantankerous maid, who performs the maid's usual door opening and serving duties and does not suffer in silence. Though she played several maids in stock, this was Bondi's only maid role on Broadway. She never played a maid in films.

On August 21, 1926, producer John Tuerk wrote to her care of Elitch Gardens, accepting her terms for doing the post–Broadway tour of *One of the Family*. They were to open September 6 at the Majestic Theatre in Brooklyn.[20] The leading players were the same, but there were some changes in the supporting cast, including future film star Robert Montgomery taking over from Raymond Van Sickle as George Adams.[21]

Bondi continued to receive good notices as Maggie. According to the *Brooklyn Standard Union*, she "brought broad comedy to the part of the aged and much badgered 'retainer.'" The *Brooklyn Citizen* thought she was "an actress who brings to mind the days of May Vokes at least to the older generation." The *Boston Globe* considered her performance at length, calling it "a gem" and making the character come alive for us: "Marvelous indeed from the knot of hair twisted in careless abandon at the top, down through the forlorn face, the rounded shoulders, the higeldy gait and the sloppy boots at the bottom." The *Boston Herald* adds to the picture: "Weather-beaten, frustrated and whining she looks and acts as old as the old man of the sea."[22]

The final proof that Bondi ran away with at least part of the show was offered by the *Baltimore Sun*, who would have remembered her well from her season with Stuart Walker at the Academy of Music in 1924, as would the audience: "Beulah Bondi, as Maggie, the aged servant who rules the Adams home and sings hymns when angry, shared applause, and deservedly, with Mr. Mitchell." The reviewer added: "Mr. Mitchell, of course, stars, but through the play moves Maggie, singing her lugubrious hymns and appearing so real that one fancies she actually has stepped from a New England farm and hopes the play will be over soon so she can get home and put the bread to rise."[23]

The *One of the Family* tour took Bondi to Brooklyn twice in September, Boston in October, and Philadelphia and Baltimore in November and kept and her busy till November 20, 1926. She then went into rehearsals for her next Broadway show, another "first year" drama, but this time of a more durable kind.

Today the Booth Theatre is still in operation at 222 W. 45th St. The same goes for the Plymouth Theatre, now known as the Gerald Schoenfeld, which stands right next door at no. 236. For two weeks in late March and early April 1927, Bondi had the novel experience for any actor on Broadway of performing concurrently in two different plays at these two theaters. Her classic embittered old maid character, Miss Pym, in *Mariners* was only seen in the first act and her equally typical landlady character, Mrs. Gorlik, in *Saturday's Children* only figured in the third act. This gave her more than enough time to go from one theater to the other and transform herself from a middle-aged, English village spinster into an aging, working-class New York boarding house keeper. Bondi was nearing 38 at the time.

It was unlikely that any producer would have thought of Bondi for *Mariners* when she was already in a play on Broadway. As it happened, both plays were being directed by Guthrie McClintic, who would also direct her in *Cock Robin* the following season and in *Distant Drums* in 1931–32. Born in Seattle in 1893, McClintic was a former actor who would become an important presence in the American theater in the middle decades of the twentieth century. In early 1927, he had just taken over as head of the Actors Theatre, which produced both *Saturday's Children* and *Mariners*. McClintic was gay and married to Broadway star Katharine Cornell, whom he directed in all her major plays.[24] McClintic had been impressed with Bondi's performance as the cleaning lady Mrs. Midget in *Outward Bound* at Elitch Gardens in 1925. When it came time to cast *Saturday's Children*, he wanted her as Mrs. Gorlik, but he could not remember her name. In a remarkable coincidence, Maxwell Anderson insisted on Bondi as Mrs. Gorlik at the same time on the basis of her performance in *One of the Family*.[25] McClintic and Bondi would become friends and he sometimes escorted her to social events. In June 1947, for example, he was her date at a Los Angeles party hosted by Cornelius "Neil" Cole II and Michael Gaszynski "with delicious cheesecake, made by Michael."[26]

Maxwell Anderson's *Saturday's Children* opened on January 26, 1927, and starred Ruth Gordon, Bondi's stock company colleague, and Roger Pryor. It was author Anderson's sixth show on Broadway, where he had had a big hit during the 1924–25 season with the drama *What Price Glory*. *Saturday's Children* was a comedy of working-class urban life in which we can recognize common film motifs of the 1950s, such as "the tender trap," "the mating game," and "the period of adjustment." Indeed, these plotlines can all be traced back to the many newlywed comedies of the 1920s. *Saturday's Children* is maybe the best of the lot, because it is deeper and more realistic than previous, more folksy and farcical incarnations, such as Frank Craven's *The First Year* (1920).

As one critic noted: "Essentially, it is the old, old story of a boy and girl who marry in haste and repent in Harlem."[27] Urged on by her married sister Florrie Sands (Ruth Hammond), young working girl Bobby Halevy (Gordon) fast-tracks a betrothal to her boyfriend Rims O'Neil (Pryor) before either of them are really ready to face the rigors of the everyday married life. By the end of the second act, the whole arrangement comes to a crashing halt. Bobby leaves the connubial home to go and live "in a house so respectable that the doors must be left open upon gentlemen callers, and the landlady is more vigilant than a library policeman."[28] The landlady is Bondi's Mrs. Gorlik, who is ubiquitous in the third act, as she pops in and out trying to keep tabs on Bobby's stream of male callers. Besides being a traffic cop, her main function is to alert Bobby's father, Mr. Halevy (Frederick Perry), to Bobby's real situation and to provide situational comedy. The dramatic irony in the play is that Bobby ends up conducting a clandestine affair with her own husband, as they discover how to put the spark back in their marriage.

Brooks Atkinson wrote: "Miss Bondi edges the part of the lodginghouse keeper with delicious comedy." It marked the first time she was "noticed" by Atkinson, who was only five years into his long tenure as the lead drama critic of the *New York Times*. As if that was not enough, Burns Mantle, drama critic of the *New York Daily News*, wrote that Bondi "has a Broadway career awaiting her as a character woman unless all signs fail." The *Brooklyn Times Union* critic felt that "as the lodging housekeeper in the final act, Beulah Bondi was simply immense."[29] Once again, Bondi had proven her ability to make the most of a small part.

Clemence Dane's *Mariners*, which opened on March 28, two months after *Saturday's Child*, was a maudlin play about the dire consequences of a sensitive, intellectual curate marrying an emotionally unstable former barmaid. Indeed, in its pervading gloom it could compare with Totheroh's *Wild Birds*, which is saying something. Bondi's Miss Pym is a stereotypical frustrated spinster, but she is more aggressive and offensive than most. As a veteran member of the church choir, Miss Pym is offended when the rector corrects her singing of an F sharp and lets loose a vitriolic attack on the poor man's absentee wife for neglecting her duties (including directing the church choir).

This time, Bondi did not rate a mention in Atkinson's review. Of the mismatched husband and wife in the drama, played by Arthur Wontner and Pauline Lord, Atkinson wrote: "By the time the second act was over last evening there were hopes that if he himself did not care to throttle her he would ask for volunteers from the audience." Another critic, though, noticed Bondi in her modest, one-act part, writing "the brilliant edge of pure mind cuts through the 'bit' assigned to Beulah Bondi."[30]

The verdict on the play was succinctly expressed by a Boston critic: "'Mariners' is depressing." "There is no quarrel with the cast," he added, "It is better than the show merits."[31] The New York run of *Mariners* turned out to be even briefer than that of Totheroh's pathetic paean to passion on the prairie. It closed after only 16 performances, meaning that Bondi shuttled between the Booth and the Plymouth for only two weeks

In late August 1927, Bondi made what would prove a tactical error when she left a hit show to take a role in what would prove no hit at all. Her thinking is easy to understand, though. She had been a part of Stuart Walker's "baby" *The Proud Princess* since the show's world premiere in Baltimore in February 1924. Now it was finally bound for Broadway, not as a straight play, but as an operetta with a book and lyrics by one of the original authors and Bondi's friend, Dorothy Donnelly, and music by Donnelly's frequent collaborator, Sigmund Romberg. Bondi was to reprise her role as the heroine's mother, Mrs. Johnson. She did not have any songs, but the part was somewhat more showy than Mrs. Gorlik.

Bondi played her final performance as Mrs. Gorlik on August 27 and was replaced by Anne Tonetti. This means that for nearly a month she acted with 27-year-old Humphrey Bogart, who took over the leading role of Rims O'Neil from Roger Pryor in early August. The two future film veterans never acted together on the big screen. Bondi opened in what was at first entitled *My Golden Girl* at the Shubert Theatre in Boston on September 5, where it played for almost a month, before its premiere at the Shubert Theatre in New York on October 6, 1927.[32] Movie star Hope Hampton was now in the lead as Mimosa "Minnie" Johnson and, like one of those "golddigger" films of the 1930s, her much older, financier husband was rumored to have put $250,000 into the show, which he hoped would make Hampton a star of the stage as well.[33] Needless to say, it did not.

Lo and behold, when New York audiences finally got to see *My Princess*, Bondi was no longer in the cast! *My Princess* turned out to be her first and only experience with being fired from a show. This happened between the Boston try-out and the Broadway opening. The explanation given was that she was "'too legitimate.'" Bondi was replaced by former vaudevillian Marie Stoddard, 15 years her senior and a very different type physically, being built on a considerably more capacious scale and vaguely reminiscent of Laura Hope Crews. To add to this indignity, with one exception, Bondi was the only replacement among the cast members in named roles. Some years later, she offered the further explanation that she had reacted to the producers "changing the play a great deal, contrary to the wishes of the author," who was ill at the time and happened to be one of Bondi's "closest friends."[34] A former stage star turned playwright and librettist, Donnelly was best known for starring in *Madame X* and for two musical comedies with Romberg called *Blossom Time* and *The Student Prince*. Donnelly died of kidney disease on January 3, 1928, at the age of 48. Like Bondi, she was unmarried.[35]

*My Princess* only ran for 20 performances and, as fate would have it, closed on the same day, October 22, as *Saturday's Children* ended its 310-performance run. In fact, the producers had done Bondi a favor by firing her. This allowed her to return to her role in *Saturday's Children*, when the company moved to the Princess Theatre in Chicago on October 24.[36] The brief run there was over by November 7 and Bondi returned to New York.[37] Guthrie McClintic had a new part for her.

On January 12, 1928, Bondi opened as Maria Scott in Philip Barry and Elmer Rice's new comedy-drama *Cock Robin* at the 48th St. Theatre, which was demolished in 1955. It would be more precise to describe this unabashed potboiler by two up-and-coming playwrights as a backstage murder mystery "whodunnit." *Cock Robin* revolves around a small, local amateur dramatic society, that has hired professional director George McAuliffe (Edward Ellis) to stage their latest production, when cast members start meeting their deaths in an untimely fashion. The play has little lasting artistic value. What is novel about it, though, is the inverted visual perspective from "behind" the stage looking towards the audience in Act II and III; and the absence of the police, the company conducting their own murder investigation under the leadership first of Julian Cleveland (Moffat Johnston), then of McAuliffe, and finally of Maria Scott.

Scott is the director's assistant, who comes in for a surprisingly large amount of vitriol from the cast members, especially the women. She is distinguished by being sharp-eyed, opinionated, and ruthlessly efficient. A middle-aged, married female cast member calls her "a very fussy, meddlesome person" and "a presumptuous, dowdy, meddlesome, little busybody." A male member of the group dubs her "the girl with the camera eye. She kodaks as she goes."[38] Thus, Maria Scott is indicative of the kind of negative feelings the single working woman might evoke at this time. The role itself is not that challenging, though she takes charge of the reconstruction of the murder scene in Act III and shows hitherto unsuspected authoritarian tendencies. Clearly, Scott intends to help her boss McAuliffe to get away with murder, by making the ironic revelation that she can hardly see even with glasses.

Despite the ephemeral quality of the play, Maria Scott was Bondi's best opportunity on Broadway to date and garnered her even more detailed critical plaudits. Brooks Atkinson wrote: "Beulah Bondi as an angular female with a camera eye and a maddening mastery of detail, and Edward Ellis as the professional coach contribute good performances to a generally agreeable evening." Burns Mantle observed that "Beulah Bondi submits another touch of character as a camera-eyed assistant." The *Brooklyn Citizen*'s reviewer quipped: "Beulah Bondi ... is splendid. However we do think the authors gave this character more than her share to keep her eye on. It will be a wonder if Miss Bondi does not suffer an acute eye strain before the end of this play's quite possible and successful engagement in this town." Finally, one reviewer felt that "the best of the playing is done by Edward Ellis, an old hand at the interpretation of the hard-boiled, and Beulah Bondi, a girl with a gift for definite and sure characterization."[39]

This time, Bondi faced stiff competition in the scene stealing category from British-born character actress Beatrice Herford, whose mock curtain speech was the decided hit of the production according to the *Brooklyn Times Union*.[40] *Cock Robin* did not prove the moneymaker the authors had hoped and closed in April 1928 after 100 performances.

Clearly, Bondi was planning her first trip abroad even before *Cock Robin* closed, as her first passport is dated March 23, 1928. She landed in the French port of Le Havre on April 30. Her hometown newspaper reported on May 1, that "a cablegram from Paris was received today from Beulah Bondy of a perfect voyage."[41] Visas and entry stamps indicate that, in addition to France, Bondi also visited Spain and Italy on this journey of a little over two months.[42] On July 7, she boarded the Berengaria bound for New York, where she arrived five days later.[43] Three weeks later, she arrived in Cincinnati to begin rehearsing a role and a play that was fast becoming a mainstay of her repertoire, namely Mrs. Johnson in *The Proud Princess*. Stuart Walker had in no way given up on the show. This was the first time Bondi acted with Walker's stock company since their contretemps in December 1924. Since then, Bondi had stormed the barricades of Broadway and conquered, which no doubt put her on a more equal footing with her autocratic former mentor.

Walker's season at the Taft Auditorium had begun on May 14, while Bondi was still in Europe. She opened in *The Proud Princess* on August 6, three days after her arrival in Cincinnati, and played it for a week in the usual stock company manner. It was followed by one week each of the plays *Nightstick*, *Kempy*, and *The Beautiful Adventure* and two weeks of *Broadway*, which was held over for a second week. In *Kempy*, Bondi reprised the role of Ma Bence, that she had played in Baltimore and Cincinnati in 1924. William Smith Goldenburg wrote: "the timid and fainty variety of the feminine of the species" is "neatly drawn, though somewhat underplayed to attain the desired effect."[44]

The heroine's grandmother, Madame de Trevillac, in *The Beautiful Adventure*, translated from the French, was one of Bondi's classic grandmother roles. In this light comedy, a runaway bride avoids a marriage of convenience arranged by her scheming aunt and with her lover seeks refuge at her grandmother's home. Madame's big scene is when she creeps to the door of what she believes to be a newlywed couple with a sprig of rosemary, only to find the purported groom sleeping in a chair outside the bedroom. She admonishes both him and her granddaughter, and effectively throws them into each other's arms to enjoy a night of premarital bliss.

The *Cincinnati Inquirer* wrote: "Beulah Bondi, always superb in character roles, gives a quaint, compelling performance as Mme. de Trevillac, the doting grandmother of Helene, who, laboring under a misconception of the circumstances, creates a situation that borders the risqué without offending any save those who have an exaggerated sense of propriety."[45]

Madame had been created on Broadway by Mrs. Thomas Whiffen in 1914, who had "a personal triumph" in the role.[46] Bondi was sometimes compared to Whiffen, who was born in London in 1845 and was active on Broadway until 1927.[47]

*Nightstick* was a brand new crime melodrama of the *Kick In* variety with no less than four authors, including the Nugents, father and son, authors of *Kempy*, whom Bondi had acted with in *Money to Burn* in 1924. The critic for the *Cincinnati Enquirer* enthused that "this is one instance where too many cooks did not spoil the broth." He called the show "Easily the most exciting production the Walker players have presented this season" and "virtually without a dull moment." He also found that "Beulah Bondi and Aldrich Bowker, as two disreputable specimens of underworld society, again exhibit unerring artistry in the interpretation of amusing characterizations, which they endow with humor and vitality."[48]

Bondi also played an underworld figure in Philip Dunning and George Abbott's "epic of night-club life,"[49] *Broadway*, which was a huge hit and ran for 603 performances in New York from 1926 to 1928. *Broadway* is an interesting play from an historical perspective, as it foreshadows so many of the elements of the crime dramas and gangster films of the 1930s. It is not half bad either from an aesthetic point of view, having some modicum of deeper meaning beyond the pure entertainment value and containing some funny characters and situations.

The role of the jaded, faded night club singer Lil Rice is not large, but it is a good comic second type role. Lil is in and out throughout the play, gets some good lines, and gives the actress portraying her a chance to play drunk and hung over in Act III. Lil even has a love interest in the gangster "Porky" Tompson (Aldrich Bowker), who prefers "a dame who can sit in a Morris chair and fill it" to the "skinny-legged, slat-sided baby pigeons" other men so often favor, and whom Lil ends up marrying one wet night after a party at the Paradise Club.[50]

Lil is described in the stage directions as a *"Prima donna type. Heavy and middle-aged with a certain amount of good looks, which, however, have long since lost their bloom."*[51] Physically, then, Bondi was not suited for this Gladys George or Marjorie Rambeau–type role. Rambeau, in fact, played Lil in the 1942 film version. Bondi was around in 1942, of course, but by that point she was about as likely to be cast as Lil as Rambeau was to play Lucy Cooper in *Make Way for Tomorrow*. Just the idea that Bondi in the 1920s was seen as likely casting as a night club singer is fascinating in itself. It makes it painfully clear how much she was constrained in the types of roles she played in Hollywood.

In what would prove the last of his many appraisals of Bondi's performances,

*Cincinnati Enquirer* drama critic William Smith Goldenburg wrote: "Hilarious comedy is provided by Beulah Bondi, and her scene with Aldrich Bowker gives adequate support."[52] Exactly two years after he penned these words, on September 4, 1930, Goldenburg died of a cerebral hemorrhage at his desk at the paper.[53]

Bondi ended her 1928 guest appearance with Walker's stock company with the final performance of *Broadway* on September 15. Three months later, she started rehearsals in New York on what would prove the most important play of her career.

A year of disaster for many—1929—was a year of triumph for Beulah Bondi. It was the year she opened in the single most important play she ever performed in and arguably the best play she ever did. *Street Scene*, Elmer Rice's gritty yet deeply emotional dissection of 1920s, lower middle-class, urban life, meant more to the development of Bondi's acting career than any other play or film. This was mainly because she acted both in the original Broadway production and the film adaptation from 1931. *Street Scene* vaulted the highly respected character actress from the stage to the screen and gave her a flying start in the medium that would be her primary arena for the remainder of her acting career. It took her career to a whole other level.

*Street Scene* was classical in taking place in a single setting and within the temporal limits of a day and a half. It was innovative in being played out literally in the street; more specifically in front of what author Rice describes as a "typical Manhattan brownstone front walk-up."[54] The drama blends the various stories of the families who live in this "average New York tenement on the grimier edge of the middle class"[55] and the life of the street from morning till night of a stiflingly hot June day and into the following, equally torrid day.

Beulah Bondi as a fan dancer? Well not quite, but her get-up here is certainly more chic, youthful, and worldly than we would ever see her in the movies. The role has not been identified, but I would guess that we see her here as Lil Rice, "The Silver-Toned Songbird" of the Paradise Night Club, in Philip Dunning and George Abbott's hit play *Broadway* at the Taft Auditorium in Cincinnati in September 1928.

Despite the ensemble feeling, with a large number of equally important characters from various ethnic and immigrant backgrounds, the main focus is on the Irish-inflected Moran family (later changed to Maurrant), consisting of stay-at-home mother Anna, stagehand father Frank, grown-up working daughter Rose, and young street urchin son Willie. In classical fashion, too, the action begins close to the climax with the whole street buzzing about the affair between Anna and the collector from the milk company, Steve Sankey; he too married with children. Frank is a violent drunk with a vicious streak and by the end of a short, tense second act, he has shot and killed both his wife and her lover. The third act depicts the capture of the murderer and the stunning speed with which people return to the minutiae of their daily lives, even after such a shocking occurrence on their very doorstep. Daughter Rose and her would-be boyfriend Sam Kaplan are left to try to make sense of it all.

This main storyline is interwoven with minor chords depicting the birth of a child, the dispossession of a family whose breadwinner has abandoned them, the sexual harassment of Rose by her boss and manager Harry Easter, and the budding yet-never-to-be romance between Rose and Sam. *Los Angeles Times* film writer Edwin Schallert gives a vivid description of the play's "huge and ample slice of life": "Youth, first of all, is seeking happiness. Crow-like, maturity looks on and caws of danger. Sordid surroundings breed more inhibitions than do gay and gladsome ones. How the 95 per cent live is here shown vividly." Robert Benchley described the play as "about as comprehensive a summary of mass existence as you could expect to find on one stage."[56]

As an avid observer and vituperative commentator on the lives of others, with nothing much happening in her own life, we find the figure Bondi was to portray so famously: Emma Jones, a curious mix of hoydenish slattern and prim and proper lower middle-class wife and mother. Mr. Jones, a nonentity given to drink, puts in a few appearances, and we also make the acquaintance of Mrs. Jones's loud, loutish son Vincent and dissolute daughter Mae. Quick to criticize others, her own children can do no wrong in her eyes.

Emma Jones is most in evidence in the long opening act. She is hardly seen or heard in Act Two and a not-so-innocent bystander in Act Three. Mrs. Jones gets the last word in the play, gossiping again, of course. Her chief function in the play is comic relief. She does not have a clear plot function in the sense that she does something decisive to hasten or hinder the oncoming catastrophe, yet indirectly her eager stirring of the pot contributes to the charged atmosphere. Frank Moran makes this clear after his capture, when he tries to explain to his daughter Rose what made him a murderer: "I'd been drinking, Rose—see what I mean?—an' all the talk that was goin' round. I just went clean off me nut, that's all."[57]

Emma Jones is tellingly described by her neighbor Anna Moran: "There's lots of people like that in the world—they never seem to be happy unless they're making trouble for somebody."[58] Many of Emma's lines are like heat-seeking missiles or poisoned darts. And they never miss their mark—as soon as the subject's back is turned. An expert on one-upmanship, Emma is ever ready with an example from her own life, if anyone tries to make their conversational mark with some experience out of the ordinary. It might be said in Mrs. Jones's defense, that she is not the only one given to gossip in the neighborhood. The Swedish-inflected janitor's wife Mrs. Olsen and German-born, Italian-married Mrs. Fiorentino, for example, are both eager to enlarge on the developing scandal in the building. The men, too, do not shy away from commentary. Yet Mrs. Jones is clearly the leader of the pack.

In preparing for her role, according to one newspaper, Bondi "went into the lower East Side and studied tenement dwellers."[59] In an interview in 1931, she reiterated that "I found my prototype in New York's East Side."[60] Strictly speaking, she was looking in the wrong part of Manhattan. Rice pointed out in his autobiography, that the play was set on the west side of Midtown, in the area known as Hell's Kitchen. More specifically, the prototype for Jo Mielziner's famous brownstone façade set was to be found at 25 W. 65th St.[61] The building is no longer there.

After being turned down by every potential producer, *Street Scene* found an unlikely sponsor in William A. Brady. Brady had once been a major Broadway producer and still owned his own theater, the Playhouse. By the late 1920s, though, he was considered a has-been and had not had a hit play in a dozen years. Brady was notoriously tight-fisted and came encumbered with a raft of hangers-on and relatives expecting handouts in the form of parts in the play. Rice cannily retained some measure of control by insisting on the right of approval of the director. When George Cukor bailed out to direct *Gypsy* instead, and no other mutually agreeable director would touch the play, Rice offered his own services, though he had never directed before. The first thing he did was to throw out all Brady's and Cukor's nepotistic hires and start the casting process over from scratch.

Rice had worked with Bondi on his recent potboiler *Cock Robin* and was determined to have her as Emma Jones, though her weekly salary was far above what Brady was accustomed to paying. Furthermore, the veteran producer did not see why they needed Bondi for what, to him, was simply a bit part. Fortunately, Rice prevailed and an agreement was reached with Bondi. As she recalled, Brady offered her only $75 a week, when she had started at $175 when she first came to New York. She was rehearsing another show at the time and was to be paid $275 a week.[62] As Rice recalled, Bondi ended up getting only half her usual salary, but a percentage if the week's receipts exceeded nine thousand dollars. This turned out to be a highly lucrative arrangement when *Street Scene* became a hit. Rice later urged Brady to sign Bondi and two of the other leads to run-of-the-play contracts, so that they would not be lured away by other producers.

As Rice remembered it, the highest salary paid any of the actors was $250 dollars a week, which may well have been Bondi's salary. Apart from Bondi, Robert Kelly as David Moran, Mary Servoss as Anna Moran, and Horace Braham as Sam Kaplan, most of the actors cast were practically unknown, certainly they were unknown to Rice, who had only seen five or six of them act before. Whenever Bondi appeared on the stage during rehearsals, Brady would say to Rice: "I don't know what we're paying that woman all that money for. It's just a bit." Bondi had been assured that she would have no direct contact with Brady, who was known for making offensive remarks to actors.

According to Equity rules, they only had 28 days to rehearse this complex, orchestral play with a cast of 50 and, in the first act alone, more than 100 exits and entrances compared to 15 or so in a conventional play. Rehearsals began in the attic of Brady's Playhouse Theatre at 137 W. 48th St. in mid–December 1928. The set was not available to rehearse in until a week before the opening. Even then it was not set up on the stage of the theater, but was erected in Brady's scene-building shop in a former movie studio in Fort Lee, New Jersey. They did not get into the Playhouse until Monday of the week they were opening. After two invitational premieres on Tuesday and Wednesday, *Street Scene* opened on Thursday, January 10, 1929.[63]

*Street Scene* was that rare thing: a critical and commercial success. Leading in the distribution of laurels, *New York Times* critic Brooks Atkinson wrote that the play "manages to be generally interesting, frequently amusing and extraordinarily authentic until the final curtain." According to Robert Benchley, "*Street Scene* would be good in any season. In this, it seems like something by Sophocles (better, if you ask us)." Rowland Field found *Street Scene* to be "exceptional in every way." Richard Dana Skinner wrote in a lengthy piece in *The Commonweal*, that *Street Scene* was "a play of extraordinary sweep, power, and intensity" and "intensely realistic." Rice was commended for the near perfection of his casting and for "something approaching genius in the handling of the huge cast." Burns Mantle summed up the critical response to the play in his "Best Plays" volume for 1928–29. "Because he [Rice] is a writer who favors the extremists and has a passion for new forms, the chances that he would produce a salable and popular success seemed slightly remote," Mantle began. Yet *Street Scene* "proved another of those exciting exceptions that make play production the fascinating gamble that it is." "Critical opinion was favorable but qualified and often restrained," while "the response of playgoers was immediate and consistently sustained through the season."[64] In March 1929, *Street Scene* was awarded the Pulitzer Prize for Drama.

Reviewers were unanimous in their praise of Bondi's efforts as Emma Jones. Starting with Atkinson again, he wrote: "Some of the acting, like Beulah Bondi's malicious gossip…, [has] time and space enough for complete fulfillment." Also influential in his day, Burns Mantle wrote in the *New York Daily News*: "Beulah Bondi does as much for Mrs. Jones as actress can do for friend and neighbor, reproducing her from eyebrows to stockings perfectly." Rowland Field thought Bondi was "superb": "Never once does she overplay a role that could easily be ruined by a less competent actress." Percy Hammond of the *New York Herald Tribune* agreed that she "never overplays a role that would tease a lesser actress to do so."[65]

According to John Anderson, Bondi "turns out a gossipy busy body with remarkable detail and rare effect." Gilbert Gabriel wrote at length: "Talk of character bits and you find yourself talking inevitably of Beulah Bondi. After that you scratch your head to remember one other young person who has made Miss Bondi's reputation for taking these small, picturesquely comic parts and working them up into such extraordinary etchings…. She is that slatternly old gossip in 'Street Scene' now, who comes out every little while to air her poodle and her evil mind. You need not be urged to watch for her."[66]

The critic for the *Brooklyn Citizen* went even further, claiming that Bondi "does the best work of her career." "For her fine acting in 'Street Scene,'" he added, "Miss Bondi deserves to be elevated to stardom." Finally, though not a theater critic per se, columnist Walter Winchell was certainly an opinion maker. He wrote that "the comedy relief is entrusted to the greatest character actress in America, Beulah Bondi. Hers was a magnificent performance." At the end of 1929, Winchell even included "Beulah Bondi's first-rate playing in 'Street Scene'" in his list of "Things I could see and hear again."[67]

Columnist James J. Geller noted in early June 1930, that Bondi was "in her eighteenth shrewish month as the harridan in 'Street Scene.'"[68] *Street Scene*'s lengthy run, which had begun at the Playhouse, finally came to an end at the Ambassador Theatre on Saturday, May 24, 1930, after 601 performances. Rowland Field pointed out that *Street Scene* was only "The 15th drama in the history of the American theatre to achieve a run of 600 performances on Broadway."[69]

Bondi was only off the Broadway boards for a week. On June 2, 1930, she opened in the Players Club's week-long revival of Arnold Bennett and Edward Knoblock's drama *Milestones* at the Empire Theatre. *Milestones* was ostensibly an attempt to encapsulate the history of the Industrial Revolution in England through a family saga extending over several generations of the Rhead family. In reality, the politics and historical "background" are just window-dressing for a play very much in the domestic tradition and dealing almost entirely with coupling and marriage in three generations of an upper-class London family. *Milestones* is a good play, but far from a great one. Despite having "a cast which is perhaps superior to any other assembled during the season for any play, by any producer," according to Richard Lockridge, even this first-rate production left Brooks Atkinson wondering "why The Players have dedicated the single week of their revival to such commonplace wares." Burns Mantle thought the play, which had been a hit on Broadway in 1912–13, still "a rather fine and observing study of those human weaknesses that make the radical of today the conservative of tomorrow."[70]

Bondi had originally been asked by the Players to portray the first-generation hero, John Rhead's mother, Mrs. Rhead, the same role she had done in her first season in stock in 1919.[71] By the time the show opened, though, she was playing Gertrude Rhead, Mrs. Rhead's daughter and John Rhead's sister. While Mrs. Rhead only appears in the first act, Gertrude Rhead is a larger and more interesting part. She is in and out in all three acts of the play and serves a type of choral function. She is also close to the ethical center of the play, as she is usually right, while the mothers and fathers are wrong, in this classic drama of parental opposition to their offspring's choice of marital partners.

Gertrude Rhead is what used to be called a strong-minded woman, who rejects her straight-laced, conservative fiancé, Sam Sibley (Warburton Gamble), even though she loves him, when he reveals his lack of respect for her as an equal. She runs the Rhead household with great efficiency, *too* great efficiency according to her mother, who fears she will not make a suitably meek and mild wife. As it turns out, she makes no wife at all, though she seems to regret breaking her engagement in later life. This materializes when she urges her beloved niece Emily (Selena Royle) to make a love match, rather than a marriage of convenience. Emily fails to follow her aunt's advice.

Gertrude Rhead, then, is also a classic spinster role in Anglo-American drama, with the stereotypical mix of disillusionment, powerlessness, depression, bitterness, leanness, and dryness. We follow her from age 21 to 73 during the 52 years of the play's development from 1860 to 1912, quite a challenge for an actress of any age. Bondi was 41, which must have made Act I a bit of a stretch! Playing 73 would have been par for the course for her, but she was not used to playing "younger." Ironically, the spinster Gertrude proves a better parent than both her sister-in-law Rose (Dorothy Stickney) and her niece Emily. Both are bad mothers, who have no true understanding, intelligence or their own point of view and defer too much to their husbands (in Rose's case) or think only of themselves (in Emily's).

Burns Mantle wrote of her performance: "Beulah Bondi, so many years hiding a comparative youth and good looks as frowsy females (she was the lady who walked the dog, you will recall in 'Street Scene'), has the Haidee Wright-Auriol Lee role of Gertrude Rhead, the spinster, and does her predecessors proud. The part is cut perfectly to her measure, and she scores with every line of it." Brooks Atkinson thought Tom Powers as John Rhead, Stickney, and Bondi were "acting in distinction in every scene."[72] The company did eight performances and then it was over. It was like doing a stock production on Broadway.

Meanwhile, by the summer of 1930 it was clear that *Street Scene* was to be presented in London's West End with several of the original New York cast members reprising their roles. Bondi was at first reported to be going along, but ended up staying at home.[73]

Margaret Moffat replaced her as Emma Jones at the Globe Theatre in London, starting September 9, 1930.[74] Clearly, Bondi felt she deserved a vacation, which was partially spent visiting friends in Stockbridge, Massachusetts, in early September.[75] Elmer Rice, who directed the London production, wrote to her ten days after the opening, as he was returning to New York aboard the S.S. France: "We were all thinking of you the first night and regretting your absence." He added that the play had had "a most thrilling reception" and he was "very happy about the whole thing."[76] It ran for five months.[77]

Beyond taking some time off, Bondi had prioritized a return to her roots over new horizons in London. On October 5, 1930, the *Cincinnati Enquirer* wrote under the heading "Guest Stars and Old Favorites Will Be Seen in Walker Casts": "An announcement of exceptional interest is the fact that Stuart Walker has secured the services of Beulah Bondi for early in the fall season."[78] When Bondi came back to Cincinnati and the Taft Auditorium in October for what would be her last hurrah with the Stuart Walker stock company, she was treated as a star. As an actress, she had outgrown her mentor and his company. She was in the big time now and had proven that she had a future on Broadway, if she wanted it. As it happened, she would soon abandon New York, too, for Hollywood. Before then, there was time for a long good-bye with her many loyal fans in Cincinnati, where she had been appearing with Walker's stock company since 1922. In heralding her arrival, the *Cincinnati Enquirer* called her "one of the most popular actresses ever introduced on a local stage."[79]

Walker was lucky and happy to have her, even if it was only for three weeks. His season had started on October 21 with Donald Ogden Stuart's new comedy *Rebound*.[80] Bondi arrived in the second week and opened on October 27, 1930, in a brand-new play written especially for her. The author was fellow Hoosier and cast member in *One of the Family*, Raymond Van Sickle. Set in a small Ohio town, *The Stand-by* was a typical "silver cord" drama in which Bondi played Mrs. Davis, "a complaining, selfish, yet strange affectionate mother" afraid of losing control over her 26-year-old daughter Cora (Leona Hogarth), if the latter enters into a relationship with a man.[81] The problem the play explored was a commonplace one in the dramas of the era, including Bondi's most celebrated film *Make Way for Tomorrow*: "To what extent may filial love be stretched and how far may the child be required to go in personal sacrifice for the parent?"[82]

George A. Leighton wrote after the gala premiere, which both Bondi's mother and the author attended, that "sincere, is the highest compliment that can be paid every phase of this drama." Fortunately, he added a few more pungent adjectives in his appraisal: "It is impressive, moving, gripping. It maintains interest; it is human; it is life as many have lived and are living." As for Bondi's performance as the hypochondriac, manipulative mother: "Beulah Bondi injected just that touch of querulousness and whiney martyrdom into the role of Mrs. Davis to arouse the audience frequently to a point of exasperation hard to repress and keep inaudible. She is a fine artist and her artistry found full expression last evening."[83]

The final verdict was that *The Stand-by* "will stand out as one of the memorable productions and the play itself as one of the distinctive dramas of the current season."[84] Stuart Walker wrote to Bondi on December 3, 1930: "You must have Ray tell you first-hand the changes that will make THE STAND-BY a good play!"[85] Bondi did not benefit from these changes and never played Mrs. Davis again. Retitled *Best Years*, Van Sickle's drama had a brief run on Broadway with Jean Adair in Bondi's role and Katharine Alexander playing the daughter. Bondi attended the world premiere of *Rain* at Grauman's Chinese

Theatre in Hollywood two days after *Best Years* opened at the Bijou Theatre in New York on September 7, 1932. When she returned to Broadway from Hollywood at the end of the year, it was in Sidney Howard's *The Late Christopher Bean*.

Ironically, Bondi did not escape playing a maid in her last season with Stuart Walker either. This time the servant was called Helen and made her presence felt in George Abbott and S.K. Lauren's new comedy *Those We Love*, which was the third week's offering of the Cincinnati stock season. *Those Who Love* was one of a slew of middle-class marital infidelity dramas from the period and its permutations of a commonplace topic need not occupy us. In Cincinnati, Victor Jory and Leona Hogarth played the ostensible leading roles, but Bondi was the star of the show. One advertisement read: "Last time Sunday: THOSE WE LOVE with Beulah Bondi."[86] According to the reviewer for the *Cincinnati Enquirer*, the role of the maid "assumes major proportions" in this play: "By way of explanation we might add that the part is portrayed by Beulah Bondi, who seems to have an uncanny knack at stealing the show. She just can't help it, for she lends distinction to any part in which she is cast. At any rate, she contributes some very welcome humorous relief to a play that leaves one with decidedly mixed impressions." "Aldrich Bowker," he added, "in the guise of a stableman, cordially cooperates with Miss Bondi in giving one of the most amusing scenes in the play."[87] As far as I know, Helen was Bondi's final maid role on any stage.

As what he must have sensed would be their final play together, Walker had chosen George S. Kaufman and Edna Ferber's *The Royal Family*, inspired by the legendary Barrymore clan of actors, here called Cavendish. The play is a mixture of screwball comedy and "marriage or career?" drama. By the end, all the many thespians in the family have decided to return to the stage, despite the various and varied misgivings that have been aired throughout the play's three acts.

Bondi played the imperious and proud leading lady and matriarch of the Cavendish clan, Fanny Cavendish, still dreaming of a return to the stage after a long illness, which she is doomed to die from in the play's final minutes. She is described in the stage directions as "Managerial, pungent, rather magnificent. Given to domineering and to reminiscence. Her clothes are rich but careless, and somewhat out-dated." "I've been a trouper all my life," she says, "and I'm going to keep on trouping." When it is suggested that her son Tony may have killed someone, her laconic response is: "Anyone we know?"[88] Fanny had been created on Broadway in 1927 by Haidee Wright and was played in the 1930 film version by Henrietta Crosman. Wright had been 60 when she played the role and Crosman was "the real thing," being 69 and a former leading lady playing a former leading lady. Bondi was 41 playing 72.

With her in the talented cast, Bondi had Leona Hogarth as her stage star daughter Julie, who rekindles the fires with an old love; Victor Jory as her matinee-idol-turned-movie-star son Tony, who makes his escape to Europe after a fracas with his director in Hollywood; and Rachel Hartzell as her granddaughter Gwen, torn between the desire for a stage career and the demands of marriage and motherhood. These players were all new to Bondi this season. In the role of the Cavendishes' hard-tried manager and producer, though, she had Aldrich Bowker. It was the last of their nearly 40 plays together, dating back to the first play of Bondi's first Walker season in 1919.

I must admit I have a hard time imagining Beulah Bondi as Fanny Cavendish. This is chiefly a testament, I suppose, to the power of typecasting in Hollywood. While Bondi certainly played many elderly ladies on the big screen, she never played an actress or a diva. The *Cincinnati Enquirer* provides the only evidence about her performance, writing: "Fannie, played by Beulah Bondi, is the patriarch of the group, regal and proud; snippy at the slightest suggestion that her acting days are over or that any of her tribe, past or present, excelled her. Miss Bondi put all of her artistry into the characterization and made it strongly appealing."[89]

From her brief season in Cincinnati, Bondi went to celebrate Thanksgiving with her parents, brother Raymond and his family in Chicago.[90] Stuart Walker wrote to her from Cincinnati: "I enjoyed your visit more than you will know but I was so upset over the rather dull audiences we had—so uninspiring."[91] By the time his stock company played its final season in Cincinnati in the spring of 1931, both Bondi and Walker were in Hollywood.

# 4

# Miss Bondi Goes to Hollywood
## *1931–1935*

"I worked with the best, I gave my best."[1]

As a character actor, or any kind of actor really, there were more or less advantageous ways to embark on a film career in Hollywood. Beulah Bondi had the benefit of starting her screen career in the best way possible. The best way possible was to have a major producer bring you to Hollywood to play a named, credited role in a major motion picture. For a character actress, it was even more advantageous if you were reprising a hit role from Broadway. Thus Bondi got a flying start when she arrived in Los Angeles on March 25, 1931, to reprise her standout role as the garrulous gossip and doting lower middle-class mother Emma Jones in *Street Scene*, the Pulitzer Prize-winning play in which she had been wowing audiences on Broadway and beyond for more than two years.[2] The film version was to be the culmination of her work on Elmer Rice's modern classic and arguably the most important role of her career, if not her most significant performance.

But first Los Angeles theatergoers got to see her in the stage version. Under the direction of the author himself, who had arrived in Los Angeles with much fanfare, rehearsals for the stage production started on March 26 and the play opened downtown at the fanciful Mayan Theater with a gala premiere on April 9.[3] *Los Angeles Times* critic Edwin Schallert raved about the production and passed "liberal laurels to.... Beulah Bondi, as the woman with the dog."[4] *Street Scene* ran at the Mayan until May 16, when it closed after 48 performances.[5]

Even after having created the role on Broadway and having played it over 1,000 times (according to one newspaper), Bondi still had to audition for producer Samuel Goldwyn.[6] By April 1, 1931, she had contracted to do the film.[7] Of the 28 actors in named roles in the Broadway production, only eight were finally asked to reprise their roles on film: Bondi as Emma Jones, George Humbert as Filippo Fiorentino, Ann Kostant as Shirley Kaplan, T.H. Manning as George Jones, Matt McHugh as Vincent Jones, John M. Qualen as Carl Olsen, Conway Washburne as Daniel Buchanan, and Eleanor Wesselhoeft as Greta Fiorentino. All five of the leads were replaced except Bondi, with Sylvia Sidney starring as Rose Maurrant (Moran in the play version), a role that had originally been intended for Nancy Carroll.[8] Estelle Taylor was now playing Rose's ill-fated mother Anna, David Landau her murderously jealous father Frank, and William Collier, Jr., her would-be boyfriend Sam Kaplan.

Bondi's film debut was gilt-edged for another reason than the prestige and security of having been brought to Hollywood by a leading producer. As she told Dennis Brown many years later, *Street Scene* was "the ideal project for me to make the transition to film." They rehearsed for two weeks before filming began. Because she already knew the part so well, she could concentrate on the special requirements of film acting. "I didn't realize the power of the microphone," she recalled. "Then I had to learn the limitations that were imposed on me by the camera. But learning about the different lenses was fun. I loved the learning."[9] When asked to compare acting on stage and screen, she said in 1937 that she found "pictures—that is the technique—is much more difficult." This was particularly the case when trying to create "the illusion of old age": "on the stage, you have the benefits of the lights and the set is at a distance from the audience, which helps immensely. With the screen ... the camera brings you uncompromisingly before your audience in close-up."[10]

Under the direction of King Vidor, production began June 10, 1931, following immediately on Goldwyn's production of *The Unholy Garden* at United Artists Studios at 7200 Santa Monica Blvd. in West Hollywood.[11] The shoot was over by late July and on August 12, 1931, the finished film was ready to be previewed by a select groups of industry

Emma Jones in Elmer Rice's *Street Scene* has commonly been regarded as Bondi's important role. It gave her her biggest personal success on Broadway and launched her film career in the best possible way, when she reprised the part in Samuel Goldwyn's production directed by King Vidor in 1931. Here Bondi is seen in the window with fellow tenant Eleanor Wesselhoeft (right), as they cast a skeptical glance at the wayward wife being played by Estelle Taylor. Only eight of the actors in the Broadway production were cast in the film. Wesselhoeft was one of them.

professionals and insiders, which included Mary Pickford, Douglas Fairbanks, Sr., and Jr., Joan Crawford, Irving Thalberg, and Norma Shearer.[12]

We get a fascinating glimpse into Bondi's mind at this pivotal point in her life in a long undated letter headed "On the Set, Monday," that she wrote to her parents during the final week of the *Street Scene* shoot in late July 1931. After describing the challenges of working "in the intense heat with the lights besides," she explains the mechanics of previewing the film and what will happen up until the time of its "grand opening." Even before the preview, she was aware that her performance was a hit: "How I wish you could both hear all the predictions and nice things which are said about my work. It would do your hearts good and I do hope they come true—so that in a small way I can repay you both for the sacrifices you both made when the way was being paved for me to become— what I have become—and what I hope to become. Each day now I hear of agents who want to sign me up." Paramount was interested. Her director King Vidor had asked what her plans were and wanted to talk to her about a new picture he was doing.[13] A New York agent had come up to her on Saturday and said "'Everyone says the picture is yours, that you steal every scene you're in.'" She continues: "word evidently is being circulated that I walk away with it [the film]—but I assure you my only hope is that I give a good per-formance—eclipsing my fellow players is not my ambition. If fine offers come from this I shall be so grateful and with any success I meet with I hope to relieve my dear ones and make life easier in a material way if possible. I assure you all the praise and predictions are not going to my head. I still realize the law of supply and demand and of earning the position I hope to achieve." In the letter, she also describes her daily routine, including taking a taxi to the studio in the morning, or a bus if she does not have to be there till 8 a.m. or 9:30. She would usually walk home in the evening, "a little over a mile," and stop for dinner at a "garden tea-room—tables under the trees," before continuing home to bed. She closes with the words "Endless—unceasing love from Daughter."[14]

*Street Scene* had its world premiere at 9 o'clock in the evening of Wednesday, August 26, 1931, at the Rivoli Theater in New York, which stood at 1620 Broadway between 49th and 50th streets. There was a throng outside and "floodlights poured their bluegrey beams all over the scene and celebrities stepped out of shining autos": "Inside the theatre the seats were filled long before the starting time, and managers and ushers had their troubles finding room for last-minute spectators, some of whom were forced to sit on the steps of the balcony."[15] Sylvia Sidney, "her dark eyes shining with excitement and happiness,"[16] made a personal appearance on the stage after the show and was introduced by Irving Pichel. Among the premiere audience were Elmer Rice; William A. Brady, the producer of the stage version; Al Jolson, Libby Holman, Tallulah Bankhead, Sinclair Lewis, King Vidor's wife Eleanor Boardman, Gary Cooper, Clare Luce, Groucho and Harpo Marx, Glenn Hunter, Judith Anderson, Claudette Colbert, and Irving Berlin.[17] Bondi attended the premiere with her mother, whom she had picked up in Valparaiso on the way.[18] For a New York actress, it must have been particularly thrilling to be able to attend the open-ing of her first film in her adopted city. "Oh, it was a great night, all right," concluded the critic for the *Brooklyn Citizen*.[19]

The film version of *Street Scene* sticks closely to the single set of the street in front of the apartment building, though there are some locations shots, including opening and closing bird's eye views and street scenes further along towards the elevated train. Most scenes, though, have the hermetic, sealed off, slightly artificial feeling of the stage set or studio production. A point was made in the press of the fact that "for the first time in

screen history ... a picture is shot in its entirety within the confines of a single set" and
that there were "no close-ups."[20] The film version also hews closely to the plot and some
of the dialogue of the play, but there is a sense of compression and simplification, particularly in some of the philosophical discussion between Rose and Sam and others about
happiness and the meaning of life. Nearly all the many characters large and small have
been retained with their original names (even if the actors playing them were not). The
only element that was truly given the "Hollywood treatment" were the over the top crowd
scenes, though one critic thought they were "handled with discretion and restraint worthy of commendation."[21] Elmer Rice himself characterized the film version as "almost an
exact replica of the play."[22]

Street Scene was a popular and critical success, garnering Goldwyn "the best reviews
of his career."[23] The columnists and film writers raved. Mollie Merrick wrote that the film
"has made the most significant impression of any talkie released in some time" and was
"the most perfectly rhythmed picture to come out of Hollywood." According to Harold
W. Cohen: "'Street Scene' has come through the Hollywood grist mill a stirring photoplay, fine, upstanding, moving and a genuine credit to its makers." He called it "the finest motion picture of the year." Walter Winchell dubbed it a "middle-class New York
skillfully painted by an Elmer Rice Rembrandt," Sue Bernardine called it "the epic of the
underdog," and Corbin Patrick described it as a "saga of the sidewalks" and "drama of
the melting pot." Philip K. Scheuer found it "uncommonly well done in all departments,"
Whitney Williams called it "a true masterpiece of motion picture artistry," and Harold
W. Cohen described it as "a stirring photoplay, fine, upstanding, moving and a genuine
credit to its makers."[24]

There were a few dissenting voices, though. Mordaunt Hall wrote in the *New York
Times*: "It is a swiftly moving production, this shadow version of 'Street Scene,' but one
that in comparison with the play always seems to be more than slightly exaggerated. It is
a good picture, but the acting lacks the naturalness of the original work and the lines are
invariably overstressed." According to Martin Dickstein, *Street Scene* might be "charged
with a certain visual monotony as a result of a too close confinement to the stage limits of the play." Though it was "a picture which commands the attention," it really was not
"much more than a carbon copy of the stage production."[25] At the end of the year, *Street
Scene* came in second after *Cimarron* in a poll of "The Ten Best Films of 1931" conducted
for the tenth time among "leading motion picture editors and critics" by *Film Daily*.
*Cimarron* got 273 votes, *Street Scene* 200 votes, and *Skippy* came in third with 178 votes.[26]

Bondi was frequently singled out for praise and got some of the best reviews of her
career for her first film. She could read that "the acting honors go to Beulah Bondi, 'The
Woman with the Dog,'" that she was "as laugh-enticing as when she portrayed this grand,
gossipy role in the stage play," and that her Emma Jones "lingers most prominently in the
memory" and "is made into a caricature without forfeiting its effectiveness."[27] Other critics used words like "superb," "striking," and "perfection itself."[28]

Mollie Merrick described her Emma Jones vividly as "some priestess of shabby
places—some clairvoyant of the sordid—some augur of implacable tragedy." Boyd Martin observed: "It is interesting to note that movie audiences appreciate the comedy of
Beulah Bondi more than any other quality in the film, and this undoubtedly is so because
Mrs. Jones is a figure so universal in philosophy that she seems an old friend." The most
detailed and acute analysis of Bondi's performance in her film debut has been penned
more recently by Frank Aversano:

Resembling a Greek chorus character, Emma Jones dominates the expository portion of the film. Lips protruding, walking as if in pain, scratching, tugging at her perspiration soaked clothes, adjusting her slip strap, and inevitably and repeatedly punctuating her caustic comments and venomous innuendo regarding every aspect of the street, its inhabitants, her neighbors, and the weather by sweeping her hand up along the back of her neck and adjusting her hair—Beulah Bondi is a joy to behold.

Her lines are never simply spoken. They are spewed forth laden with invective. Even a simple greeting becomes a condemnation; and answer to a question a barbed insinuation—nothing and no one is spared. Possessing the only obvious unethnic name, her remarks are democratically bigoted. Her judgments are sweeping anathemas. Her complaints—real or imagined—are delivered with the tone of a martyr.[29]

The only important element in the characterization Aversano fails to mention is Emma's mangy little dog Queenie, who gives her an excuse to get out of the house and hang about the streets.

On August 16, 1931, Hollywood columnist George Shaffer reported that Bondi "was heaped with so much praise when Producer Sam Goldwyn pre-viewed [*Street Scene*] to an all-star audience, that Goldwyn chased all over Hollywood the next day to sign up Miss Bondi for a part in his next special, 'Arrowsmith.'"[30] Mrs. Tozer in *Arrowsmith*, Bondi's second and final film for Goldwyn, has the dubious distinction of being the smallest role she ever played on film and the only uncredited one. Yet it is not hard to see the initial attraction for Bondi of acting in a film based on a novel by Nobel Prize-winning author Sinclair Lewis, with a screen adaptation by Pulitzer Prize-winning playwright Sidney Howard. Unfortunately, the reality of the role turned out to be much less artistically satisfying than she would have hoped.

*Arrowsmith* is the story of an idealistic, pioneering doctor, Martin Arrowsmith, who sacrifices everything, including his devoted wife Leora Tozer, to the pursuit of science and the betterment of man. In the novel, Martin's mother-in-law Mrs. Tozer only occurs in the chapters set in Leora's hometown of Wheatsylvania, North Dakota (Minnesota in the film). She is described by the narrator as "a thin, faded, unhumorous woman." Mrs. Tozer is quite benign, though, when compared with her autocratic husband and loud-mouthed, bossy son Bert and tries to milden some of the effect of Bert's ceaseless ribbing of Martin. Her most significant action in the novel is to suggest obtusely to Martin that he could open his doctor's office in the barn, which would make it easier for him to make it to meals on time and allow him to keep an eye on the house when she and the maid are out.[31]

Mrs. Tozer's lack of importance in the novel makes it unlikely that her part in the film was ever intended to be much larger than the end result. The film actually made a thin character even thinner. I would be tempted to call it a walk-on, it if were not for the fact that Bondi remains seated throughout her single scene at the family dinner table. The only significant detail retained from the novel is Leora starting to smoke to take the focus off Martin. This gives Bondi her one line in the film: "Leora, you ain't gonna smoke cigarettes?"

Production began on the film on August 17, 1931.[32] One news item suggests that Bondi's scene was filmed first to allow her to attend the New York premiere of *Street Scene*.[33] This was Bondi's only film for legendary director John Ford, who had clearly not yet hit his stride. *Arrowsmith* was "a highly unusual project for Ford," who was on loan-out to RKO from his home studio Fox.[34] Almost a decade later, Bondi was famously passed over as Ma Joad in his classic *The Grapes of Wrath*, which garnered Jane Darwell an Academy Award in 1941.

Ronald Colman, long under contract with Goldwyn, was cast as Martin Arrowsmith and Helen Hayes played Leora Tozer. Hayes, like Bondi a recent arrival in Hollywood from Broadway, was on loan-out from MGM. "Working for [Goldwyn] was the nearest I've felt in Hollywood to being back in the theatre," she recalled.[35] *Arrowsmith* was only her second film to be released in what would prove a brief early sound film career.

If nothing else, *Arrowsmith* was a useful lesson in the downside of being a Hollywood character actress. When Goldwyn offered her a long-term contract at $500 a week, she tore it up.[36] She was also offered a contract by Irving Thalberg at MGM, which she equally declined.[37] Indeed, Bondi never signed a standard seven-year contract with any studio. In 1976, she reflected that this had prevented her from being miscast and allowed her to select her own roles.[38] "I always figured that if I was a good enough actress, somebody will want me."[39] In another interview towards the end of her life, she commented further that "in the theater I had always been very particular about what roles I played, and I knew that if I started making movies I would want to continue to be every bit as particular."[40]

By the time *Arrowsmith* opened in New York on December 7, 1931, Bondi was back on Broadway rehearsing a new play, *Distant Drums* by Dan Totheroh. We recall that Totheroh's first play, *Wild Birds*, had been her New York debut at the Cherry Lane Theatre in Greenwich Village. By November 24, 1931, Bondi had contracted to do *Distant Drums* and rehearsals began the first week of December.[41] After a week of tryouts at the Shubert-Belasco Theater in Washington, D.C., the play opened on January 18, 1932.[42] The premiere was postponed one week and the venue changed from the National to the Belasco Theatre, which producer-director Guthrie McClintic and his wife Katharine Cornell had leased.[43] *Distant Drums* marked the return to the stage of Pauline Lord, who had gotten married and devoted the past two years to domestic pursuits. She had last been seen as "one of the Ninas" in O'Neill's *Strange Interlude*.[44]

Stand aside Donner Party! Eat your heart out, Mary Rowlandson! They are as nothing compared with the "grim panorama of wilderness perils"[45] Totheroh concocted in his Broadway debut. Set in the Idaho mountains (yes, indeed) in 1848, the play was inspired by the diaries of some of Totheroh's ancestors, who had followed the Oregon trail just as his characters do, though hopefully with less disastrous results. When trying to take a short cut, the party gets hopelessly lost in the mountains and is at the mercy of the local "Snake Indians." Death and disaster are all around them. The tribesmen have a somewhat unorthodox demand in return for safe passage over the mountains: they want a white woman for their old chief, the subtly named "Waiting Snake." This is when heroine Eunice Wolfhill (Pauline Lord), who has mystical powers, understands the significance of the drums that have seemed to carry such a personal message for her. Not loving her much older husband, but feeling a doomed love for a younger man, Eunice, not gladly, but willingly goes to meet her mate, I mean fate.

"She has saved us," cry the pioneers as the final curtain falls. But, as one audience member quipped: "she hasn't saved the play." Even though they tried desperately to like such a worthy effort by the ever earnest Totheroh, who had showed such promise in his first play, most critics had to concede that they had serious misgivings about his most recent effort. Brooks Atkinson remarked that he had "left the theatre with the feeling that Mr. Totheroh's imagination had never clarified the theme nor reached anything more than a perfunctory conclusion." Similarly, the reviewer for the *Brooklyn Citizen* wrote of the author that "his difficulty seems to be his inability to bring home in the last act the full meaning of what he set out to do. Some day Mr. Totheroh will write a great play."[46] Clearly, this was not it.

Burns Mantle said plainly in the *New York Daily News*: "I did not find Dan Totheroh's play as exciting as I hoped it would be. Nor as interesting." In another piece for the Tribune newspaper syndicate, Mantle said specifically of Lord's performance, that "it was while she was being starry eyed and mysterious, resenting her big husband and trying not to love a young wagoner, that I apparently lost sympathetic touch with the Totheroh message." Bondi and fellow character actress Eda Heinemann, he found, "play pioneer women truthfully." Cutting to the chase, one critic described *Distant Drums* as "a turgid, lifeless recital of the pioneer trek to Oregon." Gilbert Swan, on the other hand, concluded in a widely reprinted review, that the play was "something for the prize awarders to ponder over when the time comes."[47] *Distant Drums* did not win any awards. It only ran for 40 performances and ended February 20, 1932.[48]

It is impossible to glean from the reviews, where she was (thankfully, perhaps) barely mentioned, what Bondi's role as Mrs. Pike actually entailed, beyond being a pioneer woman, and the play has never been published. When summing up "The Season in New York" in his annual "Best Plays" volume for 1931–1932, Mantle called the play an "interesting failure" and noted that Guthrie McClintic had been "greatly disappointed" at the play's lack of success, when he had "given the drama every advantage of cast and production and the story was historically significant."[49]

When Bondi left Los Angeles after doing *Street Scene* and *Arrowsmith* and went back to New York and the stage, her future in films was uncertain. She had made a splash with *Street Scene*, but her experience with *Arrowsmith* showed that the life of a Hollywood character actress had its limitations. Bondi stayed away for seven months, but on May 4, 1932, the *Brooklyn Daily Eagle* columnist Martin Dickstein reported that she had been cast in *Rain*, which was to star Joan Crawford and Walter Huston and be produced by Feature Productions, which had also had a hand in *Street Scene*.[50] There had been a silent version with Gloria Swanson in the lead, but this was the first sound version. It remains the most authentic film adaptation of John Colton and Clemence Randolph's scandalous hit play from 1922, based on a story by W. Somerset Maugham, which gave Jeanne Eagels her first starring role.

After spending two weeks visiting her parents in Valparaiso and attending her 21-year-old niece Betty Bondy's wedding to realtor James Stuart Robinson in Chicago, Bondi left May 4 for Los Angeles via Denver to begin filming, intending to be in Hollywood "the entire summer."[51] *Rain* was directed by Lewis Milestone, who had recently won two Best Director Oscars for *Two Arabian Knights* and *All Quiet on the Western Front* and been nominated for *The Front Page*. Bondi had been experiencing the same problems in Hollywood as she had had on the stage, "convincing people that I can do a variety of things."[52] It was Maxwell Anderson, who wrote the screen adaptation of *Rain* and whom she had once convinced to let her play the landlady Mrs. Gorlik in *Saturday's Children*, who in turn convinced Milestone that she was "ideal for 'Rain.'"[53] With the exception of two short scenes, the filming of both the exteriors and the interiors took place entirely on location on Catalina Island.[54]

In *Rain*, the forces of nature battle culture and nature wins hands down. Bondi plays

Mrs. Davidson, the straitlaced wife of an equally upright missionary, Alfred Davidson (Walter Huston). The couple is stranded for ten days on Pago Pago due to a cholera outbreak and forced to share a hotel with the prostitute Sadie Thompson in a *huis clos*, "no exit"-type situation. In the role, Bondi looks painfully plain in steel-rimmed glasses and dowdy clothes. Mrs. Davidson is her husband's biggest fan and is responsible for encouraging him in the meddling and moral righteousness which will ultimately prove his downfall.

Mrs. Davidson is mostly seen at the beginning and end of the film. She nearly disappears from the central part, as her husband and Sadie struggle for control over each other. In one of her best scenes, Mrs. Davidson insists to her husband and their friend Mrs. Macphail (Kendall Lee), that there is to be no work on the Sabbath, including sewing mosquito netting, however necessary it might be under the circumstances. She is also the recipient of the heroine's famous line: "Sadie Thompson is on her way to hell!" The final image of the film is Mrs. Davidson weeping after her husband's suicide. He has cut his throat and is found in the water by the beach. She realizes her culpability in egging him on and reveals a deeper, more human side to her nature in her parting words to Sadie, "I understand, Miss Thompson. I'm sorry for him and I'm sorry for you," to which Sadie responds: "I'm sorry for everybody in the world, I guess."

The production wrapped on June 21, 1932, and *Rain* had its world premiere at Grauman's Chinese Theater on September 9 with Joan Crawford and Bondi in attendance.[55] It was probably the first Hollywood premiere of one of her own films Bondi attended. Unfortunately, the opening took place on the same day as Jean Harlow's husband Paul Bern was laid to rest after having committed suicide. According to columnist Mollie Merrick: "Cancellations from friends of the producer have been rolling in—most of them not feeling up to the strain of attending a gala premiere on the same day they attend the last services for one of the most beloved and respected executives the industry has ever known."[56] The *Los Angeles Times* noted that, because of the stark contrast between Bondi's role and her appearance at the opening in "a beautiful evening gown, fur wrap, and corsage," Robert Montgomery had failed to recognize her until she was introduced over the microphone. This despite that they had toured in the play *One of the Family* together from September to November of 1926.[57]

On September 15, columnist Edwin Schallert reported that "due to the grudging nature of whatever compliments were paid 'Rain' following its world premiere," director Milestone "has taken the picture back to the cutting room and is reassembling it." The changes were intended to give "more of a build-up to Walter Huston and Beulah Bondi's parts … and doing everything to erase the criticism of dragginess before the film hits New York and Chicago."[58] The film saw general release on October 12.[59]

On the whole, the film seems a bit anemic today and lacking in atmosphere, despite all the dripping-with-rain montages. Crawford is not half as bad as she has been made out to be (including by herself), while Walter Huston gives a wooden performance. According to Mordaunt Hall of the *New York Times*: "Mr. Huston is at his worst as the Rev. Davidson, the bigoted preacher. He walks as if he had spent years as a private in the Prussian Army." In Huston's defense, the wordless close-up, where he realizes he has been motivated by desire rather than higher ideals, is convincing. Bondi fared no better with critic Hall, who felt she "leaves nothing to the imagination in the tone in which she refers to her supposedly earnest husband. Like Mr. Huston, she loses the spirit of the role."[60]

Joan Crawford, naturally, was compared with Jeanne Eagels, but even Bondi did not escape comparisons with an earlier performer of her role. Mollie Merrick wrote on the tail end of her detailed review in the *Los Angeles Times*, that while "Beulah Bondi read her lines with a world of dry humor—Fate didn't give her that righteous spine of Blanche Friderici, but she made the most of her opportunities."[61] Friderici had played Mrs. Davidson in the 1928 silent film version. All told, Bondi's third film role met with a mixed response. The *Philadelphia Inquirer* thought she was "fairly believable as Mrs. Davidson"; the *Davenport Daily Times* thought she "deserves special mention as a member of the cast," but did not say why; the *Lafayette Journal and Courier* thought she was "outstanding"; and the *Harrisburg Sunday Courier* thought she was "superb."[62]

On September 16, 1932, a week after *Rain*'s Hollywood premier, the *Los Angeles Times* reported that, though "Miss Bondi admits to a fondness for Hollywood and film work," she had "three Broadway propositions hanging fire."[63] Bondi chose to return to New York and the stage yet again, and this time she had picked a hit. Producer Gilbert Miller's first play of the 1932–33 season was announced on September 23, 1932. It was entitled *The Late Christopher Bean* and would star Pauline Lord.[64] Three days later, it became known that the noted comic actor Walter Connolly would return from Hollywood to take the male lead in the play, while Bondi was added to the cast during the next couple of days.[65] Bondi had acted with Connolly at the Toledo Theatre in the fall of 1922, when he was 35 and she was 33. Rehearsals began around October 11, the play opened "out of town" in Baltimore on October 24 and had its premiere at Henry Miller's Theatre on October 31.[66] During the run of the play, Bondi was staying at the Tuscany Hotel, which is still operating as a hotel under the same name at 120 E. 39th St. in the Murray Hill section of New York.[67]

*The Late Christopher Bean* was the best comedy Bondi ever did on Broadway. Written by Sidney Howard, it was based on a recent French play by René Fauchois, *Prenez Garde à la Peinture* (Keep Your Eye on the Painting). More than an adaptation, Howard's version was "in effect a complete rewriting of the play in the terms of American folk comedy."[68] A master craftsman, Howard expertly preserves the classical unities of time, place, and action and makes this comedy a fine example of the well-made play tradition.

In one critic's brief summary, *The Late Christopher Bean* "concerns the sudden rise to art importance of an obscure Yankee painter some years after he has died, and the feverish competition that arises for the possession of his popular canvases."[69] The painter is Christopher Bean, the title character who never appears, as he has been dead ten years when the play opens; and the competition arises between the more or less avaricious members of the Haggett family, their devoted maid-of-all-work, Abby (Pauline Lord), and three more or less shady characters from the art world: Tallant (George Coulouris), a painter and forger; Rosen (Clarence Derwent), an art dealer; and Maxwell Davenport (Ernest Lawford), an art critic. While Abby comes into her own towards the end of the play, the focus is just as much on Dr. Haggett (Connolly), a not very ambitious or successful GP in a small New England town, who is torn between his principles, such as they are, and the demands of the women in his family; his avaricious wife, Hannah (Bondi), and two marriageable daughters Ada (Katherine Hirsch) and Susan (Adelaide Bean).

*The Late Christopher Bean*, then, is about what happens to ordinary people who get placed in extraordinary circumstances, particularly those that involve the entirely unexpected chance to obtain great wealth quickly and with little effort. As one critic wrote of Dr. Haggett: "The poor fellow has a chance to become rich and it is too much for him."[70] Mrs. Haggett was described vividly in the reviews as "the wafer-souled type of New Englander" and "an acidulous Yankee housewife."[71] For her efforts, Bondi received her usual meed of praise. We can read in the reviews, that she "presents a performance of equal comic brilliance [to Connolly]"; "does the most consistent piece of acting as the acid unrelievedly mean housewife"; is "excellent as the fretful mistress of the Haggett hearthside"; and "brings her familiar comic skill to the part of Mrs. Haggett." The comedy as a whole was described by words like "delicious" and "delightful." Burns Mantle summed up the reviewers' response: "Professional critics were generally enthused by the play without being what might be termed at all excited by it."[72]

*The Late Christopher Bean* ran for a highly respectable 224 performances at Henry Miller's Theatre and closed on April 29, 1933.[73] Despite what Mantle described as an enthusiastic rather than excited response, "the play received the third highest rating of the year's dramatic output in the vote of the Pulitzer Prize Committee"; that is, it received three votes. The Pulitzer Prize for Drama went to Maxwell Anderson's *Both Your Houses*, which got seven votes.[74]

Louella Parsons reported on April 14, 1933, that MGM had "sent from New York for [Bondi] to play in Strangers' Return [sic]."[75] Indeed, Bondi went directly from her long run in *The Late Christopher Bean* on Broadway to the *Stranger's Return* set. Production began in Culver City and on location in Chino, California, in late April 1933.[76] Though she had declined a seven-year contract at the studio, Bondi nevertheless made two films in a row for Metro in 1933.

This was Bondi's second film for director King Vidor, who had helmed her important first film, *Street Scene*. *The Stranger's Return* was less important and more conventional Hollywood fare; a family drama about a long lost granddaughter returning to her crabby old grandfather and ancestral manse, threatening the interests of the distant, fortune-hunting relatives who have encroached upon him, and emerging triumphant, though having to sacrifice her love for a married neighbor in the process.

This was the fourth negative portrayal in a row for Bondi in her first four films, as a minor villainess angling to take over 85-year-old, typically grouchy Lionel Barrymore's farm with ineffectual co-conspirators Grant Mitchell and his wife Aileen Carlyle. Bondi plays Beatrice Storr, the widow of Barrymore's nephew, while Mitchell's Allen Redfield, a pedantic, officious lawyer, is married to Barrymore's portly stepdaughter Thelma (played by Carlyle, looking like a young Maidel Turner). Grandpa Storr's only living blood relative is his granddaughter Louise (Miriam Hopkins), a good time girl fallen on bad times, who seeks refuge at Storrhaven, the family farm in Pittsville. She is the daughter of Grandpa's dead son George, who went away to the big city and never came back.

Beatrice Storr does not seem too bad at first, though she tries to insist that Grandpa eat cereal for breakfast, rather than bacon and eggs (he throws it to the chickens). As the film progresses, she becomes more and more critical of Louise's increasingly evident affair with married neighbor and heartthrob, Guy Crane (Franchot Tone), a role that was originally intended for Clark Gable.[77] This starts with her suggesting Louise should not have danced three dances in a row with Guy at the barn dance, which only makes Louise dance a fourth. Bondi imbues a fairly flat character with some degree of depth by making her subtly flirtatious in two of her scenes with Tone. She does this partly by patting her back hair (like her Emma Jones in *Street Scene*, but to different effect) and by asking if Tone will dance with her if she goes to the dance.

In the denouement, Beatrice becomes a classic villainess by trying to bribe Louise into going back where she came from, while she and her cronies do their worst to have Grandpa declared insane and committed to the state farm. It turns out old Mr. Storr has only been pretending to be addled to draw them out. He finally turns the tables on the fortune hunters in a dramatic scene with three men from the insane commission, who have come to examine him. In a scathing diatribe, Grandpa Storr calls Beatrice "You skulking, plotting, miserable woman!," as he shakes his cane threateningly at her. He revises his will on the spot, leaving nearly everything to Louise. Allen and Thelma get a house in town and Beatrice gets $1,000 provided she goes back to Des Moines ("Now get out and never come back!").

This was the first of five films Bondi did with veteran character actor and former leading man Grant Mitchell, who had been in her first show on Broadway, *One of the Family*, back in 1925–26. Here he plays the type of ineffectual, milksop male he often portrayed on the big screen. The *New York Times* found that he "fills his part with indecision" and that Bondi was "excellent as the acidulous and tight-lipped Beatrice."[78] On June 25, 1933, Bondi, Mitchell, and Robert Montgomery were invited to a reunion dinner for members of the *One of the Family* company at the home of Louise Closser Hale. Helen Hayes was also invited, as was Montgomery's wife Elizabeth.[79] Hale lived at 6766 Wedgwood Place, in the same Whitley Heights neighborhood where Bondi would later live for 40 years. Sadly, Mrs. Hale, a beloved figure in the Hollywood community and a consummate character actress, died only a month later of a heart attack brought on by heat prostration at the age of 60.[80]

In *The Stranger's Return*, Bondi's efforts as a woman moviegoers would have loved to hate were also described by the critics as "entirely life-like" and a "flawless characterization." She "etches the character of Beatrice in acid," wrote one paper, and she gave "the picture a three-dimensional touch" wrote another. If she ever saw it, Bondi would no doubt have been amused by the mix-up in a news article in the *Dayton Daily News*, which described her role as "a widow who hides an indiscreet affair behind a puritanical austerity."[81] If only! Bondi did not get to play many indiscreet widows. Her hometown newspaper, the *Vidette-Messenger of Porter County*, which always followed her career closely, carried the following advertisement on Saturday, September 2, 1933: "Monday for Three Days—BEULAH BONDI (Miss Bondi is a Valparaiso Girl, recently visited here)—Lionel Barrymore Miriam Hopkins in The Stranger's Return"; and an even larger, illustrated advert on the day of the opening, though they do not appear to have reviewed the film.[82]

When Bondi left New York for Los Angeles to do *The Stranger's Return* in the spring of 1933, she was also putting herself on the spot to be cast in the film version of her Broadway hit *The Late Christopher Bean*. Hannah Haggett turned out to be the second stage character Bondi also played in the screen adaptation. With *Tugboat Annie* and *Dinner at Eight*, *Christopher Bean* was one of MGM's desperate attempts to capitalize on the box office appeal of a dying Marie Dressler, before it was too late. It was conceived from the start as a vehicle for her and fellow 1931 Academy Award winner and MGM veteran, Lionel Barrymore, who had never been teamed up before.[83]

By mid–June 1933, Sam Wood, who had just had his contract with MGM renewed, had been chosen to direct and Bondi signed to do the picture at about the same time.[84] One wonders if Wood gave Bondi more detailed direction than he once infamously gave Flora Robson in *Saratoga Trunk*, which consisted only of the injunction to "Look at Miss Bergman, honey, look at Miss Bergman!"[85] George Coulouris also reprised his Broadway role as the artist and forger Tallant. The roles of gallery owner Rosen and art critic Maxwell Davenport were to be played by the two distinguished actors Jean Hersholt and H.B. Warner, who had been added to the cast by early August 1933.[86] By then production was well underway in Culver City.[87] *Christopher Bean* was released on November 17, 1933, and would prove to be Marie Dressler's final film.[88] She died of cancer on July 28, 1934.

To many critics, Dressler could do no wrong and the reviews were nearly all positive, including Mordaunt Hall in the *New York Times*, John Wood in the *Los Angeles Times*, and Martin Dickstein in the *Brooklyn Daily Eagle*, who usually had his eye out for attempts to give stage plays and dramas the "Hollywood treatment."[89] All the more interesting, then, to read a lengthy, detailed and convincing analysis of the failings of the film by *Pittsburgh Press* critic Florence Fisher Parry. She found that, despite the film's undoubted merits, "compared with the play from which it was adapted, it shows up crudely. What was high comedy is reduced to low comedy, what was satire is slap-stick, what was characterization is caricature." Parry noted that the film "retained the core of the plot," but cut much of the original dialogue "to make room for a 'buildup' of the part of Abby, Marie Dressler's starring role." She concluded that "if, instead of making Marie Dressler a clown to guffaw at, she had been permitted to create a genuine characterization, as genuine, let us say, as that which first won her artistic renown (the waterfront derelict in 'Anna Christie'), 'The Late Christopher Bean' would have retained all its genuineness."[90] Anyone familiar with the

*Christopher Bean* (MGM, 1933) is Bondi's "lost" film. Copies are extremely hard to come by. It was based on a play by Sidney Howard, which in turn was an English adaptation of a French comedy. This was the second time Bondi reprised a Broadway role on the big screen. She had premiered in the role of the unsympathetic, middle-class matron Hannah Haggett at Henry Miller's Theatre on October 31, 1932. Walter Connolly played her husband on stage and Lionel Barrymore in the film version. As the Haggetts' hard-tried factotum Abby, stage star Pauline Lord was replaced in the film version by Marie Dressler (right). This was Dressler's final film.

strengths and weaknesses of Dressler's "robust" screen acting technique and the exigencies of the "star system" will recognize the aptness of this analysis.

Bondi's performance was the only one in the film to meet with Parry's full approval: "Beulah Bondi was, thank heaven, retained from the play's cast in her same role of the Doctor's wife, and was superbly real. The others [in the supporting cast] were unimportant."[91] Other reviewers remarked that Mrs. Haggett was "mercilessly depicted by Beulah Bondi," that "Beulah Bondi is the only impressive member of the large supporting cast," that "Beulah Bondi plays the shrewish wife with her customary gusto," and that "Miss Bondi in a very unsympathetic role deserves praise for making it sincere." After only five films, there was a suggestion she was being typecast when one newspaper wrote: "Miss Bondi is a specialist in portraying mean spirited country housewives and appears in a made-to-order role."[92]

Bondi liked to tell a story about Lionel Barrymore from their work on this film. Old scene-stealer that he was, in one scene he kept killing off Bondi's laugh line by blandly dropping his hand in front of her face just as she was about to say it. Bondi recalled in 1947: "'I didn't say anything. I just grimly pounced on Lionel's hand just before the line, held it tight, delivered my little speech, then turned and smiled at him sweetly. He knew a defeat when he saw one and smiled back just as sweetly.'"[93]

I have already written about Bondi's long association with playwright Dan Totheroh. In the winter of 1933, she got the chance to reprise one of her stage roles on film for the third and last time, when Totheroh's play *Wild Birds* went before the cameras at RKO, starring Jean Parker and Tom Brown as the young, rustic lovers Mazie and Adam. Eighteen-year-old Parker, "climbing fast toward stardom" since her recent success as Beth in *Little Women*, replaced Dorothy Jordan in the lead when Jordan fell ill on location.[94] While Totheroh wrote several screenplays in Hollywood in the 1930s, he did not adapt his own pay for the screen, which was done by Josephine Lovett and Joseph Moncure March.

The film was directed by Elliott Nugent. Unlike most of her directors in Hollywood, who were new to her, 37-year-old Nugent was a colleague from Bondi's days in stock. He had started out as an actor and he and his father, J.C. Nugent, also wrote several successful plays together. In late July and early August 1924, Bondi had acted with father and son in one of the less successful ones, *Money to Burn*, which Stuart Walker presented in Dayton. She had also played Ma Bence, the title character's mother, in their most famous play, *Kempy*, on three separate occasions: in Baltimore in March 1924, in Cincinnati in late May and early June 1924, and again in Cincinnati in August 1928. The role of Ma Bence was created on Broadway by Jessie Crommette (who also created the role of Mrs. Grant in *The Front Page*) and played by Clara Blandick in the 1927 Broadway revival and the 1929 film version.

Even when compared with the many negative characters Bondi played early in her film career, the small-minded and suspicious Mrs. Slag was more than usually unpleasant. The transfer to the screen had not done much to make her more attractive. As one critic noted of Bondi and her screen husband, Arthur Byron, "The Slags, indeed, are dealt with unsparingly": "Mrs. Slag, in appearance and demeanour, recalls one of Macbeth's 'secret, black and midnight hags.'"[95]

Mrs. Slag was Bondi's first of many rural women in films and as such the "mother" of villainous backwoods characters like Aunt Mollie in *The Shepherd of the Hills* (1941) and Ma Bridges in *Track of the Cat* (1954). In creating the character, Bondi uses her by now familiar gesture of patting up her neck hair. She has a comic moment with departing farmhand George Marshall (Willard Robertson), who has had enough of her husband's autocratic ways, when he hesitates about whether to kiss her goodbye.

*Two Alone* was daring even by pre–Code standards. Mazie is seen nude bathing by her libidinous foster father, Mr. Slag, and becomes pregnant without the benefit of marriage. In its theme of sexual frustration on the farm and "forbidden love," *Two Alone* has shades of *Desire Under the Elms* and *Johnny Belinda*.

The cast and crew spent the second half of October on location in Sonora, California.[96] The production phase was complete on November 20, 1933, and the film was released on January 26, 1934, just as Bondi was starting work on *Finishing School*.[97] *Two Alone* was mostly well received, though a few critics, who clearly had seen the original play, described the ending as "somewhat more cheerful than that of Totheroh's play" and "slightly whitewashed." And not just slightly! Martin Dickstein pointed out that "the lad from the reformatory is not lashed to death by the cruel and lustful farmer Slag in the last act, as he was in the play. And little Maizie, the hired orphan girl, who is about to become a mother, doesn't drown herself in the well." *Wild Birds* had been given a Hollywood happy ending, in other words. The same critic found "the dependable Beulah Bondi is perfectly cast and extremely believable as the wife."[98]

Work on the *Registered Nurse* started at Warner Bros.' Burbank studios before Christmas of 1933 with Robert Florey directing, the first print was ready to be previewed by early February 1934, and the film was released April 7.[99] Miss McKenna, the remarkably nondescript head nurse at City Hospital in New York, where troubled heroine Sylvia Benton (Bebe Daniels) comes seeking employment, is second only to Mrs. Tozer in *Arrowsmith* as Bondi's least interesting role of the 1930s. Unlike Mrs. Tozer, though, Nurse McKenna does have her moments. Her appalled reaction when two wrestlers, who are visiting a local racketeer and sports promoter, start fighting in the hospital is uncommonly "broad." In this role, Bondi also plays drunk for the only time on film, when Jerry the orderly (Vince Barnett), playing bartender at an engagement party for one of the nurses, plies her with "Pink Suspender" drinks. He also wonders if she wants to try a "Bosom Caresser," that will warm her "all the way down."

Nurse McKenna's funniest scene, though, is when she and local madam, Sadie Harris, played by folksy former vaudeville star Irene Franklin, have a conversation at cross-purposes about how hard it is to keep the best girls. They always want to start for themselves, Sadie opines, sometimes even across the street. McKenna heartily agrees, being under the impression that Miss Harris has "sort of a beauty parlor." Nurses and prostitutes are not that different, the film naughtily suggests, as is underscored by the character of nurse Ethel Smith (Renee Whitney), who likes to "read" to the patients, who then reward her with valuable gifts, like diamond bracelets.

On the whole, *Registered Nurse* is an entirely unremarkable, (just barely) pre–Code film, except for the appalling amount of smoking that is being done on the job by these health professionals. Harold W. Cohen went so far as to claim that the film "achieves probably a low-water dramatic mark for the season" and notes quite accurately that "that excellent actress, Miss Beulah Bondi, is wasted in a role that could just as well have been assigned to an extra."[100]

Bondi's next film, *Finishing School*, is still a lot of fun, not so much because of Frances Dee and her love interest Bruce Cabot, but because of terrific support from second lead Ginger Rogers in full gum chewing, joke cracking, pre–Code wise gal mode (e.g.,

"If you shaved the hair off their chests you wouldn't get enough for a wig for a grape!") and because of a bevy of character actresses, including Billie Burke in fine fettle as Dee's flibbertigibbet, social butterfly mother; Theresa Harris as Burke's beautiful, beleaguered maid; Sara Haden in her usual guise as a prim, spinsterish schoolmarm; Irene Franklin as Rogers's bogus "aunt"; Jane Darwell, Bondi's future nemesis, in a tiny role as a brusque nurse; and last but not least, Beulah Bondi as the genteel but steely-edged school headmistress Miss Van Alstyne with a surname redolent of the Dutch roots of old New York.

In her first scene, Bondi gets to play straight woman to veteran comedienne Burke, who as Mrs. Helen Crawford Radcliff cannot wait to escape any responsibility for her teenage daughter Virginia (Frances Dee). Burke recalls that Bondi was a teacher back when Burke was a pupil, of literature, she seems to recall, but Bondi reminds her it was Latin. Imagine, Burke says to her daughter, your mother spoke Latin! Burke and Bondi acted together again in *The Captain Is a Lady* (1940) and *Breakfast in Hollywood* (1946), but not to such high humorous effect as here.

As soon as Burke is gone, Bondi launches into a cliché-laden, evidently insincere monologue on the school's values, which culminates in her observation, "You see, dear, we try to do all the worthwhile things." Dee soon learns that appearances are more important than realities at the school. Bondi has a good dramatic scene with Dee after she is returned to the school by her beau, Bruce Cabot, in the wee hours of the morning, where this hypocrisy is made abundantly clear. Evidently, Dee's mistake was not in lying about what she was going to do that weekend in New York, but in brazenly returning to the school and thus revealing her unorthodox behavior for all to see.

The character of Miss Van Alstyne gets darker and darker, culminating in a scene in the infirmary where Bondi correctly suspects that Dee is pregnant and tries to pressure her into admitting it. She calls Dee "cheap and vulgar," but Dee fights back as best she can, though borderline suicidal by this point. It turns out, Bondi has intercepted the letters from Cabot, making Dee

**Bondi started her film career with twelve more or less negative portrayals in a row and was in danger of being typed. Her snooty, hypocritical headmistress Miss Van Alstyne in the RKO comedy-drama *Finishing School* (1934) was the eighth of them. The turning point came two years later with warm-hearted Melissa Tolliver in *The Trail of the Lonesome Pine*, which also showcased Bondi's homespun, rustic side for the first time. It vaulted her to a whole other level as a Hollywood character actress and inaugurated the half a dozen years between 1936 and 1941 which were her most productive and rewarding period in films.**

think that he no longer cares. Rogers saves the day and Dee by calling him and love conquers all, as Dee and Cabot drive away to get married.

Bondi's appearance here is worthy of note. It looks as if she has silver or even platinum blonde hair in a finger wave hairdo (though her eyebrows are still dark) and she finally gets a chance to dress up in elegant costumes courtesy of Walter Plunkett. One paper noted: "For the first time in her screen career, Beulah Bondi wears good clothes and speaks the king's English": "Miss Bondi found that her almost perfect, highly arched eyebrows gave her a typical 'Bondi look' that she could not evade. To overcome this, she shaved off her lovely eyebrows and the studio make up expert, Mel Burns, painted new ones that are lower, less arched and a trifle wider than her own. This, and the addition of a silver gray wig, created an entirely new personality for her role as the aristocratic spinster."[101]

The production period was less than a month between January 24 and February 21, 1934, and the film was released on May 4.[102] Screenwriter Wanda Tuchock and film editor George Nichols, Jr., made their directorial debut co-directing this film, which was the only time Bondi worked with a woman film director. The *Brooklyn Daily Eagle* thought she was "excellent as Crockett Hall's strict headmistress," the *Cleveland Enquirer* wrote that she and Burke "turn out finished performances," the *Kossuth County Advance* in Iowa called her performance "as sharp and penetrating a characterization of ruthless frigidity as the screen has afforded in a long time," and the *Hammond Times* in her home state of Indiana wrote that she gave "an outstanding character portrayal."[103]

*Finishing School* was Bondi's eighth and last pre–Code film. According to Susan Doll, this comedy is clearly pre–Code in seeming to reward the heroine for her indiscretions, including getting pregnant out of wedlock, and, more subtly, for its "criticism of certain American social institutions through the characters of Miss Van Alstyne, who espouses a strict moral code, and the Radcliffs, who embody the nuclear family."[104]

On July 6, 1934, just as production was starting, the *Los Angeles Times* made a hullabaloo about the fact that Bondi, "a comparative newcomer to the screen," had been selected "from a long list of candidates" to play Garbo's mother in *The Painted Veil*, an adaptation of Somerset Maugham's sultry novel of cholera and concupiscence in China.[105] A month later, the *Times* even published a still from the film, with Garbo and Bondi, both in profile, staring each other down across a table.[106] There was no such scene in the finished film and, as it turned out, when it was released on November 23, 1934, Bondi was not in it either. So what happened?

What happened was that Bondi was replaced for the first of two times in her film career. The preview audience felt the opening scenes in Europe were too long, so the beginning of the film was condensed, which entailed reshooting some of it. Bondi was not available to do this. She visited her parents in Valparaiso October 2–7 and then went on to New York, where she was "planning to appear on the stage this winter."[107] With Bondi in New York looking for work in the theater, she had to be replaced by Bodil Rosing, giving Swedish Garbo two Danish parents, rather than one. Jean Hersholt stayed in his role as her father, Herr Koerber. This also explains why Bondi never expressed any bitterness over this episode, as she did so often about being passed over for the role of Ma Joad in *The Grapes of Wrath*. In its final incarnation, Frau Koerber is a nothing part, like Mrs. Tozer in *Arrowsmith*.

But the story does not end here. Practically every news article and review about *The Painted Veil* claims that Bondi plays Garbo's mother or includes her name in the cast list.

If you cannot recall ever having seen this scene with Greta Garbo and Bondi in a combative stance, it is because you have not. It caused a stir in the summer of 1934, when Bondi was selected in competition with several more established Hollywood character actresses to play Garbo's mother in *The Painted Veil*, to be directed by Richard Boleslawski at MGM. She gave it her best shot in a role confined to the earliest part of the film, a part which was considered too long by preview audiences. It was rewritten and reshot with Danish actress Bodil Rosing as Frau Koerber, when Bondi was not available. The amusing thing, though, is that many reviewers were not aware of the casting change and wrote as if Bondi was still in the role. Rosing gave the performance and Bondi got the credit.

The *Pittsburgh Post-Gazette* was not fooled, though. The paper pointed out that the press sheet still listed Bondi as Garbo's mother, though "the early scenes were remade entirely and Miss Bondi doesn't even appear."[108]

What is most amusing is reading the reviews that actually comment on Bondi's phantom performance as Frau Koerber. The *Salt Lake Tribune* observed that "Jean Hersholt as the heroine's father and Beulah Bondi as her mother have interesting character roles." Better yet, the *Boston Globe* reviewer writes that "Jean Hersholt and Beulah Bondi make brief appearances as the solid, homeloving parents, who want their elder daughter Katherine to marry and settle down near them." Either the reviewer was not paying attention or he had no idea what Bondi looked like. She had only made eight films by this point. Finally, the *Baltimore Sun* observed that "the entire supporting cast is comprised of familiar names" and included Bondi's name in the list.[109] Familiar names, yes, but clearly not familiar faces…. It must have been a funny experience for Bondi to get "noticed" for a performance given by another actor, but not quite so funny for Rosing.

*Ready for Love* was the first of many films Bondi did for Paramount, though far from the most interesting. Under the direction of Marion Gering, production began on July 31, 1934, just three days after the granddame of MGM and Bondi's co-star in *Christopher Bean*, Marie Dressler, died of cancer. Mrs. Burke was the first of many unsympathetic upper-class matron roles for Bondi; her function in the film a familiar one: to be the heroine's antagonist. The heroine in this case was young, attractive Marigold Tate (Ida Lupino), who is sent to the small town of Chetwattle Falls by her vaudevillian mother, Goldie Tate (Marjorie Rambeau), after she runs away from yet another boarding school for girls and to prevent her from going on the stage.

As Mrs. Burke, *née* Louella Chetwattle, Bondi is married to Ralph Remley and is the mother of the sensitive though inept poet played by Junior Durkin. The Burkes' concern is that Marigold has brought shame on the family by providing evidence for the persistent rumors that Mr. Burke's recently dead brother, Nathaniel Burke, was a philanderer. This is based on a misunderstanding, as Marigold is mourning the loss of her dog Boo-boo when she gets off the train with Burke's casket, not Burke.

Mrs. Burke overreaches herself at the Memorial Park picnic social, when she leads a mob of irate women in dunking Lupino in the lake. The hero of the piece, local newspaper editor Julian Barrow (Richard Arlen), calls Louella Burke "the leader of the mob" in his paper, the *Clarion*. This becomes a big news story across the country. With the negative publicity that accompanies it, henpecked Mr. Burke sees a way to get the upper hand, warning his wife that she may have to go to jail. His plan is to commit her to a sanatorium for a few months, laying the ground for a temporary insanity plea later, though it is probably also a thinly veiled plot finally to get rid of her. Mrs. Burke is not seen again. A humorless and stereotypically snooty woman, her only good line is about her son, who is infatuated with Marigold: "It's the Burke in him. No one in my family ever fell in love."

In *Ready for Love*, Bondi faced stiff competition from two of the most talented, rambunctious "old broads" in the business, Marjorie Rambeau and Esther Howard, though unfortunately she did not have much direct interaction with either of them in the film. There was a personal connection with Howard, who plays Goldie's sister and Marigold's former actress aunt. Howard was the widow of Arthur Albertson, who had acted with Bondi in stock in Cincinnati in 1922, and tragically committed suicide in New York in 1926 at the age of 35.[110] The two women are only seen briefly together in the big "basket social" scene, where Bondi tells Howard to stay back while she and her cronies go to give Lupino her comeuppance. While Howard had been mainly a comic second in Broadway musical comedies in the 1920s, Rambeau and been a star during the same period, before pursuing a career as a character actress in Hollywood starting in 1930. Bondi did no further films with either of them, nor with Lupino.

Like John Ford when he directed Bondi in *Arrowsmith*, William Wyler had not yet reached his "major phase" when he directed *The Good Fairy* for Universal from mid–September to mid–December 1934. He did manage, though, to elope with the star of the film, Margaret Sullavan, towards the end of the production period, despite their combative relationship on the set. Very much in the "Mittel European" romantic fantasy mode, one would have expected this to have been directed by someone more temperamentally suited, "less earth-bound,"[111] like Frank Borzage or Ernst Lubitsch. Unfortunately, Bondi never had the opportunity to work with Wyler again.

This was Bondi's first film at the studio symbolized by the revolving globe and best known at the time for horror movies and young female juvenile singing sensations like Deanna Durbin and, later, Gloria Jean. Preston Sturges, who would write the original screenplay for Bondi's *Remember the Night*, worked on the script based on Jane Hinton's English translation of a famous play from 1931 by Hungarian Ferenc Molnár about a young, naïve orphan, Luisa "Lu" Ginglebuscher (Sullavan), who goes out into the world and is variously threatened or protected by several older men, including (in the film version) Herbert Marshall, Frank Morgan, and Reginald Owen.

Bondi only has a small role at the beginning of the film, as the superintendent of the orphanage, who helps pick out Sullavan to work as an usher at a local cinema and tries to explain the facts of life to her before sending her off. The latter scene was found to be "definitely and gravely objectionable" by PCA Director Joseph Breen, who wrote to Harry H. Zehner, the assistant general manager at Universal, that the material should be deleted. "It is our thought," he continued, "that Dr. Schultz' advice to Lu should refer to her general unworldliness rather than—as is suggested in this scene—her ignorance in matters of sex."[112] All that is left of her attempt to teach Louisa the facts of life is this: "A young girl going out into the world alone cannot be too careful with the male gender." She also says: "Be brave, Louisa, the time has come for you to try your wings."

Prim and proper Dr. Schultz wears her dark hair in a bun with bangs and pince-nez, which she keeps taking off. For a moment, then, Bondi found herself playing straight woman to 25-year-old Sullavan, whom *New York Times* reviewer André Sennwald thought was "temperamentally unfitted" to playing a young, naïve orphan[113]; and perennially jocular Alan Hale as an expansive movie theater owner on the lookout for young, nubile usherettes.

Of the twelve consecutive negative portrayals with which Bondi began her film career, Dr. Schultz was the most benign. One of the few reviewers to "notice" her in this modest part found her "superbly correct." "Miss Bondi's characterization of the platitudinous mistress of the orphanage," she added, "is grand. This is the Molnar spirit of mockery and it sets the key to what should have been a cynical comedy."[114] Bondi would give a somewhat similar characterization as spinster camp director in Gloria Jean's debut film at Universal, *The Under-Pup* in 1939. *Penny Serenade* (1941) would give her a much better opportunity in the orphan and adoption racket.

The play Bondi landed when she went to New York in October 1934 and was unavailable for the retakes on *The Painted Veil* was entitled *Mother Lode*, though it turned out to be no gold mine for anyone involved. *Mother Lode*, as the title suggests, was "a drama of Virginia City in the old mining days" and was announced November 12, 1934, with the married couple Melvyn Douglas and Helen Gahagan in their first co-starring roles.[115] Douglas was also directing. This was another play by Bondi's friend Dan Totheroh, but this time he had roped in George O'Neil (known for *American Dream* from two seasons earlier) as co-author. O'Neil's cousin Barbara O'Neil (of *Gone with the Wind* fame) would have a small, unnamed role in the play. By November 20, Bondi had been engaged for a featured role.[116] Helen Freeman was also to be featured.[117] The play went into rehearsal Monday, November 26 and opened at the Cort Theatre on Saturday, December 22, 1934.[118]

Rowland Field gives an apt summary of this "saga of the soil": "It tells the story of the vast fortunes won and lost during the California mining boom and this time it is Carey Ried [Melvyn Douglas], a venturesome prospector from Connecticut, who becomes a Midas of the West only to fall from his pinnacle of affluence during Frisco's subsequent panics. The purpose of the play ... is to show that money isn't everything for Carey's wife [Helen Gahagan] sticks by her shattered husband in his time of woe and hers is a hopeful, philosophic attitude at the final curtain."[119] Carey's wife was the former saloon entertainer, Hannah Hawkins, and Bondi, by the way, played Hannah's "Ma," Kate Hawkins. What Field fails to mention is that Carey strays from the straight and narrow path in getting involved with the seductive Russian actress and blackmailer, Madame Lorska (Helen Freeman), and that the latter is soundly horsewhipped by Hannah (no doubt encouraged by her mother).

The critics were even less merciful this time, than they had been to *Distant Drums*. "[T]his reviewer," wrote one of them, "confesses that he has only the foggiest notion of what the authors intended to say." "This reviewer" was none other than Brooks Atkinson of the *New York Times*. He found, though, that "as an acidulous mother and mother-in-law, Beulah Bondi gives the crispest performance of the lot." The *Brooklyn Citizen* critic found, devastatingly, that "there is nothing of particular moment to report about this early American romance," adding that "it is convincing at almost no point." Like Atkinson, though, he found that the part of Hannah's mother was "played consummately by Beulah Bondi in a performance which is without flaws." Thus, though it must have been a poor comfort to her, Bondi fared far better than her fellow players and the play as a whole. The *Brooklyn Times Union* wrote: "Beulah Bondi plays the acidulous Mrs. Hawkins … with admirable artistry throughout the three acts." Burns Mantle thought that "Beulah Bondi was helpful as usual as a hardbitten mother-in-law."[120]

*Mother Lode* closed ignominiously on December 29, 1934, after only nine performances (two matinees and seven evening performances).[121] Incidentally, it was during the brief run of this play, that one of the landmarks of Valparaiso, the Porter County courthouse, was devastated by fire. Eva Bondy was also away from home at the time, attending her daughter's New York opening.[122]

After the failure of *Mother Lode*, Bondi stuck around in New York, no doubt hoping to get another play. She did not return to Hollywood until mid–June 1935. On her journey westward, she spent ten days with her parents in Valparaiso.[123] They had celebrated their golden wedding anniversary in 1932 and had now been married for nearly 53 years.[124] This visit was probably the last time Bondi saw her father alive. And though she may not have realized it: when she went back to Los Angeles this time, she went back for good.

While good stage roles were thin on the ground, Bondi had gotten another film assignment; this one at Fox for the first time. *Bad Boy* took less than a month to produce between mid–July and August 2, 1935, and was directed by long-term Fox employee William G. Blystone, who specialized in light comedy.[125] The screenplay was by Viña Delmar, who would go on to script Bondi's most important film, *Make Way for Tomorrow* (1937).

Films about possessive mothers were rife in the 1930s; *The Silver Cord* (1933) with Laura Hope Crews as the domineering dowager Mrs. Phelps and *Another Language* (1933) with Bondi's friend Louise Closser Hale as equally insidious and manipulative Mrs. Hallam were only two of the most notable examples. In fact, *The Silver Cord*, based on a play by Sidney Howard, lent its name to this popular motif of dysfunctional relationships between mothers and their offspring, usually their sons, which could be used to explain any number of personal and societal ills. Ultimately, there was nothing for which a bad mother could not be blamed in the 1930s! Common elements in the plots of these films were the child's potential mate threatening the mother's dominant status and her use of every means at her disposal, often including feigning illness, to get her own way.

In *Bad Boy*, Bondi's Mrs. Larkin is a fairly low-key and modest exemplar of the type and her possessive relationship is with her daughter Sally, played by Dorothy Wilson.

Mrs. Larkin can fake an "attack" at any moment, if it will get her what she wants. She does not want "pool shark" and "hoodlum" Eddie Nolan (James Dunn) around Sally any more than her husband, Fred Larkin (John Wray), does. Mr. Larkin comes home one day to find Nolan is his daughter's boyfriend and throws him out, having recently been trounced by him down at the pool hall. Mrs. Larkin much prefers Bob Carey (Allen Vincent) as her daughter's potential mate. She uses all the tricks in the book, but she still cannot prevent her daughter from seeing Nolan.

A lower middle-class example of the type, Mrs. Larkin is genteel in her speech and manner and given to "killing with kindness." She is the one who dubs Eddie Nolan a "bad boy." Mrs. Larkin was just one in a long line of Bondi's disapproving mother-in-law or potential mother-in-law characters, which started with Mrs. Tozer in *Arrowsmith*, her second film. The element of the "silver cord" was unique to this character, though one critic at the time saw a resemblance to Emma Jones in *Street Scene*.[126]

At seven o'clock in the evening of Monday, September 9, 1935, his 79th birthday, Abram O. Bondy died from hypostatic pneumonia at his home at 254 S. Valparaiso St. His front-page obituary in the *Vidette-Messenger* reported that he had been "in ill health for two years." He had retired from the real estate business five years earlier due to failing eyesight. The obituary also stated that "memorial services will not be held at this time. The body will be placed in the mausoleum at Graceland cemetery temporarily, and services held later when the family can be present."[127]

Clearly, the family member who was not present at her father's death and could not get away for an immediate funeral was Bondi herself. She was due to start two new films, which would keep her busy for the remainder of the year: *The Invisible Ray*, at Universal; and, more importantly, *The Trail of the Lonesome Pine* for producer Walter Wanger. A.O. Bondy was finally laid to rest under a simple bronze plaque in Valparaiso's Graceland Memorial Park, where he would be joined by his older brother two years later, but not by his wife or daughter.[128]

Three days after her father's death, Bondi sent her mother a typewritten letter from the Rancho Yucca Loma in Victorville, California, her favorite desert retreat at this time. "My darling," she began. "I think you must know how close I have been to you, every move and every thought have been with you and last night I wanted so much to phone but the difference in time made me hesitate.... I was thinking of you and all the day wished so much that I were there for I know, darling, the flood of memories that make the human parting hard. Our knowledge of the Law and of Truth make each experience possible but the human tie is a strong and wonderful one and we don't want to deny it. Realizing all that your life with dad has meant, the years of service for all of us, ... I know the lights and shadows which have composed the picture." Her purpose in writing the letter, it soon becomes clear, was to induce her mother to make her home with her in California:

> It is now your time to reap, my dearest, a small part of the harvest that you have sown and I want to be the one to really show you, in small part tho' it be, what your sacrifices and beautiful mother-hood have meant to me. In giving me my freedom to build my life I hope it will prove to have been one worthy of the fine example you set me, one of sharing and giving lovingly, one of construction, one which you will now be part of. If we have each learned to stand alone, as you so often have said, that was a necessary lesson for us to have but we know that in Unity there is completion and you and I have had the happiest moments of our lives together. Dad's and your lives were united for a purpose and out of that I came for one thing. Our closeness

and wonderful relationship can now continue without your feeling you are neglecting one for the other as was natural when we both needed you.

Bondi stressed all the joys and comforts they would share and that it would "mean so much to have you in the little house with me": "let us fill our lives with the joys we both can appreciate, darling and make life a Song. You have my arms around you, holding you close and closer and I eagerly await word that you want to come West…. Bless you, you wonderful woman, ever and ever—I love you."[129]

*The Invisible Ray* was the first film Bondi worked on after her father died. Production began at Universal on September 19, 1935, and a few days later her widowed mother joined her in Hollywood for a two-month visit.[130] Bondi did three films for Universal in the 1930s and none of the parts they offered her were much to write home about. The aristocratic explorer and travel writer, Lady Arabella Stevens, described in one review as "a novelist of unlovely disposition,"[131] who is also the wife of the titled scientist played by Walter Kingsford, was the best of an insignificant lot. The chance to act with the two biggest horror stars in the business, Boris Karloff and Bela Lugosi, in the same film, was not to be missed. Bondi never did another science fiction or horror film again.

Though playing a British aristocrat, Bondi does not even attempt a British accent.

In this still from Bondi's only excursion into the horror genre, Universal's *The Invisible Ray* (1936), Bondi is seen with a pensive Frank Lawton in the jungles of Africa. What we do not see is that she is wearing shorts for the first and only time in a film. Cinematographer George Robinson subtly avoided showing Bondi's knees clearly, which rather reduced the daringness of the wardrobe choice here. Bondi played a titled British lady, but made no attempt at a British accent. Maybe Lady Arabella Stevens was American.

Then again, her character may have been American-born. She is very hale and hearty and does most of the talking in her first scene, when she arrives in a tweedy tailored suit and jaunty cap with her husband, Bela Lugosi, and the young scientist Frank Lawton at Boris Karloff's castle. Later we are afforded a rare view of Bondi in shorts and a topee in deepest Africa, though the cameraman manages to avoid showing much of her knees. She hires Karloff's young wife, Frances Drake, as a personal secretary and, when he is believed to be dead, encourages her romance with Lawton. Karloff has his revenge by starting to kill the five members of the African expedition one by one. Bondi's husband is the first to die and she the second, strangled in her bed. Thus, *The Invisible Ray* stands out as being the only film in which Bondi's character is murdered.

Production on *The Invisible Ray* ended on October 25, by which time Bondi was busy working on *The Trail of the Lonesome Pine* at Paramount.[132] It had taken four years and a dozen films for Bondi finally to commit to the movie industry. Her next film would show what a wise decision she had made.

# 5

# Glory Days
## *1935–1939*

"'Give me a good supporting role, and that's all I ask,' says Miss
Bondi. 'I never want to be a star again. The life of a star, with a
few exceptions, is brief. It's like a merry-go-round—only suddenly the music stops playing. Supporting players, unless they get
typed, go on forever."[1]

After twelve negative portrayals in a row from *Street Scene* to *The Invisible Ray*,
Bondi finally got a chance to play a sympathetic role. Someone once said you had no
future as a character actress in Hollywood if you could not play sympathetic parts, so this
was a genuine turning point in her film career. Up until then, she had been doing just fine
in the wake of her fabulous debut in *Street Scene*, playing no less than a dozen "heavies" of
various degrees of weightiness, but "It wasn't until 'The Trail of the Lonesome Pine' that
she was able to win a little sympathy."[2] Her portrayal of Melissa Tolliver, the peace-loving,
long-suffering matriarch of a perpetually feuding and vengeful Kentucky mountain clan
put her on a whole other level.

*The Trail of the Lonesome Pine* was the first of three films Bondi did in 1935–36 for
longtime Paramount producer Walter Wanger's independent production unit; the other
two being *The Moon's Our Home* and *The Case Against Mrs. Ames*. The film was based
on a 1908 novel by John Fox, Jr., and was directed by industry veteran Henry Hathaway.
Production began on location at Big Bear in the San Bernardino Mountains on October 9, 1935, and ended on December 14.[3] Recently widowed Eva Bondy accompanied her
daughter on location at Big Bear for about three weeks.[4]

*Trail* was Bondi's first color film, and it was the first three-strip Technicolor feature
filmed on location. According to *New York Times* film critic Frank S. Nugent, the film
proved that "technicolor is not restricted to studios stages, but can record quite hand-
somely the rich, natural coloring of the outside world and whatever dramatic action
may be encountered in it. The significance of this achievement is not to be minimized. It
means that color need not shackle the cinema, but may give it fuller expression. It means
that we can doubt no longer the inevitability of the color film."[5]

As Melissa Tolliver, Bondi is the emotional and ethical center, not just of her bump-
tious, vengeful, male-dominated family, but of the entire film. Her spiritual presence is
felt even when she is not seen and her character is central to the regeneration of the hero,
her nephew Dave Tolliver (Henry Fonda); and through him to her husband, Judd Tolliver (Fred Stone), and even to their arch enemy, Buck Falin (Robert Barrat), head of the

neighboring, rival clan. According to one insightful reviewer, Melissa Tolliver was "holding the key to feud and the deepest emotion of the picture."[6]

In the "Prologue," Melissa gives birth to her daughter June (Sylvia Sidney) in the middle of a shoot-out between the Tollivers and the Falins. In the main part of the film, she is given a couple of powerful monologues, where she lambasts her family for their murderous hatred. The first is brought on by cousin Lena Tolliver (Fern Emmett) asking her why Melissa is brooding over the pot she is stirring. The second is occasioned by the discovery that her beloved nephew Dave is close to dying of gangrene in his arm. Her husband has resisted sending for a doctor. Engineer Jack Hale (Fred MacMurray) saves Dave's life. Ironically, Melissa preaches peace with about as much aggression as the others foment hate. *The Trail of the Lonesome Pine* is still a powerful film today and the emotion-laden plot hits a high note with the death of Melissa's young son Buddie ("Spanky" McFarland) at the hands of the Falins. At the close, Dave Tolliver explains to Buck Falin that he has come to make peace, because it is his aunt's birthday.

Reviewers found so much and so many to commend in *Trail*, that Bondi was not as often singled out for praise as she had been for *Street Scene*. Nor was she nominated for an Academy Award for this performance, though it is surely of more lasting significance than the one she gave as Rachel Jackson in *The Gorgeous Hussy*. We can read in the reviews that "Fred Stone and Beulah Bondi seem actually wrought of hillside soil, so rich and pungent are their characterisations"; that "Fred Stone and Beulah Bondi, as Pa and Ma Tolliver, give perhaps the most outstanding performances"; and that "Fred Stone, Robert Barrat and Beulah Bondi are outstanding." One local newspaper wrote that Bondi "gives a finely etched characterization which will not be forgotten." Finally, the *Pittsburgh Press* film critic intoned: "Beulah Bondi does her best work since 'Street Scene.'"[7] She was right.

Besides being Bondi's first

**While much is made of the significance of *Street Scene* and *Make Way for Tomorrow* to the development of Bondi's career, the question is if *The Trail of the Lonesome Pine* (Walter Wanger /Paramount, 1936) was not at least as important. Prior to this rustic mountain melodrama, Bondi had played a dozen "heavies" in a row, starting with viper-tongued Emma Jones in *Street Scene*. Melissa Tolliver in *Trail* was not just a good woman, but a substantial role with a major plot function and symbolic significance. Hollywood finally woke up to the fact that Bondi had a much wider range than she had been given a chance to show. In a town where you supposedly had no long-term viability as a character actress if you could not be believable in sympathetic roles, Bondi's future in films was assured.**

of many deeply felt and nuanced portrayals of sympathetic characters on film, Melissa Tolliver would be the first example of a significant sideline Bondi established playing mountain women, usually from Kentucky. Indeed, her first and her final backwoods roles (Martha Corinne Walton on two episodes of *The Waltons* in the 1970s) were her best efforts in this line. In between there were some doozies…

The final important event of 1935 was Eva Bondy moving permanently to Los Angeles to reside with her daughter. She had been appointed executrix of her dead husband's estate, which was solvent, rented out her apartment on S. Valparaiso St., and left Valparaiso by December 27.[8] She would spend her five remaining years in Los Angeles, though she made frequent visits to her hometown to "look after her property interests"[9] and to Chicago to visit her son Raymond. Raymond and Sallie Bondy had divorced in 1933, after 25 years of marriage. Sallie immediately married J.H. (Hal) Ressler and moved to Detroit.[10] Raymond would not remarry until 1940.

Bondi did two films back to back for director William A. Seiter in the first half of 1936. The films could not have been more different. While *The Moon's Our Home*, starring Margaret Sullavan and Henry Fonda, is a classic screwball comedy; *The Case Against Mrs. Ames*, starring Madeleine Carroll and George Brent, is a court room melodrama and "woman's film."

Like *The Trail of the Lonesome Pine*, both films were produced by Walter Wanger Productions and distributed by Paramount, but there was no color and no location shooting this time. The films were produced at General Service Studios,[11] which is now the Sunset Las Palmas Studios and has also been known as the Hollywood Center Studios. Founded in 1919, the studio is still located at 1040 N. Las Palmas Ave., making it "one of the oldest production facilities in Hollywood."[12] From an artistic perspective, Bondi's roles as the heroine's lady companion in the comedy and villainous antagonist in the melodrama represented a return to more stereotypical and negative roles.

On the positive side, in *The Moon's Our Home* Bondi was billed fourth after the stars and Charles Butterworth, and just ahead of Henrietta Crosman, a veteran stage actress, who gives a fair imitation of May Robson in a typical Robson role as an autocratic, upper-class grandmother. In 14 films, this was Bondi's highest billing so far. Her role as tempestuous film star Cherry Chester's live-in aunt and companion, Mrs. Boyce Medford, was considerably duller than Crosman's, though, and consisted mostly in trying to keep her unruly niece in line and dodging flying objects. Bondi disappears from the middle part of the film, where Sullavan goes incognito with Fonda at Margaret Hamilton's rural retreat.[13] She returns for the denouement back in New York. The *Cincinnati Enquirer* commented that "Beulah Bondi struggles with a colorless confidante part," while the *Chicago Tribune* thought she was "awfully funny."[14]

Screwball comedy expert Ed Sikov describes the plot as "An heiress who's also a movie star falls in love with a famous travel writer, they marry, fight, and split up, until he finally gets her in a straightjacket." He gives the film three out of three stars, which means "Classic: don't miss it" and considers it "one of the most vastly underrated films in the genre." Incidentally, he only gives *Vivacious Lady* two stars, indicating "Respectable: not first-rate, but not worth ignoring, either."[15] Contrary to Sikov, I much prefer *Vivacious Lady*, mainly because I have never been of fan of Sullavan's particular brand of hectic, high-strung haminess. *Vivacious Lady* also gives Bondi a much better opportunity; in my view, the best comedy role she ever played on film.

At least *The Moon's Our Home* gave Bondi a second sympathetic role in a row after *The Trail of the Lonesome Pine*, before she reverted to type in *The Case Against Mrs. Ames*. Her second role for Seiter was a return to the negative portrayals and the villain-and-antagonist roles that had dominated her early film career. Mrs. Livingston Ames was the upper-class mother-in-law from hell, at least if you were a pretty young widow accused of murdering her son and had a child she wanted to get her hands on. The pretty young widow in question was Hope Ames, played by British-born Madeleine Carroll in her first American film, and the child was called Bobbie (Scotty Beckett). Even after the younger Mrs. Ames is acquitted of the murder, the elder Mrs. Ames tries to get custody of Bobbie and succeeds in turning him against his mother, before ultimately losing the court battle.

On the plus side again, Bondi got to wear fanciful hats and elegant costumes by Helen Taylor, who was also the costume designer on *The Moon's Our Home* and *The Trail of the Lonesome Pine*. And the film got her noticed. The *Salt Lake Telegram* called her performance "outstanding," The *Detroit Free Press* wrote "what a vicious old hellion she makes the character," and the *Louisville Courier-Journal* observed ambiguously that "Beulah Bondi adds her experience to the hateful attributes of the mother-in-law."[16]

Sometime during the spring of 1936, Bondi returned to Warner Bros. to do a single scene in the historical romantic comedy *Hearts Divided*, directed by Frank Borzage and starring Marion Davies and Dick Powell. It would be her first period costume drama to be released. Bondi's first 15 films, then, all had contemporary settings, but in the second half of the 1930s she did a number of historical films. Borzage was one of the more high-profile directors she had worked with thus far and would direct her again many years later in *The Big Fisherman*, his penultimate film.

Bondi's single scene in *Hearts Divided* cannot have taken more than a day to shoot. Her function as Madame Letizia was to come in as a maternal *Deus ex machina* at the end of the film and resolve the conflict between her two sons, bossy big brother Napoleon (Claude Rains) and his less alpha male sibling Jerome (Powell). In an emotion-laden monologue, she pleads with Napoleon to let his younger brother marry American Betsy Patterson (Davies): "Let him have his own life to do with as he pleases, for my sake." And so it goes. Rains and Bondi would work together again on the 1957 TV version of *On Borrowed Time*, where she played her usual role of Granny Northrup and he played Mr. Brink, who comes to take her out of life.[17]

For her brief effort lasting no more than a few minutes, Bondi was billed fourteenth among the 15 credited roles. It is not immediately clear why she took on this modest assignment, but it certainly gave her an opportunity to get regally rigged out. She looks simply "mahvellous" in her Empire-style gown courtesy of Orry-Kelly. *Hearts Divided* would show producers that she could clean up nicely in a period costume drama. As a result, half her remaining films from the 1930s would be historical.

Clearly, no one expected Beulah Bondi to be the most noticed performer in the star-studded cast of Clarence Brown's *The Gorgeous Hussy*. She is not even included in the opening photo credit sequence, where Joan Crawford in her role as the innkeeper's daughter, Peggy O'Neal, is the only woman. Yet for her performance as Rachel Jackson, Andrew Jackson's rustic wife, Hubbard Keavy nominated Bondi third among the "10 best scene stealers of 1936," with Gale Sondergaard in first place for *Anthony Adverse* and Lloyd Nolan in second for *The Texas Ranger*.

More importantly, Sondergaard also beat Bondi to the Academy Award in the first year there was a separate category for "Best Actress in a Supporting Role." In addition to cinematographer George J. Folsey, who did not win either, Bondi was the only member of the *Gorgeous Hussy* cast and crew to be Oscar nominated. According to Clarke Wales, this was "one of those rare, unforgettable portrayals which come to the screen not once in a hundred pictures.... This is great acting." Kaspar Monahan wrote that "this Rachel is a thing to see." Finally, Louella Parsons observed that Bondi "stole 'The Gorgeous Hussy' right under the noses of Joan Crawford, Franchot Tone and the rest of the high powered stars in the cast."[18]

It may be that this particular performance of Bondi's has not aged as well as some of the others. Watching the film today, it is difficult to reconcile oneself to the fact that she was nominated for this relatively brief and not very demanding performance, especially when she was not nominated for her starring role in *Make Way for Tomorrow*, an infinitely better film and a much larger and more challenging role.

The first thing Rachel Jackson does on arriving at Peggy O'Neal and her father's inn in Washington, D.C., after her husband Andrew Jackson (Lionel Barrymore) has been elected senator from Tennessee, is to sit in her rocking chair and smoke a corncob pipe. And that is what she keeps on doing, in addition to telling her husband not to get "foamed up," reflecting that "they've bin usin' me to drag you down" (again to her husband), and uttering sage advice to the heroine on how to handle the capitol's catty women: "Just smile at 'em and keep on goin'." Socially ostracized for her alleged "bigamy" and plain ways, it turns out Rachel had married Jackson without realizing she was not yet formally divorced from her first husband. The couple subsequently married again to make it legal. The leader of the formidable female forces arrayed against them is DC dowager Mrs. Beal (Alison Skipworth), who refers to Rachel Jackson disparagingly as "The Backwoods Belle." With her downhome folksiness on full display, it is like Bondi is playing the foremother of Melissa Tolliver from *The Trail of the Lonesome Pine*.

This was Bondi's first of five big screen appearances with James Stewart, though they do not have any significant interaction in the film, where he plays the least favored of Crawford's many suitors. The only male star she appeared with more often was Barrymore, whom she was married to almost as often as she mothered Stewart.

Thankfully for Bondi's fans, who do not need to watch any further, Rachel Jackson dies one hour into this interminable film. If nothing else, *The Gorgeous Hussy* proves that Crawford was about as ill-suited to period costume dramas as Claudette Colbert. Howard Thompson described the film as "an overdressed and overstuffed disaster."[19] Someone else once quipped that there was "too much gorgeous and not enough hussy." Bondi remembered the film for quite another reason than the Oscar nomination and the rave reviews. It contained what she considered "the most 'risqué scene'" of her filmography. As she remembered it many years later, her mother was visiting her on the set for the first time and it just happened to be the day they were filming Bondi and Barrymore in night dress "in this huge double bed." "She didn't say anything," Bondi recalled, "but she was very surprised, I think. That was 1936, and it was the last time a double bed was allowed in a film for quite a few years."[20]

Production on *The Gorgeous Hussy* ended in late June 1936.[21] In late August, Bondi was back at Paramount, where she had done *Ready for Love* in 1934.[22] Now she would do three films in a row there, including the only film in which she starred, *Make Way for Tomorrow*. The first of these was *Maid of Salem*, set in the famous Puritan community in 1692 and starring Claudette Colbert as a free-spirited, attractive young woman, who falls in love with a dashing Virginian cavalier on the run, played by Fred MacMurray.

**Bondi with her frequent co-star Lionel Barrymore in *The Gorgeous Hussy* (MGM, 1936), where they played Andrew Jackson and his wife Rachel, dismissed by Washington society as "The Backwoods Belle." Bondi claimed that this was the last time a couple in a double bed was allowed in a Hollywood film for quite some time. Not only that, she recalled that her mother Eva had been on the set the day this scene was filmed, which she found rather awkward. How times have changed!**

Quintessentially modern in type and look, Colbert was as unsuited to playing a Puritan maid in Salem, as she would be to playing a colonial wife in *Drums Along the Mohawk* two years later. MacMurray in "Three Muskateers" style chapeau, knee britches, and rapier was equally ludicrous.

*Maid of Salem* was shot on the Paramount Ranch in Agoura and in a specially built village set on a farm four miles outside of Santa Cruz and was directed by Frank Lloyd in his only film with Bondi.[23] Indeed Bondi seldom worked twice for the same director. In the course of her 63 feature films, she had 52 different directors. If nothing else, this gave her a broad and varied experience of directors and their various personal styles and filming techniques.

Her role this time was playing Abigail Goode, a married woman with two young children. Her stern and forbidding husband Nathaniel Goode was played by Edward Ellis, who had been with Bondi in *Cock Robin* and *Distant Drums* on Broadway; and her children Ann and Nabby were portrayed by the prolific and precocious child stars Bonita

Granville and Virginia Weidler. Nineteen years her senior, Ellis was one of Bondi's most unattractive screen husbands, which is saying a lot. This was one of only two times Bondi played the mother of young children. In real life, Granville was 13 and Weidler was 10. Bondi herself was 48.

Abigail Goode is not a large or important role in *The Maid of Salem* or in Bondi's career, but she does have her own brief storyline. Out of some deeper dissatisfaction with

**Louise Dresser (left), an unidentified woman journalist, and Bondi on the set of *Maid of Salem* (1937), which was produced at the Paramount Ranch in Agoura and on location at a Santa Cruz farm between late August and early November 1936 and starred Claudette Colbert and Fred MacMurray. No two stars were less believable as a Puritan New England maiden and a Virginia cavalier. Bondi fared better as the embittered, mentally unstable Abigail Goode, who indirectly sets off the Salem witch trials. Her face was well suited to period costume dramas, though she did relatively few of them.**

her humdrum life, she is drawn to the fantastic tales of the devil, witches, and the supernatural told by her slave servant Tituba (Madame Sul-te-Wan in one of her most prominent roles). Not only Abigail is fascinated by these stories, but also her two daughters and several other women from the village. She convinces Tituba to give her some of her magic potion in exchange for a winter cloak and goes into a trance.

Later, Abigail is one of the accusers against the entirely godly and good old woman, Rebecca Nurse (Lucy Beaumont), which provokes Colbert's character Barbara Clarke to defend her and ultimately turns the community's negative scrutiny on her. Abigail's daughter Ann (Granville) is more central to the plot, as she sets off the witch hunt in a way strongly reminiscent of Arthur Miller's later play *The Crucible* by making a false and spiteful claim that Tituba has bewitched her. Fearing for her life, Tituba in turn names others, including Zeffie Tilbury as the drunken and eccentric old woman Goody Hodges.

This was the first time Bondi played a mentally disturbed women, as she would also do in *The Snake Pit* (1948). *Maid of Salem* was in the can by early November 1936 and was released February 12, 1937, in the year that would be the high point of Bondi's film career. The reviewer for the *Salt Lake Tribune* pointed to Bondi's Abigail as one of the film's "outstanding characterizations."[24] On November 21, 1936, *Los Angeles Times* film critic Edwin Schallert claimed that Paramount had made a long-term contract with Bondi on the strength of her work in *Maid of Salem*.[25] It turns out the contract was only for one year and Bondi only signed it to be able to star with Victor Moore in *Make Way for Tomorrow*. She recalled in 1972, that her contract fortunately had run out before she was forced to do anything she did not feel right for herself.[26]

*Make Way for Tomorrow* has always had its strong adherents among film critics, industry insiders, and fans of 1930s movies, but is practically unknown today among the general public. It was a critical success, but a box office failure; a fate it shares with Bondi's other great film of the 1930s, Clarence Brown's *Of Human Hearts*. Both films had a special, bittersweet place in their directors' hearts, as favorites of their own that, despite their worthiness and excellence (or maybe because of it), had not appealed to a wide audience. As we know, in Hollywood critical success without commercial success is no success at all. Jeremy Arnold has called *Make Way for Tomorrow* "one of the most unjustly forgotten pictures ever to come out of the studio system."[27]

In *Make Way for Tomorrow*, which offered Bondi the first starring role of her career, she plays Lucy Cooper a 70-year-old mother of five and a wonderful mixture of annoying old bat and sweet old biddy. Her husband Barkley "Bark" Cooper (Victor Moore) stopped working some four years before the film opens and was unable to keep making the payments on the house, so they have lost it to the bank. They have been given six months to move, but by the time the film opens and they finally tell their children, there are only a few days left. None of the children, including bachelor Robert (Ray Mayer) and Addie in California (who is never seen), can take in both parents, so the hastily made plan is that Bark will go to live with daughter Cora (Elisabeth Risdon) and son-in-law Bill Payne (Ralph Remley), while Lucy will spend three months 300 miles away with her son George (Thomas Mitchell), his wife Anita (Fay Bainter), and their daughter Rhoda (Barbara Read). Meanwhile, daughter Nellie (Minna Gombell) will concoct some plan to help them or convince her rich husband Harvey Chase (Porter Hall) to take them in, which he ultimately refuses to do. Nellie does nothing, in fact. After an eventful last day together in

New York, the separation becomes permanent when Bark goes to Addie in California and Lucy to an old age home.

Say what you will about the Hollywood film industry, then and now, it has never primarily been dedicated to making grown-up films about real problems in the real world. But that is what *Make for Tomorrow* is: A deeply felt and credible representation of the challenges of growing old and caring for elderly parents in a society with no social security and few other safety nets. Based on a bestselling 1934 novel by Josephine Lawrence called *Years Are So Long*, the film is a low-key, understated masterpiece with a script heavy on pathos, nostalgia, quotidian American tragedy, but also a charming brand of "smiling through tears" humor. It mingles elements and themes from *A Streetcar Named Desire* and *Death of a Salesman* a decade before these classic plays were written and first performed.[28]

*Miami News* columnist Eddie Cohen observed when the film came out in 1937: "It is gratifying to feel that every now and then Hollywood, with its stress of romance, strikes out and essays a drama with an adult thesis."[29] Harry Haller in the *Baltimore Sun* concurred, writing: "perhaps the most remarkable thing about Make Way for Tomorrow is that it was produced as it is. Knowing Hollywood's mimeograph methods, one would expect the film's emphasis to be placed elsewhere—on the romantic problems of the modern granddaughter or of her sophisticated parents, with the elderly couple as background characters."[30]

With no big stars in the cast, *Make Way for Tomorrow* is an ensemble piece in every sense. No single actor, character, or point of view is allowed to dominate. In a modern tragedy like this, as in the great plays of the American realist tradition of O'Neill, Hellman, Williams, and Miller, which it can well bear comparison with, no single person or faction is entirely in the right; the truth is always in between and at least two-sided. There are no cardboard villains here and no saints, no black and white, and no easy solutions. No one is entirely a winner, everyone is to some extent a loser, no matter what happens. The *Observer* of London remarked on director McCarey's evenhanded treatment of a genuine dilemma: "He is never a moralist, always an observer. He draws no conclusions, merely sets out, fairly, all the cases. He is not for the parents nor against them; the old people are often tiresome, the young people frequently unselfish. He simply sets a problem that most of us are constantly evading, and leaves it to the individual watcher to find in his own philosophy the answer to this disquieting film."[31]

A discussion of the many and important differences between the original novel and the film would take me too far afield, but let me make a few points in order to clarify the differences that make the film version stand forth as an independent and very different work from its source. The relation between novel and film here is really one of "inspired by" rather than "based on." The film is similar to the novel only in its starting point and its broader subject matter; in name only, you might say, as nearly all the main characters' names have been retained, but the characteristics they display are deeply different from one medium to another, as are the situations and plotlines used to illustrate the works' themes.

Apart from the big differences in the storyline and the various characters, then, including the personalities and appearance of the protagonists, the most significant difference between the novel and the film is the unrelentingly bleak vision of humanity and American society Lawrence presents in the novel compared with the touches of genuine human connection and comedy that Leo McCarey made such an essential part of the film. All is darkness in *Years Are So Long*, while in *Make Way for Tomorrow* there are at least some points of light, some laughs along the way, however much they stick in the throat. As the critic for the *Dayton Herald* noted: "Some of the harshness of the original tale has been strained from the picture version, but not enough to beguile you into believing that nature is a nice old gal, after all. In this manifestation she is something you cannot print."[32]

The difference in treatment can best be illustrated by the famous bridge party scene, where Lucy acts as a disruptive element at her daughter-in-law Anita's evening gathering by distracting the guests from their cards. In the novel, this is an unrelentingly bleak scene with no streak of humor, even of the blackest kind. Out of this situation, McCarey constructs one of the tragicomic centerpieces of his film. We get well-meaning and garrulous Lucy erupting on the scene, heralded by the maid Mamie's arrival with Lucy's rocking chair over her head in a completely failed attempt to be unobtrusive. Next, and in the same vein, we have granny trying to sit quietly on the sidelines, but making the chair creak annoyingly with every movement of her knitting body. Bondi came up with this bit of business herself.[33] We get Lucy's inevitable attempt to strike up a conversation with the guests, only emphasizing how out of place she is in this semi-sophisticated, urban middle-class world. Finally, we get the excruciatingly touching phone call between the old husband and wife in full hearing of the party guests, ending in Lucy's assurance to her husband, "We will soon be together for always."

Towards the end of the film, the aged couple spend a final day together in New York, choosing to forget about the family dinner at daughter Nellie's home, and instead doing only what the spirit moves them to do after a lifetime of doing their duty. They wander the streets of New York and finally return to the large, luxurious hotel, where they spent their honeymoon 50 years earlier. At the hotel's expense, they have an impromptu celebration, just the two of them, of their five decades of life and love together, just as this long period of togetherness is about to end.

Again, the novel contains only the germ of this long finale to the film. Bark and Lucy do spend a few hours together, their last it turns out, trawling the streets of Newark, not New York, and in a much less romantic and idyllic fashion. The episode takes place not at the end, but in the middle of the novel, as they are about to move to the homes of two other children than the ones they have spent their first three months with. Desperate to be together again, they try to devise a scheme whereby they might rent a little room somewhere. They even try have a look at one or two examples of what is on offer in the way of furnished rooms, but there is nothing they can afford that comes close to the minimum of comfort and cleanliness they would require.

Paramount acquired the film rights to *Years Are So Long* in June 1936.[34] By this time, the novel had sold more than 100,000 copies and was "in constant demand in public and rental libraries."[35] By July 1, Leo McCarey had been assigned to direct the film version.[36] On October 21, 1936, Louella Parsons wrote in her column: "If Paramount is really interested in getting the tops in a character actress to play the lead in 'The Years Are So Long,' why not nab Beulah Bondi—and nab her quickly. She stole 'The Gorgeous Hussy' right under the noses of Joan Crawford, Franchot Tone and the rest of the high powered stars in the cast. She has never given an indifferent performance—and I'm not her press agent, either. But I am told that Leo McCarey has almost lost his eyesight looking for a lead, so I just thought I'd try to be a little helpful."[37]

On November 16, Parsons announced that 72-year-old veteran stage and film character actor Tully Marshall would postpone his planned retirement to take the male lead in the film. She hoped "present negotiations are successful" for Bondi to be "his screen vis-à-vis."[38] Two days later, it was clear from Sheilah Graham's column that Bondi had been cast and would have as her male counterpart, not Marshall, but comedian Victor Moore in his first dramatic role.[39] Moore was best known as a headliner in vaudeville and for playing Vice President Alexander Throttlebottom in *Of Thee I Sing* and Moonface Martin ("Public Enemy 13") in *Anything Goes* on Broadway; and had thus far only assayed comic roles in films such *Swing Time, Golddiggers of 1937*, and *We're on the Jury*.[40] He was 13 years Bondi's senior and yet ten years younger than the character he would be playing. When Louella Parsons' daughter Harriet, subbing for her mother, jubilantly spread the news in her column the following week, she called Bondi "certainly the most important and popular character woman since Marie Dressler."[41] By this time, being compared to Dressler was the holy grail for character actresses. There was no higher praise.

By August 12, 1936, Viña Delmar, best known for the novel and screenplay to the film *Bad Girl* and screen writer on *Bad Boy*, which Bondi was in, had been signed to write the screenplay of the film that was still entitled *Years Are So Long*.[42] Later Howard J. Green was also involved in working on the script, though he did not receive screen credit.[43] The papers reported that he was putting the finishing touches on the screenplay just before Christmas.[44] Credit, though, was given to the writer-actor couple Nolan and Helen Leary for a dramatization of Lawrence's novel called "Years Are So Long: A Play of American Life in 2 Acts" and copyrighted September 3, 1935, which has never been published and apparently was never given a professional production.[45]

This was the first film Leo McCarey was to produce and direct for Paramount under his new three-year contract, which called for him to make two pictures a year.[46] On December 8, production on the film was reported to be "beginning right away," but was delayed by rewrites and McCarey's illness.[47] Slowly but surely, "One of the strongest casts ever assembled for a motion picture" was beginning to come together.[48] Thomas Mitchell and Louise Beavers were signed December 20, borrowed from Columbia and producer Sol Lesser respectively.[49] Mitchell would play the Coopers' eldest son George and Beavers his maid Mamie. Aline MacMahon had joined the cast by December 23 to play George's wife Anita, a professional bridge instructor.[50] Handpicked by scenarist Delmar, Barbara Read was borrowed from Universal to play George and Anita's precocious and impulsive daughter Rhoda, after making a big hit in *Three Smart Girls*.[51]

Maurice Moscovitch, a Russian-born character actor known for his debut role in the recent *Winterset*, signed up early in the new year to play a shop owner who befriends Bark Cooper while he is living with his daughter Cora.[52] Replacing Margaret Hamilton, Minna Gombell was a late arrival in the cast as the most selfish daughter, Nellie, a part written especially for her and that fits her hard-bitten blonde screen persona much better than the nitwit Nellie in the novel.[53] Then, in the first week of the new year, MacMahon suddenly had to withdraw from the production for "personal reasons" and return immediately to New York. No more specific explanation was offered by the actress and speculation was rife. MacMahon was replaced by Fay Bainter, who was flown in from New York.[54] It later became known that MacMahon's husband, architect Clarence Stein, had been critically ill in hospital.[55] He survived; in fact, he lived to be 92.[56]

On January 16, 1937, columnist Hubbard Keavy reported that production on the film had finally "got underway this week."[57] Shooting began at the beginning with the family gathering, where Bark and Lucy have to tell the children they have lost their home.[58] By

March 3, McCarey was ready to start directing the big café-ballroom sequence at the end of the film with 300 extras on "the largest set ever constructed on a studio sound stage."[59] The following day, it was announced that the film's title was being changed from *Years Are So Long* to *Make Way for Tomorrow*. McCarey had not been happy with the original title.[60] By March 14, Bainter had completed her work on film.[61] On April 26, the film was referred to as being "recently completed."[62] *Make Way for Tomorrow* opened at the Criterion in New York on Saturday, May 8, 1937, and Bondi saw the film for the first time at an afternoon showing there.[63]

Playing garrulous, exasperating but lovable Lucy Cooper in Leo McCarey's masterpiece *Make Way for Tomorrow* (Paramount, 1937) was the best opportunity Bondi ever got in films. It was an adult film on an adult theme and met with a lukewarm response from the audience. McCarey refused to tack on a happy ending and saw his tenure at Paramount come to a precipitous end. Ex-vaudevillian and film and stage comedian Victor Moore (right) assayed his first dramatic role in this film to great acclaim. McCarey called him "a male Dressler," which was high praise at the time. Despite being in her sixties, Marie Dressler had been one of the biggest stars of the early 1930s.

It took Hollywood half a dozen years and 18 films, then, to realize that one of Bondi's specialties since the beginning of her acting career was playing women much older than herself; grandmothers and other elderly women of various kinds. She described Lucy Cooper in an interview towards the end of her life as perhaps the oldest woman she had played up to that point. She must have meant, the oldest in films. The biggest challenges in enacting the role, she recalled, were "maintaining the old-lady tone of voice from take to take," "the same timbre of decrepitude"; and "keeping the character from oversweetness."[64] It was a challenge, too, when filming the big New York finale, that Bondi and Moore had worked so little together previously.[65] The whole point of the film was that they are having to live separate lives for the first time in 50 years of marriage. Suddenly, the two actors had to find a way to relate to each other on the screen that gave the illusion of a lifetime of love. Despite the odds, this succeeded brilliantly.

Bondi's starring role as Lucy Cooper garnered her the best reviews of her career in a career full of plaudits from the critics. After seeing a preview, the reviewer for the *Baltimore Sun* wrote: "Without doubt, Miss Bondi's performance is one of the finest celluloid has recorded." The *Detroit Free Press* called Moore's and Bondi's performances "nothing short of superb" and added: "Miss Bondi's Lucy is something to contemplate with reverence, so completely does she invest her every scene with a wistfulness, an eagerness, a warmth, a patience that makes it outstanding." The *Miami News* found that Moore and Bondi "play their roles with pathos, a touch of comedy and a note of realism seldom seen on stage or screen." When the *Los Angeles Times* finally had a chance to review the film in late August 1937, Grace Kingsley wrote: "Beulah Bondi's mother part is played with such faithfulness to even the smallest details, and such touches of truthfulness to life, that she never seems to be acting at all." At the same time, the *Oakland Tribune* claimed that "Beulah Bondi steps into the top rank of mother role actresses with this picture. Her direct simplicity and deliberate understatement prove more than effective; hysteria has no place in her characterization." The *Pittsburgh Press* summed it all up at the end of 1937: "The touching performances of Victor Moore and Beulah Bondi were among the best of the year."[66]

Given this chorus of approval, I feel I can permit myself to say that, however much I love *Make Way for Tomorrow* on the whole, I am not a big fan of Bondi's middle-aged performances of elderly women. I find there is something generic about them, as if she is playing "old ladyness," rather than individualized old ladies. It is a type of "old lady drag," as if the performance is being given as much by the hair, make-up, and costume, as through voice and movement. Naturally, voice and movement are also integral to the total impression. Bondi had a crackingly dry old lady voice long before she was an old lady herself and used it to great effect in these portrayals. She also had the creakily geriatric movement patterns down pat.

Granted, this discrepancy in age between the actor and the part is also a potential source of the character's humorous effect, at least for those who know Bondi was only 48 when she gave this performance. She is usually pretty cute playing an old lady, and so she is here; unless, as in *On Borrowed Time*, she is pretty dull. I think we are less easily impressed by these impersonations today, though, because we expect a higher level of realism. And then it is worth asking: What is the point, really, in a town full of talented elderly character actresses, in having a still relatively young and vigorous woman playing a little old lady?

*Make Way for Tomorrow* was not just a personal triumph for Bondi. Overall, it received more laudatory reviews than any other film she acted in. As we have seen above, encomiums seldom make for interesting reading, so let me simply summarize the critics' views using two short quotes from the beginning and the end of the film's run. According to Frank S. Nugent in the *New York Times*, *Make Way for Tomorrow* was "an extraordinarily fine picture." Mark Hellinger described it in his summary of the film year, as "a picture that was loved by everyone who saw it—but that very few went to see!"[67]

There is a general perception today that, as a result of McCarey's refusal to give in and craft a happy ending for the film, it was abandoned by the studio.[68] This impression is correct. There was no gala premiere in Hollywood or New York. The film simply opened. The film was not even shown in big Californian cities like Los Angeles and Oakland until late August 1937, months after it had opened in New York and elsewhere. There were indicators in the papers, too, that *Make Way for Tomorrow* was being given short shrift by the exhibitors. For example, we can read at the end of the review in the *Oakland Tribune* that, "because of booking requirements, the management was compelled to end the run of this unique picture abruptly."[69]

One industry observer described the film as "a truly fine picture that probably will lag far behind at the boxoffice." He ascribed this to fact that it was "listed as a second feature, billed below Shirley Temple's 'Wee Willie Winkie.'"[70] Film critic Kaspar Monahan, in discussing candidates for *Film Daily*'s "Best 10" list for 1937, says of *Make Way for Tomorrow* and Warner Bros.' crime drama *They Won't Forget*, that they "probably haven't a chance in the national poll." He explains why: "Both were considered such poor boxoffice that here and elsewhere they were shown on double-feature bills. The drums of ballyhoo did not beat in advance of their showing. Consequently the bulk of the public is probably unaware of their existence."[71] He turned out to be right in both cases. *Make Way for Tomorrow* did not make it on to the list, which was topped by *The Life of Emile Zola*, *The Good Earth*, and *Captains Courageous*.[72] It did not receive a single Academy Award nomination either.

With her standout work on *Make Way for Tomorrow* and *Of Human Hearts*, plus an annual income that year of $53,958, a substantial sum at the time, 1937 would prove the high point of Bondi's film career. The year started with columnist Mollie Merrick including among her "New Year Wishes for Film People," the hope that the new year would bring "contract artists like Elizabeth Patterson and Beulah Bondi."[73] Four days later, Hubbard Keavy praised her performance in *The Gorgeous Hussy* in a column on the biggest scene stealers of 1936.[74] George Shaffer profiled her in his column for the Chicago Tribune Press Service on January 16.[75] Philip K. Scheuer announced in the headline of his column "'Bit' Player Boom Hits Industry: Character Actors at Premium" and mentioned Bondi among the Paramount contractees.[76] And on February 7, 1937, Bondi was nominated for an Academy Award for Best Actress in a Supporting Role for *The Gorgeous Hussy*, the first year this award was handed out.[77] She was on a roll.

Bondi's income for 1937 would become public knowledge two years later when her name appeared in 1,132-page report containing a list of nearly 50,000 individuals who were paid $15,000 or more by corporations. The report had been produced at the behest of Congress by the Treasury. Bondi was no doubt mortified to see her income published in several national newspapers and on the front page of her hometown rag, the *Vidette-Messenger*. By comparison, Mandel Lowenstine, who had grown up with Bondi on N. Washington St. and was now vice president of the Central Steel and Wire Company of Chicago, had earned $60,000 that same year.[78]

More interesting yet are the comparisons we can make with other movie workers who appear on the list. Her frequent co-star Lionel Barrymore earned $132,739 at MGM; Joan Crawford, star of *The Gorgeous Hussy*, $351,538 at MGM; Claudette Colbert and Fred MacMurray, stars of *Maid of Salem*, $248,055 and $92,000 respectively at Paramount; Fredric March, star of *The Buccaneer*, $150,000 at Paramount; Clarence Brown, Bondi's director on *The Gorgeous Hussy* and *Of Human Hearts*, $139,000 at MGM; Frank Lloyd, her director on *Maid of Salem*, $166,208 at Paramount; and Leo McCarey, her director on *Make Way for Tomorrow*, $77,000 at Paramount. Among supporting players, Guy Kibbee earned $50,333, Una Merkel $50,224, Frank Morgan $84,983, and Edna May Oliver $94,458 at MGM; and her *Make Way for Tomorrow* co-star Victor Moore earned $82,785 at RKO.[79]

In late March 1937, just after filming ended on *Make Way for Tomorrow*, Bondi returned to the Mojave Desert, more specifically to the Yucca Loma Ranch in Apple Valley.[80] At an elevation of 4,000 feet, the ranch was located seven miles from Victorville, California, which in turn is 90 miles by car northeast of Hollywood. Bondi had been coming here since the mid–1930s. By the end of the decade, Yucca Loma had become the center of a colony of film folk and artists. According to Hedda Hopper, Bondi spent more time there than she did in Hollywood.[81] Fellow guests during her first years at the ranch, included David Manners, who would build his own home there and become a long-term permanent resident; Helen Mack, Walter and Ruth Pidgeon, and Stuart Walker and his life partner and adoptee Arthur H. Walker.[82] Bondi's friend Bob Balzer described life at the ranch in 1946 as "an everlasting house party for a double-dozen distinguished guests" with owner Gwen Behr as "the most radiant hostess." He made the bold claim, that there was "no place in the world where more celebrated people have flocked for recreation and relaxation."[83] Some news items suggest that Bondi owned her own ranch in the area, but I have not been able to confirm this.[84] The most reliable sources all depict her as a guest at the Yucca Loma Ranch. The ranch was put up for sale in 1955 after Gwen Behr's death in early 1954.[85]

In addition to her professional success, though, and her discovery of the charms of the desert, there was also sadness in 1937. On Tuesday, July 13 at 3:30 in the morning, Louis D. Bondy died in a hospital in Gary, Indiana, of cirrhosis of the liver. He was 84. In his heyday, Bondi's Uncle Lou had been one of the leading citizens and richest men in Valparaiso. It was a sad and lonely end to a long and successful life. Monday afternoon and purely by chance, a tenant had found Bondy semi-conscious in his apartment on the second floor of the building he had owned for decades on the corner of Lincolnway and Franklin St. No one knew he was ill.[86] Both his sister-in-law Eva Bondy and his niece Beulah were in Los Angeles when he died. It was symbolic that, during the last year and a half of his life, he, the first Bondy to move to Valparaiso, should also be the last member of the family still living there. L.D. Bondy's memorial service was held at the Bartholomew Funeral Chapel on Washington St. on Thursday, July 15, 1937. He was laid to rest next to his brother Abram in Graceland Memorial Park.[87] In a widely reprinted AP news bulletin on July 17, Bondi was reported to have inherited $30,000 from her uncle.[88] More of that later.... It would have amused him that the news bulletins of his death identified him primarily as "an uncle of Beulah Bondi."[89]

Bondi was just about to go into *The Adventures of Tom Sawyer*, which started production at Selznick International Pictures on July 18, so it is unlikely she was able to attend her uncle's funeral.[90] She was replacing her friend Elizabeth Patterson, whose option to play Aunt Polly had expired due to repeated delays in the production. Bondi worked three weeks on the film, before it was decided to replace her in turn with May Robson. According to the *Los Angeles Times*: "The last change is no reflection on Miss Bondi as she was due to start a picture at MGM."[91] The Metro production alluded to would have been *Of Human Hearts*, but that did not start filming till mid–October. As Bondi remembered it, she had simply been fired by the notoriously capricious David O. Selznick without any explanation being given.[92] 25 years later, Bondi referred to being replaced in this film, as one of "two great disappointments" of her life; the other was missing out on the role of Ma Joad in *The Grapes of Wrath*.[93]

On January 22, 1956, 32 Hollywood stars and more than 800 guests gathered to witness legendary director and producer Cecil B. DeMille receiving the Screen Producers Guild Milestone award in Beverly Hills, California. In the widely reprinted group photo of the "film greats" that DeMille had "helped to the top of the ladder," we find Beulah Bondi standing in the front row second from right between DeMille's adopted daughter, Katherine DeMille Quinn, and actor Eddie Quillan.[94]

You will easily be forgiven for not recalling what film Bondi did with DeMille, as her role is relatively modest in *The Buccaneer*, a pirate adventure film set in and around New Orleans during the War of 1812. It starred an unusually dashing Fredric March as privateer Jean Lafitte and Hungarian Franciska Gaal, in her American film debut, as Gretchen, a feisty Dutch girl, who by virtue of sheer endurance and determination gets the guy at the close of the film. Bondi did not even support the star here, but rather the second lead, Margot Grahame, the girl who does *not* get the guy.

Bondi is in her uptight, upper-class, spinster aunt and chaperone mode as Aunt Charlotte, closest relative to Lafitte's main love interest through most of the film, lovely Annette de Remy (Grahame). Aunt Charlotte is first seen at the buccaneer's sale with Lafitte's left-hand man, Dominique You (Akim Tamiroff), who tries to sell her some contraband goods. According to her niece, she cannot resist a bargain.

After the film has focused on Lafitte and Gretchen's combative relationship for most of the first hour, it finally returns to the Lafitte-Annette storyline. At 57 minutes, Aunt Charlotte bursts in on the tryst between Lafitte and Annette and ends up throwing him out of the house. She has a fainting spell when her niece tells her she wants to marry Lafitte (e.g., "Get me some sherry"). When it is later abruptly revealed to Annette that Lafitte may have been killed along with most of his men, Aunt Charlotte shows great sensitivity in saying: "It's the end I expected and the one he deserved."

Later, Aunt Charlotte shows up briefly at a couple of celebrations for General Andrew Jackson (Hugh Sothern), who with Lafitte's aid has saved New Orleans from the British forces in the Battle of New Orleans. We recall that Bondi played Andrew Jackson's corncob pipe-smoking wife Rachel in *The Gorgeous Hussy* (1936). At a reception, it is revealed that Lafitte is indirectly responsible for the tragic fate of the ship *Corinthian*, which was sunk with all aboard (save Gretchen), including Annette's sister Marie (Louise Campbell). We are not invited to share Aunt Charlotte's reactions in close-up either to Lafitte's rehabilitation in the eyes of New Orleans society, nor to the later revelation that he was indirectly responsible for her niece Marie's death, which effectively ends his affair with Annette. Bondi is last seen in a group shot comforting her niece after the shocking news.

Production began on August 12, 1937, which was DeMille's 56th birthday, and was complete by late October.[95] Naturally, given the director, the film had the largest cast of any Bondi worked on. Among the 44 credited roles, we find Spring Byington, Bondi's old friend and colleague from her days in stock. This was the closest she got to film acting with Byington, who had a Hollywood screen career to rival Bondi's. In *The Buccaneer*, Byington appears only in the opening scene of the film, as Dolly Madison fleeing the White House before the British invaders arrive, taking the Declaration of Independence and a large painting of George Washington with her. Bondi would be reunited and have an equally antagonistic screen relationship with Fredric March in *One Foot in Heaven* (1941).

Paramount gave Bondi many fine opportunities down through the years, but this was not one of them, apart from the chance to work with the legendary DeMille and to get all dolled up in Regency-style finery. It was a dissatisfying follow-up to her starring role in *Make Way for Tomorrow*, but at least it showed her versatility and how nicely she cleaned up. When DeMille pro-

Bondi cleaned up nicely, though she rarely had the opportunity to get dolled up to the extent we find her in Cecil B. DeMille's *The Buccaneer* (Paramount, 1938) starring Fredric March and Franciska Gaal. The part of Aunt Charlotte was not as spectacular as the outward trappings, though, being one of Bondi's many roles in opposition to the heroine's love match. In this case, second lead Margot Grahame ultimately does not get the guy, though Aunt Charlotte has little to do with it. Bondi had performed at the Elitch Gardens Theatre in Denver with March and his future wife Florence Eldridge during the summer of 1925.

duced a 1958 remake of *The Buccaneer* with his son-in-law Anthony Quinn directing and a new script, it was without Aunt Charlotte.

*Of Human Hearts* is one of Beulah Bondi's most moving films and the devoted mother and minister's wife Mary Wilkins one of her most finely etched characters. The film, which was originally known as *Benefits Forgot*, begins as a story about two differently devoted parents and their proud, egotistical son, but by the end the father has died and it is the relationship between mother and son that has been explored in greatest detail.

The mother-son motif was a common one in the 1930s. To the extent that the relationship was shown to be less than ideal, it was often the mother who was at fault. *Of Human Hearts* is different in that the son, Jason Wilkins (Gene Reynolds/James Stewart), is one of the most self-satisfied, self-centered, and simply annoying prats ever created on the big screen. Bondi delivers a standout performance as the mother and James Stewart is convincing, too, in the first and most important of their many mother and son portrayals. Not to forget Gene Reynolds, who bears a remarkable resemblance to Stewart and plays Jason Wilkins as a young boy with equal conviction.

As in *Rain*, Bondi was paired with Walter Huston, this time playing Ethan Wilkins, a stern, uncompromising, circuit-riding preacher Hercules in the backwoods, who feels a call from God to bring His word into the wilderness. The film opens with the couple and their young son coming from greater affluence and comfort in Maryland to Pine Hill, a rustic, pioneer Ohio village on the Ohio River across from Virginia. In a finely crafted script by Bradbury Foote based on the novel *Benefits Forgot* (1917) by Honoré Morrow, there are many revealing incidents showing Jason's selfishness. One is early on, when his mother sells two silver spoons to the grasping shopkeeper for two dollars to buy a six-month subscription to *Harper's Bazaar* for her son. He has no interest in it when he finally gets the magazines, preferring to read the local doctor's medical books.

There is a ten-year ellipsis between the family first arriving in Pine Hill and the switch to Stewart playing Jason Wilkins as an adult. Ethan Wilkins is still the minister in Pine Hill and still has a combative relationship with his strong-willed and impudent son, which finally leads to fisticuffs. This decides Jason to go away to make his fortune. After 60 minutes., then, the main storyline leaves Pine Hill, as Jason departs and goes to Baltimore to pursue a medical career, though we are shown revealing scenes from his father's death and his mother's impoverished and lonely later life.

In the end, when he has succeeded in becoming a doctor and surgeon himself, largely because of his mother's self-sacrifice, Jason is taken to task by no lesser a figure than President Lincoln (John Carradine). Mrs. Wilkins has written to the president after not hearing from her son for two years, asking if he can locate his grave for her. Jason is ordered to write to his mother every week, starting right away in Lincoln's office, or be court-martialed. This is an incredible moment in an otherwise credible film and the one jarring note objected to by some reviewers. The *Akron Beacon* Journal pointed out that "calling upon President Lincoln to turn the tide of human understanding is the film's weakest development." The *Manchester Guardian* wrote that "the introduction of President Lincoln disrupts the story and forces it to the point of bathos." Frank S. Nugent of the *New York Times* had only one criticism of the film in his laudatory review, writing that "only the ending is out of joint, disassociated from all that is gone before."[96]

One of the brilliant aspects of the script is the use of the white stallion Pilgrim as a leitmotif and foil to the characters. Pilgrim is first bought by the Wilkinses from a cruel master and becomes part of the family, until Jason asks that his mother sell him to finance his fancy new uniform as an army surgeon in the Civil War. Bondi, who is living in a simple one-room cabin with Pilgrim in an adjoining stall, does this with a heavy heart and gets $80 for him from the army. Stewart takes the money and uses seven dollars on gloves alone. This is one of the most gut-wrenching parts of the film.

The ending leans heavily on coincidence. Jason is reunited with Pilgrim when Pilgrim's new owner, Captain Griggs (Minor Watson), is wounded in the arm and is brought to Jason's battlefield hospital. Jason gets Pilgrim back for saving Griggs's arm and is able to reunite him with his mother at the close of the film in a real Hollywood ending.

An ensemble film with no stars above the title, Bondi is in effect the star of the film and, as in *The Trail of the Lonesome Pine*, its emotional center. She uses her old lady voice even when young, with its characteristically soft, lilting tones. Cinematographer Clyde

De Vinna, who had won an Academy Award for Best Cinematography in 1930, shows her Victorian face to its best advantage. Bondi looks youthful and even beautiful in her days as a still young mother. Metro's hairdressers devised a becoming center-parted, antebellum hairstyle for her, which remains unchanged in a film where no one ages very much. Bondi was 48 when she played the role.

*Of Human Hearts* was directed by Clarence Brown, who directed Bondi in both her Academy Award-nominated efforts and was himself nominated five times between 1930 and 1947. Brown owned the screen rights to the story and had waited 15 years to direct the film.[97]

The production period at the studio and on location at Agoura and Lake Arrowhead lasted from October 18 to December 20, 1937.[98] An entire village set, including "cornfields, cabbage patches and pumpkin acreage" was built at an elevation of 6,000 feet on the north shore of Lake Arrowhead, which involved 100

**Bondi is keeping warm and brushing up on her lines on the set of Clarence Brown's masterpiece *Of Human Hearts* (MGM, 1938), an ensemble film with a stellar cast including Walter Huston, James Stewart, Guy Kibbee, Charles Coburn, John Carradine, and Ann Rutherford. Bondi gave one of her most touching performances as Stewart's mother and Huston's wife Mary Wilkins. In total, she played Stewart's mother four times in films and once on television and made her last public appearance in February 1980 to celebrate him receiving the American Film Institute's Lifetime Achievement Award.**

workers and trucking all the materials for 20 miles over steep mountain roads.[99] Lake Arrowhead happened to be where Walter Huston was living at the time.[100] Guy Kibbee found a good spot to go fishing there, and Bondi and Leatrice Joy Gilbert, who played Ann Rutherford's character as a child, were reported to be "rivals for the ping pong championship."[101]

In recognition of her central role in the film, Bondi was billed third in the opening credits after Huston and Stewart and fourth in the closing credits, where Gene Reynolds got in ahead of her. Both the film as a whole and Bondi were heaped with praise. The *Greenville News* wrote: "Beulah Bondi, who has not yet received her full credit in the capital of make-believe, stole the show. With histrionic restraint and finesse she enacted a totally moving role of the mother." *Miami News* critic Eddie Cohen observed: "Beulah Bondi ... adds another to her gallery of fine screen roles, although the picture does not give her any great leeway in performance. There is something tensely dramatic about Bondi—like the despair of a Eugene O'Neill character—that adds tragedy to the sacrificing mother part." Columnist Robin Coons found: "Beulah Bondi gives another portrait worthy of the screen's leading character actress, especially in those scenes wherein she strives vainly to bring her husband and son to mutual understanding."[102]

The critic for the *Indianapolis News* had not forgotten that she "used to be here with the Stuart Walker company" and discussed her performance at length, finding that "it is the wife, and consequently Miss Bondi, who really dominates matters" and that "Miss Bondi's impersonation is extraordinary. It is one of the notable bits of acting to come out of Hollywood": "[A]fter you have watched her sterling performance you may know that the creation of character is a more abiding satisfaction to the attentive onlooker than the creation of beauty with the aid of the make-up man and the hairdresser." The *Daily Tar Heel* concluded that "'Of Human Hearts' should place Beulah Bondi among the great actresses." One of the few dissenting voices was the *Manchester Guardian*, which found that "Beulah Bondi plays the suffering mother a little too well."[103]

For her stunning, sustained performance, Bondi was nominated for an Academy Award for the second and final time. She lost to Fay Bainter for *Jezebel* in a strong field, which also included Billie Burke in *Merrily We Live*, Miliza Korjus in *The Great Waltz*, and Bondi's old friend from her days in stock, Spring Byington, in *You Can't Take It with You*. Clarence Brown considered *Of Human Hearts* one of his best films and explained its lack of commercial success with it being "a year ahead of its time," that is, ahead of *Gone with the Wind* and the Civil War interest it created.[104]

In Ed Sikov's succinct summary, *Vivacious Lady* is about what happens when "The heir apparent to a college president screws everything up by falling in love with a showgirl."[105] He does not just fall in love with her, though, he marries her after the briefest of acquaintances in New York City. The plot does not begin to thicken until the couple goes back home to Old Sharon, though, where the man, Peter Morgan, Jr. (James Stewart), sets about breaking the news to his parents, Peter Sr., and Martha Morgan (Charles Coburn and Beulah Bondi), with exaggerated consideration for their feelings and very little consideration for his wife's. For Francey LaRoche Morgan (Ginger Rogers), the lack of public acknowledgment of her marital status leads to her being shunted into the "other woman" category, as Peter is officially still engaged to Helen (Frances Mercer).

From the start, *Vivacious Lady* was pegged as a vehicle for Ginger Rogers and she in turn selected James Stewart as her leading man. During the years since *Finishing School* (1934), Rogers had become a major star at RKO after scoring hits in *The Gay Divorcee*, *Top Hat*, *Swing Time*, and most recently *Stage Door*. One of the essential elements these four enduring comedies had in common was that each had a brilliant opportunity for a comic second lead actress. In *The Gay Divorcee*, it was Alice Brady, in *Top Hat* and *Swing Time* Helen Broderick, and in *Stage Door* Constance Collier. Even though she had supported Margaret Sullavan in the classic screwball comedy *The Moon's Our Home*, Mrs. Boyce Medford was a dull lady companion role and Bondi was unlikely casting as a comic second in films.

Indeed, it turns out Bondi was not the studio's first choice to play Martha Morgan. Ultra-genteel and velvet-voiced Fay Bainter had originally been cast as James Stewart's mother, but production was halted in late April 1937, after Stewart fell acutely and painfully ill with what was variously reported as an attack of arthritis, a sore throat, and a "neck infection." Once he recovered, it was time to return for *Of Human Hearts* at his home studio MGM and *Vivacious Lady* was put on the back burner.[106] By the time production finally resumed in mid–December 1937,[107] Bainter was busy with *Jezebel* at Warner's. The *New York Times* reported that Pauline Lord, Leona Roberts, and Kathleen Lockhart were being considered to replace her.[108]

Bondi was finally signed for the part in late December 1937, at the same time as Charles Coburn signed up to play her husband, replacing Donald Crisp, who was also busy in *Jezebel*.[109] Both Bondi and Coburn came directly from major roles in *Of Human Hearts* at MGM, which had also starred James Stewart, and the standout performance she had given there no doubt put her in contention for the juicy part in the RKO comedy.

Martha Morgan is arguably the most important comedy role of Bondi's film career, a career which admittedly did not contain many comedy roles. This is ironic, considering that during her busy days in stock Bondi had primarily been known and celebrated as a comedienne.

She first appears as Mrs. Morgan 27 minutes into the film, after the plot has moved from New York to the college town of Old Sharon, where Bondi's husband is college president and where her son works as an associate professor of botany. Mrs. Morgan has a fainting spell almost immediately, when she comes upon her husband and son having a violent quarrel in a sort of comedy version of Walter Huston and Stewart's troubled father-son relationship in *Of Human Hearts*. Apparently, Mrs. Morgan cannot stand excitement, and this prevents her son from telling her that he is married to Francey, even after he has told his father.

Not long after this, we encounter Mrs. Morgan in the powder room of a club during a prom dance, where she first meets Francey without knowing who she is. In this intimate, all-female space, Martha seems an entirely different person. She is vibrant and alive with a twinkle in her eye. She compliments Francey on her pantyhose, asking where she got them. She even asks Francey for a cigarette. Discovering that Francey only has one left, she divides it in two and they smoke together while continuing their tête-à-tête, which is only interrupted by Hattie McDaniel, in her usual guise of a maid, telling Mrs. Morgan that her husband is waiting outside. Martha Morgan is about to leave still smoking her cig, when the maid reminds her that she'd better "snuff out that snipe."

After her first two scenes, then, the film has left us with an entirely conflicting conception of who Martha Morgan really is, which might be the sign of a fundamental flaw in the screenplay. In this case, it exactly the point: that Mrs. Morgan is not the same person in all circumstances. Discovering who she really is, how she has coped with a domineering husband for 30 years, and witnessing the moment when she finally has had enough are integral to the enjoyment of the film, which contrasts the long haul of the elder Morgans' marriage with the as yet short-lived and unconsummated marriage of Peter and Francey.

Mrs. Morgan does not discover the true nature of Francey's relationship with her son until she seeks her out in her apartment. Peter's fiancée Helen has told her she has seen Peter climbing down the fire escape from Francey's apartment in the middle of the night ("There's only one way to handle a woman like that. Helen, I'm getting up!"). Thinking Mrs. Morgan already knows, Francey reveals that she is married to Peter and Martha Morgan takes it surprisingly well ("You know, I think I'm going to feel fine"). She even asks for another cigarette. It turns out her weak heart and fainting spells have for three

**Yes, indeed, to the right we find Hattie McDaniel with *Gone with the Wind* and her Academy Award still in the future, though not far in the future. She only shows up in *Vivacious Lady* (RKO, 1938) for about a minute, as a maid who comes into the powder room to tell Bondi her impatient husband is waiting outside and reminds her to ditch the cigarette she has been sharing with daughter-in-law Ginger Rogers. Bondi did too few comedy roles in films and Martha Morgan was her best opportunity in the comic vein. She claimed to have based her performance on the beleaguered wife of a college professor she had known back home in Valparaiso.**

decades been a survival strategy for dealing with her pompous, egotistical, and autocratic husband.

This is Bondi's big scene in the film (starting at 1 hour and 6 minutes) and culminates in her famously and convincingly dancing the "Big Apple" with Francey and Keith (James Ellison), Martha's ne'er-do-well, playboy nephew. According to one contemporary news item, this dance was "the craze in Hollywood" and Bondi was really worried about having to learn it. Everyone broke up when she tried it the first time.[110] At any rate, the three dancers are surprised by the arrival of Mr. Morgan and Martha's "cover" is blown. When her husband calls her to heel, she finally rebels. In fact, she leaves him after an emotional monologue about all she has suffered and sacrificed down through the years for the good of the college ("Coming? I'm going!").

We finally find Mrs. Morgan teary-eyed in the train compartment next to Francey in an extended split scene, where an increasingly dazed and confused train waiter, Willie Best, is witness to the emotional turmoil of the two women, as they both try to eat a ham sandwich and ask for a cigarette. They are reunited and comfort each other, before Peters Sr., and Jr., arrive on the scene, having stopped the train by parking their car across the tracks. Ironically, Mr. Morgan uses the same fake illness strategy to get into wife's compartment and elicit her sympathy, as she has used for years to manipulate him.

The *Chicago Tribune* wrote that Bondi did a "beautiful job." The *New York Times*, which gave the film a glowing review overall, wrote that "Beulah Bondi ... is an excellent foil for Mr. Coburn, with his magnificent monocle and intellectual snobbism."[111] She was an excellent foil for Ginger Rogers, too, and gave her a run for her money as the "vivacious lady."

Bondi spent part of the summer of 1938 working on her third film for Warner Bros., under the direction of Anatole Litvak.[112] *The Sisters* was based on a recent novel of the same name by Myron Brinig about three sisters born and raised in Montana, the choices they make, the paths they follow, and, of course, their men. Brinig is an interesting though now forgotten writer, who often focused on his native state of Montana and Jewish American life in his more than 20 novels, though there is no Jewish emphasis in *The Sisters*. He also created one of the first major gay characters in an American novel in two volumes of his family saga *Singermann* (1929) and *This Man Is My Brother* (1932).

While the three sisters are given equal billing in the novel, in the film version the main focus is on the eldest sister, Louise Elliott (Bette Davis), and her difficult life with her hotheaded and impulsive, alcoholic sportswriter husband, Frank Medlin (Errol Flynn). Having followed Frank to San Francisco and finally been abandoned by him, poor Louise also has to contend with the 1906 earthquake, only aided by her colorful neighbor Flora Gibbon (Lee Patrick). Louise pursues a secretarial career both out of want and need. Back home in Silver Bow, Montana, is her middle sister Grace (Jane Bryan), who marries Louise's former fiancé and has a son; and her devoted parents Rose and Ned Elliott, played by Bondi and Henry Travers. Ned is a pharmacist and lives over the store. The third and most conventionally beautiful sister is Helen (Anita Louise), who makes a career of "marrying up" and lives a life of luxury on the world stage.

**Bondi looks genteel and benevolent in this still portrait from Warner Bros.' 1938 drama *The Sisters*, where she played mother to Bette Davis, Jane Bryan, and Anita Louise and wife to Henry Travers for the first of two times. Bondi had a "period face," which lent itself well to costume dramas. Bondi and Travers were not given much to do here, besides acting as a sort of chorus commenting on their daughters' unfolding lives.**

For Bondi, this was not a major role by any means. The elder Elliots stay in Silver Bow and are most visible in the early part of the film, though they later form a sort of chorus, commenting on their daughters' lives both near and far. Notably, Bondi is seen in night dress in bed with husband Travers, as she had been seen previously with Lionel Barrymore. A columnist wrote in late June 1938, that the "Only way the situation could be handled to the satisfaction of the Hays office … was to put them in twin beds."[113] Twin beds or not, the beds are clearly not standing apart. In addition to double beds being taboo, there was also a ban on metal knitting needles on the set, "after several scenes had been spoiled by the click of the needles striking each other." Bondi was one of the knitters.[114]

On October 13, 1938, the day before *The Sisters* was released, Bondi hosted a private screening of the film for her friends.[115] While *The Sisters* has its moments, including any scene with an over the top Lee Patrick or her equally "colorful" mother, Laura Hope Crews, Bette Davis in a rare role as a good little woman can be tiresome. Few critics had anything to say about Bondi's performance here. The *San Bernardino County Sun* thought she and Travers did "superlative work as the girls' parents" and the *Honolulu Advertiser* found them "truly excellent in their sincere portrayals."[116] It was on this shoot that director Litvak asked Bondi to do a scene again seven times without offering any comment or criticism. "Finally, after seven takes, and a bit exasperated, she turned to him and told him that she didn't mind doing the scene, but would he please offer some comment." That is when he said: "'I just love to watch you act.'"[117]

*The Sisters* wrapped in early August 1938 and on Saturday, August 27, Bondi had to rush to the Indio, California, desert location of Warner's *They Made Me a Criminal* to replace 80-year-old May Robson, who had broken her arm in a "freakish accident."[118] Robson had tripped over her dog in her Beverly Hills home the previous day and would be unable to work for at least two weeks.[119] This was a foreshadowing of how Bondi would meet her end more than 40 years later. It is interesting, too, that these two actresses, more than 30 years apart in age, would be seen as interchangeable at this time. Born in Australia, Robson was a top-tier character woman with a slew of film credits to her name and was for many years the oldest actress to have been nominated for an Oscar. That was for her leading role in *Lady for a Day* in 1934. No doubt Bondi's performance in *Make Way for Tomorrow* had something to do with how the producers viewed the two women. And maybe the studio thought Bondi less likely to have an accident. At any rate, redoing all Robson's scenes was estimated to cost $60,000.[120] The role was, predictably, one of a grandmother, though this one atypically runs a date ranch in Arizona.

*They Made Me a Criminal* was the first film in which John Garfield was starred. His starring career might have been brief, though, as he and Bondi were involved in a car accident on the set. Garfield was at the wheel, he hit the wrong pedal, the car went backward instead of forward, and they ended up in a ditch. Though they were "tossed heels over head into the back seat," thankfully they both "were only bruised."[121] I suppose Garfield was not the worst guy you could get tossed around with. Bondi also got to act with the Dead End Kids, who played her helpers on the ranch. Apparently, she loved working with them, even when they made snowballs out of mashed potatoes and threw them at each other, one of them hitting her instead.[122]

During their ten-day sojourn in Palm Desert, the thermometer stood at a sizzling 120 degrees.[123] Frank Miller describes the grueling conditions Bondi was working under: "The cast and crew had to cover their heads and torsos with netting between shots to protect themselves from gnats, which swarmed constantly. Temperatures rose so high in the afternoon that cast members passed out. Eventually, they had to do all their shooting in the morning. The afternoon temperatures were so high they would have melted the film in the cameras."[124] As we have seen, by this time Bondi was an aficionado of the desert, so she was probably able to handle the heat better than most.

Incredibly, after all of this, Bondi was finally found to be "not the right type" and "didn't look old enough." The studio decided to go back to Robson at an added cost, this time, of $150,000.[125] Bondi herself had been "filled with misgivings about the role into which it [Robson's accident] boosted her," as she couldn't see anyone but Robson playing it.[126] One newspaper explained further that "she is inclined to shy from the motherly-grandmotherly type, admitting frankly that she is more at home when she can snap at people and take an occasional bite out of them."[127] Which sounds a lot like May Robson…. At any rate, the studio ultimately agreed with Bondi and her work with John Garfield and the Dead End Kids never reached the screen. On September 19, 1938, Robson wrote to her from the California Hospital to thank her for "your beautiful flowers and your sweet little note."[128] By October 10, Bondi was visiting Valparaiso on her way to a well-deserved vacation in New York City.[129] She was also working on her autobiography at this time, though nothing came of it.[130]

You would be hard put to find more gruesome family entertainment from the 1930s, than *On Borrowed Time*, a vaguely metaphysical fantasy in which an entire family is wiped out. After a young boy's parents are killed in a car accident, his grandparents take responsibility for raising him, all the time worrying about what will happen to him after they die. The solution to this dilemma turns out to have the boy die too!

Basically, a love story between a grandfather and grandson, Bondi plays the least interesting leading role of the grandmother, Nellie Northrup, who tries to keep her grumpy, wheel-chair-bound husband, Julian "Gramps" Northrup (Lionel Barrymore), and her unruly grandson Pud (Bobs Watson) in line. In a rare opportunity for low-profile, prolific character actress Eily Malyon, she plays the straitlaced, avaricious maternal aunt Demetria Riffle, who wants control over Pud and the $50,000 he has inherited. She is a "pismire" according to the two surviving Northrup men (a pismire being the most evil ant there is), while Granny tries to defend her as an upstanding, Christian woman.

Granny Northrup is subject to fainting spells and has a weak heart. When Demetria comes over to spread gossip about the Northrups' hired help, Marcia Giles (Una Merkel), having been seen kissing a boy on a bench and insists that Bondi fire her, Gramps reacts. He calls his wife a fool for listening to the "viper" Demetria's idle gossip and says he is disappointed in her. Demetria is thrown out of the house for the first of two times and Nellie takes to her bed for the first of two times. The second time, she never gets up again.

In a later scene, Nellie is a shocked witness (with Demetria) to her husband and grandson stalling in their car right in front of the church, as it is letting out after the service, a vivid reminder that they should have been in church themselves, rather than going on a fishing expedition. This leads to another spat between the elderly Northrups, which is ended only by Nellie's demise. At 38 mins., Cedric Hardwicke as the personification of death, Mr. Brink, comes to fetch her as she is knitting in bed. Nellie asks permission to finish the mitten she is working on, which she receives.

This was the fourth of no less than six films Bondi did with the MGM veteran Barrymore, making him her most frequent male co-star. She was married to him in three of the pictures, the two previous times being *Christopher Bean* (1933) and *The Gorgeous Hussy* (1936). She told Hedda Hopper on the set of *On Borrowed Time*: "I feel like a member of the Barrymore family."[131] Born in 1878, Barrymore was in bad shape and having to use a wheel-chair by this stage, though he would live till 1954. The studio heads wanted to replace him with Frank Morgan, but he convinced them he could do the role.[132] Bondi recalled to Jordan R. Young that "he was on drugs then. He was very ill."[133] She probably did not know that one of the drugs was cocaine.

Helmed by Harold S. Bucquet, production *On Borrowed Time* began at MGM on April 3, 1939, the same day *Mr. Smith Goes to Washington* started shooting at Columbia's Sunset Gower studios.[134] A news item noted that between the two films, Bondi was working with no less than five members of the Watson family, Bobs Watson being the youngest of the five brothers.[135] By the time filming ended in mid–May, production had begun on *The Under-Pup* at Universal.[136]

For her second granny performance and a role where she is seen in less than half the film, Bondi was billed third after Barrymore and Hardwicke, which is an indicator of her strong standing in the film industry at this time. Because of her high billing, Bondi's performance was widely "noticed," and she received excellent reviews. The *Philadelphia Inquirer* found that she "gives a warmly human characterization of the grandmother," while the *Cincinnati Enquirer* thought she "contributes some of the finest work of the year" and "is an excellent tired old lady granny." The *Los Angeles Times* also lauded her efforts, writing: "No less effective [than Barrymore and Hardwicke] is Beulah Bondi in the briefer role of the grandmother. She is, in fact, thought superior to Dorothy Stickney of the stage version, and her assignment, lacking in inherent sympathy as it is, is therefore the more difficult, and as she plays it, the more triumphant." Unintentionally hinting at the somewhat generic quality of her performance (and the script), at least as compared with *Make Way for Tomorrow*, the *Nebraska State Journal* wrote that "Beulah Bondi is nearly everybody's grandmother, as she is Bobs.'" Last but not least, the Warren, Pennsylvania *Times Mirror* thought she was "at her finest."[137]

Bondi did three very different films for Universal in the 1930s: a romantic comedy, a science fiction horror film, and a musical. The musical was *The Under-Pup*, a light-hearted juvenile film set in an exclusive girl's camp and designed to showcase the warbling prowess of Universal's new discovery, 13-year-old Gloria Jean in her film debut.

Bondi's relatively modest role as a professional working woman was most closely akin to the orphanage director she had played in *The Good Fairy* (also at Universal) and a comedic counterpart to the headmistress in *Finishing School*. Bondi plays Miss Thornton, the genteel, spinsterish camp director, who with the assistance of the girls and their Purple Order of the Penguins selects an underprivileged girl from New York City to attend camp that summer. The girl is Gloria Jean's character Pip-Emma Binns, who soon wreaks havoc in the camp with her curious, working-class ways, include gambling.

Bondi's characterization, particularly her high-voiced, fluty way of speaking, is absolutely hilarious, especially in the opening scene. Where she describes the glories of the camp to the poor girls in church. She keeps on insisting that she is *Miss* Thornton, though there is a suggestion in the final shot of her and the camp doctor, played by Samuel S. Hinds, that she may not be "miss" much longer.

Bondi signed up for the role on May 8, 1939, the day production got underway at Universal under the direction of Richard Wallace.[138] The production period partially overlapped with both *On Borrowed Time* and *Mr. Smith Goes to Washington* and ended in mid–July 1939.[139] Hedda Hopper reported an anecdote from the set. When Bondi had worn her wristwatch with the face on the inside, director Wallace insisted on reshooting the scene with the watch on the outside of her wrist. According to Wallace, "All old maid's faces are worn on the outside, Beulah."[140] This was not an important film for Bondi, but it gave her yet another chance to impersonate an elegant, grandiloquent spinster, who in contrast to Dr. Schultz and Miss Van Alstyne, gets to reveal her human side when Pip-Emma shows her some affection.

On July 2, 1939, in an article on how "veteran actors make practically a clean sweep of fat supporting character roles," Boyd Martin observed that "Miss Bondi is very much in demand."[141] In a news item printed in the *Lansing State Journal*, Bondi went on the record as wanting to play more sympathetic roles: "Nasty roles are the more tempting roles to play but Beulah Bondi wants no more of them. At least for the time being."[142] She got her wish.

The year she turned 50—1939—was a busy one, by her standards, with work on four different productions, compared to five in 1936, four in 1937, three in 1938, and four in 1940. While she ended up working for all the major studios during the 1930s, she did not get to Columbia until the end of the decade. *Mr. Smith Goes to Washington* was the first of her four films for the studio located at 1458 N. Gower St. in the heart of Hollywood, where boss Harry Cohn ruled supreme. Producer and director on the film was Frank Capra, who already had a string of hits with *Lady for a Day*, *It Happened One Night*, *Mr. Deeds Goes to Town*, *Lost Horizon*, and *You Can't Take It with You*. Production lasted from April 3 to July 7, 1939, though Bondi cannot have spent many days on the set.[143]

On April 23, we can read in Jean Craig's "Movie Memos" column, that "Beulah Bondi, Valparaiso, Indiana's contribution to the films, has been chosen by Columbia for one of the principal roles in the new Frank Capra picture."[144] This was either gross exaggeration or Bondi's part landed mostly on the cutting room floor. Of all the middle-class mothers Bondi played in the '30s, this was the least interesting, with the exception of Mrs. Tozer in *Arrowsmith*. In *Mr. Smith Goes to Washington*, she plays Stewart's mother in a film for the third of four times and the widow of an idealistic newspaper editor, who was shot and killed while trying to uncover crime and corruption. Ma Smith stays back home and tries to get out Stewart's Boy Rangers paper after he goes to Washington, which becomes all the more important when Edward Arnold's media empire tries to sway public opinion and stop freedom of speech.

To be honest, this is practically a non-speaking part. Ma Smith has exactly three lines in three separate scenes: greeting governor Guy Kibbee when he comes to their home to ask Stewart if he will become the new senator; responding to a call from Jean Arthur to use the scout paper to spread the word about Stewart's filibuster in the senate and his attempt to unmask graft and corruption in his home state; and finally the line "Children hurt all over the city. Tell Jeff to stop," spoken to Arthur over the phone. She is present in one other scene, which is the banquet given in Stewart's honor, where she is seated at his right hand at the main table, but has no lines.

In her few appearances, Bondi is dressed neatly and simply in a cotton print dress with a lace collar and wears her dark hair, streaked with grey, in a loose bun. For this brief effort, she was credited eighth and even given a stand-in.[145] Bondi's laconic comment on her efforts here are worth recording. She recalled in 1980: "I had to do very little in that movie, other than look concerned, which I think I did very well."[146] *Mr. Smith Goes to*

*Washington* was Bondi's last film to be released in the 1930s. Capra would give her a better part in *It's a Wonderful Life*.

Though released early in the new year and the new decade, Mitchell Leisen's finely crafted comedy-drama *Remember the Night* was the final film Bondi worked on in the 1930s.[147] Work on her fifth film for Paramount was scheduled to begin on the studio lot at 5555 Melrose Ave. in Hollywood on August 3, 1939, about a month after production ended on *Mr. Smith Goes to Washington*.[148] The production phase of the film only took 34 days and Leisen brought it in $46,000 under the budget of $634,000.[149] Bondi was paid $5,000 for two weeks' work.[150]

Based on an original screenplay by Preston Sturges, who was soon to embark on his celebrated run as a writer-director, the film deals with a young assistant district attorney, John Sargent (Fred MacMurray), who gets more than professionally interested in a lady shoplifter, Lee Leander (Barbara Stanwyck). Bondi was billed third as MacMurray's

Mrs. Sargent in *Remember the Night* (Paramount, 1940) was one of Bondi's good mothers, which increased in number relative to the bad ones as her career progressed. Mrs. Sargent is between a rock and a hard place in this film, where she is concerned that the young woman her son Fred MacMurray is becoming enamored of will not make a suitable wife for an up-and-coming assistant district attorney. Bondi had two of her best scenes in films with Barbara Stanwyck. One was in *Remember the Night* and the other was ten years later in *The Furies*. They were directed by Mitchell Leisen and Anthony Mann respectively. In the background here is the always amusing Sterling Holloway, who plays the goofy hired hand Willie.

doting down home mother. Mrs. Sargent worries about his future when he falls in love with the defendant he is prosecuting in a larceny case and brings her home for Christmas to the farm outside Wabash, Indiana, where Mrs. Sargent lives with her unmarried sister Emma and ne'er-do-well hired hand, Willie, played with customary aplomb by Sterling Holloway.

In a perfectly cast film, Aunt Emma was played by Bondi's friend from her days in stock, Elizabeth Patterson. Patterson's career is an interesting parallel to Bondi's. She had been in sound films since 1929, after doing a couple of silents, but never quite reached the eminence of her 14-year younger colleague in the character actress field. In comparison with Bondi, she was only paid $2,500 for her work on *Remember the Night*.[151] This despite the fact that Paramount was Patterson's home studio, where she made a staggering 36 films between 1929 and 1949. In total she acted in nearly 100 films in a career that lasted till 1960, but few of her roles had the size and significance of Bondi's. The high point of Patterson's screen acting was reached when she played Miss Habersham in *Intruder in the Dust* (1949), based on William Faulkner's novel of the same name. She is also well worth watching in *A Bill of Divorcement*; *Go West, Young Man*; *The Cat and the Canary*, *Tobacco Road*, and *Bright Leaf*. Patterson is remembered today as Mrs. Trumbull, the neighbor in 11 episodes of *I Love Lucy* in the mid–1950s.

No doubt Bondi and Patterson spent some of their waiting time on the set reminiscing about their years with the Stuart Walker stock company. Indeed, in a remarkable coincidence, the man himself, Stuart Walker, could have shared in their reminiscences, as he was an associate producer at Paramount at this time.[152] According to columnist Harold W. Cohen, Bondi and Patterson, "a couple of old-timers from the stage," were the only ones to recognize Lillian Gish when she lunched at the Paramount commissary in August 1939.[153] *Remember the Night* was Bondi's only film with Patterson.

In the "good guy drawn in by shady lady" plot, there were similarities to *Rain*, but the setting and atmosphere could not be more different and the denouement in *Remember the Night* was considerably less disastrous. There were shades of *Waterloo Bridge* in the mother's concern for how a potential daughter-in-law's bad reputation will impact on her son's life and career, though, again, homespun Mrs. Sargent could not have been more different from aristocratic Lady Margaret Cronin. Both are basically sympathetic women, who feel they have to play the "heavy" to protect their sons from potential harm. Bondi initially refuses to believe that Stanwyck could ever have stolen anything. In a Mrs. Malaprop moment, she insists that "she's probably a hypochondriac." Later, she puts her foot in it, when she says to Stanwyck in preparation for a bazaar: "Why the men are so tight, you have to pick their…." In her decisive scene with her potential daughter-in-law, after telling her how hard MacMurray has worked to get where he is today, she says subtly: "I don't think we should allow anything to spoil it for him now." As she leaves the room, having attained her goal, she asks: "You do love him, though, don't you?" In 1972, Bondi recalled in a letter that she had always admired Stanwyck and worked well with her, but "thought Barbara was somewhat impersonal when the day's work was finished."[154]

In the Bondi canon, *Remember the Night* is distinguished by being one of two of her films set in her home state of Indiana. By the time Paramount had given the Hoosier state the Hollywood treatment, though, it could have been any rural midwestern community. Bondi's home looks more like a suburban ranch style house than a traditional farmhouse. Despite the vagueness of the setting, Indiana papers approved of Hollywood's efforts to portray their state. The critic for the *Indianapolis Star*, Corbin Patrick, noted with pride:

"Natives will appreciate its tribute to the warm, friendly, homespun brand of hospitality dispensed in a modest Indiana farm home in striking contrast with the cold treatment the characters receive when they find themselves innocently stranded for a night in Pennsylvania."[155]

The film was released in mid–January 1940, but did not open in Valparaiso till Friday, May 10.[156] In connection with the film's release on DVD in 2009, entertainment writer Susan King dubbed *Remember the Night* "the best holiday film you've never heard of."[157]

As the year 1939 and the decade drew to a close, there was yet time to do one more film and a role Bondi wanted desperately to play. Twentieth Century–Fox was filming John Steinbeck's classic novel *The Grapes of Wrath* and Bondi coveted the central role of the family matriarch Ma Joad, a character strongly related to her Melissa Tolliver in *The Trail of the Lonesome Pine*. According to the papers, Bondi was not studio chief Darryl Zanuck's first choice to play the role. "Zanuck is known to have set his heart on Alice for the assignment," wrote columnist Harold Hefferman in early August 1939, Alice being Alice Brady, the daughter of *Street Scene*'s Broadway producer William A. Brady. There were concerns, though, about the state of Brady's health. "If Alice isn't available," Hefferman added, "then the plum will almost certainly fall between Beulah Bondi and Aline MacMahon."[158]

At what would prove the end of her brilliant but all too brief film career, Alice Brady—a hypersophisticated Broadway star and former flibbertigibbet in classic screwball comedies like *Our Man Godfrey*—had scored big as folksy, salt of the earth women in the Fox period dramas *In Old Chicago* and *Young Mr. Lincoln*. She had even won an Oscar for her performance as Molly O'Leary in the epic of the Chicago fire of 1871. By this time, though, Brady had returned to New York to seek treatment for her cancer, which finally killed her on October 28, 1939.

With Brady out of the running, Bondi was tagged as the favorite. Sheilah Grahame wrote in her "Hollywood Today" column on August 10, 1939, that "Walter Brennan will probably be Grampa Joad with Beulah Bondi as Maw Joad."[159] Bondi did two tests for director John Ford, who assured her she was the only one being considered for the role at that point. Bondi became suspicious, though, when the actor who had made the test with her revealed that he had tested with five other actresses. "I knew then that there had been prevarication," Bondi told Frank Aversano in 1979. "I knew instantly that I would not play the role."[160]

On September 7, 1939, Darryl F. Zanuck, vice president in charge of production at Twentieth Century–Fox, wrote her a note that she kept till the end of her days. He thanked her for making a test for *The Grapes of Wrath* and added tersely: "Your test was excellent from the standpoint of performance, but I sincerely feel that from the matter of appearance it did not correctly coincide with the requirements of the role."[161] She had lost the part.

Philip K. Scheuer wrote in his column in the *Los Angeles Times* on Monday, September 11: "The pre-weekend brought news that Ma Joad, keystone in the arch of the family, would be interpreted by motherly Jane Darwell."[162] Darwell was a contract player at Fox and had done no less than 35 films for the studio at this point. She had worked away in small, thankless roles for years, but had also played the leading role in *Star for a Night* (1936). Darwell was ten years older than Bondi. The age difference would not have mattered, but physically the two women were very different. Bondi would later claim that

Darwell was the wrong type: "I don't think Ma Joad should've been so portly, so well fed." Though Ford told her she was "the best one for the role," it turns out he saw things differently.[163] According to his biographer, Scott Eyman, it was Ford who cast the deciding vote for Darwell, because he "wanted something more expansive and more of an earth-mother."[164] Bondi deeply resented being lied to.[165]

She vented some of her spleen in a conversation with Hefferman early in 1940, which prompted him to weigh in on the studio's choice in his Hollywood column: "Many addicts of John Steinbeck's 'Grapes of Wrath' were sorry Beulah Bondi wasn't cast in the Ma Joad mother role of the movie version. She seems to have been born for that particular assignment. Ma was a forlorn, gaunt, hungry-looking picture of misery in the book. But, much to the surprise of Hollywood and a few hundred thousand readers, the ma of the movie turned up as a jolly, well-fed individual—Jane Darwell, a good actress, but in appearance certainly not the sort of person Steinbeck wrote into his fiery pages."[166] It is not difficult to hear Bondi's own point of view being channeled here. She made it clear in another interview from 1940 that, though she had "spent three days at a migratory camp getting the 'feeling' for her test," she "didn't begrudge [Darwell] the part." She added magnanimously: "I think Jane Darwell was magnificent in 'The Grapes of Wrath.'"[167]

Undoubtedly, playing Ma Joad would have been a brilliant capstone to Bondi's 1930s film career. Instead, losing the role made the decade end on a sour note. It did not help matters that Jane Darwell won an Academy Award for her performance. To judge from the number of times Bondi reverted to this episode in later life, it was her most negative experience, maybe the only really negative experience she had during her more than three decades in the movie industry. Her final word on the matter was: "Nothing good ever came of a lie."[168]

# 6

# Bondi's War

## *1940–1945*

"I watch people and wonder what shaped them, what happened? I don't sit in judgment. I'm just interested in humanity."[1]

The first important event in Bondi's life of the new year and the new decade was signing to play Myrtle Webb in the filmatization of Thornton Wilder's Pulitzer Prize-winning drama *Our Town*.[2] Mrs. Webb is the wife of the Grover's Corners newspaper editor Charles Webb and the mother of Emily and Wally Webb. According to producer Sol Lesser, who had paid Wilder $45,000 for the screen rights, Bondi was the only actress considered for the role.[3]

*Our Town* had opened at Henry Miller's Theater in New York on February 4, 1938, and stayed there and at the Morosco Theater for 336 performances. The role of Mrs. Webb was originated by Helen Carew and her neighbor Julia Gibbs was played on the stage by Evelyn Varden, who would be in *Hilda Crane* with Bondi on Broadway in 1950. These two classic turn-of-the-last-century middle-class wife and mother roles went to Bondi, then, and to Fay Bainter, a former Broadway star and top-tier character actress in Hollywood since 1936. She had been nominated and won an Academy Award for Best Actress in a Supporting Role for *Jezebel* in 1939, beating Bondi for *Of Human Hearts*. This was one of the more inexplicable votes of the Academy, surely, but Bainter was a fine actress, who was also nominated for *White Banners* in the leading actress category in the same year as *Jezebel*; and for her final film, the 1961 remake of *The Children's Hour*, where she played Amelia Tilford.

Only Martha Scott, who made her Broadway and screen debut as Emily Webb; Frank Craven as the narrator and the druggist Mr. Martin; and Doro Merande as Mrs. Soames reprised their stage roles in the film version. Fellow character actress Merande, born in 1892 in Kansas, bore a superficial resemblance to Bondi and a strong one to Margaret Hamilton. She followed a different career path than either of them, though, sticking with the stage and basing herself in New York, where she lived for years at 119 E. 39th St., right across the street from the Tuscany Hotel, where Bondi stayed during the run of *The Late Christopher Bean*. Merande would show up again in *The Snake Pit*, but was little used in Hollywood. Like Bondi, she never married. Mrs. Soames in *Our Town* was her signature role ("Oh, I do love a wedding, don't you?").

The film version of *Our Town*, which went into production in mid–January 1940, was directed by Sam Wood, produced by Sol Lesser's independent production company, and released through United Artists on May 24, 1940. The author himself adapted the play for the screen with the help of Harry Chandlee and Frank Craven, who was also a playwright. In fact, Bondi had done three of Craven's plays during her stock company days in the 1920s. The role of Bondi's husband, Mr. Webb, was played in the film by Guy Kibbee and the Webbs' neighbor Dr. Gibbs was played by Thomas Mitchell. In the central role of George Gibbs, created on Broadway by Frank Craven's son John Craven, we find William Holden.

At 27, goggle-eyed Martha Scott was a little long in the tooth to be playing a high school girl. It was not easy either having to compete with blazing beauty of William Holden at 21. As one columnist pointed out: "She hasn't beauty ... but she has everything else."[4] While the leads were new to Bondi, she had what amounted to an old school reunion with director Wood (*Christopher Bean*), cinematographer Bert Glennon (*Bad Boy*), and the other major cast members: Kibbee (*Rain, Of Human Hearts, Mr. Smith Goes to Washington*), Bainter (*Make Way for Tomorrow*), Mitchell (*Make Way for Tomorrow, Mr. Smith Goes to Washington*), Merande (*Bad Boy*), and Stuart Erwin (*The Stranger's Return*), who played the ubiquitous milkman Howie Newsom. Hollywood was beginning to feel like home.

Bondi gives one of her best wife and mother performances in *Our Town* and is completely convincing in the role. She has two particularly good scenes: the first with her friend and neighbor, Julia Gibbs (Bainter), where the latter dreams of selling a family heirloom to finance a trip to Paris, France with her husband; and one with her daughter Emily, who wants to know if she is pretty enough "to get people interested" in her. When Emily keeps harping on the question of her own physical attractiveness, her mother finally utters her best line in the film, which is taken verbatim from the play: "You're pretty enough for all normal purposes." The reviewer for the *Boston Globe* wrote after world premiere of the film in that city on May 23, 1940: "Beulah Bondi ... gives a brilliant and true portrayal, particularly in the emotional scenes with her daughter."[5]

Even in intimate conversational scenes, Mrs. Webb is always doing things: stringing beans, shelling peas or unraveling yarn. As to the realism of Bondi's and Bainter's technique, Craven pointed out to Hedda Hopper when she visited the set: "They're not acting, they're living those parts. They're stringing beans, their hands look as if they've done that kind of work. Nails broken down without polish."[6] In the film, Mrs. Webb lends her voice to the small church choir with Mrs. Gibbs and Mrs. Soames. According to one news article, the actors did their own vocal work in the film and practiced singing hymns a full day before the choir scene was shot, but another article revealed that Bainter had refused to sing and was "dubbed in by the sound department."[7] Speaking of voices, maybe the most striking part of Bondi's characterization here is the use of her highest, driest register, shrill as a whistle, especially when she calls the children down to breakfast. Bondi looks handsome with her thick black hair rolled up on either side of her oval face in a becoming turn-of-the-last-century style.

*Our Town* was as close to experimental as Bondi's films got, with expressionist camera angles, lighting, and music, especially in the scenes with the town's troubled drunkard and choir director, Simon Stimson. It was a timely reminder of the play's themes, that the actor who played Stimson, 44-year-old Philip Wood, died of a heart attack just as the production was winding up in early March 1940.[8] The score by modernist master Aaron Copeland is simply beautiful, as is the set design by legendary designer William Cameron Menzies.

As an adaptation of an instant modern classic, *Our Town* begins and develops well.

For anyone who knows and loves the original play, though, where Emily dies in childbirth in the third act and returns to relive her twelfth birthday, it is hard to see the tacked on happy ending of the film as anything but a cop out. Wilder surprisingly bowed to pressure to let Emily live and to pretend that the entire previous segment depicting her death, burial, and afterlife was only a bad dream, a feverish vision. According to film critic Robin Coons, Wilder "warmly approved the change." Wilder's rationale for this about face, as he told producer Lesser in one of the 41 letters and 18 telegrams they exchanged during production, was that "on the stage Emily was a figure in an allegory, her death a fact to be accepted, as death must be accepted by all. In the film, Emily has become a human being, known and loved by the audience. To have let her die here would have been needlessly cruel."[9] Lesser explained to a group of journalists who visited the set: "There is so much sadness in the world today. If people leave the theatre feeling sorry that Emily had to die so young, the picture might be too depressing. We tried both endings at out-of-the-way-theatres, and got this reaction."[10]

As newspaper editor's wife and mother of two, Myrtle Webb in *Our Town* (Sol Lesser, 1940), Bondi was playing a woman of her mother's generation, while her screen daughter Emily Webb (Martha Scott) belonged to Bondi's own generation. Though set in New Hampshire, Grover's Corners was not unlike Valparaiso, Indiana, in size and demographics. Thus, this classic example of early twentieth-century Americana gives us a vivid impression of what Bondi's upbringing in a quiet college town would have been like. Bondi, though, never met a George Gibbs; or, if she did, she did not marry him.

Despite the botched ending, Bosley Crowther, who would give many of Bondi's films of the 1940s short shrift, was highly enamored of the film. He described it as "a picture which utilizes the fullest prerogatives of the camera to participate as a recognized witness to a simple dramatic account of people's lives." Crowther did not directly address the change in the ending, but it was warmly approved of by other critics. Wood Soanes, for example, while recognizing that the change was "a concession to the moviegoer's persistent demand for happy endings," thought it "a concession that is critically sound." Robin Coons thought it was a "gratifying departure" from the original.[11] Thornton Wilder sent Bondi a telegram from Orlando, Florida, before the premiere: "I was proud when they told me you'd be in it and now I'm happier than ever. A thousand thanks."[12]

In early April 1940, the census was taken. The record shows Bondi living with her 79-year-old mother Eva at 14412 Greenleaf

Street in Sherman Oaks, a home she rented for $238 a month. Also living with them was Ada Bertrand, their 38-year-old, widowed African American maid, who hailed from Colorado. Despite having worked in films for nearly a decade, Bondi is listed as "actress theatrical." The census also shows that she was paid $27,000 for 12 weeks work in 1939, while Bertrand worked the entire year for $780. Bondi, who would turn 51 on May 3, gave her age as 46.[13] Bondi had lived in this relatively small home covered in white shingles and stucco since about 1935. It stood in lushly landscaped grounds with a tennis court, swimming pool, summer house of lath covered with red rambler roses, rock garden, and four fish pools. The guest room and her mother's room were downstairs, and Bondi's "suite" of rooms upstairs. In 1940, she had many paintings on display by her friend, the Mexican painter and muralist Alfredo Ramos Martinez (1871–1946).[14]

In this candid from 1940, part of a publicity campaign designed by the press agent Louis J. Allemann, Bondi is seen at the front door of her Sherman Oaks home. She lived at 14412 Greenleaf St. from about 1935 till 1941. Her mother Eva lived with her until her death in 1941. Bondi then moved to Hollywood and a Spanish Revival house in Whitley Heights, which would be her home for 40 years.

The only time there is room for a lot of character actresses in a classic Hollywood film is if it is set in an old age home, a school, or a convent. The "Grandma" segment of *If I Had a Million*, starring May Robson, is one classic example, but *The Captain Is a Lady* goes it one better. On paper, it looks very promising. Beulah Bondi, Helen Broderick, Billie Burke, Cecil Cunningham, Marjorie Main, *and* Helen Westley, all in one film! How can it go wrong? Well, it does. So much talent, so much experience, used to so little effect.

*The Captain Is a Lady* was the second of Bondi's "starring" vehicles, though here, as in *Make Way for Tomorrow*, she had to take second place in the billing to her male co-star. Charles Coburn had been in Hollywood since the mid–1930s, after spending more than three decades on Broadway. He would come into his own in the 1940s, with three Academy Award nominations and a win for *The More the Merrier* in 1943. We recall that Coburn had been paired with Bondi previously—and more successfully, I might add—in *Vivacious Lady*. This was quite a different setting, a small harbor town called Glousterport; and a more modest socio-economic background for the married couple they played: the captain of the title, Abe Peabody, and his devoted wife Angie.

The film's starting point was similar to *Make Way for Tomorrow*, with the elderly couple losing their home of 30 years and wondering where they will go and how they will stay together. The nearest old age home is only for "ladies," and that is how Abe becomes "Old Lady 31," the title of the 1909 novel by Louise Forsslund and the 1916 play by Rachel Crothers on which the film was based. Despite the intriguing title, let me hasten to disappoint those who have not seen the film, that *The Captain Is a Lady* is no pioneering exploration of transgender identity or early equal rights manifesto. This has not prevented modern writers from claiming that Coburn dresses as a woman to get into the home.[15] That would have been something to see and might have livened things up considerably, but unfortunately there is not a stitch of cross-dressing in the film.

After initial opposition from some of the residents, Abe is able to move in with Angie and the plot really gets rolling when the presence of one man among so many women leads to jealousy, gossip, and intrigue. All through this, Bondi is Coburn's ever faithful, devoted, and hopeful "angel in the house." Coburn is not at his best trying to be folksy and "just one of the boys," even when he spends at least as much time trying to be one of the girls. In fact, no one is at their best in this sentimental, cliché-ridden claptrap, least of all Bondi, who is mired in a type of all-forgiving, all-trusting, totally passive role, where she can do nothing for herself, but trust in providence and her improvident, bungling moron of a husband. There is no old lady drag here, so Angie seems too young to be in an old age home and much younger than Abe.

Billie Burke, as a resident with an unlikely romantic interest in a toupee-challenged Clem Bevans, does not look like someone who needs to be in a home either. At age 55, she was five years older than Bondi. As Blossy Stort, she supports Helen Broderick's motion to admit Abe to the home and even offers the Peabodys her double room. Broderick, as former actress Nancy Crocker, becomes Abe's drinking buddy and Pinochle partner. One news item reported that she thought she was "the baby of the troupe," only to discover "to her horror that Beulah Bondi was younger."[16] She was not. In fact, Bondi turned 51 during the shoot and Broderick was only 48.

Cecil Cunningham, a well-to-do widow in full dowager regalia, and her sidekick, Marjorie Main, who is paying her way at the home by cooking, are initially against admitting Abe to the home, but then change their minds. Cunningham was 51 and Main was 50. All these vigorous women look as if they need to be in a home about as much as Jane Fonda. In fact, at age 65, Helen Westley is the only one who looks old enough to be in a home and she is the one running it! There are, though, a bunch of genuinely elderly extras and "under fives," who sit around or totter about, creating an appropriately aged atmosphere. One of them is puckish, height-challenged Dorothea Wolbert, who, like Bondi, had her scenes deleted from *The Painted Veil*.

It was a quick and intense shoot at MGM between April 18 and May 9, 1940, under the direction of 35-year-old Robert B. Sinclair.[17] This was Bondi's only film with Broderick, Cunningham, and Westley, who died 1942. Burke had been in *Finishing School* (1934) and would show up again in *Breakfast in Hollywood* (1946), though she and Bondi had no significant interaction there. Main was soon to join Bondi on the *Shepherd of the Hills* set at Paramount, where she played a blind grandmother who regains her sight. Bondi said of working on *The Captain Is a Lady* at the time, that they had had "so much fun on the set": "'Miss Westley, an old trouper, can say the naughtiest things while looking completely innocent.'"[18] Sometimes fun on the sound stage does not translate into fun on the screen.

As production on *The Captain Is a Lady* came to a close in May 1940, Bondi had to turn her attention to other pressing matters. I teasingly mentioned in the previous chapter, that when Bondi's uncle, Louis Bondy, died in the summer of 1937, she inherited $30,000. It was not quite as simple as that, as the dispositions of Louis's 1933 will gave rise to a court case that would not be decided until three and a half years after his death. The cause of the conflict was that Louis had left his estate equally to his sister Rose Hirschman and to his brother Abram Bondy. As we recall, Abram predeceased him, and the fault on Louis's part was that he never updated his will to indicate what he wanted to happen to the half of his estate he had left to his brother. Should it go to his brother's widow? Should it go to Abram's two children? Should it be divided equally between all his living blood relatives? This is the stuff that lawsuits are made of.

The branch of the Bondy family that had not been mentioned in the will, the four surviving children of Louis's long deceased sister Estelle Bondy Flexner, saw an opportunity to share in the inheritance. According to the *Vidette-Messenger*, they were "attacking the will on the ground that they are entitled to a portion by reason of the fact that L.D. Bondy died intestate as to the clause in the will devising one-half of the residue of the estate to A.O. Bondy." Beulah Bondi, her brother Raymond, aunt Rose Hirschman and Rose's daughter Leola Sure, on the other hand, were contending that "by reason of A.O. Bondy's death, Mrs. Hirschman is entitled to all the residue of the estate."[19]

This was a noble stance on the part of Bondi and her brother, but maybe they felt that Rose needed the money more than they did. Louis was a rich man and a substantial property holder in Valparaiso. His estate was estimated to be worth between $75,000 and $100,000, so the stakes were high for most of his relatives, who had modest or average incomes.[20] For Bondi, of course, the situation was different, being at this point probably even richer than her late uncle. But she had a clear sense of right and wrong and a clear idea of where Uncle Louis's money should go, and it was not to her older first cousins Vivian Flexner, Cora Rhode, Olive Power, and Aimee Flexner.

The oldest and the youngest Flexner cousins, Vivian who was 64 and Aimee who was 55, were both unmarried, though Aimee spent more than 20 years living with another woman, Carolyn H. Rich. Both Vivian and Aimee worked as legal stenographers their entire lives. By 1940, they had lived in Portland, Oregon, for more than 30 years. Cora Flexner Rhode, born in 1877, had also worked all her life, as a stenographer, clerk, and executive in the military, and had been married to private investigator Carl A. Rhode for 40 years. They lived in Chicago and had no children. Finally, there was Bondi's most original and intrepid cousin Olive, born in St. Louis in 1880, who had made a career of "marrying up." By 1940, she was a widow; her fourth and final husband, Harold Morgan Power, from a wealthy Placer county, California family, having died in the Philippines in 1936. Sixty-year-old Olive Flexner Power was now living in Portland, near her sisters. Bondi herself turned 51 just a week before the case came up for trial.

I could be wrong, but my impression is that Bondi was not close to the Flexner branch of the family, even before the estate case put an added strain on the family ties. As I have indicated, the roots of this estrangement may have gone all the way back to the separation of Gabriel and Mary Bondy in the 1870s. It may have been exacerbated by Abram's decision to marry Eva Marble, who was a Presbyterian, back in 1882. Both Abram's sisters had married within the faith and Louis, of course, had not married at all.

Nearly three years after Louis D. Bondy's death, then, it was finally time for the case to be tried. It came up before Judge Mark B. Rockwell on Friday, May 10, 1940, the day after production ended on *The Captain Is a Lady* and, as it happened, the day *Remember the Night* opened at the Premier cinema in Valparaiso.[21] Bondi was probably more focused on the trial. The 63-year-old judge was a farmer's son from Pennsylvania, who had originally come to study law at Valparaiso University in 1902, stayed on to practice law in the city, and had been on the bench of the Porter County Superior Court since 1931. He lived at 605 Lincolnway, just two houses down from the old Roessler house at no. 601, which had been turned into apartments by this time, and next door to the Benton house at no. 607.[22]

Though Rockwell heard the opposing arguments in May, he did not render a ruling until Friday, November 30, 1940. In his ruling, "the death of Abraham O. Bondy prior to the death of Louis D. Bondy, the part of the residue of the estate that would have been inherited by Abraham O. Bondy became intestate property and goes to the next of kin."[23] This meant that Rose Hirschman, in addition to the half the estate she had already inherited, received one third of A.O. Bondy's half, while Beulah and Raymond received one third together, and the four daughters of Estelle Bondy Flexner one third together.[24] By this point, though, "the residue of the estate which was in controversy" had been reduced in value to about $20,000, still a lot of money at the time. As a comparison, the judge presiding over the case had an annual income of $4,200 in 1939.[25] Carl Rhode had earned $1,950. None of the Flexner sisters reported any income to the census enumerator, though Vivian and Aimee were working full-time as stenographers. Bondi had earned $27,000 in 1939.

No one was happy with the ruling, so the various parties involved filed a motion for a retrial on December 28, 1940, on the basis that the ruling was "contrary to law" and "not supported by the evidence."[26] At the time of the ruling, Judge Rockwell himself had "informed attorneys that he would like to see the case appealed to a higher court."[27] The end of the story, though, is that the request for a retrial was withdrawn in early 1941, so the parties must have decided to abide by the judge's decision or reached some other form of agreement.[28] Several of the heirs would not have long to enjoy their legacies. Bondi's Aunt Rose, her daughter Leora, and Bondi's cousin Aimee Flexner all died during the next three and a half years. Judge Rockwell retired from the bench due to ill health in 1944 and died from the effects of a stroke two years later.[29]

Even without any filming, the summer of 1940, the first summer of the war, was unusually busy for Bondi. She had three movies in the theaters all through the summer: *Remember the Night, Our Town,* and *The Captain Is a Lady. Our Town* was released in May and producer Lesser kept her busy promoting the film. Even before the film's release, there was a radio broadcast on May 6 with the major cast reprising their roles.[30] On May 23, there was a gala premiere at two Boston movie theaters with Bondi, Frank Craven, Guy Kibbee, Fay Bainter, Thornton Wilder, producer Lesser, and composer Aaron Copeland in attendance and interviews via a radio hook-up outside the Loew's State Theatre. The mayor of Boston and the governors of both New Hampshire and Massachusetts hosted receptions for their fellow New England governors and local business leaders. On the evening of the premiere, autograph seekers halted traffic on Arlington St. and Massachusetts Ave., outside the Ritz-Carlton hotel, where the celebratory dinner was held, and also outside the movie theaters. To the premiere, Bondi wore a black "Spanish matador" style jacket with gold braiding down the arms, under it "a dinner gown of rose and beige," and had her hair pulled back from her face.[31] It was "raining cats and dogs."[32] Bondi was escorted to all the social events by New Hampshire governor Francis P.

Murphy, a Republican born in 1877, who was the 64th governor of his state from 1937 till 1941 and, upon his death in 1958, still the only Roman Catholic to be elected to that office in New Hampshire.[33]

Bondi intended to visit with her friends in New England after the Boston premiere and stayed with the landscape artist Robert Strong Woodward (1885–1957) at Shelburne Falls, before she was suddenly called back to do retakes on *The Captain Is a Lady*. She hopped on the first plane to Los Angeles, worked all day and all night on the retakes, went to sleep for 24 hours at her home in Van Nuys, and then flew back to Boston. There she was reported to be having "the time of her life."[34]

On Saturday, June 8, 1940, Bondi and her mother flew from New York to Miami to attend Raymond Bondy's wedding to Frances Miller Cadle, an elementary school teacher born in Minnesota, but a long-term resident of Florida. The wedding took place at 4:30 p.m. on Sunday at the home of Mrs. Charles S. Ewing, 4501 Prairie Ave., with the Rev. Frank E. Harlow of the Boulevard Christian church performing the ceremony, followed by a reception. Raymond's daughter and son-in-law were also among the guests.[35] Raymond was 56, while the bride was about 40 and had a 14-year-old daughter from a previous marriage.

Duty called again and Bondi was needed for a personal appearance in New York. She stayed in her usual suite at the Lombardy Hotel at 111 E. 56th St., that she had not occupied in five years.[36] On Thursday, June 13, 1940, at 11 a.m. Bondi and Fay Bainter were named honorary mayors of the model village "Town of Tomorrow" at the World's Fair in New York.[37] During a stay in New York that allowed plenty of time for shopping and seeing old friends, Bondi even found time to spend the day people watching at Coney Island. Legendary columnist Walter Winchell observed "Fay Bainter and Beulah Bondi trading smiles with Mayor LaGuardia at the British Buttery—oomph begins at 40."[38]

Another major event of the summer was that Bondi hired a New York publicist, Louis J. Allemann, who had offices at 200 W. 54th St.[39] Allemann's major effort as Bondi's publicist was putting out two issues of the "Beulah Bondi Bulletin." The first, August issue was a lavish, 14-page, magazine-size publication with dozens of recent candid photographs and press articles Allemann was hoping newspapers would carry or at least quote from. A note reads: "Mats or glossy prints will be sent without cost on request." The first issue of the bulletin was sent to 3,000 motion picture editors and columnists in daily and Sunday newspapers across the United States.[40] On September 11, 1940, Allemann wrote to his client: "Thanks millions for trying to get me some other accounts. A RICH actress would be all right, but rich or poor, if they are just half as nice and wonderful as you I would be glad to have them."[41] Their collaboration only lasted till November 1940.[42]

While in New York, Bondi got an invitation from her *Captain Is a Lady* co-star Charles Coburn to star as Mrs. Wiggs, "the cabbage patch optimist," in *Mrs. Wiggs of the Cabbage Patch*, the opening play of the Mohawk Drama Festival at Union College in Schenectady, New York. This role had been created by Madge Carr Cook on Broadway back in 1904 and had been played by Pauline Lord in a rare screen appearance in 1934. The play and the seven-week festival, which had been co-founded by Coburn in 1935 and was still being overseen by him, opened on Tuesday, July 16, 1940. Percy Kilbride played the role of Mr. Stubbins, the comic bachelor character played by W.C. Fields in the first sound film version.[43] The play ran till Saturday, July 20 and was followed by Cornelia Otis Skinner in *Biography*.[44]

On July 31, 1940, Bondi arrived in Valparaiso for a brief, surprise visit "to spend a

Bondi and her two-time screen husband Charles Coburn are seen here at the Mohawk Drama Festival, which he had founded and directed at Union College in Schenectady, New York, in July 1940. Coburn, who was a dozen years older than Bondi, had lost his beloved wife Ivah Wills Coburn in 1937. Bondi's close female friends hoped in vain that there might be some real life romantic potential in their professional relationship. When Coburn finally remarried in 1959, he chose a wife many years his junior and fathered his seventh child in his eighties.

few hours dining and chatting with friends." She came on from Chicago and brought a friend, Maida Butler, of that city. Born in Lincoln, Nebraska, in 1892, Maida was a housewife, whose husband Albert worked in advertising. She had two grown daughters.[45] Floy Brownell held a "steak fry" at her Colonial Revival home at 703 Washington St., so Bondi could more easily meet people. The guests included such old friends as Marie Windle, Anadell Lowenstine, Louise Bartholomew, and Ada Bartholomew. Later, they were joined by their husbands and children, including mayor C.L. Bartholomew, who gave Bondi the keys to the city. The *Vidette-Messenger* wrote: "today the children of these friends are telling their pals 'I saw a real movie actress last night.'" Bondi planned to leave for Los Angeles on Sunday and expected to begin a new picture on September 1. The party was over by 9:30 p.m. She was given a police escort with sirens blaring on her way out of town and back to Chicago.[46]

Having spent the better part of the summer on the east coast, it was time to return home for her next film. Henry Hathaway's *The Shepherd of the Hills* was an unabashed and, most would agree, ultimately unsuccessful attempt to rekindle the flame of his hit film *The Trail of the Lonesome Pine*, produced in 1935 and released in 1936. Including the director and Bondi, 15 members of the cast and crew worked on both films at Paramount; *The Shepherd of the Hills* being in production there between early September and mid–November 1940. Bondi must have looked forward to her guiding spirit and mentor from her stock company days, Stuart Walker, being the producer of the film. Sadly, Walker had to retire due to ill health in July 1940 and was replaced by William LeBaron during pre-production, whom in turn was replaced by Jack Moss.[47] Columnist Harold W. Cohen simply noted, that Walker had "checked off the Paramount lot."[48] On March 13, 1941, Walker died of cerebral thrombosis and hypostatic pneumonia at his home at 824 N. Whitter Dr. in Beverly Hills. He was 61 years old.[49]

Like *The Trail of the Lonesome Pine*, *The Shepherd of the Hills* was in Technicolor and involved location shooting in the same part of the San Bernardino National Forest. It was Bondi's second color film. For Bondi, though, there was a big difference from *Trail* in that, this time, she would be symbolizing the negative forces at work in her Ozark mountain clan and community, rather than the positive ones. It is as if her character Mollie Matthews is the negative alter ego of Melissa Tolliver or is what Melissa might have turned into under different circumstances. Bondi plays the hard-hearted, superstitious, vengeful, and suspicious matriarch of the Matthews clan and the aunt of protagonist and anti-hero "Young Matt" Matthews (John Wayne). According to Grandma Becky (Marjorie Main donning the old lady drag this time), "her soul's et up with hate." Mollie tirelessly tries to place the blame on others for her own misdeeds and ceaselessly spurs her menfolk on to remove the curse on the family by avenging the wrong that has been done to them. The wrong done was that Sarah, Bondi's sister and Wayne's unwed mother, was impregnated by a man, who then disappeared.

Mollie's most important plot function is to sell Sarah's abandoned property, "Moaning Meadow," for $1,000 to Daniel Howitt (Harry Carey), a stranger who inveigles himself into the community, without discussing it with her nephew. Not surprisingly, Mr. Howitt turns out to be Sarah's former lover and Young Matt's long lost father, who was in prison for killing a man and did not even know Sarah was pregnant. For once, being jailed for manslaughter turns out to be a useful excuse!

This was Bondi's only film with James Barton, famous for portraying Jeeter Lester in the record-breaking Broadway production of *Tobacco Road*. Here he portrayed her weak, downtrodden husband, who finally has had enough and lets rip at his wife in a torrent of recrimination and invective. The turning point for Mollie comes when she accidentally shoots and mortally wounds her own disabled son Pete (Marc Lawrence). This happens in a scuffle, where Pete tries to prevent Young Matt from killing his father, by now a respected and beloved member of the community known as "the Shepherd of the Hills." Harry Carey has the spiritually uplifting role here, that Bondi had in *The Trail of the Lonesome Pine*, while Bondi embodies the negative forces that were not symbolized by any single character in *Trail*, but distributed among most of the backwoods folk. When Pete dies, Mollie is driven mad with grief and makes a flaming circle of kerosene all around his body, which soon engulfs the wooden cabin obliterating both of them.

If nothing else, *The Shepherd of the Hills* inspired one of the most amusingly satirical reviews ever written of one of Bondi's films. I only wish I had the space to quote it in its entirety. According to Harold V. Cohen, "the movies have seldom committed a more dreary libel on the good, respectable moonshiners of the mountain country." He adds that the "the actors get in the way of the scenery, and the story gets in the way of the actors. Unfortunately, nobody got in the way of the picture and it's at the Penn." As for our subject of interest: "Miss Beulah Bondi is properly mean and nasty as the old hag who fuels the ancient feud with frequent if terribly uninspired declamations of vengeance."[50]

Other critics were willing to take the film and Bondi's performance seriously. The *Akron Beacon Journal* wrote: "Beulah Bondi's performance as the vengeful aunt, hiding her own frailties in a campaign of murder, has the film's strongest role and plays it well and lending conviction to the warped quality of mind and soul she is asked to portray." According to the *Honolulu Advertiser*: "Beulah Bondi is an able exponent of the witch type and is frighteningly realistic." Yet the *New York Times* concluded: "Paramount has wasted the talents of some excellent actors in the film."[51] Bondi was one of them. To see what she really could do with a warped and twisted rural matriarch, it is better to watch her in William A. Wellman's misunderstood masterpiece *Track of the Cat* from 1954.

When Bondi stepped onto the set of *Penny Serenade* at Columbia in November 1940, it was two years since she and director George Stevens had started on *Vivacious Lady* together at RKO.[52] The stars this time were Cary Grant and Irene Dunne, who previously had been paired to such fine effect in Leo McCarey's classic romantic comedy *The Awful Truth* (1937) and more recently in *My Favorite Wife* (1940). *Penny Serenade* was an entirely different and more lachrymose film in which Grant plays Roger Adams, a somewhat difficult and impulsive newspaper man, who buys a small local newspaper; and Dunne his hard-tried wife Julie. The main part of the film is narrated as a series of flashbacks, where Julie listens to records from their romance and marriage before intending to leave her husband and home forever.

Even before Julie meets and marries Roger, it is her fondest wish to have a child. She loses the child she is carrying during an earthquake in Tokyo and learns not long afterwards, when the couple has returned to San Francisco, that she will not be able to have another. Enter Bondi as Miss Oliver, the head of the Child Placement Bureau in the city, who helps the Adamses find a child to adopt. Miss Oliver is a wonderful role in which an apparently unmarried woman lives vicariously through the Adamses and makes them feel as if the baby they receive is meant especially for them. She first appears 48 minutes into the two-hour film and has seven scenes in total. Bondi looks very slim and trim here in tailored suits and fancy, unconventional hats. She wears pince-nez, which she keeps taking off and putting on, as she did as Dr. Schultz in *The Good Fairy*.

Among the five professional women Bondi portrayed, Miss Oliver is the most interesting, with Miss Van Alstyne in *Finishing School* coming in second. The difference between them, apart from their character traits, is their function. As we have seen, Miss Oliver is a helper, while Miss Van Alstyne is a "harmer"; that is, Miss Oliver tries to assist the protagonists in obtaining their goal, while Miss Van Alstyne creates obstacles to the heroine's pursuit of happiness, which in a romantic comedy, even one with dark undertones, means happiness in marriage. In her "helper" role in *Penny Serenade*, Miss Oliver has a male counterpart in Edgar Buchanan as Applejack, the Adamses' trusty, crusty unmarried male friend, who works as a printer at the newspaper. The credits read "With Beulah Bondi and Edgar Buchanan." Credits like "With so and so" can be a status marker for an actor, but it can also be a way of sugaring the pill of being pushed further down the credit list. As it happens, in this film Bondi was billed third and Buchanan fourth, though his is the larger role.

Personally, I find *Penny Serenade* curiously claustrophobic, with its obsessive focus on Grant and Dunne, to the near total exclusion of any other characters. Even Bondi and Buchanan have little in the way of a backstory. As Boyd Martin pointed out: "Edgar Buchanan, as an old printer, and Beulah Bondi seem to be the only important supporting players in a cast composed almost entirely of the two stars."[53] Yet I am fascinated by Bondi's performance here, because I imagine that in playing Miss Oliver she is revealing more of her own personality than in any other film role. Indeed, I wonder if this was not the character most similar to Bondi's own appearance, style, and demeanor in real life. Outwardly, they have things in common: two unmarried women of a certain age, totally

Bondi often made a point of how she never played herself in films; that she always hid her own personality in her characterizations. Nevertheless, I imagine the closest she ever came to playing a woman not unlike herself was in creating the adoption agency worker Miss Oliver in *Penny Serenade* (Columbia, 1941). There is something about the way Miss Oliver looks and behaves, that reminds me of Bondi's own appearance and demeanor *in propria persona. Penny Serenade* suffers from a claustrophobic focus on its two stars, Irene Dunne and Cary Grant, but Bondi has her moments and was billed third for her efforts. The item she is holding in her hand is her pince-nez, which she uses to great effect in the film.

wrapped up in their work; elegant, even chic. Inwardly too, we see similarities: the serenity, the warm sympathy; a note of sternness or command, if necessary; self-containment, reticence, and sensitivity to shocks and strong impressions; a suggestion of shyness; a certain degree of conventionality, but no cant or prudishness; a desire to please. This is how a journalist described Bondi in 1932, when she was 43: "She is one of the foremost exponents of charm, possessing the prerequisites that are commonly considered to determine woman's power to attract. She is chic without being obvious, delightfully refreshing and intelligent, with a wit and humor that would cause any man to be hard put to recall that she portrays grandmothers in most of her work before the camera."[54] Bondi herself insisted that "no one has ever seen the real Beulah Bondi on stage or screen."[55]

*New York Times* critic Bosley Crowther failed to capture the full effect of her performance in *Penny Serenade* in his low-key comment that "Beulah Bondi is sensible as an orphanage matron," though he does add the word "heart-warming" to his brief description. Edna B. Lawson described her performance somewhat better, when she wrote: "Beulah Bondi is excellent as the fairy godmother from the orphanage. Her character is a combination of institutional propriety and instinctive kindliness."[56] As Miss Oliver, Bondi is more than these things, though. She is luminous.

For Bondi, the busy year 1940 came to a close with a vacation on a ranch in the Mojave Desert, playing Edison's mother in a radio broadcast of "Young Tom Edison" with Mickey Rooney on *Radio Theater*, praise for her Christmas card being the "cutest" from columnist Ed Sullivan, and *Shepherd of the Hills* director Henry Hathaway calling her "the greatest character actress in Hollywood."[57]

The year of 1941 would turn out to be one of the most difficult years of Bondi's life. Granted, her life was devoid of tragedy, but it was no doubt a challenge for her to lose the one individual who had meant the most to her development and given her the most emotional support throughout the 52 years of her life. Eva Bondy had turned 80 on January 19 the previous year. For the five years since her husband's death, she had lived quietly with her daughter in Sherman Oaks, occasionally visiting old friends and looking after her properties in Valparaiso and also staying in close touch with her son Raymond and his family in Florida.

Eva was particularly keen to keep up with the activities of the Valparaiso Woman's Club, which had been such an important part of her life. In 1939, she sent a special letter to be read at the celebration of the cancelling of the club's debt, reminding them that the Sarah Porter Kinsey Memorial was the only club house in Indiana bearing a woman's name.[58] On October 17, 1940, at the 30th annual convention of the Tenth district of Indiana federation of Women's clubs in Brookston, Indiana, Eva Bondy had been awarded a medal for "having served the longest in federation work in the district." She was not present to receive the award.[59]

Eva lived to hear the judge's long delayed ruling in the Bondy estate case and shared in the final decision to withdraw the motion for a retrial in early 1941. *Penny Serenade* was released on April 24, 1941, and was Bondi's final film to open while her mother was still alive. In early May, Eva Bondy had a cerebral hemorrhage. She had been suffering from chronic arteriosclerosis for three years.[60] In late May, Bondi wrote to her friend Stella Spooner in Valparaiso about her mother's stroke and gradually worsening condition.[61] Uremia set in not long after and Eva Susanna Marble Bondy died on Monday, June 9, 1941, at 12:15 a.m. at her and her daughter's home in Sherman Oaks. Her death certificate listed her occupation as "poet."[62]

Eva Marble Bondy's memorial service was held on Thursday, June 12 at 3 p.m. at Pierce Bros. Valley Chapel, 6153 Van Nuys Blvd.[63] Her cremated body had already been, in the words of her pastor, "Unostentatiously ... returned to the elements from which it came." He told the mourners present at the ceremony that "it was her wish that we meet without her outworn body being present. She never allowed its facilities to imprison her spirit. She was ever reluctant to acknowledge its restrictions. Though it housed her for more than fourscore years, it never mastered her." Gordon Chapman also said of her: "she found in her heart none of the narrowness that makes bondslaves of some of us. The Bible was but one of God's voices. Her sensitive soul found the voice of the Divine where others passed unseeing by."[64] On June 20, Eva Bondy was memorialized at the annual meeting of the Valparaiso Woman's Club, including a written remembrance from her pastor in Los Angeles.[65]

After her mother's death, Bondi gave up her house in Sherman Oaks and lived for a time at 6754 Wedgewood Place in Whitley Heights, just down the street from Louise Closser Hale's former home.[66] By October 1942, she had moved to a house in the same neighborhood, where she would live for the remainder of her life.[67] 6660 Whitley Terrace is 2,726 square foot, two bedroom, four bathroom Spanish Revival home built in 1926, that, outwardly at least, looks little changed since Bondi lived there. Its street frontage is chiefly distinguished by a large, squat, round tower. The walls are white stucco and the roof is tiled in red. According to one gossip column, Bondi had a new cook, "a real southern mammy from West Virginia," to go with her new house.[68] In one of the first mentions of Bondi's new home in the press, columnist Bessie M. Gant described it as "a sanctuary for birds as well as her friends."[69] Tab Hunter remembered it as being "filled with religious artifacts and beautiful, old, elegant oak furniture. So tasteful and real, not the work of some uptight decorator. Understated, just like Beulah herself."[70] The house had previously been the home of writer James Hilton, actor Joseph Schildkraut, and Rosalind Russell.[71]

It would have been a help to Bondi to have a film set to go to after her mother's death. Production on *One Foot in Heaven* started at Warner Bros. only a week or so after Eva Bondy passed away, though Bondi may not have been needed immediately for her relatively limited role in the film. She had signed to do the film before her mother died.[72] It would also have been reassuring that her director was familiar to her, Irving Rapper having directed Bondi's previous film at Warner Bros., *The Sisters*, in 1938. Not only that, for once she was also working with familiar leading actors. Fredric March had starred in *The Buccaneer* at Paramount in 1937 and, more recently, Martha Scott played Bondi's daughter in *Our Town*. Now they were playing an idealistic Methodist minister, William Spence, and his hard-tried but ever faithful wife Hope, in a film based on a best-selling memoir by Hartzell Spence about his father.

Bondi appears in the long Denver segment of the film, as a rich, snobbish, widowed parishioner, Mrs. Lydia Sandow, who starts going to the Baptist church after March has tea with her gardener, Harry Davenport, and refuses to promise that he will never to do it again. Mrs. Sandow is head of the parsonage committee and her father built the church. When the leaks in the parsonage roof have reached double digits, March seeks her out at her palatial home, but she is not in, which is how he ends up talking to Davenport instead.

Lydia Sandow is one of Bondi's unsympathetic, upper-class dowager-antagonist roles, like Mrs. Livingstone Ames in *The Case Against Mrs. Ames*, which was the first of them. Mrs. Sandow is younger than Mrs. Ames, though, and more spoilt and pettish, and just a little bit coquettish. It Is indicative of Bondi's standing in the industry at this point, that she is billed third in the large cast with several other well established and prestigious supporting players, like Gene Lockhart, playing a wealthy parishioner who opposes March's plan to build a new church; Bondi's stage colleague from way back when, Grant Mitchell, as another member of the church board; and, last but not least, former Broadway star and veteran character actress Laura Hope Crews, as Lockhart's wife, who sings in the less than euphonious church choir and is none too thrilled about March's plan to replace it with a children's choir.

Despite her billing, Bondi only has two scenes in *One Foot in Heaven*, in addition to being seen in the crowd in the finale. Her part arguably is smaller than that of Lockhart, who is billed fourth, and Crews, who is billed seventh. This was Bondi's third and final film with Lockhart, who had been in *The Gorgeous Hussy* and *Of Human Hearts*; her fourth out of five with Grant Mitchell; and her second with Laura Hope Crews, who was at the end of her film career and died in 1942. Unfortunately, the two veteran actresses had no scenes together in *The Sisters*, nor did they here.

In her first scene more than an hour into the film, Bondi arrives at the parsonage dripping with dead foxes and wearing a velvet cloche hat with a decoration on top that looks like a cabbage to take March to task for socializing with the "help." It is interesting that Bondi has conceived a look for Mrs. Sandow that is far from typical dowager regalia and more akin to the "arty" style of her later Miss Horn in *Our Hearts Were Young and Gay* (1944). Bondi's second scene is near the end of the film's seemingly interminable 108 minutes. Mrs. Sandow comes back repentant because she feels "out of it," and is forgiven by her minister when she gives a large sum of money for a memorial window to her husband Thaddeus, an organ, and chimes for new church building.

*One Foot in Heaven* was the final film Bondi worked on before the Japanese attacked Pearl Harbor on December 7, 1941, and the United States entered the war. *Watch of the Rhine* was the first film she worked on after. It is so much finer and deeper than the average homefront film, that it hardly seems like a homefront film at all. No doubt this is because it is an adaptation of a hit Broadway play by Lillian Hellman, a play that, like *Street Scene*, just misses being great. *Watch on the Rhine* ran for 378 performances at the Martin Beck Theater from April 1, 1941, to February 21, 1942, and provided veteran actress Lucile Watson with one of her signature roles as Fanny Farrelly, the wealthy widow of a Washington, D.C., judge and the ultimate insider. In the course of the play, Fanny gets "woken up" to the realities of war and the geopolitical situation in 1940, when her daughter Sara, who married a German, Kurt Muller, and has raised three children with him in Europe, finally returns to her native land after a 17-year absence. A former engineer, Kurt Muller is a fighter in the anti-fascist resistance. He needs rest and relaxation in the supposedly safe environment of his wife's luxurious family home, but it turns out that even in the quiet, prosperous suburbs of the nation's capital, there is no escaping the long arm of the Nazis.

Bondi was cast as Anise, a role created on Broadway by Eda Heinemann, who did a string of plays there between 1908 and 1963, including playing Cousin Lily in the original production of O'Neill's *Ah, Wilderness!*, but only did one, uncredited role in films. Anise is Fanny Farrelly's paid companion and general factotum and, with the exception of the butler Joseph, the least interesting of the eight adult roles in Hellman's play. Of French origin, born in the "Bas-Rhin" according to her own report, Anise, according to Sara, has been in the family since before she was born. Fanny calls Anise a "snooper," but is not averse to making use of the information Anise provides, including updates about Fanny's son David (Donald Woods) and his unfolding affair with their long-term house guest Marthe de Brancovis (Geraldine Fitzgerald), married to the sinister Romanian aristocrat and former diplomat Teck de Brancovis (George Coulouris).

For once, Bondi is overshadowed by another character actress. Canadian-born and ten years Bondi's senior, Watson had a raft of Broadway credits and had been a top-tier character woman in Hollywood since 1934, when she made her screen debut in *What Every Woman Knows*. Among her major film roles are Mrs. Morehead in *The Women* (1939), Lady Margaret Cronin in *Waterloo Bridge* (1940), Mary Kimball in *My Reputation* (1946), and Celia Fenwick in *Harriet Craig* (1950). Watson was Oscar-nominated for her

**With the notable exception of *The Captain Is a Lady*, which was set in a retirement home for women, Bondi seldom had much competition in the character actress field in her films. In *Watch on the Rhine* (Warner Bros., 1943), though, based closely on a hit play by Lillian Hellman, she came up against a tour de force performance by top-tier New York actress Lucile Watson (left). Born in Canada in 1879, Watson had created the role of the wealthy Washington widow and matriarch Fanny Farrelly on Broadway in 1941. Bondi was relegated to the much less interesting role of Fanny's French-inflected companion Anise and for once had to see herself beaten at her own game.**

performance in *Watch on the Rhine*, retired from films and returned to Broadway in 1950, and died in 1962.[73]

Production on *Watch on the Rhine* started at Warner Bros. on June 9, 1942, and ended August 22.[74] It marked the screen directorial debut of Herman Shumlin, a major Broadway producer and director closely associated with Hellman, who had also directed the Broadway production. Watson, Paul Lukas as Kurt Muller; Eric Roberts, who played the Mullers' youngest son Bodo; and Frank Wilson, the butler, reprised their stage roles on film. So did George Coulouris, Bondi's co-star from both the stage and screen versions of *Christopher Bean*. In the role of Sara Muller, Bette Davis replaced Mady Christians. Davis, too, was familiar to Bondi, of course, from *The Sisters*, which they had done together in the summer of 1938. In the intervening four years, Davis had triumphed in standout films like *Dark Victory*, *All This, and Heaven Too*, *The Letter*, and *Now, Voyager* and had been nominated for no less than five Academy Awards and won for *Jezebel*.

The screenplay by Hellman's longtime companion Dashiell Hammett, to which she contributed additional dialogue, hewed close to the original in what Bosley Crowther described in the *New York Times* as "an almost literal adaptation."[75] One of the few differences from the play is that Sara is 38 in the film, rather than 41, and has been away 17 years rather than 20.[76] We can see how Davis, who was only 34, might have bridled at playing a woman of over 40, even though she could not avoid playing the mother of three children, including two teenagers. *Mrs. Skeffington* was still in the future. There is a lot of two and fro in the second act of the play, which lags a bit, about the Muller's youngest son Bodo trying to repair Anise's heating pad, which has been left out of the film. Anise is absent from the entire climactic third act of the play and the latter part of the film, where Kurt Muller is forced to kill Teck de Brancovis to prevent him from endangering Kurt's own life and those of his fellow resistance fighters in Europe, whom Kurt is going over to help escape Nazi imprisonment.

The stage drama is played out on the single set of the Farrelly living room, while there is some opening up in the film. It starts with the Mullers' train journey and crossing the border from Mexico; at one point we see Fanny in her chauffeur-driven car with her talkative friend Mellie Sewell (Mary Young) going into town on some errands; and we witness Teck de Brancovis playing cards at the German embassy in Washington. There is also an unnecessary sort of epilogue, where eldest son Joshua Muller (Donald Buka) prepares to go after his father to Europe.

The play ends with Fanny's famous line to her son David about being "shaken out of the magnolias" and her saying that she wants to go up to Anise. "I like Anise best when I don't feel well," she adds.

Bosley Crowther called *Watch on the Rhine* "one of the fine adult films of these times." He thought Bondi was "very good" in her minor role. Edwin Schallert thought she "does a quaint impersonation effectively." Mildred Martin thought Anise was "capably handled." Kaspar Monahan thought Bondi "fit into the pattern of the drama splendidly." Finally, Len G. Shaw thought she "adds some comedy touches."[77] Not bad for a not very good role in a very good film.

In October 1942, seven years after *Bad Boy* and three years after the *Grapes of Wrath* debacle, Bondi was back at Twentieth Century–Fox and set to do her first World War II film from the war front rather than the home front. Granted, Bondi's bête noir Darryl F. Zanuck was not involved in the film, which was directed by German-born John Brahm, better known for his TV work than his films, including 12 episodes of *The Twilight Zone* in the 1960s.

Bondi was billed fourth as Madame Bonnard, the wife of French farmer Lee J. Cobb and the mother of Annabella and a son, Pierre, who was killed fighting the Allies in Northern Africa, having been forced into the German army. When British resistance fighter John Sutton becomes the family's uninvited guest on a commando mission to destroy a local munitions factory, Sutton pretends to be Pierre to hide his true identity.

According to her husband, Madame Bonnard has "not been quite right" since her son died. Bondi's big scene, if you can call it that, is when wily German officer Howard Da Silva tricks her into showing him photos of her son, confirming his suspicions that Sutton is an impostor. As a result, Bondi and her husband are summarily executed by firing squad with their friends, neighbors and co-conspirators Ann Codee and Marcel Dalio, mother and son, while daughter Annabella is a powerless witness to the foul deed. Not surprisingly, this makes her see the Allied-Axis conflict in a different light and from there on out she is on the right side.

Though Bondi's French-accented English is passable, in fact, better than in *Watch on the Rhine*, her husband Cobb can only stretch himself to sounding vaguely mid–Atlantic. The film generally sounds like an episode of *Hallo! Hallo!*, including the German officers. Or maybe, given chronology, it is *Hallo! Hallo!* That sounds like *Tonight We Raid Calais*. At any rate, you almost expect someone to pull out the "Fallen Madonna with the Big Boobies" at any moment. Somewhat surprisingly, John Sutton never says "I vil say dis only wans." Bosley Crowther and I are in agreement about the general air of unreality about the film. He wrote in his *New York Times* review: "All we can say is that this picture … is a piece of thoroughly obvious fictionizing, done in an artificial way, and that it carries about as much sense of reality as a puppet pantomime."[78] And just to be clear: the film, whose working titles were *Project 47* and *Secret Mission*, has nothing to do with raiding Calais.

Bondi did not appear on Broadway during the 1940s, but she did perform in one-off performances or short runs of plays elsewhere. Nothing was happening on the film front in the first half of 1943, so in early June she appeared in Thornton Wilder's popular one-act play *The Happy Journey to Trenton and Camden* presented by the Brentwood Service Players under the direction of James Whale. Bondi played the central role of Ma Kirby and joining her in the cast were Byron Foulger as her husband, Rennel Lasky and Norman Wilnor as her children, Rose Hobart as her married daughter, and Matt McHugh as the stage manager. McHugh had played Bondi's loud and unpleasant son, Vincent Jones, in *Street Scene*. An interesting precursor of *Our Town* with a minimalist set and stage manager character, just like in Wilder's later classic, the play simply depicts the mundane moments of a family's drive from Newark to Camden, New Jersey, to visit a married daughter and sister, who has just had a stillborn child. There were shades of Mrs. Webb about Ma Kirby with her homely adages and firm opinions, easily ruffled feathers, and general air of conventionality. Katherine von Blon wrote in the *Los Angeles Times*, that "Beulah Bondi, as the mother, gave an unforgettable performance in which humor and pathos were never far apart."[79] The play was repeated in late July and in mid–August 1943.[80]

In the second half of 1943, Bondi worked on three films in a row at Paramount, her entire output for that year. The films were *Our Hearts Were Young and Gay*, *I Love a Soldier*, and *And Now Tomorrow*. Bondi had signed to do the first of these by July 5, 1943, and shooting began on August 24 under the direction of Lewis Allen.[81]

*Our Hearts Were Young and Gay* was a wafer-thin romantic comedy based on a 1942 book by actress and writer Cornelia Otis Skinner and her friend Emily Kimbrough, which depicted their youthful escapades on a post-college trip to Europe in 1923. Cornelia was played by ill-fated starlet Gail Russell and Emily by pert Diana Lynn, tagged in one review respectively as the "ghost-haunted heroine of 'The Uninvited'" and the "'miracle' child of 'Morgan's Creek.'"[82] The two girls encounter Bondi and Alma Kruger on the ship bound for Europe, as travel companions and possible life partners Abby Horn and Ethel Lamberton. Cornelia's mother, played by Dorothy Gish in her sound film debut, wants her to "get attached to some nice older women," but Emily's dismissive response, after Bondi and Kruger have made a social overture towards them, is to say that they "don't want to get stuck with them."

Miss Horn was actually the first non-working spinster Bondi played on the screen. There is an arty and intellectual feeling about her, conveyed mainly through how she looks. Abby Horn wears large Spanish-style combs in her black hair and is partial to embroidered velvet jackets. She wears a distinctive tricorn hat in her first scene, as she and Mrs. Lamberton are standing next to Cornelia and Emily at the ship's railing and leering at them with undisguised admiration. In a curious digression, at one point on the crossing Miss Horn reveals her deep zoological knowledge of whales.

The lavender ladies' plotline, if you can call it that, revolves around the loss of Mrs. Lamberton's purse, which Cornelia has hooked onto a coat hanger she is carrying without noticing and which stewardess Anita Sharp-Bolster puts away in a chest of drawers in the girls' tiny, overcrowded cabin. There is a long, farcical segment, after the girls have found the missing purse, where they try to get it back into Kruger and Bondi's cabin. The older ladies keep showing up and interrupting them. When they finally succeed, it turns out they have put it in Miss Horn's suitcase, where Emily's love interest Tom Newhall (Bill Edwards) finds it. As a result, the two older women get embroiled in a heated discussion about which of them is the most absentminded. Mrs. Lamberton ends up going to a psychiatrist in Switzerland to cure her forgetfulness!

This was Bondi's only film with veteran character actress Kruger, a vastly experienced Broadway actress 18 years her senior, who had a distinguished film debut as Amelia Tilford in Samuel Goldwyn's *These Three* in 1936. She had had to be satisfied with much smaller roles since then, most recognizably as head nurse Molly Byrd, Lionel Barrymore's helpmeet, in no less than 14 of the 16 films of the Dr. Kildare-Dr. Gillespie series. Kruger retired from films in 1947 and died in 1960 at age 88. Like Bondi, she never married.[83]

Though production ended on October 21, 1943, *Our Hearts Were Young and Gay* did not premiere until October 12 the following year.[84] The critic "A.W." for the *New York Times*, possibly Alexander Woollcott, concluded that it "may be as durable as a nosegay of forget-me-not but it is just as charming."[85]

On August 5, 1942, Bondi's friend, the portrait painter Joseph Cummings Chase (1878–1965) wrote to her from his studio in New York's fabled Chelsea Hotel: "Beulah darlin' up to her good works, as usual, doing all those kindnesses for the soldier lads who have our so-great admiration."[86] During the war years, Bondi was actively involved in various charities, volunteering, and supporting the soldiers on the home front. Hedda Hopper wrote in her column on October 1, 1943: "Beulah Bondi isn't an ingénue but she works harder than most of them. Acting in 'Their Hearts Were Young and Gay' in daytime, spends evenings at Playtime Theater, helps at three different canteens weekly, and joins the Grey Ladies for another day at various hospitals."[87] She trained as "grey lady" at the Cedars of Lebanon hospital. Hopper reported again, in early 1944, that patients were "pretty happy that an actress is writing letters and running errands for them."[88] In 1945, she was doing "her home-front part as a 'Gray Lady'" at the Birmingham General Hospital in Van Nuys.[89]

Bondi also sold war bonds and volunteered at the Hollywood Canteen. On Tuesday, August 10, 1943, for example, she joined Mrs. Lewis Stone, Mrs. Edward C. Warner and other representatives of the League for Crippled Children in selling war bonds in the "Victory Window" of I. Magnin's department store.[90] She also held luncheon meetings at her home for the League for Crippled Children, a charity she supported for decades.[91] For her work at the Hollywood Canteen on Sunday afternoons doling out coffee and sandwiches from behind the snack bar, fashion guru Travis Banton designed a special frock for her to wear, as he did for fellow volunteers Marlene Dietrich, Claudette Colbert, Billie Burke, and four others. All eight dresses were different, but had in common "extra large pockets" that could be filled with "feminine trivia such as compacts, lipsticks and what-not."[92]

While Bondi was finding personal fulfillment in various charities and war work, her screen characters also reflected the then current need, even the pressure, to "get involved." Etta Lane in *I Love a Soldier* is one of Bondi's "self-centered old woman finds meaning in life by helping others" roles. Bondi could play this type of dignified, aging spinster with both hands tied behind her back. All she had to do was look aristocratic or sympathetic, as the situation demanded. Here she offers typical support, in every sense of the word, for stars Paulette Goddard and Sonny Tufts, including opening her San Francisco mansion to GIs on the couple's encouragement and housing Goddard's pregnant friend with a husband who is MIA.

Things get rolling when Tufts seeks out Bondi to give her his fellow soldier and her dead nephew Richie's effects and tell her how he died. Goddard, whom the dead nephew pretended was his girlfriend after they had been on one date, comes with Tufts to break the news. At first Bondi does not want to see them, as she is distraught with grief and not seeing anyone. Tufts criticizes her for wallowing and says she is nothing like the "tough old bird" his friend told him about. Richie killed 21 Japanese soldiers before he died heroically, he tells her, though it later turns out this is what Tufts did, not Richie. Tufts even gives Bondi his own medal, pretending it was Richie's. Bondi finally ends up crying on Tufts's shoulder. He admits that Richie never called her a tough old bird, but she interjects: "But I am, a tough old turkey." She also admits that "I feel so alone."

Bondi does not turn up again until 48 minutes in, by which time she has opened up her palatial home to soldiers and anyone else who needs a place to stay. At a crucial juncture in the on-again-off-again Goddard-Tufts romance, we get the classic spinster sob story about not living while she could. In this case, Bondi sent her "young man" away to war 40 years earlier without marrying him, because they "didn't want to take the risk." Thus, she never used her wedding veil, he never came back, and she never loved anyone else. Bondi urges Goddard to marry Tufts, even though Goddard has just witnessed a friend lose her husband in battle. As the *Sydney Morning Herald* put it, Bondi "wins her round to a gather-ye-rosebuds-while-ye-may line of thought."[93] The last we see of her, Bondi helps Tufts to look for Goddard when he hears from his wife that she has divorced him and obtains a special leave to get married again.

Production on *I Love a Soldier* partially overlapped with the earlier *Our Hearts Were Young and Gay* and the later *And Now Tomorrow*, so Paramount was keeping Bondi busy during the last three months of 1943. This was her only film for director Mark Sandrich, best known for his 1930s romantic comedies *The Gay Divorcee*, *Top Hat*, *Follow the Fleet*, and *Shall We Dance*, all starring Fred Astaire and Ginger Rogers. Bosley Crowther's succinct response to *I Love a Soldier* was: "Heaven forbid that the home front should ever be so thoroughly mixed up!" He did not see fit to mention Bondi's presence in the movie, nor did many other reviewers. Kaspar Monahan took the time to observe that "Beulah Bondi, a fine actress, is wasted in the empty spinster role." The reviewer for the *Jackson Sun*, on the other hand, wrote that "few will fail to be effected by the warmth of 'Etta Lane' (Beulah Bondi), the wealthy spinster who waited too long for her man in the last war." Edwin Schallert stayed neutral: "Beulah Bondi is accountable for a fine character part."[94]

By late 1943, Bondi had cornered the market on playing "maiden ladies" in films, having done three in a row for Paramount. Emily Blair in *And Now Tomorrow* was the third and least interesting of them, though it marked the only time Bondi played a captain of industry on the big screen. The film starred Loretta Young as a deaf heiress, also called Emily Blair, and Alan Ladd as a young doctor, Merek Vance, born on the wrong side of the tracks, who, through a risky and experimental new treatment, succeeds in curing Emily of both her deafness and her snobbery and wins her heart in the process. *And Now Tomorrow* marked the return of Ladd to the big screen, after a year in the army. The director was Irving Pichel, a former actor, in his only outing with Bondi. Production was underway from December 13, 1943, till mid–February 1944, though the film was not released until November 1945.[95]

Bondi's role as Young's and her naughty sister Susan Hayward's closest living relative and the head of the family's textile mill in the New England town named for them must largely have landed on the cutting room floor. She is given practically nothing to do in what remains but stand around looking elegant and dignified and directing traffic at social events. We gather that Aunt Em is miffed not to have been told that Ladd was experimenting on her niece. In her only semi-moment, more than an hour into the film, she seems gravely concerned when Young has a negative reaction to an injection of Ladd's serum. She is wearing a peignoir no less and displays some emotion, but why would we care, since we know nothing about her? It is symptomatic of her narrative insignificance, that in the AFI catalogue's 670-word summary of the plot, Aunt Emily is not mentioned at all.

Bondi has a terribly fluty voice in this and says things like "I'll see you children before you go?." In a flashback scene to a Christmas celebration with Santa distributing

In Irving Pichel's woman's film *And Now Tomorrow* (Paramount, 1944), starring Loretta Young and Alan Ladd, Bondi was given little to do as Young's aunt, beyond directing traffic at parties and looking regal. What was unusual, though, was that her character, Emily Blair, was head of the family business, a textile mill in the New England town named for the family. It was the only time Bondi played an industrialist, though we never get to see her at work.

gifts from the Blairs to the children of the town, Bondi is seen on the steps of the Blair mansion in an elegant mink coat and matching hat. These may have been her own, as character actresses frequently wore their own clothes and she is wearing a similar coat with Joan Crawford shoulder pads in a candid taken outside her home in 1940.

Speaking of apparel: Young wears a series of incredible hats in the film, that might either serve to save her from drowning or to receive satellite TV signals, especially the stadium-sized dish she is wearing when she first encounters Ladd at a train station. "And now tomorrow" is Young's final line to Ladd and the final line of the film. Bosley Crowther, as usual, does not fail to be quotable. On Young: "Whatever it was this actress never had, she still hasn't got." On Ladd: "plays the doctor with a haughty air that must be tough on his patients—and is likely to be equally tough on yours." On *And Now Tomorrow* as a whole: "a very stupid film."[96] Bondi, thankfully for her, is overlooked yet again.

With a title that would be more suited to Bondi's later picture *Back to Bataan*, *She's a Soldier Too* was produced at Columbia, which previously had cast Bondi in high-profile pictures like *Mr. Smith Goes to Washington* (1939) and *Penny Serenade* (1941). This was not a high-profile picture. Originally entitled *Soldiers in Slacks*, this typical homefront film also has all the hallmarks of a B movie, which can explain why for the first and only time in her career, Bondi was at the top of the bill. Lucy Cooper in *Make Way for Tomorrow* is often said to be her only starring role, but that is not strictly correct. This 67-minute, low budget film, which consists almost entirely of interior shots, was produced in just 16 days on the Columbia lot at 1438 N. Gower St. in Hollywood in March 1944.[97] Director William Castle, later known for horror films like *House on Haunted Hill*, *Strait-Jacket*, and *I Saw What You Did*, had been the dialogue director on *Penny Serenade*. The film was released in late June and shown in theaters as a second feature in select company with such classics as *The Hairy Ape*, *Cobra Woman*, or the Hopalong Cassidy feature *Bar 20 Rides Again*.[98]

*She's a Soldier Too* revolves around the elderly, patrician, spinster Kittredge sisters, Agatha (Bondi) and Julia (Ida Moore), and their bachelor brother Jonathan (Percy Kilbride), who still live in the old family home from 1768 at No. 17 in Philadelphia. They are set in their ways and Agatha dominates her siblings, being the killjoy of all time. Sixty-eight-year-old Jonathan is an amateur inventor (naturally, they are descended from Benjamin Franklin) and serves as the family butler and man of all work.

One night at midnight, there is an unexpected ringing on the doorbell. It turns out to be a cab driver, nicknamed Taxi (Nina Foch), with a pregnant woman, who is about to give birth and urgently needs a roof over her head. The young mother dies in childbirth and there is no way of tracing the father, Mr. Jones, so the Kittredge sisters are more or less coerced by the dashing local doctor Bill White (Jess Barker) into fostering the child.

At the same time, the bank threatens to foreclose on the Kittredge mansion, which is mortgaged to the hilt, and sell it to two businessmen who want to turn it into a factory for inner soles. There is a housing shortage and Taxi concocts a plan to save the house by converting it into a boarding house for women working in the war industry. Agatha is forced to agree, but makes herself as unpleasant as possible in her dealings with the boarders. Some of her characteristic pronouncements are "We have a duty to perform and will perform it dutifully regardless of how distasteful it is to us" and "I believe I've asked repeatedly for decorum in this drawing room." Of the informal and jovial Dr. White, Agatha says: "A physician's business is to heal, not to entertain. I would feel safer if he wore a beard." He in turn nicknames Agatha "Baby Face."

Bondi (left) was top-billed in *She's a Soldier Too* (1944), which was probably the only way in which Columbia could get her to do this low budget B movie about the regenerative power of a baby, a kind of World War II "Luck of Roaring Camp." As Agatha Kittredge, the old maid of all time in a patrician family fallen on hard times, which consisted also of her hard-tried siblings Ida Moore (right) and Percy Kilbride, Bondi reached new heights of unpleasantness and disdain, something she did well and dispensed liberally to family members, boarders in her home, and visitors alike. For ten years or more after her death, Hollywood studios kept on hoping they would discover the new Marie Dressler, but even Bondi failed to repeat Dressler's stunning success with film audiences. At center above is Jess Barker.

Finally, one of Jonathan's inventions, a knee lock that can be used in the landing gear of a new air force bomber, pans out. With the $15,000 check, Agatha is able to evict all her tenants and they can return to their old way of life. Jonathan, though, has had enough. After telling his sister that she is "the enemy," he packs up and leaves. Taxi and the baby's father, Charles Jones (Lloyd Bridges), have married and come to get the baby. As the door closes on "the two old zombies," as Charles dismissively calls them, Julia sighs: "Now we're all alone." This final loss occasions a sudden change of heart in Agatha. She asks the young couple and their baby to stay and for Taxi to find all their old tenants as well. The film ends on Christmas Eve, when Jonathan returns while a big party is underway at the Kittredge mansion. As a surprise gift, he gets Ralphie, the Collie dog he had to give away at the beginning of the film, because Agatha did not want him in the house.

Percy Kilbride had not yet found his calling as Pa Kettle with Marjorie Main as Ma Kettle at Universal. He would also show up in *The Southerner* (1945) and *Mr. Soft Touch* (1949) with Bondi. This was her only film with Ida Moore. The warm and sympathetic Julia Kittredge was an unusually large role for the Kansas-born Moore, who was a recent arrival in Hollywood and was on a much less exalted plane than Bondi as a character actress. Moore has a nice scene when she sings her favorite "Brahms Lullaby" to the baby, while Agatha and Bill White listen in silence.

In 1964, acidulous UPI Hollywood correspondent Vernon Scott pointed out that *She's a Soldier Too* was the only one of William Castle's many films that did not contain at least one murder. He added: "With stars such as [Beulah Bondi and Percy Kilbride] Castle really didn't need a homicide. It was a form of suicide."[99]

Following *Watch on the Rhine*, *I Love a Soldier*, and *She's a Soldier Too*, *The Very Thought of You* was the fourth and final homefront film Bondi made during World War II. It was helmed by Delmer Daves, who would later direct Bondi in *A Summer Place* (1959), and went before the cameras at Warner Bros. starting March 6, 1944, and ending in late April.[100] According to Lorraine LoBianco, what made this film different from the typical homefront film was the realistic focus on the strains and challenges for parents and spouses left behind when their sons and husbands went off to war.[101] Was not that what all homefront films were about?

Specifically, *The Very Thought of You* relates the wartime romance between a former academic turned sergeant, Dave Stewart (Dennis Morgan), and a working girl from a lower middle-class Pasadena family, Janet Wheeler (Eleanor Parker in her first leading role at Warner Bros.), who currently is employed in a parachute factory. Bondi plays Parker's crass, negative, and controlling mother, Harriet Wheeler, "a dyspeptic, suspicious creature."[102] She was the second in a trio of possessive mothers Bondi portrayed on the screen, starting in a minor key with Mrs. Larkin in *Bad Boy* (1936) and culminating with the monstrous Letty Bridges in *Track of the Cat* (1954).

In addition to Parker and Bondi, the dysfunctional Wheeler family consists of husband and father Henry Travers (also married to Bondi in *The Sisters*), daughters Andrea King and Georgia Lee Settle, and married son John Alvin and his wife Marianne O'Brien. One of Bondi's central scenes is the elder Wheelers' 28th wedding anniversary dinner, with Mrs. Wheeler competing with Mrs. Hallam in *Another Language* as far as making her children feel bad, particularly her daughter Janet.

Mrs. Wheeler's chief function in the film is to strongly disapprove of her daughter's romance and later marriage to Dave. For a "silver cord" mom, a son or daughter-in-law is a potential threat to her dominance over her child. Mrs. Wheeler goes so far, with the collusion of her daughter Molly (King), as to hide Dave's letters to Janet from the front. By the end, Mrs. Wheeler has "come 'round" to some extent and, as a conciliatory gesture, makes a fricassee.

The verdict of the *New York Times*: "Quite a bit of pap the Warners have cooked up here, and quite a distasteful and irritating picture is 'The Very Thought of You.'" Few reviewers had anything to say about Bondi's efforts. According to Tom Birks, "Miss Beulah Bondi as the nagging, vitriolic Mrs. Wheeler, has the movie goers hoping that someone will put poison in her coffee." The *Jackson Sun* found that "the characterization of Beulah Bondi, as Janet's mother, seems particularly harsh and unbelievable." Corbin Patrick thought Bondi and Travers were "first rate" and George L. David thought they were "good."[103]

Just as production on *The Very Thought of You* was coming to an end, Bondi's 81-year-old aunt, Rose Hirschman, died on April 29, 1944, in Milwaukee, where she had lived her entire married life. You will remember that Aunt Rose inherited the larger part of her older brother Louis's fortune after he died in 1937 and the estate case was finally settled in 1940. Her final years, though, were marked by sadness. Her only child, Leola Hirschman Sure, predeceased her in 1941 and Rose's son-law, Dr. Julius Sure, died in 1943.[104] Leola was only the second woman appointed to the University of Wisconsin board of regents, where she served from 1922 to 1928.[105] In 1930, she had married Dr. Julius Hilton Sure, a widowed obstetrician and gynecologist born in Russia, when she was 46 and he was 51.[106] On her death, Rose's estate amounted to $15,000. She left bequests to the Milwaukee Home for the Aged Jews, Mt. Sinai Hospital (where her son-in-law had worked for decades), Milwaukee Children's Hospital, the University of Wisconsin, and to her nephew Raymond Bondy.[107] Rose Bondy Hirschman was the last of Bondi's aunts and uncles to pass away.

*The Southerner* is the point in Bondi's career where granny drag meets Grand Guignol and the result is outrageous. I count her grandmother here, as the only total miss of her film career, while recognizing that director Jean Renoir needs to take his part of the blame for not reigning her in. It is not that her character is not amusing or amazing as a kind of sideshow or grotesque entertainment, but Bondi's acting style here is grossly out of keeping with that of the naturalistic leads Betty Field and Zachary Scott and with the serious and lyrical tone of the film as a whole. Her performance would have fit right in in *Tobacco Road*, but not here. At times, it even looks like co-star Scott is thinking "Wow, she's really pulling out all the stops on this one!"

*The Southerner* is a cotton-picking *Grapes of Wrath*, a low key, passably realistic film about the struggles of a young family of sharecroppers trying to eke out a living on a small Texas farm through the four seasons with their various challenges and rewards. Sam Tucker (Scott) and his wife Nona (Field) have two children, Jot (Jay Gilpin) and Daisy (Jean Vanderwilt), and also share their home with Sam's grandmother, Kitty Tucker. Kitty is one of the most ornery, evil-minded, exasperating old women ever portrayed on celluloid. She is a human being reduced to her most primitive instincts by the onslaught of old age and poverty in combination and makes having lost three children to "spring sickness" (aka pellagra) sound like an achievement. According to the *Sydney Morning Herald*, she "has outlived patience but not her appetite for soft food and sweet hot drinks."[108]

Granny Kitty is first encountered gorging herself on fox grapes with her great-granddaughter Daisy, who teases her with a dead snake. Next, she is less than thrilled with the ramshackle farmhouse where her son and daughter-in-law have brought her to live. At first, she refuses even to come in and remains rocking in her chair on the back of the truck till it starts to rain cats and dogs. Granny does not have much in the way of worldly possessions and is keenly distressed when Sam wants to cut up half of her best blanket for a warm coat for Daisy, so she can go to school in winter without catching her death of cold. Nona knows how to handle her and Granny is finally mollified by Nona's offer to get her some wild honey. Granny Kitty's presence in the remainder of the film is more benign. The last we hear from her, in the ending, is that she is "Goin' back to the house an' just set and wait for my call to glory."

Still at the height of her film career, Bondi was billed fourth after Scott, Field, and J. Carrol Naish as Devers, a particularly nasty neighbor, in her only film for director Jean Renoir. On the set at General Services Studios, where production started on September 6, 1944, and at various rural California locations,[109] Bondi was reunited with Percy Kilbride, who had played her brother in *She's a Soldier Too*, and who plays a storekeeper here and her daughter-in-law Blanche Yurka's new husband.

Though they had no scenes together, Bondi may also have been reunited, after more than a dozen years, with Estelle Taylor from *Street Scene*. Taylor's film career had stalled in the early 1930s and *The Southerner* would prove her final film. She plays an older woman who comes on to Sam Tucker in a bar, but meets with no response. Taylor died of cancer in 1958 at the age of 63. Last but not least, Bondi was reunited with Betty Field from *The Shepherd of the Hills*. Since that 1940 production, Field had married *Street Scene* writer Elmer Rice, so it was a small world. *The Southerner* was a film more worthy of Fields's considerable acting talents than *The Shepherd of the Hills*.

Production on *The Southerner* ended in early November 1944 and the film premiered in Boston on August 1 and New York on August 25, 1945.[110] Surprisingly, no review I have read called Bondi out on her ridiculous histrionics in this film. In fact, she got some of the best reviews of her latter career. Robert H. Allen of the *Cincinnati Enquirer* thought "Beulah Bondi as Granny is all that possibly could be asked." He added: "She has some pat dialogue, and with an almost physical literalness she is Granny." *Akron Beacon Journal* theater editor Betty French wrote that Bondi's performance was "Perhaps the most impressive portrayal of all." The *Quad-City Times* thought her role was "delightfully played." Dorothy Raymer of the *Miami Daily News* wrote that Bondi "steals every scene she's in." Don Birks of the *Pittsburgh Sun-Telegraph* agreed about the scene-stealing, in fact he thought she almost stole the entire picture and "provides what few chuckles there are."[111]

Incredibly, the *Sydney Morning Herald* thought Bondi gave "her best performance on record." Donald Kirkley of the *Baltimore Sun* went completely overboard, writing that Bondi "gives a performance that may well win the Academy Award for the best supporting role of the year, and would get our vote if we had one." Bondi was not nominated. Edwin Schallert of the *Los Angeles Times* thought she was "remarkable as the complaining Granny." Even the critic for the *New York Times* listed her among the supporting players who contributed "vigorous characterizations." Only customarily plain-spoken Kaspar Monahan at the *Pittsburgh Press* allowed some small note of criticism to slip into his review, when he wrote that "'Granny' is more of a caricature than a real person." He was quick to add, though, that Bondi "gives a crackling performance."[112]

I think this chorus of approval can chiefly be explained by the fact that Bondi was unrecognizable in the role, a kind of "Charlize Theron in *Monster* effect," where critics are too easily impressed by the outward trappings of the character without asking whether it serves the needs of the film. I also think Bondi benefited from her established reputation as a middle-aged actress specializing in playing little old ladies. She was 55 when she gave her most exaggerated granny performance.

Bondi's second film from the war front rather than the home front was *Back to Bataan*, a better opportunity and a better film, on the whole, than the French-inflected *Tonight We Raid Calais*. *Back to Bataan* had better production values, location shooting, and a big star at the helm: John Wayne as Col. Joseph Madden, not to mention budding star Anthony Quinn as Madden's right-hand man. It was produced at RKO and directed by Edward Dmytryk, yet another of the many "man's man" directors Bondi worked well with down through the years, including John Ford, Sam Wood, Henry Hathaway, and William A. Wellman.

Originally entitled *The Invisible Army*, this late war film is set in the Philippines, Bataan being a peninsular province on the island of Luzon, across the bay from Manila. *Back to Bataan* attempts a capsule history of both the Japanese invasion and the American and Filipino recapture of the Philippines and incorporates real historical events leading up to the freeing of the prisoners of war held by the Japanese in the Cabanatuan camp on January 30, 1945. Production on the film was underway as this military offensive was taking place, so the ending had to be changed to reflect an altered reality.[113]

Readers who have not seen the film may be curious to know how Bondi could have a role to play in all of this and even manages to be billed third after Wayne and Quinn. As one of only two women in the cast, she plays Bertha Barnes, an upright and forthright spinster schoolteacher working in the Philippines, who is witness to Japanese atrocities and later joins the American and Filipino guerrilla forces under leadership of Wayne's Colonel Madden. According to one source, there was a "prim schoolteacher ... who commanded 110 Filipinos in effective resistance."[114] Bondi's hometown newspaper reported that she was portraying "a sort of composite of three American women now living in the islands, who were among 1,200 teachers sent there by the United States in 1910 to offer free education to the Filipinos."[115]

Bertha Barnes is first encountered on the day Balintawak Public School must close, as the Japanese are coming and will be billeted in the school. When the Filipino principal, Buenaventura J. Bello (Vladimir Sokoloff), her former pupil, refuses to lower the American flag, the Japanese commanding officer, played by Abner Biberman, orders that he be strung up on the same flagpole. In Hollywood's ethnic logic of the day, you have a Russian playing a Filipino and a Jewish American from Milwaukee playing a Japanese. *C'est la guerre!*

Miss Barnes first encounters Madden and his ragtag band of not so merry men, when she is brought to safety in the jungle. She is appalled that they are not immediately going into the village to avenge Bello's death and gives them a piece of her mind and his stirring epitaph. As it happens, Madden's guerrilla fighters are on an important mission of their own and entering the village will jeopardize it. When that mission is completed, they go into the village, hang the Japanese officer responsible for Bello's death, and give Bello a proper burial. A bossy, brave, imperious pain in the neck, Miss Barnes is ubiquitous in the jungle encampment, nursing the sick and the wounded, urging a lovesick Andrés Bonifácio (Quinn) to eat, encouraging and admonishing. Her sidekick is her former pupil Maximo Cuenca ("Ducky" Louie), a boy who makes himself useful by stealing a radio from the Japanese and who wants to be a scout. He is finally captured by the Japanese and mortally wounded when he grabs the steering wheel of the truck he is sitting in, causing it to drive off the road. Miss Barnes is at his side when he dies, after apologizing for never learning how to spell liberty. She is last seen tearing down the Japanese flag from the blackboard of a schoolhouse and wiping out the Japanese symbols. Her token gesture, which by this point can be called a mannerism, is the stroking up of her back hair. In a 1932 interview, Bondi had noted: "The unpardonable acting sins are mannerisms."[116]

Production at RKO took place between November 6, 1944, and early March 1945.[117] The *Los Angeles Times* was under the impression that Bondi's character would be "one of the people to meet death in 'Invisible Army.'"[118] Maybe that was the original idea. Bondi's performance met mostly with a perfunctory but positive critical response, being variously described as "excellent," "characteristically acid and stouthearted," "her usual acid self," "excellent," and "outstanding." The *Newark Advocate*, thought Bondi "went a trifle over-board in ordering the colonel and his men around" and the *Pittsburgh Post-Gazette* wrote harshly that "only Miss Bondi ... strikes a phoney note, and that could be either in her own playing or in the way her role has been written." I particularly love the review that mixes up Bondi's and Filipino actress Fely Franquelli's roles, claiming that Bondi plays Anthony Quinn's "sweetheart" Dalisay Delgado, "the beautiful yet supposedly dangerous traitor." That would have been something to see! Bosley Crowther took a dim view of the film as a whole, which he thought "a cheap and meretricious conception of the ordeal of the Philippine patriots and of the Americans who stayed behind to aid them" and "a juvenile dramatization of significant history."[119]

# 7

# Bondi's Peace
## *1945–1949*

"The whole world is my archive."[1]

When Bondi returned to Valparaiso on Monday, July 23, 1945, it was five years since her flying visit with her friend Maida Butler on July 31, 1940. This was an uncommonly long time for her to be away from her former home, but wartime fuel shortages, a busy schedule of film work and charity work, and the fact that Louis Bondy's heirs had sold most of his properties in Valparaiso can explain her lengthy absence. Since her last visit, Bondi's friend Maida Searles Butler had died at the age of 51. That happened in her home town of Chicago on May 3, 1943.[2]

By this time the war was nearly over and it was summer, but Bondi still only had time to stay over for one night with her old friend Louise Bartholomew at her home at 508 Napoleon St. The Bartholomews held an informal open house for about 50 guests. Avery B. Weaver reported in the *Vidette-Messenger*, where the visit was front page news: "Miss Bondi, charmingly gowned in a black and white sheer with white accessories and wearing a brushed up coiffure, sparked emotion in greeting her many friends." Bondi vouchsafed that she "would like nothing better than return to the legitimate stage" and was reading two scripts for forthcoming Broadway productions.[3] It would be another five years until Bondi returned to the New York stage.

This summer offered yet another opportunity for Bondi to walk down memory lane. For the first time since her graduation in 1907, she returned to her alma mater Frances Shimer College in Mount Carroll, Illinois. She came the last weekend in July with her brother Raymond and his stepdaughter, Marion Cadle, who had just turned 19 and was enrolling at Shimer in the fall. Bondi had the opportunity to visit with two old school friends, who still lived in the area, and stayed with the Ward Weldmans.[4] That same weekend, Bondi was also the guest of Myrtle Norton Walgreen, widow of Charles R. Walgreen, who founded the drug store chain, and matriarch of the Walgreen family. Dr. Albin Bro, president of Shimer College, was also a guest at Mrs. Walgreen's estate Hazelwood in Dixon, Illinois, which is only 40 miles from Mount Carroll.[5]

After her summer outings, it was time to go back to work on a new film in mid–August 1945.[6] Annie Reed in *Breakfast in Hollywood* is one of Bondi's most endearing little old lady roles. Bondi has her decked out in a flowered print dress with white ruffled blouse, a brooch at her throat, steel-rimmed spectacles, a flat, dowdy hat, white gloves, and a purse. Annie is not unlike Lucy Cooper from *Make Way for Tomorrow*. She has an old dog called "Tippy." On the way to attend a radio broadcast of "Breakfast in Hollywood" with popular host Tom Breneman at his restaurant "Tom Breneman's," the 82-year-old widowed Hollywood resident is hit by a car at corner of Hollywood and Vine, but insists on continuing on to her destination.

As Annie, Bondi was billed third after Breneman playing himself and Bonita Granville as Dorothy Larson, a young woman from Minneapolis, who comes to Los Angeles looking for her soldier fiancé, because has stopped writing to her. Granville had played Bondi's daughter in *Maid of Salem* back in 1936 and now at 22 was nearing the end of her film career. Oscar-nominated for *Three Three* the same year Bondi was nominated for *The Gorgeous Hussy*, they had both lost to Gale Sondergaard for *Anthony Adverse*.

Born in Waynesboro, Pennsylvania, in 1901, Tom Breneman is forgotten today, but his 30-minute radio show was a "one of ABC's most popular daytime shows" in the 1940s, with an estimated daily audience of ten to twelve million listeners. It began as "Breakfast at Sardi's" and was renamed "Breakfast in Hollywood" in 1943. An ordinary-looking man with what was described as a "baby face" and grey hair, Breneman was charming and affable and loved engaging in witty repartee with the members of his largely female audience. His AP obituary described how "He had a neat way of making the audience love his jibes, sometimes almost insulting. He kissed old ladies and they ate it up."[7]

By the time the film was produced between mid–August and early September 1945, under the direction of Harold Schuster, Breneman had opened a restaurant next door to present-day 1555 Vine St., named it for himself, and broadcast the program from there. *Breakfast in Hollywood* is basically a recreation of one of Breneman's broadcasts with several musical numbers, which were not a part of the show, and added fictional storylines of Breneman getting involved in sorting out the lives of some of his audience members. He is first seen picking up a sailor, Ken Smith (Edward Ryan), in his car on his way to work. The sailor becomes the male love interest of the piece and ends up paired with Granville.

Seated with Bondi during the broadcast is the irrepressible Zasu Pitts as Elvira Spriggens, a maiden lady originally from Pomona and now living in Hollywood, who is vying for Breneman's attention and desperate to win his "Most Outrageous Hat" contest. When Pitts says she came alone because she did not want to embarrass anyone, Bondi responds helpfully: "Why don't you put a clove in your mouth and then nobody will know you've been drinking." Breneman is about to try on her hat, when Pitts is upstaged by Hedda Hopper, famous for her outrageous headgear, and this time sporting a goldfish bowl on her head. Bondi tries to comfort Pitts, but she leaves the restaurant brokenhearted. Pitts had been with Bondi in *Two Alone* in 1933.

Also present in the audience is Billie Burke, whose husband Raymond Walburn is running out on her with some young ladies, but finally gets caught red-handed. In one of those curious film coincidences, it was Walburn who hit Bondi with his car in the opening of the film. Burke wins back her wayward husband by going through the then current version of an extreme makeover. Initially, Burke, who was once a star on Broadway and the glamorous widow of Flo Ziegfeld, is practically unrecognizable without makeup, in a rare appearance as a dowdy, middle-class housewife. Her distinctive helium voice is in place, though. Burke had had two good scenes with Bondi in *Finishing School* in 1934 and also showed up in *The Captain Is a Lady* in 1940.

Annie Reed wins the orchid as the oldest member of the audience present at age 82. She introduces herself to Breneman as "Anna Reed from Hollywood, California" and gives as good as she gets in the conversation with the popular host. After the show is over,

Annie has a fainting spell in the lobby and Breneman later finds time to visit her at home and to tell her to pull herself together. It turns out, despite having a son and a grandson, Mrs. Reed is yet another one of Bondi's lonely old women without a purpose in life. Nobody needs her, she says, but Tippy, and he has lived his life too.

The saving grace for Annie is getting herself involved in a plan to unite the two young leads Granville and Ryan in the bonds of matrimony. She follows developments by phone. Naturally, the boy gets the girl and all is well. It is heartening to see that such a busy man as Breneman could find the time to involve himself so extensively in the personal lives of his audience members. Breneman died suddenly of a heart attack one morning in April 1948, as he was getting ready for work and eager fans were already lining up at the restaurant to get into the day's broadcast. He was only 46.

*Breakfast in Hollywood* is a charming and amusing time capsule. Reviewers had kind words for Bondi's sixth performance as an elderly woman, writing that she "turns in a top-notch bit of acting," "is the most convincing," and "easily wins acting honors," and that her role was "beautifully played."[8]

Production on *Breakfast in Hollywood* ended just as World War II came to a close with the Japanese surrender on September 2, 1945. "If there were any doubts that the war

**Zasu Pitts (left) was known for the type of fluttery old maid roles on the screen, that Bondi had often played on the stage. Here the two women are seen in *Breakfast in Hollywood* (Golden Pictures, 1946), a topical feature built around a broadcast of Tom Breneman's popular radio show. Bondi's little old lady role was most akin to Lucy Cooper in *Make Way for Tomorrow*, though entirely comedic. Breneman, seated comfortably here between Pitts's Elvira Spriggens and Bondi's Annie Reed, died of a massive heart attack in April 1948 at the age of 46.**

was over for Hollywood," Bob Thomas noted in his column, "they were dispelled last night at the opening of 'Spellbound.' The movie crowd put up a whopping show that has not been equaled since Pearl Harbor." Maybe not the most fortunate of comparisons.... Among the stars on display at the Cathay Circle Theater were Henry Fonda, Jimmy Stewart, Clark Gable, Lana Turner, Gregory Peck, Alan Ladd and, last but not least, "two youngsters together: Charles Coburn and Beulah Bondi."[9]

Bondi was given some good opportunities at RKO, but *Sister Kenny* was not one of them. In fact, playing Rosalind Russell's mother Mary Kenny is in a dead heat with Mrs. Tozer in *Arrowsmith* as her most insignificant role. Though she was billed fifth, Bondi and screen husband Charles Dingle are given practically nothing to do and appear only in the earliest part of the film, when their daughter Elizabeth Kenny is young. Their most important scene is at the kitchen table trying to surprise Elizabeth with the early arrival of her boyfriend, played by Dean Jagger. Otherwise, they mostly stand around looking either worried or pleased, depending on what their daughter is getting up to. This did not prevent Wood Soanes of the *Oakland Tribune* from feeling they had made "important contributions."[10]

No one even halfway attempts an Australian accent in this biopic about a nurse who pioneered a new treatment for infantile paralysis, despite adamant opposition from the male-dominated medical establishment. It was Bondi's only film for Dudley Nichols and the only time she supported Rosalind Russell. From Bondi's perspective, *Sister Kenny* is only significant for being "the first time in 24 years," that she was "unable to report for the first day of an assignment." As Hollywood columnist Harrison Carroll explained, she had fallen and torn a ligament in her foot.[11]

Though she lived a long and healthy life, Bondi seems to have become increasingly accident prone. On January 1, 1946, Harrison Carroll reported "Beulah Bondi injured again." This time she had fallen over a trunk and sprained her back and would have to cancel her trip to Florida.[12] What really happened was that she strained her back while packing for the trip by lifting a too heavy suitcase. She was laid up for two weeks and the journey had to be postponed. She was determined, though, to make the trip in mid–January 1946 to visit her brother Raymond and his wife Frances, who lived at 1901 SW 13th St. in Miami. "This time I decided I was really going to get here, and here I am," she told a reporter. The *Miami News* claimed she had not been to Florida in eight years, which was incorrect, as she had attended her brother's wedding in Miami in June 1940. In the same interview, she "branded as 'untrue' reports that she and actor Charles Coburn were engaged." Coburn was a widower. On the screen, though, she had had "more husbands than I can count": "All were charming gentlemen and there were no divorces."[13] Bondi stayed with her brother and sister-in-law for several weeks, extending her stay to be able to attend the Miami opening of *Breakfast in Hollywood* at the Lincoln Theater on February 9, where she was interviewed over the radio by Eve Tellegen and entertained a group of her friends.[14] Bondi then went to stay with friends at their beach cottage on San Carlos Island, before returning to Miami to attend the Pressman's Ball.[15]

Back home in Los Angeles by early March 1946, Bondi signed to do what may well be her most familiar film role today: James Stewart's mother, Ma Bailey, in *It's a Wonderful Life*.[16] This is far from being one of her most interesting or impressive performances, but such are the vagaries of fame and fate. Yet it was a better opportunity than playing Stewart's mother in her previous Frank Capra outing, *Mr. Smith Goes to Washington*, and did have the added interest of showing both her dominant screen personas—the helpful and sympathetic and the harmful and unsympathetic—in the same character and the same film. Bondi is "warmly sympathetic"[17] as Stewart's mother in the "real life" main storyline, and is transformed into a harridan of a landlady in an imaginary scene from what life would have been like in Bedford Falls had George Bailey never been born. Ironically, Bondi never played a real landlady in any film.

In the early part of the film, Bondi's Ma Bailey is mostly "atmosphere," homely atmosphere, both around the family dinner table and at the wedding between Stewart and Donna Reed. She has one scene to herself with her son, where she tells him Reed is back home from school and encourages him to call on her. On the church steps, as Stewart and Reed leave to go on their honeymoon, she says to her maid Lillian Randolph: "Annie, we're just two old maids now," to which Annie responds: "You speak for yourself, Miz B." Then she goes missing from the long middle section of this 210-minute film.

When Bondi returns at 1 hour 55 minutes, it is for her big scene as Mrs. Bailey turned crabby, evil-minded landlady, who tells George Bailey that the boarding house is full and she does not take strangers anyway and that Uncle Billy is in an insane asylum and that is where he, George, probably belongs as well. Finally, Ma Bailey is present with practically the entire cast at the Christmas Eve finale singing "Silent Night" and "Auld Lang Syne." For her efforts here, Bondi was billed sixth after the stars, Lionel Barrymore, Thomas Mitchell, and Henry Travers, which was respectable given the limited nature of her role.

Bondi would have enjoyed making the film, as it brought together a wide swathe of the actors she had worked with during her first 15 years in Hollywood. The set would have been like old home week for her. First and foremost, *It's a Wonderful Life* was her fifth and final film with James Stewart and the fourth time she played his mother, though, I think, the only time he kisses her on the lips. It was also her fifth film with Lionel Barrymore, her frequent screen husband (in *Christopher Bean*, *The Gorgeous Hussy*, and *On Borrowed Time*), though they were not hitched here and did not have any scenes together. Her husband this time, albeit only for the first half hour of the film, before he peremptorily dies, was another five-time co-star, Samuel S. Hinds, who had played the camp doctor in *The Under-Pup* and sits holding hands with Bondi at the end of that film.

Bondi had yet another of her former screen husbands on the set, Henry Travers, who had watched with her the unfolding lives of their three daughters in *The Sisters* and had a considerably less harmonious marital relation with her in *The Very Thought of You*, in addition to being in *Ready for Love* and *On Borrowed Time*. Dithering, ineffectual Uncle Billy in *It's a Wonderful Life*, Thomas Mitchell, had played her son in *Make Way for Tomorrow* and her next-door neighbor in *Our Town*, and was also in *Mr. Smith Goes to Washington*. More peripherally, we have Ward Bond in his fifth and final film with Bondi, as the genial local policeman and George Bailey ally, Bert; and H.B. Warner in his third and last, as the formerly cantankerous and grief-stricken shopkeeper Mr. Gower. This was only 1946, though, and it does make one wonder about the absence of character actors of this caliber in her many remaining films. Only Barrymore would show up again, in *Lone Star* in 1951, where he and Bondi had a quasi-marital relation as Andrew Jackson and his caregiver Minniver Bryan.

The Walt Disney film *So Dear to My Heart* was a long time in the making and represented a new departure for Disney, as the animated sequences only make up about 12 of the film's 82 minutes. The live action sequences were produced on location at Porterville, Tulare, and Hot Springs, California, between May 15 and August 23, 1946, with retakes in February and March 1947.[18] The film was not ready to preview, though, in Chicago, until November 29, 1948, and the official premiere was on January 19, 1949. That was at the Indiana Theater in Indianapolis with Bondi in attendance.[19] Including the promotional tour she went on in January 1949,[20] Bondi was involved in this project off and on for nearly three years, the longest commitment to a single film production she ever made.

The production period partially overlapped with that for *It's a Wonderful Life* at RKO. One contemporary news item related that Bondi had had to travel 275 miles from Porterville, where she was on location for *So Dear to My Heart*, to do a sequence with James Stewart for *It's a Wonderful Life*. She arrived in Encino at midnight, worked till 4:30 a.m. and then headed back to Porterville.[21] As in *Make Way for Tomorrow* and *The Captain Is a Lady*, Bondi found herself in second place in the credit list, after her male co-star, in this case Burl Ives. *So Dear to My Heart* was the last film in which she got this top billing. After this, her name began to slip further down the credit list.

The film takes place in 1903 and is set mainly on the small Kincaid farm near Fulton Corners, Indiana, where Granny Kincaid lives with her orphaned grandson Jeremiah "Jerry" Kincaid (Bobby Driscoll), her mule General Jackson, various other livestock, and the black lamb Danny (named for the legendary racehorse Dan Patch), who becomes her grandson's best friend. The film is mainly about the boy and his ram and how he dreams of making Danny a champion. His Uncle Hiram (Burl Ives) aids and abets him in this endeavor, while Grandma Kincaid is considerably more ambivalent to Danny's rambunctious presence in her well-ordered home. She is finally won over, though, and Jerry gets his long-awaited chance to enter Danny at the county fair. According to one reviewer, Bondi and Driscoll "make dramatic sparks fly."[22]

Bondi gives a fine, nuanced performance as a stern but loving grandmother, raising her grandson alone, without any explanation of how this came about. Granny says quite profound things like "Nothing's born afraid," when Jerry points out that the newborn black lamb is not scared of him at all. To Tildy (Luana Patten), Uncle Hiram's young daughter and Jerry's constant companion, she says: "Honey, it's time you learned not to go settin' your heart on the daydreams of menfolks."

As far as grandmother roles go, this was more arduous than one might imagine. According to columnist Mae Tinee, preparing for the role involved learning "a good many new tricks," including plowing with a mule, operating a spinning wheel, carding and weaving, and square dancing; and working from dusk till dawn on a scene in a rain storm, where she was looking for her lost grandson, and which involved 14 changes of clothing.[23] At one point, Bondi got to sing a rousing duet with Ives and she square danced, too. The last time she hot footed it was in *Vivacious Lady*, but that was quite a different and more urbane form of dancing.

As Granny Kincaid, Bondi's hair is in a topknot and she uses steel-rimmed glasses, but fortunately there is no granny drag here in the form of a wig or other overt appurtenances of old age. I was particularly struck at one point by Bondi's radiant smile, which lights up her whole face when she finds Jerry and Danny asleep together in the barn. It was so unfamiliar and unexpected, it served as a reminder of how seldom she smiled like that on film.

Among the cast, Bondi was reunited with Harry Carey from *The Shepherd of the Hills* in his final film. He plays the judge who gives Jerry and Danny the Special Award of Merit at the Pike County Fair, after he has awarded the Blue Ribbon to another ram. He says to the boy and the large gathering at the fair: "It's what you do with what you got that counts." Carey died from a multitude of ills on September 21, 1947, at the age of 69, four months before the film was released.

This visually appealing film was Bondi's third in Technicolor and her second film set in her home state of Indiana, though it was not any more distinctively "Hoosier" than *Remember the Night* had been. It might have given her a head start, though, on the competition for the role, that she was a Hoosier herself; Walt Disney surely being alive to the promotional possibilities if one of his stars was from the state where the film was set. Disney had based part of his adaptation of a children's novel by Sterling North on his own memories of his boyhood in Missouri.[24]

I will let two industry observers represent opposing views of the film and Bondi's performance this time. Hedda Hopper described *So Dear to My Heart* as "the best thing Beulah has ever done," adding that, "in my opinion, she deserves a special Oscar."[25] Myles Standish disliked the film entirely, calling it "a concoction of crude, unabashed hokum, sticky as cheap candy and artificially pretentious as a paper-lace valentine." He felt Bondi was "competent," but that both she and Ives "haven't been given adequate material." Bobby Driscoll's performance as Jerry he found "completely phony."[26]

In early November 1946, Bondi returned to the stage in one of the mainstays of her career, *On Borrowed Time*, at El Patio Theater in Los Angeles under the auspices of Players' Productions. Predictably, she played Granny Northrup and, less predictably, "Gramps" this time was played by Boris Karloff. Karloff and Bondi had been in *The Invisible Ray* together back in 1935. Frank Morgan played Mr. Brink, Margaret Hamilton Demetria Riffle, and Tommy Ivo the boy Pud. Ivo went on to become a child star at Republic. The play was directed by Herbert Rudley. Edwin Schallert hailed it as Karloff's "finest footlight interpretation," *Arsenic and Old Lace* included. Schallert described Bondi as "a fair match" for Karloff, "as long as she is on the stage, which is all too brief a time." Her performance was "one of simplicity and reality."[27] Hedda Hopper found Karloff "mighty convincing," Bondi did "her usual super job," and Ivo had "talent scouts drooling."[28]

*High Conquest*, directed by Lewis Allen, was a high-altitude drama about the dangers of climbing big mountains while involved in a love triangle between two men and one woman. The leads were Anna Lee, Gilbert Roland, and Warren Douglas. A lot was made of the live footage of the legendary Matterhorn, where the director spent nine weeks shooting 60,000 feet of "terrific scenery," but the actors never got anywhere near Switzerland. In a September 1946 interview, months before production started at Monogram, Allen frankly admitted that the lead actors "haven't started to work yet," but that he had still "got the picture half finished." In other words, the star of this film was the scenery. Allen also admitted that "most of that mountain climbing is done by doubles."[29]

So, we do not need to picture future world traveler Bondi climbing any Swiss mountain peaks to make this film. She and her fellow actors were safely ensconced at Monogram's studio at 4376 Sunset Dr. for the entire production period, which lasted from December 6, 1946, till early January 1947.[30] From the summary of the plot in the American Film Institute catalogue and the one review that has anything to say about her performance, I gather her part as Clara Kingsley was not a large one. In the only newspaper to "notice" Bondi in this role, we can read: "Beulah Bondi does a clever piece of acting as a scatterbrain American, who never gets to climb the Matterhorn."[31] The AFI synopsis intriguingly suggests that Roland "fends off the advances of novice climber Clara

Kingsley."[32] Flibbertigibbets and sex-starved women were not commonplace in Bondi's film repertoire, so Clara Kingsley is unique in that regard.

I also have a rare film still of Bondi from the set looking like a female impersonator in hilarious Swiss Alpine drag with a debonair, bearded, pipe-smoking man, who looks very much like Errol Flynn. Prior to the film's release in the summer of 1947, Hedda Hopper described it as "a Monogram sleeper with some of the most wonderful scenery ever."[33] The question is if it ever woke up, buried as it was as the second feature on a double bill.

1947 was the year Bondi's film career began to slow down. With no films in the offing, she flew to Hawaii on what would prove the first of many trips to the islands. She had been encouraged to visit by Edward G. Robinson and his wife and had several other friends who had been to Hawaii as well. She arrived on March 26 and stayed at the Halekulani Hotel on Waikiki Beach in Honolulu. She was given a royal welcome by the press and the locals.[34] Columnist Lucille Leimert reported that "when Beulah Bondi flew off to Honolulu the other night, she already had six dinner engagements for the first six nights on the island."[35] On April 15, Bondi travelled on to Maui for a three-day visit, this time in company with her childhood friend Gertrude Polk and Root Sommers, who worked for the Bureau of Internal Revenue.[36] Bondi also visited Kauai and the island of Hawaii.[37] Hedda Hopper reported that she was "having the time of her life in Honolulu": "she got her greatest thrill in trying to photograph the inside of the crater of Haleakala volcano on Maui island from the air."[38] Bondi extended her stay till May 15 and celebrated her 58th birthday with friends on Oahu, before she and Gertrude Polk flew back to the mainland.[39] She had retakes to do for *So Dear to My Heart*.[40] Production on *The Snake Pit* started in mid–July 1947.[41]

There is not much that needs to be said about Bondi's cameo in support of Olivia de Havilland in *The Snake Pit*, a film I once described as taking "the scenic route through every available postwar psychiatric treatment."[42] This was her second film for director Anatole Litvak, who had helmed *The Sisters* at Warner Bros. back in 1938. Bondi's bête noir Darryl F. Zanuck produced this at Twentieth Century–Fox, so clearly Bondi did not let her pique at losing the role of Ma Joad get in the way of an acting job seven years later. It was her third and final film for Fox.

Bondi appears briefly a little over an hour into the drama, as a fellow patient in the mental institution where de Havilland's heroine Virginia Stuart Cunningham is being treated. Mrs. Greer is a woman with delusions of grandeur. She claims her husband is very rich and that General Pershing is a cousin from a minor branch of the family. When Mrs. Greer brags further that she owns the Hope diamond, de Havilland responds that she owns the "Hopeless" emerald in one of the film's few witty moments. This was Bondi's only film with de Havilland, who died in Paris in 2020 at age 104.

Among her half dozen rich, upper-class dowager roles, Hester Rivercomb in *The Sainted Sisters* is of less than middling interest and not much energy needs be expended on describing it. Set in 1896, the film stars Veronica Lake, in her final film as a Paramount contractee, and Joan Caulfield as two con women on the run, who hide out in Grove Falls, a Maine town bordering on Canada. There good-hearted sculptor and stone-cutter Barry Fitzgerald takes them in and slowly but surely brings about their regeneration and reintegration into society, first by secretly giving away their ill-gotten gains to worthy citizens and causes in the local community and later by dispensing their largesse with the sisters' full knowledge and approval. Bondi plays a domineering small town grandee, who has commissioned a marble mausoleum from Fitzgerald, "a monument to ugliness," as he terms it, for herself and her dead husband. She also owns the house he and his young female guests are living in. Mrs. Rivercomb bosses everyone in the town around, including Sheriff Tewilliger (William Demarest), who says, behind her back, that "what she needs is a boot in the bustle."

Bondi is not given much to do until 35 minutes into the film. Her nephew and sidekick, and Joan Caulfield's love interest, Ray Walker, wants her to invest $30,000 in a power plant to "light up the Falls" with water power. A big believer in the adage that "the Lord helps them who helps themselves," Hannah Rivercomb pledges $15,000 towards the project, if the town can raise the same amount, which the sisters then quickly proffer. The intricacies of the film's trivial plot need not occupy us further, but naturally all turns out well in the end. Mrs. Rivercomb is to some degree regenerated from her selfishness and parsimony and love conquers all with Lake uniting with George Reeves and Caulfield with Walker.

This middle-grade film was expeditiously produced at Paramount between mid–October and late November 1947 under the direction of William D. Russell, who only helmed seven feature films before turning his talents to television.[43] Bondi was billed sixth, behind the female stars, Fitzgerald, Reeves, and Demarest, which was a little low for her at this stage of her career. The film was universally panned by the larger urban newspapers. Philip K. Scheuer did not pull any punches in the *Los Angeles Times*, when he wrote on May 7, 1948: "I would unqualifiedly label it the poorest example of an alleged 'A' picture to come from a major studio so far this year." He continues: "As for the performers, whatever embarrassment they may have felt at finding themselves in such a lifeless travesty has now been shared, I can assure them, by this portion of the audience." We can imagine Bondi's toes curling as she read this. Adding insult to injury, Leonard Mendlowitz wrote in the *Pittsburgh Sun-Telegraph*: "Scene stealers Beulah Bondi and William Demarest have nothing to steal, as 'The Sainted Sisters' offers little enough for its stars, let alone its supporting players."[44]

The possibility of a return to Broadway and stage was becoming a recurring theme in interviews and news items about Bondi as the 1940s progressed. Harold Heffernan let it be known through his column in mid–December 1947, that "a good stage offer wouldn't be turned down." "Beulah's a mother type and those roles are running out in the movies," he added.[45] Yet the right vehicle for Bondi's long-awaited Broadway comeback was not forthcoming.

With film offers thin on the ground, Bondi satisfied herself with a return to the stage on the West coast instead. July 6–11, 1948, at the La Jolla Playhouse, she played Fabia in a summer stock production of Robert Sherwood's *The Road to Rome*, starring Wendell Corey as Hannibal and Eve Arden as Amytis.[46] Bondi had never acted with either of them on film. The play had been a big Broadway hit for Jane Cowl and Philip Merivale in 1927. The La Jolla production was directed by Norman Lloyd, a fellow actor who was in *The Southerner* and *The Black Book* and who is still alive as I write at age 105.

*The Road to Rome* may described as a romantic comedy in Roman togas and is about as accurately Roman as the Magic Castle is medieval. It is also an anti-war satire in which "Amytis [Arden], pleasure-loving wife of Roman Dictator Fabius Maximus [Donald Curtis], … uses her generously endowed charms, fortified by social conscience, to save Rome from Hannibal [Corey]'s Carthaginian army."[47] Fabia, created on Broadway by Jessie Ralph, is Fabius Maximus' mother and Amytis' mother-in-law and is described as "a cross, narrow-minded old lady whose world is her home. For all her 73 years, she is brisk and vigorous and rules the establishment with an iron hand."[48] A typical Bondi dowager and mother-in-law "heavy" role, in other words. Fabia only appears in the first act.

Bondi's comeback on Broadway looked like it was about to happen in late July 1948, when she signed to do Edward Chodorov's new play *Signor Chicago*, inspired by the Brothers Quintero's Spanish drama *The Women Have Their Way*.[49] *Signor Chicago* was on again and then off again, back and forth on the Broadway horizon for more than a year, yet ultimately never made it there with or without Bondi.

Along with films like *Arrowsmith*, *Registered Nurse*, and *Sister Kenny*, *Mr. Soft Touch* is a minor film in the Bondi canon, in fact it is hard to understand that a character actress of this caliber was needed for such an innocuous role in such a mediocre film. Or that Bondi was interested in playing it. Yet, as we have seen, after some busy war years, work in film was becoming scarcer by the end of the 1940s. In fact, the downward curve of Bondi's film career—and that of many of her breed of character actresses—had begun. When production started almost simultaneously on *Mr. Soft Touch* at Columbia and *The Black Book* at Eagle-Lions Films in mid–August 1948, she had not worked on a film since *The Sainted Sisters* in November 1947.

*Mr. Soft Touch* is a rousing, salubrious, cautionary tale of how much trouble can be caused by do-gooders, especially when they let former night club owners hole up in their settlement house. Evelyn Keyes is Jenny Jones, the do-good social worker, and Glenn Ford is Joe Miracle, the object of her do-gooding. He needs to keep himself and $100,000 safe for 24 hours until he can get a ship out of San Francisco. Ford has taken the money, which is his own, from the safe in the River Club, which he used to own and which has been taken over by the mob while Ford was away doing his patriotic duty in World War II.

As Clara Hangale, Bondi has a limited role as the head of the settlement house where Keyes works and has a few innocuous encounters during the final 40 minutes of the film with the two stars and with her trusty fellow worker Clara Blandick. In her most important scene, relatively speaking, she gives Keyes the third degree about her relationship with Ford, a man who carries a gun. "It is personal, isn't it? Send him away, Jenny, he'll bring you mischief, mark my words." As is her habit by this point in the film, Blandick comes rushing in with the latest news, this time to say that none of the phones are working.

For her brief and entirely mundane efforts, Bondi was billed fourth after the stars and John Ireland and ahead of her frequent co-stars Percy Kilbride and Blandick. In fact, this was her fifth and final film with Blandick, but the first where they had any significant screen interaction. Blandick's role as an elderly co-worker at the settlement house is as large as Bondi's and was one of her final three film roles. She and Bondi worked on the film at Columbia between August 9 and September 23, 1948, and had two directors: Gordon Douglas and Henry Levin.[50] It was the last time Bondi worked at Columbia.

*The Black Book*, a suspenseful, convoluted, semi-historical drama of the French Revolution also known as *Reign of Terror*, saw Bondi back with producer Walter Wanger a dozen years after she had done *The Trail of the Lonesome Pine*, *The Moon's Our Home*, and *The Case Against Mrs. Ames* for him in 1935–36. In the intervening years, Wanger had produced films like *Stagecoach*, *Foreign Correspondent*, *Scarlet Street*, and the disastrous *Joan of Arc*, been president of the Academy of Motion Pictures Arts and Sciences, and divorced his first wife and married Joan Bennett. His going to jail for shooting Bennett's lover was still in the future. The film was directed by Anthony Mann before he had hit the big time and produced at Eagle-Lion Films between mid–August and early October 1948.[51]

For her efforts as a rural grandmother, Bondi was billed eighth, a sign that she, inevitably, was beginning to slip down the credits list. The extremely complex plot of imposture and deceit, told with telegrammatic brevity, revolves around revolutionary leader Maxmillian Robespierre's small black book containing a death list of persons he considers to be "enemies of France." He claims to have misplaced it and charges hero and secret agent Charles d'Aubigny (Robert Cummings), who is pretending to be Robespierre's new public prosecutor Duval, with recovering it. Robespierre is played devilishly well by Richard Basehart.

Bondi's Grandma Blanchard does not appear until one hour into the film, when Cummings and co-conspirator Arlene Dahl stop at her rural farmhouse while making their escape by carriage from the terrors of Paris. The elderly woman wants to know if they have had their supper. Cummings responds rather rudely that they just want a bed. She has two young boys and a girl with her, her grandchildren and the children of her son Pierre and his wife Marie, comrades of Cummings.

Robespierre (Basehart) and his guardsmen suddenly show up in force. "We're looking for a man and woman; traitors to the republic," he tells her, as he regards her grandchildren under the covers with suspicion. She responds: "Well, you won't find them in that bed." Basehart tells her that her son and daughter-in-law have been arrested for treason and will be executed the following day. She says she knows nothing. He demands food and wine. Though Basehart tries to tempt her youngest grandson with a horse and promises he can become a soldier, the child senses danger and does not give anything away: "I didn't see anybody!" When Bondi mutters "Swine!" under her breath, Basehart hears her, but she claims to have said "More wine?"

Then, as she is about to place a pillow on the cot so Basehart can take a nap, she sees the black book lying there. Quickly, she hides it under the pillow. Cummings and the children create a diversion, so Dahl can come in and grab the book. The couple make their getaway on horseback. We are not invited to contemplate Bondi and the children's fate after this. This is undoubtedly the most tense and exciting scene in the film. I am tempted, though, to say that Bondi's performance is mostly being given by her voluminous cloth cap, which looks like it is wearing her, rather than the other way around.

The year of 1948 was the last year in which Bondi worked on more than two films. After completing work on *Mr. Soft Touch* and *The Black Book* in late September and early October 1948, she went immediately to work at Universal. Bondi did not make her finest films for Universal, but even by Universal standards—and with two Universal "Tammy" films still in the future—her final release of the 1940s was a low point. *The Life of Riley* is an inept, dull, not very funny comedy about the trials and tribulations of the little man. It starred William Bendix, reprising his role from a popular NBC radio series of the same name, as Chester A. Riley, a riveter at an aircraft production company. Rosemary De Camp played his long-suffering but ever supportive wife Peg. The war was over, Rosie had gone back to the kitchen, and the riveting was now being done by men.

As Miss Martha Bogle, Bondi has a medium-sized role as landlady to the Riley family, which includes their pretty daughter Babs (Meg Randall) and precocious son Junior (Lanny Rees). Miss Bogle's threat to sell the Rileys' house from over their heads leads to a major turning point, where Babs believes she has to sacrifice herself and enter into a marriage of convenience with her father's boss's son, Burt Stevenson (Mark Daniels), to save the family's fortunes and her father's already tarnished reputation. To add to the not so comic complications, Miss Bogle lives right next door with her hunky nephew and premed student, Jeff Taylor (Richard Long), Babs's main love interest in the film. Bogle wants her nephew to be a surgeon and then she can die happy.

In one scene, Miss Bogle appears in a robe and curlers after one of her many baths. According to her nephew, she takes baths all the time, which is the only thing she has in common with Blanche DuBois. Seeking forgiveness for being late with the rent, Riley presents her with a bouquet of flowers: "Yellow chrysanthemums, they bring out your complexion." Miss Bogle soon realizes they are from her own garden and calls him a robber. Riley's excuse is that he got them from Babs (who got them from Jeff): "My daughter, she's the robber. I was only the fence!." Miss Bogle's best scene is when she tells Riley she is selling the house for $8,000 and asks him to put up the "For Sale" sign on the front lawn. He thinks she means her own home, until he notices the sign is in his garden.

In the big climax, Miss Bogle is violently opposed to her nephew marrying Babs and greatly relieved when Babs says she is marrying the boss's son instead. Martha Bogle even shows up at the wedding, which turns out to be no wedding at all. The boss's son has his own dark motives in marrying Babs. He wants to get his hands on his $23,000 trust fund to pay off gambling debts, but is foiled at the last moment when the Rileys, father and son, overhear a revealing conversation via the intercom. Ultimately, Babs gets the man of her dreams and Riley can return to his working-class cronies, including James Gleason as his buddy Gillis, having saved the family's honor and the house.

This was Bondi's only film with Bendix, DeCamp, Gleason, Randall, Long, and director Irving Brecher, and I think we can be glad of it. Bosley Crowther wrote a scathing review in the newspaper of note. "Certainly no notable expansion of the comedy horizons of the screen is achieved by bringing the buffoonery of the Rileys to it from the radio," he remarked.[52] Once again, Bondi was the only major player to escape his vitriol by virtue of not being mentioned at all.

A promotional tour for *So Dear to My Heart* started 1949 busily and took her to several cities, including Indianapolis, Cincinnati, Nashville, Lexington, and Louisville[53]; and making rag dolls for fellow actor John Beal's new store, The Actors Hobby Market. Bondi had started making the rag dolls for the League for Crippled Children and supplied them with 65 a year according to one news article.[54] She had worked with Beal on a *University Playhouse* radio production of Katherine Ann Porter's *Noon Wine*, which was broadcast over NBC on August 20, 1948, and repeated January 29, 1949; and Beal had done the voice-over narration as the adult Jerry in *So Dear to My Heart*.[55] Beal's somewhat quirky business idea was to sell actors' handiwork from a tiny shop "sandwiched in between Tom Breneman's Restaurant and the Radio Room, a filmland pub." The only requirement for the sales items was that they "must be made by persons connected with the show business." All the sales items were on consignment and the idea was primarily to help out-of-work actors find an extra source of income. Bondi's dolls were "in constant demand at the Mart" and sold for a good price.[56] The shop opened in November 1948 and closed on June 30, 1950.[57]

It was after the tour was over, or as it was winding down, that Bondi spent a few days in Chicago seeing old friends. She had previously visited Myrtle Walgreen at her estate Hazelwood in late July 1945. This time, Bondi stayed with Mrs. Walgreen at her home at 4441 Drexel Blvd. in the North Kenwood section of Chicago, where Walgreen hosted a reception for "some 50 guests" in her honor on Tuesday, January 25, 1949, from 3 to 7 p.m. The *Dixon Telegraph* waxed eloquently about the food and decorations: "The dining room table was very beautiful, the covering being an Italian lace cloth upon which rested a large centerpiece of lavender iris and pale yellow jonquils in a silver basket. Lighted white tapers in tall silver candlesticks shed a soft light which always gives a pleasing effect to any tea table. The refreshments were varied and delicious." Bondi was described as "an old friend of Mrs. Walgreen."[58]

The next day, Bondi had lunch with some of her closest Valparaiso friends in the Pump Room of the Ambassador East Hotel in Chicago. Present were Louise Bartholomew, Ada Bartholomew, Floy Brownell, and Marie Windle and *Chicago Tribune* columnist Mae Tinee, who had come to interview Bondi. There is an interesting description of this lunch by Tinee, which gives a vivid picture of Bondi as she was approaching 60. Entitled "Beulah Bondi Engaging Off Screen or On," Tinee described her as "a winsome person, with a gentle, quiet manner, a sincere interest in people and a sprightly sense of humor." Her Valparaiso friends "were full of gossip about former schoolmates, the progress of their children and grandchildren, and were ready listeners to the actress' bits of information about the pleasures and problems of movie making." Bondi "smilingly denied" all the rumors her friends had heard "mostly concerned with the talk of the possibilities of marriage": "Like women the world over, they've been trying for years to talk her into matrimony, she just shook her head at them and finally said 'Don't you girls EVER give up?'"[59]

On September 2, 1949, Hedda Hopper reported that Bondi had "read three plays she loves." One was *Second Spring*, written for her by Bill Mercer: "Story's about a globetrotter gal, who leaves her two children in the security of New England. When she comes home, she finds they have grown stodgy and dull with all that security, and through her example she breathes new life into them." *The Man* was a suspense story by Mel Dinelli, best known for *The Spiral Staircase* and *The Window*. "It's a humdinger!" Bondi said.[60] On November 18, Harold V. Cohen reported that Bondi was to open in *The Man* at the Nixon Theater with Peggy Ann Garner, Don Hanmer, and Robert Emhardt.[61] The play opened January 19 at the Fulton Theater in New York, with Dorothy Gish in Bondi's role. It ran for 92 performances.

While considering options for her long-awaited stage comeback, Bondi was able to squeeze in two film productions before the year and the decade were over. The films were produced at roughly the same time, but Bondi's parts were limited enough to make it possible to do both. *The Baron of Arizona* had a slight head start on *The Furies* and got underway on November 1, 1949, at the newly built Nasser Studios on Sunset Boulevard under the direction of Samuel Fuller.[62] This was Bondi's first and only film for Fuller and with the two stars Vincent Price and Ellen Drew.

Vladimir Sokoloff, though, who this time was credited in third place, just above Bondi, was familiar to her from *Back to Bataan*. There he had played the Filipino headmaster who is hanged by the Japanese for refusing to lower the American flag at his school when they come to take over. Another familiar face on the set was Robert Barrat, who had played the head of the Tollivers' rival backwoods clan, Buck Falin, in *The Trail of the Lonesome Pine*, and a pirate captain in *The Buccaneer* who ignores Fredric March's direct orders and sinks an American ship with Bondi's niece on board, so she and her fiancé both die. Cinematographer on *The Baron of Arizona* was the legendary James

Wong Howe in his only outing with Bondi. Apparently, there were some exterior shots filmed on location at Florence, Arizona, before the production ended in late November, a month before *The Furies* wrapped at Paramount.[63]

*The Baron of Arizona* is a suspense-filled period crime drama in which Vincent Price as the bogus "Baron of Arizona" tries to falsify papers to prove that a little girl he has "adopted" is Sofia, Baroness de Peralta, the rightful heir to the territory of Arizona through a deed granted her ancestors by the king of Spain. Sofia as a child was played by Karen Kester and as an adult by Ellen Drew. Bondi's role as Loma Morales is a modest one. A former teacher at Las Vegas College, she is hired by Price as Sofia's governess to give her the necessary polish in what is yet another Pygmalion story. Loma appears mainly in the ear-

liest scenes of the film and mostly in montage with no dialogue. She reappears in the trial scene, where she sits with Sofia's foster father Pepito Alvarez (Sokoloff) and later Price thanks her for all she has done for Sofia. This is practically a non-speaking part.

The role of Loma is interesting, though, for being the only time Bondi played an Hispanic role on film. Bondi had probably avoided ethnically coded roles up until this point out of fear that she would be marginalized if she played up her "ethnic" features. This was a marked difference from her early days on the stage, where she had played both Native Americans and African Americans in various contexts. Her *Back to Bataan* co-star Vladimir Sokoloff, born in Russia, played the Mexican Pepito this time. Clearly, in the ethnic logic of Hollywood at the time, he looked exotic enough to play anything but an African American. At any rate, Hedda Hopper reported on November 14, that Bondi was "loving her role in 'The Baron of Arizona.' She has some amusing scenes with Vladimir Sokoloff."[64] One wonders what happened to them…. They certainly did not make it into the final cut.

The Baron's plan, which involves an extended stay in Spain

Throughout her years in Hollywood, Bondi studiously avoided any role with an ethnic slant. Clearly, she was afraid that her dark hair, eyebrows, and eyes and olive skin might be seen as "exotic" and limit her opportunities at a time when minority meant marginal. Loma Morales in *The Baron of Arizona* (Deputy, 1950) was about as far as she was willing to go in portraying a non–Anglo-American character on the screen. During her days in stock, it was quite another matter. There she played a variety of women of color in a way that would not be acceptable today. At a time when theater companies were not integrated, the only way to have a Native American, Latino, African American or other minority character in a play was to have a white actor play the part.

to falsify two land grant books, almost succeeds, but is finally foiled by Pepito revealing, what he promised Sofia's parents one day to reveal, that she has "Indian blood." The Baron is sentenced to six years hard labor for fraud. In the final scene, Loma is visible waiting in the carriage with Sofia and Pepito, when Price is finally released from prison.

After five films in a row of variable quality and with few chances for Bondi to shine, the decade ended on a high note when she was cast in Anthony Mann's noir Western masterpiece *The Furies*. Production started on November 9, 1949, but Bondi did not join the cast until December, after production on *The Baron of Arizona* was over.[65] She was billed seventh in a small but significant role as a banker's wife, Emily Anaheim, who helps Barbara Stanwyck late in the film, when she is trying to get an extension on her father's loans and take over the family ranch, "The Furies."

Mrs. Anaheim appears in the San Francisco segment as a hostess at a party, married to one of the bankers Stanwyck needs on her side. Bondi's lecherous husband, Old Anaheim, played by the prolific but seldom credited character actor Charles Evans, wants to escort Stanwyck home from the party, but she will have none of it. While this is playing out, Stanwyck gives Bondi a significant, conspiratorial look. Her hostess follows her out and thanks her for giving the old man the brush off. Stanwyck's says she realized during the course of the evening, that Mrs. Anaheim was the one to reckon with if she was to get her father a 90-day extension on his mortgage. Bondi responds: "You're a clever one. I don't control the Anaheim Bank, but I do control Mr. Anaheim." Stanwyck: "And have I reckoned with you?" Bondi: "I like a clever woman. I'll help you." Her last words as they part at the carriage are: "He's a faithless husband, but he is my husband." This is an effective and well-acted scene, in which Bondi and Stanwyck demonstrate that sometimes you do not need the old boys network, but in fact the old gals…

In the next scene, Bondi comes rushing into her husband's bank office, after he has turned down Walter Huston's request for an extension. Huston, who is estranged from Stanwyck at this point, says he has no daughter, when Bondi mentions she has met her. To her husband, Bondi says: "I think T.C. can have till 10 tomorrow morning, don't you?" He reluctantly agrees. Huston responds: "Thanks, Emily, how is she?" "Your daughter? Oh, fine!" The acting is so good in Bondi's two scenes here, that it sends shivers down your spine. It appears that Bondi's role had been enlarged after the end of the production period on December 23, 1949. She had gone to New York to negotiate a possible appearance in Mel Dinelli's *The Man* and to spend the holidays there, when she was hastily recalled to the west coast.[66] There was no Mrs. Anaheim at all in the novel by Niven Busch on which the film was based. There T.C. Jeffords manages to negotiate an extension with Anaheim and some other bankers without any outside, female intervention.

It was ten years since Bondi had done *Remember the Night* with Stanwyck, where they also seemed to have a special rapport on the screen. In the meantime, Stanwyck had been nominated for three Academy Awards for *Ball of Fire*, *Double Indemnity*, and *Sorry, Wrong Number*, but they had eluded her. *The Furies* was Bondi's third and final film with Walter Huston, who had played her husband both in *Rain* and *Of Human Hearts*. He died on April 7, 1950, of an aortic aneurysm, two days after his 67th birthday. While *The Furies* was Bondi's last film produced in the 1940s, it was Huston's final film of all and was released after his death.

# 8

# It Was a Wonderful Life

## Later Career and Final Years

"Someone told me I should write my life story. My life story wouldn't interest anyone. It's too happy. It's really been a wonderful life."[1]

Both quantitatively and qualitatively, there was little in Bondi's latter career that could compare with the 1930s and '40s. The last 30 years of her long life were less about work and more about enjoying the fruits of her labors, as she transformed herself into a world traveler, pursued her other hobbies and interests and dedicated herself to a small circle of family and friends. Bondi only made ten feature films during her final three decades. She returned to Broadway after a long absence in 1950 and worked intermittently in the live theater until 1957. She also did some work in television. By 1963, she had officially retired, though she did a handful of high-profile television roles in the 1970s. To a question about what had happened to Beulah Bondi, columnist Mike Connolly responded in 1962: "Beulah is very wealthy, having made most of her moola during the era of low taxes, and is now on a rock-hunting expedition in Egypt."[2] When a young actress, Bondi had found a Boston investment firm to help manage her money and they did so for more than 50 years.[3]

Let us resume our account in the early 1950s. Bondi had been trying to find an appropriate vehicle on Broadway for some time, when she finally landed the role of the mother in a new drama called *Hilda Crane* in August 1950.[4] A month later, she was busy rehearsing the play in New York, according to Louella Parsons.[5] After out-of-town try-outs at the McArthur Theatre in Princeton, New Jersey, and the Locust Theatre in Philadelphia, *Hilda Crane* opened at the Coronet Theatre in New York on November 1, 1950. It was 16 years since Bondi last appeared on Broadway.

Referred to by one critic as a "sex drama,"[6] *Hilda Crane* would prove the final Broadway play of Samson Raphaelson, an advertising man turned short story writer and playwright best remembered today for writing the story and the play on which the first talking film, *The Jazz Singer*, was based. Raphaelson had his biggest successes on Broadway with *The Jazz Singer* in 1925–26, *Accent on Youth* in 1935, and *Skylark* in 1939–40. He also wrote or co-wrote several screenplays in Hollywood, including *Trouble in Paradise*, *The Shop Around the Corner*, *Suspicion*, and *Heaven Can Wait*.

The title role in *Hilda Crane* was played by Jessica Tandy, following directly on her standout success as Blanche DuBois in *A Streetcar Named Desire*. The play was directed by Tandy's husband Hume Cronyn and produced by Broadway composer Arthur Schwartz

174

as his second venture into producing. Finding it difficult to cast the play in New York, Schwartz flew to Los Angeles to court his favorite actors, including Bondi, whom were all working in films at the time.[7] In one of those vagaries of fate, Schwartz caught up with Bondi on her way back to a friend's house to pick of a film contract that she had forgotten and was intending to sign. She never signed it, heading back to Broadway instead.[8]

After 11 years in New York, two failed marriages and several affairs, and with only a mink coat to her name, Hilda Crane sees herself forced to return to her childhood home in the small college town of Winona, Illinois, where her widowed mother, Mrs. Crane (Bondi), still lives in the family home. Faced with the choice between rekindling an affair with an attractive former lover, literature professor Charles Jensen (Frank Sundstrom), or finding security in a marriage of convenience with the stolid and dependable self-made-man Henry Ottwell (John Alexander), Hilda ultimately follows her conventional mother's advice and marries the latter, with disastrous results.

As one critic framed the central question posed by the play: "What happens ... to these independent, traditionless women who are too restless to find happiness, even contentment, in marriage and who are not sufficiently aggressive or talented to achieve successful careers?"[9]

Hilda Crane was clearly a heroine in the tradition of Hedda Gabler and Blanche DuBois, of Kate Chopin's Edna Pontellier and Edith Wharton's Lily Bart. Yet she had little of the vitality and depth that made those classic portrayals of women chafing against the constraints of contemporary gender norms come alive and invoke our sympathy. As one critic wrote, she was "basically neither a likable nor an admirable woman."[10] Another noted: "Hilda is too adolescent, too lacking in warmth, to engage your feelings."[11]

In an article in the *New York Times* published shortly before the play's premiere, Raphaelson described his play as "the story of how marriage and love and death happened, at least in this case, to stem from the fumbling, painful efforts of a woman and her mother to understand each other and themselves."[12] Mrs. Crane was Bondi's most important dramatic role on Broadway. She is described in the stage directions as "a well-bred American small-town mother, neat, composed, old-fashioned, pleasantly severe." In her own admission to Henry Ottwell in the opening scene, after having seen each other only three times in 11 years, she and her daughter are "still strangers to each other."[13]

Despite the author's emphasis on the mother-daughter relationship, the best supporting role was that of Hilda Crane's mother-in-law and arch nemesis, Mrs. Ottwell, played with vim and vigor and thinly veiled vulgarity by Evelyn Varden. One critic wrote that she "practically steals the show."[14] Though she had begun her career as an ingénue, Varden made her biggest impact on Broadway as a character actress between 1934 and 1955. She was also memorable in films like *Pinky*, *Phone Call from a Stranger*, and *The Bad Seed*.[15] Fortunately, Varden got to reprise her standout performance in *Hilda Crane* in the 1956 film version, directed and written by Philip Dunne and starring Jean Simmons, while Bondi was replaced to little effect by Judith Evelyn. We know Bondi was in Hollywood and available when the film was made in January and early February 1956. She did not begin work on *Back from Eternity* until March.

On Broadway, *Hilda Crane* received decidedly mixed reviews. Brooks Atkinson thought the play was "admirably acted" and "well written," but added that "there is no getting away from the fact that the heroine is a tiresome, irritating egotist, and that Mr. Raphaelson's writing and thinking are not original enough to give his play about her much interest or significance." He found that, "as Hilda's patient mother, Beulah Bondi acts with force, pride and decision." Atkinson concluded devastatingly that the heroine "does not seem worth the trouble that Mr. Raphaelson and Miss Tandy have taken to put her on the stage."[16] UP drama editor Jack Gaver agreed when he wrote that the play was "theatrically effective most of the time without seeming to have any value at the end. It interests you, yet leaves you cold."[17]

The response to Bondi's performance from other critics was positive yet subdued. They described it in words like "quiet bitterness," "quiet authority," "comforting assurance," and "as crisp and assured as ever."[18] Gaver wrote that Bondi "grows in effectiveness as the play progresses, more by what she doesn't say or do than by any speech or action." The raves were reserved for Varden. Linton Martin thought both actors turned in "perfectly priceless performances" and Gaver called Mrs. Crane and Mrs. Ottwell "two of the most reprehensible mothers ever seen on a stage." Louis Shaeffer objected that "neither Hilda nor her mother is very well explained."[19] This is more true of Mrs. Crane, I think, than it is of Hilda, and it weakens the fabric of the play.

In an interview with columnist Mark Barron published on the day of the final performance, Bondi explained that the Winona, Illinois, of the play was just the kind of quiet college town she had grown up in: "She found most of her guidance in playing this role from her own experience in a quiet, respectful Indiana community." Bondi added: "Back in my childhood in Indiana, I found that you are either 'a good girl' or 'a bad girl.' … And in my experience around Broadway and Hollywood I think the same judgements of character still holds true."[20]

*Hilda Crane* closed on December 31, 1950, after a modest 70 performances. With no new play on offer, Bondi returned to Hollywood. *Lone Star* was the only film she worked on in 1951, a year distinguished by being the first since she started in films two decades earlier that she was off the screen. Indeed, *Lone Star* was her first film of the 1950s, a decade in which she only worked on seven films. Directed by Vincent Sherman, it was a good opportunity for her at this stage in her career. Many character actresses would have given an arm and a leg to be supporting not one but two of MGM's legendary male stars; in fact, arguably the two most important stars of their respective generations (at least who were still working): Clark Gable and Lionel Barrymore.

In his and Bondi's sixth and final film together, Barrymore was back playing Andrew Jackson. It was his last dramatic role, though he would show up playing himself in the "docudrama" *Main Street to Broadway* in 1953, the year before he died. Given the number of times Andrew Jackson shows up in Bondi's films, we can almost wonder if the seventh president had some special place in her heart. Bondi played Jackson's wife, the "Backwoods Belle" Rachel Jackson, in *The Gorgeous Hussy* (1936), had a more peripheral relationship with him as an upper-class member of his social circle in New Orleans in *The Buccaneer* (1938), and now in *Lone Star* would play a fictitious character, Jackson's cousin and caregiver in old age, Minniver Bryan.

Minniver Bryan's function here is to be a confidante both to Jackson and to the man he hopes will help bring the "Lone Star" state into the union, Devereaux Burke, "a rough Texas adventurer-cattleman"[21] with no small degree of Rhett Butler in him, played by the now 51-year-old Clark Gable. Miss Bryan is evident from the first scene, at Jackson's home in Nashville, Tennessee, when Luther Kilgore (James Burke) comes in all excited that Sam Houston has made a speech against annexation and Minniver tells him she has kept the news from Jackson. "I don't want to see him go to his grave any sooner than the Lord intended," she tells Kilgore. By the way, dependable character actor James Burke was

Bondi supported many of the great stars of the 1930s and '40s, but few were greater than Clark Gable (left). Their common vehicle *Lone Star* (MGM, 1952) was not great, but at least Bondi got more screen time here than was usual for her during the 1950s, a period when both Hollywood filmmaking and Bondi's career were in a decline. In *Lone Star*, a mix of western, biopic, and period costume drama, Bondi played Lionel Barrymore's caregiver and Gable's confidante and was billed fifth.

in seven of Bondi's films from *The Trail of the Lonesome Pine* (1936) to *The Unholy Wife* (1957), making him probably her most frequent co-star, though they did not always share screen time.

It was not long after production started on May 16, 1951, that Hedda Hopper reported that Bondi had suffered a fall from a horse and was now wearing a brace for her back. According to the gossip columnist, "It wasn't fair to ask Beulah Bondi to ride a horse."[22] I am pretty sure no force on earth would have gotten 62-year-old Bondi up on a horse, if she did not feel up to it and accidents will happen. Production on the film was over by late June and may have involved location shooting in Texas for Bondi, as her character more or less follows Gable around wherever he goes.[23] For her sterling efforts here, Bondi was billed fifth after Gable, Ava Gardner, Broderick Crawford, and Barrymore, followed by Ed Begley in a "with Beulah Bondi and Ed Begley" type credit listing. This was Bondi's only film with Gable and Gardner and director Sherman.

In her only film produced in 1952, *Latin Lovers*, a terminally dull, Technicolor romance set in New York and Brazil and directed by veteran Mervyn LeRoy, Bondi was cast as an unnamed analyst, who tries to help John Lund in his wooing of Lana Turner. A hard-nosed heiress and businesswoman worth 37 million dollars, Turner also spends time on the therapist's couch, though a different therapist, trying to sort out her feelings for Lund. Bondi features in two scenes, both with her patient, and wears her very dark hair in a bun. In the first, she gives him advice to be gentle and patient when proposing, which turns out to be just the opposite of what Turner wants and needs. The second time around, Bondi reverses her position on forcefulness in proposing, but it is too late. All ends well, though, when Lund marries Turner's secretary, played by Jean Hagen, and Turner gets hitched to quintessential Latin lover Ricardo Montalban. Few reviewers did more than mention Bondi's presence here, though the *Los Angeles Times* took time to note that it was "pleasing to see Beulah Bondi in one of the psychiatrist assignments."[24] In fact, this was the last time she played a professional woman on the big screen.

Production on *Latin Lovers* began at MGM on December 2, 1952, and ran till mid–January the following year. Bondi likely did her scenes early, before she broke her leg in a fall on the ice in Yosemite National Park on Christmas Eve and then, undeterred, started on a pre–Broadway tour of Paul Osborn's *On Borrowed Time* on December 29.[25]

Nellie Northrup, the grandmother in *On Borrowed Time*, was not Bondi's most important role, but it was certainly her most recurring one, as she played in not only in the 1939 film version, but also on the stage at various times, on radio in 1952, and on television in 1957. *On Borrowed Time* was the lachrymose love story between grandfather and grandson in which the grandmother is largely "de trop," as the French say. She conveniently dies in the middle of the story, leaving Gramps and Pud to battle on against their mortal and immortal foes: rapacious, stiff-necked Aunt Demetria and death in the figure of Mr. Brink. One might have wished Bondi had devoted her energy to a more worthy vehicle and a more interesting role, but there were not many good alternatives or more interesting parts available by the early 1950s.

As we have seen, Bondi had played Granny at the El Patio Theatre in 1946, where her "significant other" had been Boris Karloff. Then in the summer of 1951, she teamed up with her *Make Way for Tomorrow* co-star Victor Moore to present *On Borrowed Time* at the famous local theater in La Jolla with Leo C. Carroll as Mr. Brink, Kay Hammond as Demetria Riffle, and David John Stollery as Pud.[26] A Broadway revival was mooted at this time.[27] In fact, New York audiences would not see this production until February 10, 1953, when it opened at the 48th Street Theatre after tryouts in San Francisco and Boston. Bondi had done *Cock Robin* at the 48th Street Theatre back in 1928.

Bondi had turned 50 during production on the film version directed by Harold S. Bucquet in 1939. Now she was nearing 64. Theresa Loeb Cone wrote after the San Francisco premiere at the Alcazar Theatre on December 29, 1952, that "Beulah Bondi contributes a jewel-like bit as an understanding if somewhat shrewish grandmother."[28] After her Christmas Eve fall in Yosemite, Bondi had a cast on her broken leg during the San Francisco run. This was a lesser hindrance than it might seem, as she only appeared in the first act and it was decided that she would be wheelchair-bound, just as Lionel Barrymore had been in the film.[29] In his rave review, the *Boston Globe*'s critic thought Bondi, "that consummate mistress of character portrayal," was "a perfect choice for Granny."[30] Walter F. Kerr wrote that Bondi "makes the most of her brief opportunities."[31] John Chapman called her "lovely and touching."[32] Jack Geiger thought she deserved praise, but "couldn't match the Moore-Stollery combination."[33] Brooks Atkinson's final notice of Bondi was that she "acts Gramps' tired, mistrustful wife with a sweetness that is never cloying."[34]

Despite laudatory reviews that predicted a long run, *On Borrowed Time* only ran a week longer than *Hilda Crane* had in 1950. It closed on April 18, 1953, after 78 performances. Victor Moore died of a heart attack on July 23, 1962, at the age of 86, while Bondi was working on her final film *Tammy and the Doctor*.[35]

Bondi had one more go around with *On Borrowed Time* on November 17, 1957, when she did a one and a half hour, "colorcast" version on the seventh season of the TV drama anthology series *Hallmark Hall of Fame*, directed by George Schaefer. She was joined in the cast by Ed Wynn as Gramps, Claude Rains as Mr. Brink, Dennis Kohler as Pud, and Margaret Hamilton as Demetria Riffle.[36] The episode was well received. Columnist Jack O'Brian wrote that "Beulah Bondi as Granny was as right as her crusty, lovely old role could insist" and Donald Kirkley thought she was "a fortunate choice."[37] He might just as well have said she was an *obvious* choice.

While *On Borrowed Time* was Bondi's last Broadway show, it was not her final stage appearance. It was while she was playing in *On Borrowed Time* in San Francisco in January 1953, that the *Oakland Tribune* reported that Dan Totheroh was writing a play especially for her.[38] It was to be based on a semiautobiographical novel by Jean Bell Thomas called *The Traipsin' Woman* from 1933. The title referred to the nickname Thomas had been given when she worked as a journalist in her home state of Kentucky and started reporting on court cases from the rural counties of Appalachia. Her travels would make Thomas an authority on the rich musical life and cultural traditions of eastern Kentucky. Bondi had known Thomas since the 1920s.[39]

Bondi did not open in the play until August 1, 1957, as part of the Denver Drama Festival held at the University of Denver.[40] Jean Thomas attended a performance, as did columnist John Chapman.[41] He reported: "As a play it wasn't so much, being gentle folk stuff with little kick; but as a production it was admirable. It was all outdoors, with the stage backed up against a building and the audience sitting in folding chairs arranged on the gentle slope of a lawn."[42] An amateur production with a backstage crew consisting of entirely of students, *The Traipsin' Woman* was Bondi's final stage play. It was the fourth play she did by Totheroh, who died in Oakland in 1976.

William A. Wellman's *Track of the Cat* from 1954 is one of the most highly wrought and visually stunning films in the Bondi canon. Fifteen years earlier, when working on another film, Wellman hit on the idea of making a black and white movie in color by designing a set and using costumes that were almost entirely black and white, so that the only color was the sky, the evergreen trees, the actors' skin tones, and a few carefully placed, symbolic splashes. One of these was star Robert Mitchum's red mackinaw jacket, symbolizing "the danger he creates"; another, young romantic lead Diana Lynn's yellow blouse, symbolizing "the cheer she brings in other lives," but surely also open to alternative interpretations.[43] One article at the time pointed out that "even the chickens in a barnyard scene are Minorcas, mottled black and white fowl."[44] According to Wellman, "The story lends itself to the no-color idea…. Stark, realistic. You'll see the faces, eyes, the pigment of skin; nothing extraneous to 'annoy' or 'interest' you; no flowers, gowns, jewelry, pretty scenery as such. Just people."[45]

The result is stunning in its stark simplicity. When combined with the new widescreen technology of CinemaScope, the film develops as a series of striking tableaux. CinemaScope had the disadvantage that it could make the human actors look small and insignificant, swamped in the grandeur of the surrounding landscape. When this is part of the message of the film—that human trials and tribulations are as nothing when compared with the eternal truth and beauty of nature—the photographic technology works in harmony with the film's theme.

In addition to its visual appeal, *Track of the Cat* has a small, tightly knit, perfectly configured ensemble cast of only eight players enacting a storyline that, though it teeters on the edge of cliché and stereotype, also has a mythical, timeless quality. Bondi plays Letty Bridges, matriarch and ruler of her northern California ranch, with Robert Mitchum as her favorite son Curt; William Hopper her thoughtful, sensitive son Arthur; Tab Hunter her callow, youngest son Harold; Teresa Wright her frustrated, unmarried daughter Grace; and British-inflected Philip Tonge her ineffectual, alcoholic husband.

Letty Bridges is somewhat reminiscent of Mollie Matthews in *The Shepherd of the Hills*, only about 20 years older and living on a California mountain ranch, rather than being mired in the backwoods of Kentucky. And unlike Mollie, Letty is still capable of growth and change. She likes to read her Bible and is the most possessive mother Bondi

**Bondi had a treasure trove of costumes and props, which she used to advantage throughout her career. She must have been waiting for just the right moment to use this tatty terry robe worn with a black full-length skirt over it. *Track of the Cat* (Wayne-Fellows, 1954), directed by Walter Wellman, was the finest film of her latter career. It is a visually stunning picture shot in color as if it were black and white. Plotwise it is not quite as stunning, but it is totally dominated by Bondi in her final incarnation on film of the mountain matriarch she had so often embodied. Tab Hunter (middle) and William Hopper (right) played two of her three sons. Robert Mitchum was the third. Hunter became a personal friend and fondly remembered her in his 2005 memoir *Tab Hunter Confidential*.**

ever played, doing what she can to disrupt the budding romance of her handsome son Harold and his plain-faced girlfriend Gwen Williams (Diana Lynn), who has come on a first visit to the ranch. Letty suggests Gwen, whose family lives in a "gopher home" (she says), may be a gold digger. And besides, Gwen is two years older than Harold, whom Letty considers too young to marry.

The central symbol of the film is the legendary panther, thought to be black, who is never seen, "a vague and complex symbol of Evil or Hate or what you will."[46] In the Bridges' local idiom, of course, the panther is a "painter." He kills first the Bridges' cattle and then eldest son Arthur Bridges half an hour into the film. While middle son Curt is engaged in a struggle to the death in the wilds of northern California, the rest of the family enact a domestic drama within the claustrophobic four walls of the Bridges homestead, mourning and burying Arthur, and squabbling over who should stay and who should go. Harold, in particular, is torn between his love and desire for Gwen, and his loyalty to his aging parents, who need him more than ever when first Arthur and then Curt dies in the course of the film.

Unlike Mollie Matthews, then, Letty Bridges slowly comes to recognize and admit to her own culpability and the need for change. In Arthur's burial scene, strikingly shot upwards from the bottom of the freshly dug grave, Letty reflects, "All the things I could say, seems to me I could have said them when he was alive." Later, when Curt has been found dead at the bottom of a ravine, Ma Bridges says: "I done wrong. Curt has to come home. He can't die with my sin on his soul. It was my doin.' Whatever he done, he done to please me."

The film was co-produced by John Wayne for the production company he shared with Robert Fellows and was shot between June 14 and late July 1954, starting with two weeks on location at Mount Rainier in Washington state, before the cast and crew headed to Stage 22 at Warner Bros.[47] One UP news item made much of the fact that director Wellman had wanted Bondi for Ma Bridges based on having seen her in *The Trail of the Lonesome Pine*: "He asked her to come in to discuss the role with him and then refused to believe that the woman who came to his office was the same Beulah Bondi he'd seen in a picture some years ago. 'It's always been like that,' said Miss Bondi, ... 'I finally convinced him and he gave me the part. I'm very happy about it, as it's a challenge—Ma Bridges is such a mean old woman.'"[48] Wellman was known as a "man's director" and "'Wild Bill' Wellman," who voiced his opinions loudly and in strong language. When Wellman's "first comments on her acting ... were expressed in adjectives that Beulah Bondi accepts from no one," she objected immediately, saying "she would take his direction, but she would not listen to it expressed in vulgarisms." Wellman apologized.[49]

Bondi formed a special bond with Tab Hunter on the set, that he remembered fondly half a century later in his autobiography *Tab Hunter Confidential*.[50] But even back in 1954, he had been full of praise of his screen mother. One news item read "Bondi Tops Glamor Girls." According to this brief interview with Hunter, "one of Hollywood's most eligible young men ... finds in Beulah Bondi many of the fascinations of the 'ideal date.'" He added that "many a present day glamor doll could learn much from Miss Bondi. She has deep tolerance, kindliness and understanding—a rare combination of qualities."[51]

Though the reviews were decidedly mixed, *Track of the Cat* was the last film in which Bondi's performance was widely commented on and widely commended. Whatever the critic's thought of the film as a whole, most of them recognized the extent to which Bondi's unique presence had contributed to the total impact of the film. R.H. Gardner of the

*Baltimore Sun* was one of them. "'Track of the Cat' is a minor artistic triumph," he wrote, "combining the realism of a Grant Wood painting with the horror of an Edgar Allan Poe short story." He found that the characters "have a sort of unholy festering sickness about them that reminds one of O'Neill's 'Mourning Becomes Electra.'" Gardner was not afraid to make bold claims for the film: "story-wise, it is probably the best movie ever made in CinemaScope." About the individual performances, he commented: "Robert Mitchum does well as the unfortunate Curt, but the real star of the piece (excepting Mr. Wellman of course) is Beulah Bondi, who makes the part of the mother as wretchedly real as a sink-ful of dirty dishes."[52]

Gardner's colleague at the *Baltimore Evening Sun*, Gilbert Kanour, found that the real star of the picture was director of photography William H. Clothier. Kanour was ecstatic about the film's visuals: "Never, in looking at several hundred photoplays a year, have we seen such artistry." He found that Letty Bridges, "a hard-bitten, sanctimonious old dame fond of quoting the Old Testament," was "acted with uncomfortable precision by that grand Beulah Bondi."

Theresa Loeb Cone of the *Oakland Tribune* observed tartly: "I don't know if the book explained much about the characters' background and motivations, but the movie certainly doesn't." Nevertheless, she found "the individual acting stints are extremely impressive, especially in the case of Beulah Bondi as the Bible-reading, narrow-minded farm woman."[53]

Mildred Martin of the *Philadelphia Inquirer* also had a lot to say about *Track of the Cat*. On the downside: "Everybody talks and talks in this—even to himself when no one else is about. And the more they talk, the less one is likely to understand, although some-where along the line the impression comes over that the whole world is a mysteriously lurking black panther waiting to spring at the throat of the unwary." She found that "the weird drama constantly promises more of profound moment than is ever delivered." But she had fine words for Bondi: "Outstanding, towering above all of the others with one of the film's more comprehensible performances, is Beulah Bondi as Mrs. Bridges, whose strength of character and unbending religious conception of what is right apparently proves the family's undoing."[54]

Edwin Schallert of the *Los Angeles Times* thought Bondi dominated the plot and found that "her somber scenes of sorrow are powerful." Lillian Blackstone wrote in the *St. Petersburg Times*: "The best job of acting is done by Beulah Bondi, an unforgettable char-acter as the mother of a misfit family and the wife of a drunken man."[55]

*New York Times* critic Bosley Crowther's largely critical analysis is worth quot-ing at length. He admits that the film has its moments, "usually when Miss Bondi as the pinch-lipped mother takes command and browbeats her brood of frightened weak-lings by the very force of her hard, determined will": "Then a feeling of tragic frustration seeps out of the CinemaScope screen, and the shadow of an O'Neill character flickers on the fringe." "But," Crowther continues, "for the most part, Mr. Wellman's big screen picture seems a heavy and clumsy travesty of a deep matriarchal melodrama or a West-ern with Greek overtones. And the business of the brother hunting the panther in the great big CinemaScope outdoors, while the family booze and blather in the ranch-house, has the nature of an entirely different show." In the final analysis, *Track of the Cat*, in Crowther's considered opinion, "has no psychological pattern, no dramatic point. There's a lot of pretty snow scenery in it and a lot of talk about deep emotional things. But it gets lost in following some sort of pretense. The cat goes this way and O'Neill goes that."[56]

Surprisingly, Crowther has not a word to say about the artfulness and novelty of the film's cinematography and mise en scène.

Despite the reasonable demurs discussed above, I now consider *Track of the Cat* to be among the half dozen of Bondi's most important films. It is the only one of Bondi's films I have had to radically reassess in connection with writing this book. In my 2006 profile of Bondi, I wrote: "Tab Hunter fans will be the only ones to enjoy this inept, snow-bound, noir Western, and even they should probably turn off the sound."[57] Well, like Ma Bridges, I wuz wrong. I suspect that others will see this film in a new light in the coming years, if they have not already, in the same way as the 1950s melodramas of Douglas Sirk have long since have been reevaluated and upgraded to high art worthy of the most searching critical attention.

While Bondi had secured a new passport in January 1953, she did not get to use it till 1955. This year marks the beginning of her life as a world traveler. She had been to Europe in 1928, but between then and 1955, she vacationed in the United States, with the Mojave Desert, Hawaii, and Florida as three favorite destinations. I have documented one foreign trip during these years: a car trip to Mexico and Guatemala in the spring of 1950.[58]

Given that she was born in 1889, when Benjamin Harrison was president and Queen Victoria still had a dozen years left on the throne, and came of age during a time when there were many more restrictions on women's freedom than there are today, at least in the Western world, I imagine that Bondi must have been one of the most well-travelled American women of her generation. She was energetic, unafraid, and endlessly curious about people and places. Not only that, by the mid–1950s, she had the means and the time available to become a first-class globetrotter in every sense: she travelled in style and she travelled literally around the world. She once explained: "my main reason for liking to travel is the people."[59]

Bondi is known to have visited the following countries (in some cases several times): Australia, Cambodia, Dahomey, Denmark, Egypt, Ethiopia, Fiji, France, French Polynesia (Tahiti), Germany, Greece, Guatemala, Hong Kong, India, Indonesia, Italy, Jordan, Kenya, Lebanon, Lichtenstein, Malaysia, Mali, Mexico, Nepal, New Zealand, Niger, Nigeria, Norway, Peru, Portugal, Senegal, South Africa, Spain, Sudan, Switzerland, Syria, Taiwan, Tanzania, Thailand, Tunisia, Turkey, Uganda, the United Kingdom, and Yugoslavia. Once the necessary air travel had transported to her chosen, far-away travel destinations, her favorite way to see things was renting a car and driving off the beaten path. She drove herself and kept till the end of her days the international driver's license she had obtained in July 1955.[60]

Bondi's first major journey in 17 years was mainly a trip around the Mediterranean, which took to her to Tunisia, Egypt, Lebanon, Syria, Turkey, Greece, Yugoslavia, Italy, England, France, Switzerland, and Lichtenstein, in roughly that order.[61] She arrived in the port of Tunis on April 22, 1955, and returned home aboard the Nieuw Amsterdam from Le Havre, arriving in New York on September 3, 1955.[62] According to Louella Parsons, she had turned down two films to make the trip: "It's something she's planned for a long time."[63]

It was a funny coincidence that Bondi's first film after her six-month trip was one that prominently featured foreign travel. Of the two films she made back to back for John Farrow's independent production company and directed by him in 1956, *Back from Eternity* was superior to *The Unholy Wife*, which is not saying a lot. Bondi had signed to do the film by February 23, 1956, and production started at soon-to-be defunct RKO on

March 5, lasting until April 26, on which date Farrow wrote to her: "both your acting and your manner were an example to us all."[64] Some of the airport scenes were filmed on location at Long Beach Municipal Airport.[65]

Part of the 1950s fascination with airports and airplanes, one of the charms of *Back from Eternity* is the opportunity to observe all the paraphernalia and local color of commercial airline travel in its infancy. But the aviation angle is only a starting point for the story. Once the various passengers on a flight to Boca Grande have been introduced and brought together at the airport in Panama, the stage has been set for an adventure story of life and death in the deepest jungles of South America. Needless to say, the flight never gets to Boca Grande. After a brief lunchtime layover in San Dimas, they hit a terrible thunderstorm on their final stretch to their destination and make a crash landing in what the captain, Robert Ryan, describes as "one of the most isolated areas anywhere." The sole stewardess has been sucked out of the door to her death, but Ryan, the co-pilot Keith Andes, and all nine passengers have miraculously survived without a scratch.

Among these passengers, we find elderly Professor Henry Spangler and his wife Martha, played by Cameron Prud'Homme and Bondi. Born in 1892, Prud'Homme was primarily a stage and radio actor and only did five films over a period of 33 years starting with *Abraham Lincoln* in 1930.[66] Mr. and Mrs. Spangler are far from being the main focus of the film, which is more concerned with the romantic potentialities of Anita Ekberg, a blonde bombshell with a dubious past and no valid citizenship, and troubled, alcoholic pilot Ryan; and dashing co-pilot Andes' budding romance with Phyllis Kirk, who is on the trip with her increasingly boorish and unsympathetic fiancé Gene Barry; not to mention the possibility that they may have their heads shrunk at any moment! The plane also contains the young son of a mob boss, played by Jon Provost of *Lassie* fame, being brought to supposed safety by one of his father's henchmen, Jesse White; and a convicted assassin, Rod Steiger, being brought to Boca Grande for execution by bounty hunter Fred Clarke.

Bondi establishes her character in the first two minutes of the film, as a bossy, bourgeois yet not unsympathetic wife, who keeps her husband under tight control. No *arroz con pollo* for him on the layover in San Dimas; rather, toast and an egg is what she orders for him to eat. We later learn that the Spanglers have been married for 42 years and have one child. After the crash, Bondi is put in charge of the cooking. Her husband fears there may be hostile natives, but says nothing to the others, except Steiger, who knows the area even better than he does. Clarke is the first to hear the ominous beat of drums. We later learn that when the drums stop, an attack is imminent. Back at the airport in Panama, the airport manager (Bondi's frequent co-star James Burke) calls off the search after a few days.

Finally, the plane is miraculously repaired and ready to fly, but with only one engine working it can only hold four adults plus the child Tommy. By this time both Clarke and White have been killed by the natives, leaving eight adults and one child. When the captain suggests women and children first, Bondi says "I think the women ought to have the right to make a choice, too, as well as the men." Steiger draws his gun and says he is the only one who can decide logically and objectively, since he is doomed to die one way or the other. The Spanglers decide that they will sacrifice themselves and ask Steiger to leave them behind, "as a favor." After the plane has successfully lifted off, Steiger uses the last two bullets to kill the elderly couple to save them from being taken alive by the cannibals, leaving himself at their mercy.

Bosley Crowther of the *New York Times* quipped: "All in all, there is little about this picture to encourage even the fancy to take wing."[67] After a lengthy summer holiday, Bondi unexpectedly found herself doing her second film with Steiger for Farrow's independent production company, again with Farrow directing. The production started with two weeks of location shooting in the Napa Valley in September 1956 for a film originally entitled *The Lady and the Prowler*. The shoot was centered on the Beringer Winery and vineyards near St. Helena, the fictional locale of the 1956 episode of *Climax!* on which Jonathan Latimer's screenplay was based.[68]

I took a stern view of this film in 2006 and have not seen any reason to reassess that evaluation since then.[69] *The Unholy Wife* is to Bondi's career what *Dear Dead Delilah* was to Agnes Moorehead's: a film admirers of the actress wish she had never done. This plum came to her as a result of Ethel Barrymore, the original incumbent, being "forced to relinquish it because of the rigors of location filming," meaning specifically "the extreme heat customary at this time of the year in the Napa Valley."[70] At the age of 67 and 14 years after May Robson's death, Bondi was still considered an appropriate replacement for much older actresses. Barrymore was 77. Bondi's personal liking for director Farrow may have clouded her judgment in taking on this assignment. She told Hedda Hopper during the production period on *The Unholy Wife*: "He's so pleasant to work with. Always knows what he wants, so naturally you give it to him."[71]

Set in the Northern California wine country and focusing on a wealthy vineyard owner, Paul Hochen (Steiger), his nefarious wife Phyllis (Diana Dors in her American feature film debut), and her lover, rodeo star San Sanford (Tom Tryon), the plot involves the tritest type of love triangle and more twists and turns than Lombard Street in San Francisco. Bondi plays Steiger's aged, nervous old mother Emma Hochen, who spends most of her screen time wandering around in an old housedress complaining of "noises" and worrying about prowlers. In a striking first, Bondi has a simultaneous stroke and heart attack towards the end of the film, when she discovers that daughter-in-law Dors has framed her son for Dors' accidental killing of his neighbor, friend, and grape supplier, Gino Verdugo (Joe De Santis), whom Dors mistook for her husband, the intended victim of the crime.

Bondi loses the ability to speak, but manages to revenge herself on Dors by taking a couple of extra pills right before her daughter-in-law gives her one, making it look as if Dors has killed her. Justly and ironically, then, Dors is framed herself—hoist by her own petard! She is tried, convicted, and sentenced to death for the killing of Emma Hochen. The film itself is framed by Dors' first-person narration to her brother-in-law, Father Stephen Hochen (Arthur Franz), as she awaits her execution.

By the time *The Unholy Wife* was finished, RKO had ceased all operations, so the film was released by Universal. Thus, it cannot be blamed for hastening RKO's demise. One would have liked to know what Bondi thought of the new brand of buxom, bottle-blonde stars she was currently supporting—first Anita Ekberg, now Diana Dors—but, unfortunately, she left no record of that. The reviewer for the *New York Times*, on the other hand, left no doubt about what he thought of the film as a whole, calling it "a dull, unholy mess, and an absolute waste of anyone's time. Including, we might add, that of the two principals."[72]

Even before *The Unholy Wife* shoot ended, Bondi was planning her first trip around the world.[73] The journey did not get underway, though, until February 1958. In the meantime, Bondi made a six-week excursion to Hawaii accompanied by her friend Neely

Powers from Ocean Springs, Mississippi.[74] Arriving in Honolulu on March 27, 1857,
Bondi probably also spent time with one of her local friends, the artist Juanita Vitousek,
and planned the extensive journey they would be taking together the following year.[75]
Vitousek was born Juanita Mabel Judy in Silverton, Oregon, in 1890 and grew up in California. Both her parents, Martin and Frederica Judy, were teachers and her father also
worked as a Methodist minister for many years.[76] Juanita Judy met Royal "Roy" Arnold
Vitousek when they were both living in Healdsburg, California, they married in 1914 and
had three children. The couple moved to Hawaii in 1917, where for 20 years Roy was a
prominent local politician for the Republican party and during three different periods
Speaker of the House of the Hawaii Territorial House of Representatives. Roy Vitousek
died suddenly of coronary thrombosis on April 3, 1947, aged 56, while Bondi was on her
first trip to Hawaii. The Vitouseks owned a gorgeous property at 4623 Kahala Ave., front-
ing directly on Hunakai Beach beyond Diamond Head, where they had lived since 1935.
They also owned a macadamia nut farm at Kona on the Big Island. While raising her family, Vitousek developed into a fine painter of landscapes and "one of Hawaii's best known
watercolor artists."[77] As a rich, independent, like-minded supporter and confidante, Juanita Vitousek played the same role in Bondi's life as the New Jersey banker Mary Roebling
would play in Agnes Moorehead's starting in the 1960s.

On what was her first genuine trip around the world, Bondi started from Hawaii
with Vitousek February 7, 1958. Their first stops were in Japan and Hong Kong. In Asia,
they also visited Thailand, Cambodia, India, and Nepal. This was followed by a month in
the Belgian Congo, Uganda, Zanzibar, and South Africa, including the four main animal
reserves, before they flew to Europe for stops in Italy, Portugal, Spain, Austria, and Norway. They boarded the Swedish liner Stella Polaris for a cruise to North Cape, before taking an SAS flight over the North Pole from Copenhagen to Los Angeles, arriving home on
July 9. According to Vitousek, the high points of the trip were their visits to Angkor Wat
in Cambodia, Nepal, and Zanzibar.[78]

In her column for September 22, 1958, Louella Parsons wrote that she was "very
glad that we are going to see Beulah Bondi on the screen once again." "She's always been
a favorite with me," Parsons added graciously. Bondi was just back from a trip around the
world and "had a ball on her sabbatical." She was looking forward to her mother-in-law
role in *The Big Fisherman* for director Frank Borzage and producer Rowland V. Lee.[79]
Bondi had done a one-scene role for Borzage as Napoleon's mother in *Hearts Divided*
back in 1936. This would be his final film.

As far as Hollywood biblical epics go, *The Big Fisherman* was less successful then and
is less well known now than, say, *Ben-Hur*, which came out the same year and "revolu-
tionized the genre,"[80] or *The Robe*, based on a novel by the same author, Lloyd C. Douglas.
Howard Keel starred as the disciple and fisherman Simon Peter and Susan Kohner played
an Arabian-Jewish princess in a tortuous romantic subplot that ultimately hijacks the
entire film. It should have been called *The Big-Haired Fisherman*, as the male star is sporting a bouffant of epic proportions.

Bondi first appears 51 minutes into this three-hour marathon, as Hannah, Peter's
dead wife's mother, who keeps house for him. Keel positively towers over her. Their first
scene together is simply ludicrous—more classic "in-law" situation comedy than ancient
epic—as Peter explains that he "can't stand anymore today" and is "long on temper and
short on help," having let his employees and fellow fishermen John and James go, because
of their bad attitude. In their place, he has hired a ragamuffin, runaway boy, played by

As the stern yet loving mother-in-law of the widower and future disciple Simon Peter (aka The Big Fisherman), played by Howard Keel, Bondi casts a disapproving eye at the "dirty boy" her son-in-law has brought home. Susan Kohner is no boy, but rather an Arabian-Jewish princess in disguise and on a mission to avenge her mother's death. Kohner's incredibly convoluted plotline threatens to derail *The Big Fisherman* (Centurion/Walt Disney, 1959) entirely, as does "The Big Hair" that the Big Fisherman is sporting throughout. The film as a whole is a Big Bore.

Susan Kohner, who is really a princess in disguise. Hannah reluctantly takes the boy in, but soon realizes she is a girl when Fara is forced to get out of her filthy, flea-ridden clothes. Hannah lends Fara her dead daughter's clothes and jewels in what is quite an abrupt change of heart. Two of Hannah's deathless lines are "I will not have this dirty boy in the house" and "Have you got lice? Fleas?" Fara admits to both.

Peter is not equally thrilled to discover Fara is a woman and wants her to go, but now Hannah insists that she stay. She is seen intermittently as a sort of sidekick to Fara, who is on a quest to avenge her mother's death but gets sidetracked when she comes under the benevolent influence of "the Nazarene." Hannah's big scene comes at two hours 14 minutes, when she is raised up from her deathbed ("Hannah! Hannah! Arise!"), after Peter prays for her in Fara's presence. We do not see her again after that. Swaddled in Hollywood's idea of authentic period costume, Bondi spends the film looking as if she has constipation.

Billed only ninth in this, Bondi nevertheless rated some mentions in contemporary reviews. One paper wrote that "Beulah Bondi impresses as Hannah." The *New York Times* noted Bondi as one of several supporting players who "contribute passingly effective bits to this Biblical panorama." The critic for the *Arizona Daily Star* concluded her negative review with this encomium: "Beulah Bondi, a reliable old-time actress, did the most effective bit when she was raised from the dead. In this little gem of a scene she contributed a real glow which gave actuality to the Master's words."[81]

Bondi went directly from the set of *The Big Fisherman* to location shooting for her next film. Under the heading "Beulah's Back," Hedda Hopper reported on February 24, 1959, that "Beulah Bondi had a time for herself on a six months jaunt around the world, now signed by Warners for the dowager role in 'A Summer Place.'"[82] Production on the film that has been deemed "the definitive Hollywood statement on teen love" had begun the previous day and ended on April 24.[83] *A Summer Place* was written, produced, and directed by Delmer Daves, who had directed Bondi in *The Very Thought of You* in 1944. It was Bondi's eighth and last film for Warner Bros. As Hopper pointed out, she was cast in a typical upper-class dowager role. Mrs. Hamilton Hamble is the godmother of troubled, alcoholic Bart Hunter (Arthur Kennedy), who, with his still attractive wife Sylvia (Dorothy McGuire), runs a seaside boarding house in his once wealthy family's ancestral manse in Maine. During the summer in question, Sylvia's former lover, Ken Jorgenson (Richard Egan), returns to his old haunts with his wife Helen (Constance Ford) and daughter Molly (Sandra Dee). The rest is history (or melodrama).

Mrs. Hamilton Hamble plays a significant role in the first half of the film. In the scene of the Jorgensons' arrival at Pine Island, she embarrasses Ken by remembering him as the lifeguard who had an affair with Sylvia. "Did you marry that pretty thing you were always teaching to swim?" she asks. She does not seem to be quite all there in the beginning, but later appears to have recovered her marbles. Mrs. Hamble's major segment begins 30 minutes into the movie, when she discovers a leak in her bathroom ceiling, right over one her "conveniences," which causes her "some difficulty." When Sylvia tells her her husband Bart is not the practical type, Mrs. Hamble enlists the help of Ken, whom she still addresses as "lifeguard." Her plot function here is to give Ken and Sylvia an excuse for a tête-à-tête in the attic. She even overhears them rekindle their affair through the vent in her room, which "acts as a sort of megaphone," and later tries to dissuade her godson's wife from straying from the straight and narrow. Bondi's character uses a cane, but hardly seems to need it. She has a big jigsaw puzzle on the table in her room and a canary in a large cage. She looks handsome and grand in this film, though the Technicolor makes it appear as if everyone has yellow teeth.

Helen Bower in the *Detroit Free Press* called this "a sprightly character bit as an elderly, forthright relative."[84] John Springer, who wrote the first lengthy consideration of Bondi's film career in *Films in Review* in 1963, thought Mrs. Hamilton Hamble "the bit part which best exemplifies Bondi's acting ability."[85] For me, this is an oddly disjointed character, who does not come together. Is she a semi-senile old biddy or a wise old owl? The confidential conversation she has with McGuire and the advice she gives her makes no sense at all. This is the fault of Daves's screenplay, rather than Bondi's performance. Clearly, the one to watch in this is Constance Ford. As Sandra Dee's bigoted, nouveau riche, sexually repressed mother, she is a riot and a half. Among her many peculiar notions is blaming her husband's Swedish blood for her daughter's "cheap" behavior.

Given Bondi's disapproval of the increasingly permissive atmosphere of American films in the 1960s, it is ironic that she features so prominently in what the *New York Times* described as "one of the most laboriously and garishly sex-scented movies in years" and the *Baltimore Sun* headlined a "Hollywood 'Sex Horror.'"[86] I can think of no better symbol of the deterioration of the American film industry, than that an actress who had supported all the great stars of the 1930s and '40s found herself by the end of her career supporting the likes of Sandra Dee in three of her four last films.

Dr. Raymond Marble Bondy died in Fort Lauderdale on July 31, 1959, at the age of 75. He had had a serious illness in June 1957, but rallied.[87] This time, he succumbed. Raymond's entire family, including his sister, was at his bedside when he passed at the Holy Cross Hospital. Funeral services were held three days later at the Fairchild Chapel.[88] At age 70, Bondi was the sole surviving member of her birth family. Her closest living relative was now her niece Elizabeth Beulah Bondy Robinson, known as Betty. Betty was 49 and lived with her husband James Stuart Robinson and 23-year-old daughter Elizabeth in a modest apartment building on Chicago's South Shore.

The new decade began on an upbeat when Bondi was awarded a star on the Walk of Fame at 1718 Vine St. in Hollywood on February 8, 1960. Yet her professional future was not promising. By the early 1960s, options for character actresses of Bondi's stature were severely limited in films, especially if they were not comfortable with the level of explicitness (they might have called it the vulgarity) of many of the then current offerings. Bondi made only three films in the 1960s, all in the early part of the decade, and they turned out to be the final three feature films of her career. It is maybe not surprising that two of them were anodyne "Tammy" films for producer Ross Hunter at Universal, where she had first done *The Good Fairy* in 1934. The first of the series had been *Tammy and the Bachelor*, starring Debbie Reynolds back in 1957. Now four years later, the second outing starred Bondi's *A Summer Place* co-star Sandra Dee as the homespun, spunky, amateur philosopher, riverboat-residing heroine Tammy Tyree with a "muffin-thick bayou drawl."[89]

As it turns out, Bondi is the only saving grace of *Tammy Tell Me True*, which was directed by Harry Keller and was in production by January 1961.[90] She plays Annie Rook Call, a rich widow embittered by the accidental death of her son. In her own words, "Since my son was killed, I've been like a ship stuck on a sand bar." The plot revolves around Tammy's attempt to get some "book learnin'," so that she can stay on a level with her boyfriend Pete, who has gone off to agricultural college and not written to her since. Naturally, Tammy is accompanied by her pet goat Nan on her quest for knowledge at a local college. Tammy initially hopes to rent a room in Mrs. Call's capacious home, but it is Mrs. Call who ends up moving into Tammy's houseboat, the "Ellen B": "I'm going to love your river, Tammy." Riverboat life takes Annie Call back to her childhood on her uncle's palatial shantyboat on the Mississippi. Mrs. Call soon recovers her *joie de vivre* and throws her sleeping pills out the window. Sunrise finds her in a shirt and slacks having no luck catching a cat fish, while Tammy gets one right away. "Well, I'll be Rotterdamed!" says Annie. Indeed, Mrs. Call transforms herself into "Shantyboat" Annie to hide her true identity from loquacious Captain Joe (Cecil Kellaway) and her avaricious, controlling niece Suzanne (Julia Meade), who has made her life a misery.

Surprisingly, perhaps, this underwhelming film turned out to be an opportunity for Bondi to display her folksy and grand side at the same time, just as she showed her up-and downsides in *It's a Wonderful Life*. She even got to have a subtle flirtation with veteran character actor Cecil Kellaway, who was four years her junior and had played the family doctor in *And Now Tomorrow*. The *Los Angeles Times* called Bondi's Mrs. Call "the most substantial performance" in the film. The *Oakland Tribune* thought she was "sporadically funny."[91]

In the spring of 1961, after she was done with *Tammy Tell Me True*, Bondi returned to Hawaii for a month. This time she was the house guest of Juanita Vitousek. Several parties were given in Bondi's honor and she and Vitousek also spent time at the latter's summer home in Kona on the island of Hawaii.[92] Sheilah Graham referred to Bondi in her column at the time as "That traveling lady."[93]

At the end of November 1961, Bondi got a new passport, which was always a sign that she was planning a foreign jaunt. But before she went off on what would be her second trip around the world, she squeezed in a brief appearance in *The Wonderful World of the Brothers Grimm*, reporting at MGM in January 1962.[94] While Bondi was unlikely to have played a gypsy in a realistic drama film, where gypsies only figured on the margins, playing a gypsy in a fairy tale was something different altogether. Not that this was a very large part, consisting as it does of one scene lasting only a few minutes of the total two hours and 15 minutes devoted to picturizing the Brothers Grimm and three of their more obscure fairy tales. Bondi's gypsy occurs in the "Dancing Princess" segment, starring Russ Tamblyn as The Woodsman, who lives in the forest all alone and hopes to win the heart of the king's daughter, played by Yvette Mimieux.

Bondi's appears 16 minutes into the film. When Tamblyn stops by the cave of the lonely gypsy, whom no one has ever given a word of kindness but him, she sees his heart and his quest in the cards. "When others have scoffed, you alone have smiled," she says meaningfully. She gives him a cloak of invisibility, as a token of her gratitude. "It will hide you from men's greed and protect you from their envy," she says. He gives her a kiss on the cheek in return. As he leaves, a raven alights on her shoulder and this is the last image we have of Bondi in this film.

George Pal directed the fairytale segments and left the biographical segments to Henry Levin, who had directed Bondi in *Mr. Soft Touch* back in 1948. The *Wonderful World of the Brothers Grimm* has the distinction of being "the first dramatic story film shot and exhibited in the 3-camera Cinerama format."[95] Bosley Crowther was unimpressed: "nothing especially new or notable in the way of motion-picture entertainment—or even Cinerama entertainment—has been accomplished here."[96] This was the last of Bondi's ten films for Metro-Goldwyn-Mayer. The first of these was *The Stranger's Return* 30 years earlier. All told, MGM had given her some of her best opportunities and high-profile roles, including *The Gorgeous Hussy*, *Of Human Hearts*, *On Borrowed Time*, and *The Captain Is a Lady*.

While Bondi did not need to go on location in Germany for her small role in *The Wonderful World of the Brothers Grimm*, she had much more ambitious travel plans at this time. Her new passport in hand, she started her journey in Cairo in late February 1962. This trip also included stops in Greece, Lebanon, Jordan, Malaysia, Indonesia, Fiji, French Polynesia (Tahiti), Australia, and New Zealand. It was while she was in New

Zealand, that she received the call from Ross Hunter to do *Tammy and the Doctor*. She arrived home on June 30, 1962, and was ready to begin work July 8.[97]

It would have been nice to say Bondi ended her more than 30-year film career with a bang, but it was more a whimper. In her last feature film role, she returned to the bucolic world of Tammy Tyree, again as Annie Call, this time with a heart condition that requires an operation at a hospital in Los Angeles. Tammy tags along (but not the goat this time) and naturally there are both romantic and other "developments." Once again, Tammy was played by Sandra Dee and the film was helmed by Harry Keller. The title was *Tammy and the Doctor* and the doctor was Peter Fonda in his film debut. Much like Ethel Barrymore at the end of her illustrious career, Bondi spends almost the entire film in the horizontal position. That does not prevent her from finding love with a rich, crotchety fellow patient played by Reginald Owen.

The year of 1963 saw the release of Bondi's final film and also what could have been her final appearance on television, the Season 7 premiere episode of *Perry Mason* entitled "The Case of the Nebulous Nephew." Bondi's television career was of long duration, but never prolific, lasting as it did from the late 1940s until 1976 and consisting only of

**Bondi's stellar film career ended not with a bang but with a whimper with *Tammy and the Doctor* (Universal, 1963), her second "Tammy" outing in support of Sandra Dee. That an actress who had supported all the greats from Hollywood's Golden Age would end up like this is a sad fact. To make matters worse, Bondi spends most of her screen time as Annie Call in the horizontal position. It was probably a poor comfort that she was given a love interest in the form of Reginald Owen.**

about two dozen appearances. She never had a recurring role on a series, which turns out to have been a conscious choice on her part. She recalled in an interview in 1976, that she had said no to a role in a series because "she couldn't be certain what would happen to her part as the show progressed."[98]

There is evidence that she started working in television as early as 1949. She is mentioned in an article on "A new kind of movie-making," televised films, which is "springing up fast," as one of several actors who "work for the screen actors' guild minimum for speaking parts—$55 a day." The article does not say what specific TV movie she may have played in; or if she appeared in the one nationally sponsored TV series that is mentioned: the drama anthology series *Your Show Time*, sponsored by the American Tobacco Company, which ran on NBC from January to July 1949 and consisted of "filmed dramatizations of classic short stories."[99] On November 12, 1950, we know Bondi and Jessica Tandy did a scene from *Hilda Crane* as part of the weekly half-hour variety show *Showtime, U.S.A.*, a "plug for Broadway."[100] The date of the broadcast varied according to the area. In Los Angeles, it aired on December 1.[101]

Among Bondi's earliest TV appearances, we also find her playing a grieving mother in a 1952 episode of the NBC dramatic anthology series *The Doctor* called "The Guest" (#1.10). Charles Bronson played a bank robber on the run trying to convince Bondi that he had known her son, who was killed in Korea. Robert Aldrich directed the episode, which Hedda Hopper referred to in her column as Bondi's "TV film debut."[102] Bronson was only one of the many exciting young actors she worked with in television, which included Betsy von Furstenberg, Tom Tryon, Mala Powers, Bobby Driscoll, Gigi Perreau, Kim Stanley, Inger Stevens, Patty Duke, and Richard Thomas.

During the 1950s, in addition to *The Doctor*, Bondi made guest appearances on *Medallion Theater*, *Alfred Hitchcock Presents*, *Front Row Center*, *Goodyear Playhouse*, *General Electric Theater*, *Zane Grey Theater*, and in three episodes of *Climax!*. The year of 1957 was her busiest year in television, when she played featured roles in five different episodes of four different shows. In the early 1960s, she did *Playhouse 90*, *Play of the Week*, *Harrigan and Son*, *Wagon Train*, *The Best of the Post*, *Route 66*, *Alcoa Premiere*, and *Perry Mason*.

Nearly all these shows were dramatic anthology series, an important genre of programming in the early days of television. Despite the absence of the comedy roles, which we have seen dominated her stage career, we might claim that Bondi played a somewhat broader range of roles in television than she did in films. In an episode of *Alfred Hitchcock Presents* from 1955, "Our Cook's a Treasure" (#1.8), for example, she played a cook-housekeeper called Mrs. Sutton and was given above-the-title star billing with male co-star (and her employer in the episode) Everett Sloane. Based on a story by Dorothy L. Sayers, the plot revolved around whether or not Mrs. Sutton was a serial killer on the loose trying to poison her boss. Bondi never played servants in films. The closest she got was the lady companion Anise in *Watch on the Rhine*. Bondi played a housekeeper role not unlike Anise in her only TV movie, a thriller with supernatural overtones called *She Waits* from 1972, starring Patty Duke and directed by Delbert Mann. Her employer this time was her *Summer Place* co-star Dorothy McGuire.

On the opposite end of the social scale, Bondi played a countess in her third and final appearance on *Climax!*, which was also her last TV appearance of the 1950s. "Hurricane Diane" (#4.10) was the story of "a young man suspected of the homicide of a girl named Diane who finds himself stranded in a hotel with the sheriff and the dead girl's fiancé during a violent hurricane." The countess is another of the hotel guests trapped in this "huis clos" situation (with a murderer on the loose) by a hurricane that bears the same name as the dead woman. Jeffrey Hunter, Vanessa Brown, Brian Keith, and Noah Beery, Jr., co-starred with Bondi.[103]

In a 1960 *Playhouse 90* dramatization by Horton Foote of William Faulkner's short story "Tomorrow" (#4.12), Bondi played a rural midwife, Mrs. Hulie. The drama starred Richard Boone and Kim Stanley as two star-crossed lovers in mid-life and related how Boone fails in his attempt to raise Stanley's infant son after her death giving birth to the child. This episode was more widely reviewed than Bondi's other TV appearances, probably due to the cachet of Foote and Faulkner and the CBS dramatic anthology series of which it was a part. Tim Brooks and Earle Marsh write: "Of all the fine dramatic-anthology series to grace television in the 1950s, *Playhouse 90* was the most ambitious and remains the standard against which all the others are judged."[104]

Bondi's old friend and colleague Elizabeth Patterson also had a featured role in this episode, though the two women did not have any scenes together. Patterson died of pneumonia in 1966 at the age of 90. Critics wrote that she and Bondi contributed "vivid vignettes" and were part of an "excellent supporting cast" and "supremely human in their roles," while the episode as a whole was described as "an odd and occasionally poignant little drama," "a fairly successful depiction of the Nobel Prize author's murky, brooding realm of decadent chivalry," and "a touching and extended dialogue between a pair of courageous innocents."[105]

Beyond the occasional cooks, housekeepers, midwives, and countesses, Bondi mostly played character types on television that closely resembled her most familiar film roles. For example, she portrayed a classic upper-class mother-in-law from hell in an episode of the adventure series *Route 66* called "Burning for Burning" (#2.13) in 1961; a middle-class Connecticut matron in "The Hands of Danofrio" (#2.9) on *Alcoa Premiere* in 1962; and a typical proud, domineering dowager on a highly convoluted episode of *Perry Mason* called "The Nebulous Nephew" (#7.1) in 1963. Her daughter-in-law and sparring partner on *Route 66* was ill-fated Swedish actress Inger Stevens (playing a Swedish actress); Telly Savalas starred as a famous sculptor wrongly believed to be dead in the *Alcoa Premiere* episode; while the "nebulous nephew" was played by Ron Starr.[106]

Predictably, there were traditional mother roles for Bondi in TV too. A 1956 episode of the full-hour CBS drama anthology series *Front Row Center* called "Finley's Fan Club" (#2.1) revolved around "the hero worship of an internationally famous writer-lecturer, Finley Fitzpatrick, by a small group that meets in an Omaha grocery store. The focus of this adoration is Finley's mother (Beulah Bondi)." William Bakewell played her son and Diana Lynn and Eddie Bracken co-starred.[107]

Rural matriarchs were part of Bondi's television repertoire, too, as in a 1956 episode of *Goodyear Playhouse* called "Ark of Safety" (#5.27), "a drama telling of an old woman's hatred which feeds a feud and of a young preacher's perseverance in trying to end it." The story was set in the Tennessee mountain country. Bondi called her character "a real meanie." Andrew Duggan played the preacher.[108]

In a 1957 episode of *Climax!* called "Circle of Destruction" (#3.14), Bondi played the mother of an escaped convict, played by Dale Robertson, "whose ruthless disregard for the well-being of those who love him finally results in his own destruction."[109] One reviewer had a field day with what he saw as the blatant implausibilities of the plot in what he called "the clinker of the week." "Mixed up in this calamity" was Beulah Bondi, he wrote, "our heart bled for this fine actress who had to keep asking 'I wonder what went wrong?'"[110]

In a 1957 episode of the western series *Zane Grey Theater* entitled "Black Is for Grief" (#1.26), Bondi played the concerned mother of Tom Tryon, who returns from the Civil War to discover his murdered wife, Mala Powers, had been running out on him. Director Lewis Allen had directed Bondi in *Our Hearts Were Young and Gay* back in 1944. In a 1960 episode of *Play of the Week* called "Morning's at Seven" (#1.29), Bondi was starred with Ann Harding, Dorothy Gish, and Ruth White as four sisters whose daily lives are turned upside down when White's son Hiram Sherman finally brings home his fiancée of 15 years, Eileen Heckart. This original teleplay was by fellow Hoosier and author of *On Borrowed Time*, Paul Osborn.[111]

Not to forget that Bondi came out of retirement in 1971 to put in a fifth and final appearance as James Stewart's mother in an episode of the one-season *Jimmy Stewart Show* entitled "The Identity Crisis" (#1.7). She was vacationing on a ranch in Colorado, when the call came. As Stewart later recalled, "she didn't want anything to do with it. She said she was retired and enjoying her fishing, 'but if Jimmy wants me to do it, I'll do it.'"[112] Bondi cancelled all her engagements, flew back directly on a Sunday and "on Tuesday she was at work on the show, her lines learned, her three costumes ready."[113] Bondi and Stewart had not seen each other in 15 years. Except for an episode of *Harrigan and Son* in 1960, this was her only role in a TV situation comedy and gave her a rare opportunity to dress up as an elegant Nob Hill granddame. Bondi looks small and frail and uses a cane, but her face and expression are radiant. Stewart is sporting one of the worst toupees ever made.

In 1976, Bondi even got a lick at playing Abraham Lincoln's mother before it was all over; that is, Sarah Bush Lincoln was strictly speaking his stepmother. Hal Holbrook played the sixteenth president in the celebrated miniseries entitled simply *Lincoln*. Bondi was everything the role required in the episode "Crossing Fox River," where Lincoln comes to call on his stepmother in her rustic cabin at the end of her long life and they visit his father's grave. In an interview with TV and radio columnist Steve Hoffman, Bondi referred to Holbrook as "one of our finest actors": "Few can compare with him."[114]

Bondi also played her share of grandmothers and eccentric old ladies on the small screen. Early on, she played the title role in a 1953 episode of *Medallion Theater* called "Gran'ma Rebel" (#2.8), "a drama set in Dixie revolving around a family's desire to see a grand dame, with only two hours to go, live to be 100 years old."[115] Gran'ma Rebel had the distinction of being the oldest character Bondi ever played. Jackie Cooper and Betsy von Furstenburg co-starred and the show was broadcast live from CBS studios in New York.[116]

In January 1955, before her first major trip abroad since 1928, Bondi starred in an episode of *Family Theater*, hosted by Jack Bailey, called "Slaughterhouse Row": "a 'who-dunnit' type of story that concerns an elderly lady, whose peculiar habit of spending her nights riding streetcars arouses the interest of an inquisitive reporter." "Gradually, a forgotten era of a half century ago is unfolded as the newsman gets his story." The episode was written and directed by John T. Kelley.[117]

Bondi's eccentric little old lady character "Silver Annie" Huxley was the focus of an episode of *General Electric Theater* in 1957 called "The Town with a Past" (#5.21) in which the actress was reunited with James Stewart for the first time since *It's a Wonderful Life* ten years earlier. Annie refuses to sell her played-out silver mine to a railroad company and Stewart's wandering cowboy character Britt Ponset gets mixed up in the dispute.

Stewart had made his TV debut in 1955 in a previous episode of this Sunday night CBS dramatic anthology series.[118]

In a rare comedy role, Bondi played an eccentric elderly millionaire who wants to make her cat rather than her dog the beneficiary of her will in an episode of the ABC Friday night sitcom *Harrigan and Son*. The episode was called "Non Compos Mentis" (#1.11). The 1960–61 show starred Pat O'Brien and Roger Perry as father and son, both lawyers, and depicted the challenges they faced working in the same legal firm.[119]

In January 1961, Bondi had the opportunity to contribute to one of the most successful Western series of all time. Her episode of *Wagon Train* was called "The Prairie Story" (#4.19). It starred "Jan Clayton as a woman unable to endure the pressures of crossing that sea of grass; and Beulah Bondi as a woman on her second crossing who accepts the dangers, refusing to cringe from them."[120]

The short-lived Western series *Dirty Sally* was a spin-off from *Gunsmoke* and starred 62-year-old fellow character actress Jeanette Nolan in the title role and Dack Rambo as her sidekick Cyrus. Bondi made a guest appearance in the sixth episode, entitled "Too Long to Wait," of the series' first and only season, as "an old blind woman living alone in the wilderness, waiting for her grandson to return home so she can die in peace."[121]

**Even when Bondi was in her 30s, she was known for playing old ladies. Inevitably, age and time had caught up with her and by the mid–1950s elaborate old lady makeup was no longer necessary. This portrait is from her first, 1974 appearance on *The Waltons* in the third season opener called "The Conflict" in which she played Aunt Martha Corinne for the first of two times. Bondi had turned down the part of Grandma Walton, which had gone to her friend Ellen Corby. Always liking to be in control, Bondi did not want a recurring role in a series, because she could not know how the character would develop.**

Finally, Bondi also put in a few appearances in typical spinster and maiden aunt roles. In the first of three different episodes of the suspense series *Climax!*, "The Secret of River Lane" (#2.18), Bondi played the favorite aunt of a young man, played by Bobby Driscoll, who is suspected of having fatally shot a schoolmate in a hunting accident.[122] "Antidote for Hatred" (#1.20), which first aired on *Best of the Post* on December 8, 1960, dealt with Bondi's Miss Newton, who "adopts a Hungarian refugee in the hopes that she can supplant her love for the hatred the boy carries in his heart."[123]

Despite some solid and varied performances in the 1950s and '60s, Bondi saved the best for last. She gave two of the finest performances of her career playing the same character on two separate episodes of *The Waltons* in the 1970s. Her performance as a crotchety yet lovable elderly relative of the family on the Season 5 episode "The Pony Cart" is best remembered, because she won a Primetime Emmy Award for it in 1977 and it turned out to be her final appearance as an actress. She had actually played the same character previously in the double episode entitled "The Conflict," which opened Season 3. Martha Corinne Tyler Walton is the quintessential Bondi character; the supreme and final embodiment of the many rural women, both good and bad, she had played down through the years. In playing this character, Bondi attained a degree of realism and depth that is simply stunning. She was 87 when she did "The Pony Cart." No better finale to her career could be imagined than that performance and the Emmy she so deservedly won for it.

For eight years, then, between 1963 and 1971, Bondi was not seen on the large or the small screen. In 1964, she undertook her last major foreign trip, which was a wide-ranging exploration of the African continent. She arrived in France August 14 and landed in Johannesburg three days later. Between then and her return to the United States via France on October 24, she visited South Africa, Kenya, Tanzania, Senegal, Niger, Ethiopia, Sudan, Nigeria, Dahomey, and Mali. She claimed to have covered 40,000 miles on this trip.[124]

Though she made her last lengthy trip abroad when she was 75, she continued to travel to Hawaii and internationally until she was 87. She celebrated President Tito's 80th birthday in Yugoslavia in 1972.[125] She motored around Alaska in the summer of 1975, the summer she filmed her episode of *Lincoln* with Hal Holbrook.[126] She spent Christmas that year in Lima, Peru.[127] In January 1976, she traveled to Taiwan for two weeks as part of an American delegation, then went on to Hong Kong for a few days on her own.[128] Finally, in April 1976 she went back to Africa for the fifth time, with her niece Elizabeth Robinson and her family.[129] She turned 87 while she was there. She said in an interview that year: "I believe Africa is my favorite continent although I also like the Middle East. It's always nice to go back to places and see them again."[130] Though she had five years left to live, it was her final trip abroad.

Bondi made her last trip to Valparaiso in May 1978 and received a Doctorate of Laws degree from Valparaiso University at its 104th commencement.[131] There was a sense in which she had never left the town in which she was raised. When she returned this final time, none of her circle of lifelong female friends were there to greet her. Marie Timmons Windle, Louise Banister Bartholomew, Floy Binyon Brownell, and Daisy Temple Lowenstine were all dead. Only Ada Roessler Bartholomew was still living, but she was in an Indianapolis nursing home. She died on September 10, 1979, at the age of 91.[132] Bondi was the last of "the girls," as she was the last of the cousins.

Bondi made her last public appearance on February 27, 1980, when she was on hand when James Stewart received the American Film Institute's Lifetime Achievement Award at the Beverly Hilton Hotel. Bondi, Grace Kelly, and Ruth Hussey were the only women who spoke.[133]

Bondi lived at 6660 Whitley Terrace till the end of her days. In an interview in 1976, she confidently stated: "I expect to stay here."[134] By that time, her closest companion was her maid, who had worked for her for 16 years.[135] Her home was described as "a treasure trove of art works, sculpture and general memorabilia collected from all over the world."[136] She did not give up driving till she was 90.[137]

Bondi had an iron constitution and could probably have lived to be a 100, but she was accident prone. On January 2, 1981, she was admitted to hospital for treatment for broken ribs suffered in a fall. She fell when trying to avoid stepping on "her beloved Mr. Cat."[138] Bondi died from "pulmonary complications" at the Motion Picture and Television Country House and Hospital in Woodland Hills on Sunday, January 11 at the age of 91.[139] A memorial service was held four days later in the Louis B. Mayer Memorial Theater at Woodland Hills. It was attended by some 200 people and included eulogies by Bondi's *Waltons* co-star Richard Thomas and her director on *Mr. Smith Goes to Washington* and *It's a Wonderful Life*, Frank Capra.[140] A great spirit had passed out of the world.

# Chapter Notes

## Preface

1. Bondi quoted in Cobey Black, "Who's News with Cobey Black: The Magical Life of Beulah Bondi," *Honolulu Star-Bulletin* (April 1, 1957), p. 13.
2. Quoted in Richard Lamparski, *Whatever Became of...?* 8th Series (New York: Crown, 1982), p. 33.
3. Joan Crosby and Dick Kleiner, "The World of Television," *Columbus Republic* (August 3, 1974), p. 4.
4. "Beulah Bondi, Noted for Screen Characterizations, Studies Unusual Types," unidentified clipping [1938] (NYPL).
5. Phil Potempa, "The Beloved Mother: Beulah Bondi," in Stephen Cox, *It's a Wonderful Life: A Memory Book* (Nashville, TN: Cumberland House, 2003), p. 67.
6. Jordan R. Young, *Reel Characters: Great Movie Character Actors* (Beverly Hills, CA: Moonstone Press, n.d.), p. 61. In another interview, she explained: "I can't sit on the set and play gin rummy and socialize. I have to go to my dressing room and be quiet and, as I say, *hang on*." See Dennis Brown, *Actors Talk: Profiles and Stories from the Acting Trade* (New York: Limelight Editions, 1999), p. 152.
7. Lydia Lane, "Beulah Accents the Positive," *Los Angeles Times* (December 4, 1977), p. 5.
8. Robert Lawrence Balzer, "Al Fresco on the Rum: The Spirit of the Buccaneers Is Still the Life of the Party," *Los Angeles Times Magazine* (May 17, 1987), p. 32.
9. A.J. Greene, "Everybody's Mother," unidentified clipping (January 1947) (WCFTR).
10. Dick Kleiner, "Looking Back on a Charmed Life," *Lowell Sun* (January 2, 1974), n.pag.
11. Tom Green, "Beulah Bondi Back on Screen at 80," *Camden Courier-Post* (January 25, 1972), p. 21.
12. Lamparski, *Whatever Became of...?*, p. 33.
13. Lamparski, p. 33.
14. Irene Thirer, "Beulah Bondi Sees Self on Screen at Criterion," unidentified clipping [1937] (NYPL).
15. William H. McKegg, "More Than Actress," *Picture Play* (June 1937) (WCFTR).
16. Tab Hunter with Eddie Muller, *Tab Hunter Confidential: The Making of a Movie Star* (Chapel Hill, NC: Algonquin Books of Chapel Hill, 2005), p. 98.
17. McKegg, "More Than Actress."

## Chapter 1

1. Bondi quoted in Jo Mannies, "Beulah's Debut 47 Pages Long," *Vidette-Messenger* (April 13, 1976), p. 1.
2. Quoted in Chris Burkett, "Beulah Bondi Wows Shimer," *Quad-City Times* (April 11, 1976), p. 3A.
3. This appears in Abram Bondy's 1920 U.S. Census record, which records his mother's mother tongue. See "United States Census, 1920," database with images, *Family Search* (https://familysearch.org/ark:/61903/1:1:MF4C-WVG: accessed 12 May 2020), A O Bondy, Valparaiso Ward 2, Porter, Indiana, United States; citing ED 142, sheet 3A, line 50, family 71, NARA microfilm publication T625 (Washington, D.C.: National Archives and Records Administration, 1992), roll 460; FHL microfilm 1,820,460.
4. While we know from direct evidence that Mary came from the German province of Saxony, the evidence linking her specifically to Geisa in Saxony is indirect but strong. We know that her older brother Elias M. Rosenblatt was born in Geisa on February 22, 1822, because it is engraved on his grave marker in Chicago's Zion Gardens. See Elias M. Rosenblatt, findagrave.com. We also know that her niece Henrietta Rosenblatt (Lindauer), Elias's daughter, was born in Geisa, in 1850. I am operating on the assumption that Mary was born in the same town as her brother and where he raised a family until they immigrated to the United States in 1862. The document showing Henrietta was born in Geisa is her son Arthur Lindauer's birth record. See "Illinois, Cook County, Birth Certificates, 1871–1940," database, *Family Search* (https://familysearch.org/ark:/61903/1:1:Q239-7LDV: 18 May 2016), Henrietta Rosenblatt in entry for Arthur Mayer Lindauer, 25 Jul 1879; Chicago, Cook, Illinois, United States, reference/certificate 207186, Cook County Clerk, Cook County Courthouse, Chicago; FHL microfilm.
5. Mary Rosenblatt Bondy's year of birth is consistent in all the available public records and

1825 is also the year given on her grave marker. The 1900 U.S. Census gives the month of her birth as July. The exact date is given in her death record, as are the names of her parents. See "United States Census, 1900," database with images, *Family Search* (https://familysearch.org/ark:/61903/1:1:M9MG-BBK: accessed 11 May 2020), Mary Bondy, Center Township Valparaiso city Ward 3, Porter, Indiana, United States; citing enumeration district (ED) 83, sheet 3A, family 65, NARA microfilm publication T623 (Washington, D.C.: National Archives and Records Administration, 1972.); FHL microfilm 1,240,398; "Wisconsin, Death Records, 1867–1907," database, *Family Search* (https://familysearch.org/ark:/61903/1:1:XLN3-129: 10 March 2018), Mary R. Bondy, 1907; citing Death, Milw., Milwaukee, Wisconsin, Wisconsin State Historical Society, Madison; FHL microfilm 1,310,334; Mary Bondy, findagrave.com.

6. The 1900 U.S. Census provides information on year of immigration and number of years in the United States. See "United States Census, 1900," Mary Bondy.

7. In several censuses, Gabriel's place of birth is given as Germany, but the 1870 U.S. Census gives "Bohemia," just as it gives "Saxony" for Mary Bondy. See "United States Census, 1870," database with images, *Family Search* (https://familysearch.org/ark:/61903/1:1:MDVY-M8S: 19 March 2020), Gabriel Bondy.

8. This appears in Abram Bondy's 1920 U.S. Census record, which records his father's mother tongue. See "United States Census, 1920," A O Bondy.

9. According to the 1850 and 1860 U.S. Census, Gabriel was born in 1815. According to the 1870 census, he was born in 1812. Finally, according to the 1885 Iowa State Census and his obituary, he was born in 1805, which seems the most likely. See "United States Census, 1850," database with images, *Family Search* (https://familysearch.org/ark:/61903/1:1:M4CP-J89: 4 April 2020), Gabriel Bandy, Southwark, ward 3, Philadelphia, Pennsylvania, United States; citing family 1013, NARA microfilm publication M432 (Washington, D.C.: National Archives and Records Administration, n.d.); "United States Census, 1860," database with images, *Family Search* (https://familysearch.org/ark:/61903/1:1:MWDY-DF5: 19 March 2020), Gabriel Bondy, 1860; "United States Census, 1870," Gabriel Bondy; "Iowa State Census, 1885," database with images, *Family Search* (https://familysearch.org/ark:/61903/1:1:H47K-CMM: 2 December 2019), Gabriel Bondy, Davenport, Davenport, Scott, Iowa; citing p. 6, 1885, State Historical Society, Des Moines; FHL microfilm 1,020,181; "Died," *Davenport Sunday Times* (November 29, 1885), p. 4.

10. This appears from the 1900 U.S. Census. See "United States Census, 1900," Mary Bondy.

11. Evidence for these years of birth is given below.

12. "United States Census, 1850," Gabriel Bandy; "United States Census, 1860," Gabriel Bondy; "United States Census, 1870," Gabriel Bondy; "Iowa State Census, 1885," Gabriel Bondy.

13. "United States Census, 1860." Gabriel Bondy.

14. Abram Bondy's year and place of birth are given in his 1882 marriage record. See "Michigan Marriages, 1868–1925," database with images, *Family Search* (https://familysearch.org/ark:/61903/1:1:NQS8-NXB: 2 April 2020), Adolph O. Bouder and Eva Marble, 1 Aug 1882; citing Marriage, Cassopolis, Cass, Michigan, Citing Secretary of State, Department of Vital Records, Lansing; FHL microfilm 4032366. For the exact date, see "A.O. Bondy Is Dead at 79; Ill 2 Years," *Vidette-Messenger* (September 10, 1935), p. 1.

15. "United States Census, 1870," Gabriel Bondy.

16. "Iowa State Census, 1885," Gabriel Bondy.

17. "Bondy," *Davenport Sunday Democrat* (November 29, 1885), p. 1.

18. "Died," "The Late Mr. G. Bondy," *Davenport Democrat* (November 30, 1885), p. 1. Isaac Fall was a 40-year-old minister and Jewish rabbi, who lived at 1034 W. 3rd St. in Davenport with his wife Helen and two children. See "Iowa State Census, 1885," database with images, *Family Search* (https://familysearch.org/ark:/61903/1:1:H4WF-G2M: 2 December 2019), Isaac Fall, Davenport, Davenport, Scott, Iowa; citing p. 4, 1885, State Historical Society, Des Moines; FHL microfilm 1,020,180.

19. Information on Estelle and Leopold Flexner from "United States Germans to America Index, 1850–1897," database, *Family Search* (https://familysearch.org/ark:/61903/1:1:KD3F-T3J: 27 December 2014), Leopold Flexner, 07 May 1866; citing Germans to America Passenger Data file, 1850–1897, Ship New York, departed from Bremen, arrived in New York, New York, New York, United States, NAID identifier 1746067, National Archives at College Park, Maryland; "Iowa, County Marriages, 1838–1934," database, *Family Search* (https://familysearch.org/ark:/61903/1:1:KCWL-N97: 25 September 2017), L. Flexner and Estelle Bondy, 17 Apr 1872, Davenport, Scott, Iowa, United States; citing reference vol. 4, page 234, county courthouses, Iowa; FHL microfilm 1,004,415; "United States Census, 1900," database with images, *Family Search* (https://familysearch.org/ark:/61903/1:1:M9LN-77D: accessed 17 May 2020), Estelle Flexner in household of Leopold Flexner, Davenport Township, Precinct 1 Davenport city Ward 5, Scott, Iowa, United States; citing enumeration district (ED) 133, sheet 3A, family 47, NARA microfilm publication T623 (Washington, D.C.: National Archives and Records Administration, 1972.); FHL microfilm 1,240,458; "United States Census, 1910," database with images, *Family Search* (https://familysearch.org/ark:/61903/1:1:MLBS-DMP: accessed 17 May 2020), Estelle Flexner, Portland Ward 2, Multnomah, Oregon, United States; citing enumeration district (ED) 131, sheet 5A, family 9, NARA microfilm publication T624 (Washington, D.C.: National Archives and Records Administration, 1982), roll 1285; FHL microfilm 1,375,298; "United

States Passport Applications, 1795–1925," database with images, *Family Search* (https://familysearch.org/ark:/61903/1:1:QV5Y-GY67: 16 March 2018), Leopold Flexner, 1913; citing Passport Application, Pennsylvania, United States, source certificate #3296, Passport Applications, January 2, 1906–March 31, 1925, 181, NARA microfilm publications M1490 and M1372 (Washington, D.C.: National Archives and Records Administration, n.d.); "Personal," *Davenport Democrat and Leader* (July 3, 1908), p. 11.

20. "United States Census, 1880," database with images, *Family Search* (https://familysearch.org/ark:/61903/1:1:MHS7-MD7: 19 August 2017), Mary Boudy in household of L D Boudy, Valparaiso, Porter, Indiana, United States; citing enumeration district ED 140, sheet 462C, NARA microfilm publication T9 (Washington, D.C.: National Archives and Records Administration, n.d.), FHL microfilm 1,254,305.

21. "L.D. Bondy Dies at Age 84: Succumbs in Gary Hospital Early Today," *Vidette-Messenger* (July 13, 1937), p. 1.

22. "United States Census, 1900," Mary Bondy. 101 N. Lafayette St. is now a parking lot.

23. "Wisconsin, Death Records, 1867–1907," Mary R. Bondy; Mary Bondy, findagrave.com.

24. "National Register of Historic Places Registration Form: Rising Sun Historic District" (August 2005), p. 93. https://secure.in.gov/apps/dnr/shaard/r/254b1/N/Rising_Sun_HD_Ohio_CO_Nom.pdf.

25. "Rising Sun Historic District," https://en.wikipedia.org/wiki/Rising_Sun_Historic_District.

26. Her birth month and year is given in the 1900 U.S. Census and the year corroborated by other sources. See "United States Census, 1900," database with images, *Family Search* (https://familysearch.org/ark:/61903/1:1:M9MP-73C: accessed 17 May 2020), Melissa Marble in household of Aldolph O Bandy, Center Township Valparaiso city Ward 2, Porter, Indiana, United States; citing enumeration district (ED) 82, sheet 7A, family 152, NARA microfilm publication T623 (Washington, D.C.: National Archives and Records Administration, 1972.); FHL microfilm 1,240,398.

27. "United States Census, 1830," database with images, *Family Search* (https://familysearch.org/ark:/61903/1:1:XHPY-5RL: 12 August 2017), Jacob Fisher, Randolph, Dearborn, Indiana, United States; citing 169, NARA microfilm publication M19 (Washington, D.C.: National Archives and Records Administration, n.d.), roll 27; FHL microfilm 7,716; "United States Census, 1840," database with images, *Family Search* (https://familysearch.org/ark:/61903/1:1:XHBV-ZX9: 15 August 2017), Jacob Fisher, Dearborn, Indiana, United States; citing p. 74, NARA microfilm publication M704 (Washington, D.C.: National Archives and Records Administration, n.d.), roll 77; FHL microfilm 7,723; Jacob Fisher, Susannah Hawk/Hock Fisher, findagrave.com.

28. "Indiana Marriages, 1811–2007," database with images, *Family Search* (https://familysearch.org/ark:/61903/1:1:XXVC-T2P: 11 March 2018),

Daniel Clark and Melissa Fisher, 01 May 1845; citing Ohio, Indiana, United States, Marriage Registration, Indiana Commission on Public Records, Indianapolis; FHL microfilm 004455441.

29. "Indiana Marriages, 1811–2007," database with images, *Family Search* (https://familysearch.org/ark:/61903/1:1:XXVC-YLH: 11 March 2018), Jonathan W Marble and Melissa Clark, 27 Jun 1849; citing Ohio, Indiana, United States, Marriage Registration, Indiana Commission on Public Records, Indianapolis; FHL microfilm 004455441.

30. For Jonathan Marble's year of birth, see U.S. census data 1840–1870 cited below. His father was probably Nathan Jonathan Marble (1757–1834). Nathan is buried in Union Cemetery in Rising Sun. See "United States Census, 1830," database with images, *Family Search* (https://familysearch.org/ark:/61903/1:1:XHPY-RSV: 12 August 2017), Nathan Marble, Randolph, Dearborn, Indiana, United States; citing 173, NARA microfilm publication M19 (Washington, D.C.: National Archives and Records Administration, n.d.), roll 27; FHL microfilm 7,716; Nathan Jonathan Marble, findagrave.com.

31. "Indiana Marriages, 1811–2007," database with images, *Family Search* (https://familysearch.org/ark:/61903/1:1:XXTL-JZZ: 8 December 2017), Jonathan W Marble and Eleanor Clark, 17 Oct 1833; citing Dearborn, Indiana, United States, Marriage Registration, Indiana Commission on Public Records, Indianapolis; FHL microfilm 004476631; "United States Census, 1840," database with images, *Family Search* (https://familysearch.org/ark:/61903/1:1:XHBV-ZV8: 15 August 2017), Jonathan Marble, Dearborn, Indiana, United States; citing p. 83, NARA microfilm publication M704 (Washington, D.C.: National Archives and Records Administration, n.d.), roll 77; FHL microfilm 7,723.

32. Information on Sallie R. Marble Hughes from "United States Census, 1850," Sally R Marble in household of Jonathon Marble; "United States Census, 1860," Sarah R Marble in entry for J W Marble; "United States Census, 1870," database with images, *Family Search* (https://familysearch.org/ark:/61903/1:1:MXXT-4G5: 19 March 2020), Sarah Hughs in entry for William Hughs, 1870; "United States Census, 1880," database with images, *Family Search* (https://familysearch.org/ark:/61903/1:1:-MH9W-VSK: 14 August 2017), Sallie R Hughs in household of William H Hughs, Lincoln, Hendricks, Indiana, United States; citing enumeration district ED 146, sheet 663B, NARA microfilm publication T9 (Washington, D.C.: National Archives and Records Administration, n.d.), FHL microfilm 1,254,283; Sallie R. Hughes, William H. Hughes, findagrave.com.

33. Information on Wilson Clark from "United States Census, 1850," Wilson Clark in household of Jonathon Marble; "United States Census, 1860," W D C Marble in entry for J W Marble; "United States Census, 1870," Wilson Clark in entry for Jonathan Marble; "United States Census, 1880," database with images, *Family Search* (https://familysearch.org/ark:/61903/1:1:MH93-VMJ: 14 August 2017),

Wilson D Clark, Sheridan, Hamilton, Indiana, United States; citing enumeration district ED 36, sheet 358D, NARA microfilm publication T9 (Washington, D.C.: National Archives and Records Administration, n.d.), FHL microfilm 1,254,281; "Adams Township," *Noblesville Independent* (April 24, 1880), p. 1; "Local Summary," *Noblesville Independent* (April 5, 1895), p. 5; Wilson Daniel Clark, Margaret Scott Clark, findagrave.com.

34. "United States Census, 1850," database with images, *Family Search* (https://familysearch.org/ark:/61903/1:1:MHJB-D2L: 4 April 2020), Jonathon Marble, Rising Sun, Ohio, Indiana, United States; citing family 239, NARA microfilm publication M432 (Washington, D.C.: National Archives and Records Administration, n.d.); "United States Census, 1860," database with images, *Family Search* (https://familysearch.org/ark:/61903/1:1:MXH5-3J3: 19 March 2020), J W Marble, 1860; "United States Census, 1870," database with images, *Family Search* (https://familysearch.org/ark:/61903/1:1:M6W2-VTB: 19 March 2020), Jonathan Marble, 1870.

35. "United States Census, 1860," O M Marble in entry for J W Marble; "United States Census, 1870," Olive Marble in entry for Jonathan Marble; "United States Census, 1900," database with images, *Family Search* (https://familysearch.org/ark:/61903/1:1:MMY9-4R2: accessed 17 May 2020), Olive M Coffelt in household of John Coffelt, Elmerdaro Township (part) Hartford city, Lyon, Kansas, United States; citing enumeration district (ED) 67, sheet 5A, family 104, NARA microfilm publication T623 (Washington, D.C.: National Archives and Records Administration, 1972); FHL microfilm 1,240,487.

36. "United States Census, 1860," E S Marble in entry for J W Marble; "United States Census, 1870," Eva Marble in entry for Jonathan Marble; Eva Marble Bondy, *Worldkins* (Los Angeles: The Ward Ritchie Press, 1962), p. 119.

37. Jacob Fisher, Susannah Hawk/Hock Fisher, findagrave.com.

38. Bondy, *Worldkins*, p. 8. The dedication is included in the expanded version of her poems published in 1962 with "Ohio Country" erroneously replacing "Ohio County."

39. "United States Census, 1850," database with images, *Family Search* (https://familysearch.org/ark:/61903/1:1:MHJD-5S4: 4 April 2020), Henry D Pollock in household of Thomas D Pollock, Logan, Fountain, Indiana, United States; citing family 837, NARA microfilm publication M432 (Washington, D.C.: National Archives and Records Administration, n.d.); "United States Census, 1860," database with images, *Family Search* (https://familysearch.org/ark:/61903/1:1:M4FX-V3F: 19 March 2020), Henry D Pollock in entry for T D Pollock, 1860; "United States Census, 1870," database with images, *Family Search* (https://familysearch.org/ark:/61903/1:1:MXXK-CMK: 19 March 2020), Henry D Pollock in entry for T Davis Pollock, 1870.

40. "United States Census, 1880," database with images, *Family Search* (https://familysearch.org/

ark:/61903/1:1:MHMB-Z1J: 24 August 2017), Olive Pollock in household of Henry Pollock, Logan, Fountain, Indiana, United States; citing enumeration district ED 69, sheet 14C, NARA microfilm publication T9 (Washington, D.C.: National Archives and Records Administration, n.d.), FHL microfilm 1,254,277; *Hartford News* (July 3, 1890), p. 3; "Death of Henry D. Pollock," *Hartford Call* (July 4, 1890), p. 3.

41. *Hartford News* (July 3, 1890), p. 3; "Death of Henry D. Pollock," p. 3.

42. "Local," *Hartford News* (May 22, 1890), p. 3.

43. John Martin Coffelt, findagrave.com.

44. "Coffelt-Pollock," *Hartford News* (February 1, 1894), p. 2.

45. Summons, *South Kansas Tribune* (April 20, 1910), p. 8; "District Court Cases," *South Kansas Tribune* (August 10, 1910), p. 8. The same summons was also published in the paper on April 27, May 4, and May 11, 1910.

46. His third wife was Viola V. Coffelt. Though she was six years older, she survived him and died in 1927. See "Kansas Marriages, 1840–1935," database, *Family Search* (https://familysearch.org/ark:/61903/1:1:Q2MY-3QLC: 14 January 2020), John Coffelt, 1912; "Kansas State Census, 1915," database with images, *Family Search* (https://familysearch.org/ark:/61903/1:1:QGR4-1SRW: 13 October 2019), John C Coffelt, Caney, Montgomery, Kansas, United States; citing Caney, Montgomery, Kansas, United States, 42, 23, Kansas Historical Society, Topeka; "Personal Items," *Caney News* (July 5, 1912), p. 5; John Martin Coffelt, Viola V. Coffelt, findagrave.com.

47. "United States Census, 1900," Melissa Marble in household of Aldolph O Bandy.

48. "United States Census, 1910," database with images, *Family Search* (https://familysearch.org/ark:/61903/1:1:M2YX-L4P: accessed 17 May 2020), Melissa Marble in household of William W Pollock, Kansas Ward 10, Jackson, Missouri, United States; citing enumeration district (ED) ED 138, sheet 6B, family 141, NARA microfilm publication T624 (Washington, D.C.: National Archives and Records Administration, 1982), roll 787; FHL microfilm 1,374,800.

49. *Neosho Valley Times* (May 8, 1914), p. 1.

50. "Death of Mrs. Olive Pollock," *Independence Daily Reporter* (March 17, 1919), p. 1; *South Kansas Tribune* (March 19, 1919), p. 5; Olive Marble Pollock, findagrave.com.

51. "United States Census, 1920," database with images, *Family Search* (https://familysearch.org/ark:/61903/1:1:MZ75-FZP: accessed 17 May 2020), Helen Pollock, Detroit Ward 1, Wayne, Michigan, United States; citing ED 27, sheet 12A, line 14, family 190, NARA microfilm publication T625 (Washington, D.C.: National Archives and Records Administration, 1992), roll 802; FHL microfilm 1,820,802.

52. "United States Census, 1880," database with images, *Family Search* (https://familysearch.org/ark:/61903/1:1:MXKP-DFD: 17 August 2017), Eva Marble in household of George Doadenhoffer,

Danville, Vermilion, Illinois, United States; citing enumeration district ED 211, sheet 368C, NARA microfilm publication T9 (Washington, D.C.: National Archives and Records Administration, n.d.), FHL microfilm 1,254,255.

53. "United States Census, 1880," A O Boudy in household of L D Boudy.

54. Advertisement, *Chicago Tribune* (May 24, 1903), p. 52.

55. "A.O. Bondy Is Dead at 79," p. 1.

56. "Michigan Marriages, 1868–1925," Adolph O. Bouder and Eva Marble, 1 Aug 1882; *Valparaiso City Directory 1893* (Chicago: Kraft and Radcliffe, 1893), n.pag.; "United States Census, 1900," Aldolph O Bandy; *Bumstead's Valparaiso City and Porter County Directory 1902* (Chicago: Bumstead, 1902), p. 60; *Bumstead's Valparaiso City Directory 1905* (Chicago: Bumstead, 1905), p. 60; "United States Census, 1910," Abraham C Bundy.

57. "Michigan Marriages, 1868–1925," Adolph O. Bouder and Eva Marble, 1 Aug 1882.

58. Bondy, *Worldkins*, p. 119.

59. "Illinois, Cook County Birth Registers, 1871–1915," database, *Family Search* (https://familysearch.org/ark:/61903/1:1:N772-G57: 10 March 2018), Raymond M. Bondy, 22 Mar 1884; citing v 9 p 16, Chicago, Cook, Illinois, Cook County Courthouse, Chicago; FHL microfilm 1,287,728.

60. "Pennsylvania, Philadelphia City Births, 1860–1906," database with images, *Family Search* (https://familysearch.org/ark:/61903/1:1:-VBYC-R92: 25 September 2019), Rachael Bondy, 04 Aug 1862; citing Birth, Philadelphia, Philadelphia, Pennsylvania, United States, City of Philadelphia, Department of Records, Pennsylvania; "Jacob L. Hirschman, Old Newspaperman, Succumbs," *Wasau Daily Herald* (March 24, 1930), p. 6; "Obituary: Jacob L. Hirschman," *Wisconsin Jewish Chronicle* (March 28, 1930), p. 5.

61. "Illinois, Cook County Marriages, 1871–1920," database, *Family Search* (https://familysearch.org/ark:/61903/1:1:N7DC-QZK: 10 March 2018), Jake L. Hirschman and Rose Bondy, 20 Dec 1882.

62. "The City: Personal and General," *Chicago Tribune* (December 21, 1882), p. 8.

63. "Social Amenities: Hirshman—Bondy," *Daily Inter Ocean* (December 21, 1882), p. 4.

64. "United States Census, 1910," database with images, *Family Search* (https://familysearch.org/ark:/61903/1:1:MPVF-MKQ: accessed 18 May 2020), Rose E Hirshman in household of Jacob L Hirshman, Milwaukee Ward 4, Milwaukee, Wisconsin, United States; citing enumeration district (ED) ED 37, sheet 7B, family 154, NARA microfilm publication T624 (Washington, D.C.: National Archives and Records Administration, 1982), roll 1723; FHL microfilm 1,375,736; "United States Census, 1920," database with images, *Family Search* (https://familysearch.org/ark:/61903/1:1:MFKK-LWX: accessed 18 May 2020), Rose E Hirschman in household of Jacob L Hirschman, Milwaukee Ward 16, Milwaukee, Wisconsin, United States; citing ED 183, sheet 8A, line 33, family 197, NARA microfilm publication T625 (Washington, D.C.:

National Archives and Records Administration, 1992), roll 2002; FHL microfilm 1,822,002; "United States Census, 1930," database with images, *Family Search* (https://familysearch.org/ark:/61903/1:1:-X992-BQ4: accessed 18 May 2020), Rose Hirshman, Milwaukee (Districts 1–250), Milwaukee, Wisconsin, United States; citing enumeration district (ED) ED 226, sheet 11B, line 58, family 42, NARA microfilm publication T626 (Washington, D.C.: National Archives and Records Administration, 2002), roll 2593; FHL microfilm 2,342,327; "United States Census, 1940," database with images, *Family Search* (https://familysearch.org/ark:/61903/1:1:K729-RBQ: 29 July 2019), Rosa Hirschman in household of Julius H Sure, Ward 18, Milwaukee, Milwaukee City, Milwaukee, Wisconsin, United States; citing enumeration district (ED) 72–406, sheet 5B, line 65, family 118, Sixteenth Census of the United States, 1940, NARA digital publication T627. Records of the Bureau of the Census, 1790–2007, RG 29. Washington, D.C.: National Archives and Records Administration, 2012, roll 4558; "Jacob L. Hirschman, Old Newspaperman, Succumbs," p. 6; "Obituary: Jacob L. Hirschman," p. 5.

65. Information on Leola Hirschman Sure from "United States Census, 1910," Leola M Hirshman in household of Jacob L Hirshman; "United States Census, 1920," Leola M Hirschman in household of Jacob L Hirschman; "United States Census, 1930," database with images, *Family Search* (https://familysearch.org/ark:/61903/1:1:X992-FNY: accessed 18 May 2020), Leola H Sure in household of Julius H Sure, Milwaukee (Districts 1–250), Milwaukee, Wisconsin, United States; citing enumeration district (ED) ED 227, sheet 30B, line 52, family 40, NARA microfilm publication T626 (Washington, D.C.: National Archives and Records Administration, 2002), roll 2593; FHL microfilm 2,342,327; "United States Census, 1940," Leola Sure in household of Julius H Sure; "Two Regents Are Named by Blaine: Miss Leola Hirschman Is Appointed to Board of Regents of University," *Madison Capital Times* (May 2, 1922), p. 1; "Mrs. Sure, Former U.W. Regent, Dies," *Madison Capital Times* (May 3, 1941), p. 1; "Former Regent, Mrs. Sure, Dies," *Wisconsin State Journal* (May 4, 1941), p. 2; Leola Hirschman Sure, findagrave.com.

66. "Personal," *Davenport Democrat* (October 17, 1898), p. 1.

67. "Oregon Death Index, 1903–1998," database, *Family Search* (https://familysearch.org/ark:/61903/1:1:VZ4R-Q2J: 11 December 2014), Estelle B Flexner, 1917; from "Oregon, Death Index, 1898–2008," database and images, *Ancestry* (http://www.ancestry.com: 2000); citing Portland, Oregon, certificate number 2343, Oregon State Archives and Records Center, Salem.

68. "United States Census, 1920," Leopold Flerner in household of Everett Francis, San Jose, Santa Clara, California, United States; citing ED 168, sheet 4A, line 1, family 86, NARA microfilm publication T625 (Washington, D.C.: National Archives and Records Administration, 1992), roll 147; FHL microfilm 1,820,147; "California Death

Index, 1905–1939," database with images, *Family Search* (https://familysearch.org/ark:/61903/1:1:-QK91-J6N8: 8 November 2017), Leopold Flexner, 09 Oct 1923; citing 45730, Department of Health Services, Vital Statistics Department, Sacramento; FHL microfilm 1,686,045.

69. Information on Vivian Flexner from "Iowa, Delayed Birth Records, 1850–1939," database with images, *Family Search* (https://familysearch.org/ark:/61903/1:1:Q246-3521: accessed 17 May 2020), Vivian Flexner, 14 Nov 1875, Davenport, Scott, Iowa, United States; citing reference ID 103491, State Historical Society of Iowa, Des Moines; Family Search digital folder 101693744; "United States Census, 1880," Vivia Flexner in household of Lee Flexner; "United States Census, 1900," Vivian Flexner in household of Leopold Flexner; "Iowa State Census, 1905," database with images, *Family Search* (https://familysearch.org/ark:/61903/1:1:-QVM5-JD83: 16 March 2018), Vivian Flexner, Scott, Iowa, United States; citing card #D925, State Historical Department, Des Moines; FHL microfilm 1,430,621; "United States Census, 1910," Vivian Flexner in household of Estelle Flexner; "United States Census, 1920," database with images, *Family Search* (https://familysearch.org/ark:/61903/1:1:-M48F-WBM: accessed 17 May 2020), Vivian Flexner, Portland, Multnomah, Oregon, United States; citing ED 101, sheet 4B, line 88, family 102, NARA microfilm publication T625 (Washington, D.C.: National Archives and Records Administration, 1992), roll 1501; FHL microfilm 1,821,501; "United States Census, 1930," database with images, *Family Search* (https://familysearch.org/ark:/61903/1:1:-XCSQ-12V: accessed 17 May 2020), Vivian Flexner, Portland (Districts 271–553), Multnomah, Oregon, United States; citing enumeration district (ED) ED 372, sheet 7B, line 84, family 240, NARA microfilm publication T626 (Washington, D.C.: National Archives and Records Administration, 2002), roll 1952; FHL microfilm 2,341,686; "United States Census, 1940," database with images, *Family Search* (https://familysearch.org/ark:/61903/1:1:-VRTR-L88: 7 February 2020), Vivian Flexner, Tract 28, Portland, Portland City Election Precinct 233, Multnomah, Oregon, United States; citing enumeration district (ED) 37–317, sheet 3B, line 73, family 77, Sixteenth Census of the United States, 1940, NARA digital publication T627. Records of the Bureau of the Census, 1790–2007, RG 29. Washington, D.C.: National Archives and Records Administration, 2012, roll 3390; "Oregon Death Index, 1903–1998," database, *Family Search* (https://familysearch.org/ark:/61903/1:1:VZHM-N4R: 11 December 2014), Vivian Flexner, 1962; from "Oregon, Death Index, 1898–2008," database and images, *Ancestry* (http://www.ancestry.com: 2000); citing Multnomah, Oregon, certificate number 16365, Oregon State Archives and Records Center, Salem.

70. Information on Aimee Flexner and Carolyn H. Rich from "Iowa Births and Christenings, 1830–1950," database, *Family Search* (https://familysearch.org/ark:/61903/1:1:XVHW-Y61: 13 January 2020), Flexner, 1884; "United States Census,

1900," Amy Flexner in household of Leopold Flexner; "United States Census, 1910," Annie Flexner in household of Estelle Flexner; "United States Census, 1920," Annice Flexner in household of Vivian Flexner; "United States Census, 1920," Carolyn H Rich in household of Vivian Flexner; "United States Census, 1930," database with images, *Family Search* (https://familysearch.org/ark:/61903/1:1:-XCSQ-P79: accessed 18 May 2020), Aimee Flexner, Portland (Districts 271–553), Multnomah, Oregon, United States; citing enumeration district (ED) ED 372, sheet 7A, line 17, family 215, NARA microfilm publication T626 (Washington, D.C.: National Archives and Records Administration, 2002), roll 1952; FHL microfilm 2,341,686; "United States Census, 1930," Caroline H Rich in household of Aimee Flexner; "United States Census, 1940," database with images, *Family Search* (https://familysearch.org/ark:/61903/1:1:VRTT-DRC: 26 July 2019), Aimee Flexner, Tract 28, Portland, Portland City Election Precinct 257, Multnomah, Oregon, United States; citing enumeration district (ED) 37–350, sheet 1B, line 75, family 22, Sixteenth Census of the United States, 1940, NARA digital publication T627. Records of the Bureau of the Census, 1790–2007, RG 29. Washington, D.C.: National Archives and Records Administration, 2012, roll 3391; "United States Census, 1940," Carylon Rich in household of Aimee Flexner; "Oregon Death Index, 1903–1998," database, *Family Search* (https://familysearch.org/ark:/61903/1:1:VZHK-FKC: 11 December 2014), Aimee Flexner, 25 Jul 1943; from "Oregon, Death Index, 1898–2008," database and images, *Ancestry* (http://www.ancestry.com: 2000); citing Portland, Oregon, certificate number, Oregon State Archives and Records Center, Salem; "Oregon Death Index, 1903–1998," database, *Family Search* (https://familysearch.org/ark:/61903/1:1:VZ47-XWB: 11 December 2014), Carolyn H Rich, 09 May 1960; from "Oregon, Death Index, 1898–2008," database and images, *Ancestry* (http://www.ancestry.com: 2000); citing Multnomah, Oregon, certificate number 6432, Oregon State Archives and Records Center, Salem.

71. Information on Cora Flexner Rhode and Carl A. Rhode from "United States Census, 1880," Cora Flexner in household of Lee Flexner; "United States Census, 1900," Cora Flexner in household of Leopold Flexner; "Iowa, County Marriages, 1838–1934," database, *Family Search* (https://familysearch.org/ark:/61903/1:1:XJVD-6K3: 10 February 2018), Carl A Rohde and Cora Flexner, 27 Aug 1900, Davenport, Scott County, Iowa, United States; citing reference Vol 1 Lic # 13756 p 91, county courthouses, Iowa; FHL microfilm 1,004,421; "United States Census, 1910," database with images, *Family Search* (https://familysearch.org/ark:/61903/1:1:-MKZL-HXH: accessed 18 May 2020), Cora Rohde in household of Carl A Rohde, Chicago Ward 25, Cook, Illinois, United States; citing enumeration district (ED) ED 1084, sheet 3B, family 84, NARA microfilm publication T624 (Washington, D.C.: National Archives and Records Administration, 1982), roll 268; FHL microfilm 1,374,281; "United

States Census, 1920," database with images, *Family Search* (https://familysearch.org/ark:/61903/1:1:-MJQ1-PBT: accessed 18 May 2020), Cora F Rohde in household of Carl A Rohde, Chicago Ward 25, Cook (Chicago), Illinois, United States; citing ED 1435, sheet 3A, line 13, family 70, NARA microfilm publication T625 (Washington, D.C.: National Archives and Records Administration, 1992), roll 341; FHL microfilm 1,820,341; "United States Census, 1930," database with images, *Family Search* (https://familysearch.org/ark:/61903/1:1:-XS5K-63D: accessed 18 May 2020), Cora F Rohde in household of Carl A Rohde, Chicago (Districts 2877–2908), Cook, Illinois, United States; citing enumeration district (ED) ED 2892, sheet 4A, line 2, family 76, NARA microfilm publication T626 (Washington, D.C.: National Archives and Records Administration, 2002), roll 493; FHL microfilm 2,340,228; "United States Census, 1940," database with images, *Family Search* (https://familysearch.org/ark:/61903/1:1:K497-CPX: 18 December 2019), Cora F Rohde in household of Carl A Rohde, Ward 48, Chicago, Chicago City, Cook, Illinois, United States; citing enumeration district (ED) 103–3098, sheet 9B, line 70, family 210, Sixteenth Census of the United States, 1940, NARA digital publication T627. Records of the Bureau of the Census, 1790–2007, RG 29. Washington, D.C.: National Archives and Records Administration, 2012, roll 1019; "Oregon Death Index, 1903–1998," database, *Family Search* (https://familysearch.org/ark:/61903/1:1:VZ48-CJ9: 11 December 2014), Cora F Rohde, 19 Jul 1959; from "Oregon, Death Index, 1898–2008," database and images, *Ancestry* (http://www.ancestry.com: 2000); citing Multnomah, Oregon, certificate number 9378, Oregon State Archives and Records Center, Salem; "Oregon Death Index, 1903–1998," database, *Family Search* (https://familysearch.org/ark:/61903/1:1:VZ4P-RFS: 11 December 2014), Carl A Rohde, 13 Sep 1957; from "Oregon, Death Index, 1898–2008," database and images, *Ancestry* (http://www.ancestry.com: 2000); citing Multnomah, Oregon, certificate number 10928, Oregon State Archives and Records Center, Salem; "Social Events," *Davenport Daily Democrat* (August 28, 1900), p. 5; Cora F. Rhode, Carl A. Rohde, findagrave.com.

72. Information on Jefferson Flexner and Blanche Wolf Flexner from "Iowa, County Births, 1880–1935," database, *Family Search* (https://familysearch.org/ark:/61903/1:1:XVDN-JHW: 1 April 2020), Flexner, 23 Mar 1883; citing Iowa, United States; county district courts, Iowa; FHL microfilm 1,004,408; "United States Census, 1900," Jefferson Flexner in household of Leopold Flexner; "United States Census, 1910," database with images, *Family Search* (https://familysearch.org/ark:/61903/1:1:MPNB-S9J: accessed 17 May 2020), Jefferson E Flexner, Adkin, McDowell, West Virginia, United States; citing enumeration district (ED) ED 67, sheet 9A, family 163, NARA microfilm publication T624 (Washington, D.C.: National Archives and Records Administration, 1982), roll 1686; FHL microfilm 1,375,699; "United States

Census, 1920," database with images, *Family Search* (https://familysearch.org/ark:/61903/1:1:MNKR-WNL: accessed 17 May 2020), Jefferson E Flexner, Huntington Ward 6, Cabell, West Virginia, United States; citing ED 36, sheet 6A, line 22, family 124, NARA microfilm publication T625 (Washington, D.C.: National Archives and Records Administration, 1992), roll 1951; FHL microfilm 1,821,951; "Illinois, Cook County Deaths, 1878–1994," database, *Family Search* (https://familysearch.org/ark:/61903/1:1:QL45-1SF9: 17 March 2018), Leopold Flexner in entry for Jefferson E Flexner, 27 Oct 1924; citing Cook, Illinois, United States, source reference, record number, Cook County Courthouse, Chicago; FHL microfilm; "Mr. and Mrs. J.E. Flexner Spend Honeymoon Here," *Davenport Daily Times* (December 28, 1907), p. 6; "Death Notices: Flexner," *Davenport Daily Times* (October 28, 1924), p. 6; Jefferson E. Flexner, findagrave.com.

73. Information on Olive Power and Harold Morgan Power from "United States Census, 1880," Ollie Flexner in household of Lee Flexner; "United States Census, 1900," Olive Flexner in household of Leopold Flexner; "United States Census, 1920," Olive Francis in household of Everett Francis; "Philippines Marriages, 1723–1957," database, *Family Search* (https://familysearch.org/ark:/61903/1:1:-FN63-CM8: 15 February 2020), Olive F Francis in entry for Harold Morgan Power, 1930; "United States Census, 1940," Oliva F Power in household of Vivian Flexner; "United States Social Security Death Index," database, *Family Search* (https://familysearch.org/ark:/61903/1:1:JT4Q-8MS: 20 May 2014), Olive Power, Feb 1972; citing U.S. Social Security Administration, *Death Master File*, database (Alexandria, Virginia: National Technical Information Service, ongoing); "Large Attendance: Scott County Teachers at Normal Institute," *Davenport Times* (July 6, 1899), p. 3; Harold M. Power, findagrave.com.

74. Information on Edward, Helen, and William Pollock from "United States Census, 1910," database with images, *Family Search* (https://familysearch.org/ark:/61903/1:1:MKD4-NXC: accessed 17 May 2020), Edward Pollock, Mazon, Grundy, Illinois, United States; citing enumeration district (ED) ED 54, sheet 1A, family 14, NARA microfilm publication T624 (Washington, D.C.: National Archives and Records Administration, 1982), roll 290; FHL microfilm 1,374,303; "United States Census, 1920," database with images, *Family Search* (https://familysearch.org/ark:/61903/1:1:MJ7K-BVM: accessed 17 May 2020), E D Pollock, Chicago Ward 32, Cook (Chicago), Illinois, United States; citing ED 2038, sheet 6B, line 82, family 135, NARA microfilm publication T625 (Washington, D.C.: National Archives and Records Administration, 1992), roll 351; FHL microfilm 1,820,351; "United States Census, 1930," database with images, *Family Search* (https://familysearch.org/ark:/61903/1:1:-XSL1-YMN: accessed 17 May 2020), Edward D Pollock, Chicago (Districts 0751–1000), Cook, Illinois, United States; citing enumeration district (ED) ED 751, sheet 10B, line 86, family 173, NARA

microfilm publicaison T626 (Washington, D.C.: National Archives and Records Administration, 2002), roll 448; FHL microfilm 2,340,183; "Illinois, Cook County Deaths, 1878–1994," database, *Family Search* (https://familysearch.org/ark:/61903/1:1:-Q2MD-GR1M: 18 March 2018), Edward D Pollock, 17 Sep 1934; citing Chicago, Cook, Illinois, United States, source reference, record number, Cook County Courthouse, Chicago; FHL microfilm; Edward Pollack, Bertha Pollack, Christine E. Pollock, findagrave.com; "United States Census, 1920," Helen Pollock; "United States World War I Draft Registration Cards, 1917–1918," database with images, *Family Search* (https://familysearch.org/ark:/61903/1:1:K66F-DB8: 25 August 2019), William Wiley Pollock, 1917–1918; "United States Passport Applications, 1795–1925," database with images, *Family Search* (https://familysearch.org/ark:/61903/1:1:QV5B-WS59: 16 March 2018), William W Pollock, 1920; citing Passport Application, Texas, United States, source certificate #59677, Passport Applications, January 2, 1906—March 31, 1925, 1275, NARA microfilm publications M1490 and M1372 (Washington, D.C.: National Archives and Records Administration, n.d.); "United States Census, 1930," database with images, *Family Search* (https://familysearch.org/ark:/61903/1:1:-XCH9-NY4: accessed 17 May 2020), William Pollock, Bartlesville, Washington, Oklahoma, United States; citing enumeration district (ED) ED 1, sheet 11B, line 54, family 277, NARA microfilm publication T626 (Washington, D.C.: National Archives and Records Administration, 2002), roll 1938; FHL microfilm 2,341,672; "United States Census, 1940," database with images, *Family Search* (https://familysearch.org/ark:/61903/1:1:KHMP-55V: 15 May 2020), William W Pollock, Ward 4, Detroit, Detroit City, Wayne, Michigan, United States; citing enumeration district (ED) 84–175, sheet 7A, line 34, family 198, Sixteenth Census of the United States, 1940, NARA digital publication T627. Records of the Bureau of the Census, 1790–2007, RG 29. Washington, D.C.: National Archives and Records Administration, 2012, roll 1845; "California Death Index, 1940–1997," database, *Family Search* (https://familysearch.org/ark:/61903/1:1:VPCZ-2YN: 26 November 2014), William Pollock, 10 Nov 1968; Department of Public Health Services, Sacramento.

75. "At Valparaiso College: Commencement Exercises to Take Place Thursday Evening," *Indianapolis Journal* (August 12, 1903), p. 7.

76. "Valparaiso," *Lake County Times* (May 27, 1908), p. 1.

77. "Michigan, County Marriages, 1820–1940," database with images, *Family Search* (https://familysearch.org/ark:/61903/1:1:VNK5-V99: 11 May 2018), Woodbridge George Cary and Fanny Bel Toles, 24 May 1882; citing reference ID, various county clerks and libraries, Michigan; FHL microfilm 2,240,469; "Michigan Births, 1867–1902," database with images, *Family Search* (https://familysearch.org/ark:/61903/1:1:NQ8W-DQH: 12 August 2019), Sarah W. Cary, 16 Sep 1887; citing item 2 p 268 rn 106, Benton Harbor, Berrien,

Michigan, Department of Vital Records, Lansing; FHL microfilm 2,320,847.

78. "United States Census, 1900," database with images, *Family Search* (https://familysearch.org/ark:/61903/1:1:M912-Q54: accessed 21 May 2020), Sarah Cary in household of Fannie Cary, Benton Harbor city Ward 1–2, Berrien, Michigan, United States; citing enumeration district (ED) 55, sheet 11B, family 222, NARA microfilm publication T623 (Washington, D.C.: National Archives and Records Administration, 1972); FHL microfilm 1,240,702.

79. "New York State Census, 1855," database with images, *Family Search* (https://familysearch.org/ark:/61903/1:1:K6Q2-NW3: 13 March 2018), William Cary, E.D. 2, Clayton, Jefferson, New York, United States; citing p. 4, line #13, family #126, county clerk offices, New York; FHL microfilm 895,241; "United States Census, 1860," database with images, *Family Search* (https://familysearch.org/ark:/61903/1:1:MC7F-FM4: 19 March 2020), William M Cary, 1860; Woodbridge George Cary, findagrave.com, including obituary; "Mackinac Women Tars Date Back to 1905," *Chicago Tribune* (August 7, 1916), p. 10.

80. "United States Census, 1910," database with images, *Family Search* (https://familysearch.org/ark:/61903/1:1:MKD3-B8V: accessed 21 May 2020), R M Bondy, Union, Fulton, Illinois, United States; citing enumeration district (ED) ED 99, sheet 13A, family 316, NARA microfilm publication T624 (Washington, D.C.: National Archives and Records Administration, 1982), roll 288; FHL microfilm 1,374,301; "Brevities," *Benton Harbor News-Palladium* (January 20, 1910), p. 5.

81. "United States Social Security Death Index," database, *Family Search* (https://familysearch.org/ark:/61903/1:1:VMH1-3NB: 20 May 2014), Elizabeth B Markert, 29 Jun 2009; citing U.S. Social Security Administration, *Death Master File*, database (Alexandria, Virginia: National Technical Information Service, ongoing).

82. "Mackinac Women Tars," p. 10; "United States Census, 1920," database with images, *Family Search* (https://familysearch.org/ark:/61903/1:1:-MJ3W-7L3: accessed 21 May 2020), Raymond Bondy, Chicago Ward 7, Cook (Chicago), Illinois, United States; citing ED 405, sheet 7B, line 78, family 183, NARA microfilm publication T625 (Washington, D.C.: National Archives and Records Administration, 1992), roll 315; FHL microfilm 1,820,315.

83. *Southtown Economist* (November 25, 1927), p. 3.

84. "Engagement Is Made Public," *Vidette-Messenger* (March 31, 1932), p. 10; "Local Brevities," *Vidette-Messenger* (April 19, 1932), p. 3; "Mrs. James S. Robinson," *Chicago Tribune* (April 24, 1932), p. 82.

85. "Personals," *Benton Harbor News-Palladium* (August 18, 1943), p. 3; *Detroit Free Press* (June 18, 1944), p. 36; "Mrs. J.H. Ressler," *Lancaster Intelligencer-Journal* (July 20, 1967), p. 2. The first source I have found that refers to Sallie Bondy as

Mrs. Ressler is her father's June 1933 obituary. See Woodbridge G. Cary, findagrave.com.

86. "Illinois, Cook County, Birth Certificates, 1871–1940," database, *Family Search* (https://familysearch.org/ark:/61903/1:1:QGCF-3FD6: 18 March 2018), Elizabeth Louise Robinson, 27 Apr 1935; Chicago, Cook, Illinois, United States, reference/certificate 15102, Cook County Clerk, Cook County Courthouse, Chicago; FHL microfilm; "United States Social Security Death Index," Elizabeth B Markert.

87. "Illinois, Cook County, Birth Certificates, 1871–1940," database, *Family Search* (https://familysearch.org/ark:/61903/1:1:Q239-ZZBL: 18 May 2016), Beulah Bondy, 03 May 1889; Chicago, Cook, Illinois, United States, reference/certificate 249937, Cook County Clerk, Cook County Courthouse, Chicago; FHL microfilm.

88. "Beulah Bondi Dead at 92," *Vidette-Messenger* (January 12, 1981),p. 1.

89. Based on information from the *Bumstead's Valparaiso City and Porter County Directory 1902.*

90. *Valparaiso City Directory 1893*, n.pag.; "United States Census, 1900," Aldolph O Bandy; *Bumstead's Valparaiso City and Porter County Directory 1902*, p. 60; *Bumstead's Valparaiso City Directory 1905*, p. 60; "United States Census, 1910," Abraham C Bundy.

91. "Valparaiso, Indiana May 1886" (New York: Sanborn Map Publishing, 1886); *Valparaiso City Directory 1885–86* (Valparaiso, IN: Talcott and Tevis, 1885), p. 113.

92. "United States Census, 1930," database with images, *Family Search* (https://familysearch.org/ark:/61903/1:1:X4B7-CPX: accessed 20 May 2020), Abran O Bondy, Valparaiso, Porter, Indiana, United States; citing enumeration district (ED) ED 9, sheet 8A, line 47, family 132, NARA microfilm publication T626 (Washington, D.C.: National Archives and Records Administration, 2002), roll 622; FHL microfilm 2,340,357.

93. "Trinity Fund Drive Sunday," *Vidette-Messenger* (November 3, 1967), p. 9; "OK Variances for 2 Churches," *Vidette-Messenger* (February 22, 1968), p. 1; *Vidette-Messenger* (December 19, 1968), p. 17; http://tlcvalpo.com/about-us/our-history/.

94. http://tlcvalpo.com/about-us/our-history/.

95. Bondi's 4th grade notebook with "Columbia School" on the cover is found among her papers in the Margaret Herrick Library (BBP 2.25).

96. Rollie Bernhart, "Tears Shed as Columbia Comes Down," *Vidette-Messenger* (March 2, 1965), p. 1, 6.

97. https://www.fpcvalpo.org/history.

98. "United States Census, 1900," database with images, *Family Search* (https://familysearch.org/ark:/61903/1:1:M9MP-DXQ: accessed 23 April 2020), Gertrude Polk in household of Caleb C Polk, Center Township Valparaiso city Ward 2, Porter, Indiana, United States; citing enumeration district (ED) 82, sheet 3B, family 72, NARA microfilm publication T623 (Washington, D.C.: National Archives and Records Administration, 1972); FHL microfilm

1,240,398; *Bumstead's Valparaiso City and Porter County Directory 1902*, p. 126; *Bumstead's Valparaiso City Directory 1905* (Chicago: Bumstead, 1905), p. 127.

99. "Deaths in Indiana: Valparaiso," *Indianapolis Star* (August 20, 1923), p. 17.

100. "Ten Years Ago: January 26, 1918," *Vidette-Messenger* (January 26, 1928), p. 2; "United States Census, 1930," database with images, *Family Search* (https://familysearch.org/ark:/61903/1:1:-XCNN-L7C: accessed 23 April 2020), Gertrude J Polk in household of Henry T Polk, Santa Barbara, Santa Barbara, California, United States; citing enumeration district (ED) ED 19, sheet 22A, line 44, family 249, NARA microfilm publication T626 (Washington, D.C.: National Archives and Records Administration, 2002), roll 214; FHL microfilm 2,339,949; "United States Census, 1940," database with images, *Family Search* (https://familysearch.org/ark:/61903/1:1:K9DP-3BJ: 12 February 2020), Gertrude J Polk in household of Henry Polk, Ward 5, Santa Barbara, Judicial Township 2, Santa Barbara, California, United States; citing enumeration district (ED) 42–27, sheet 64B, line 75, family 365, Sixteenth Census of the United States, 1940, NARA digital publication T627. Records of the Bureau of the Census, 1790–2007, RG 29. Washington, D.C.: National Archives and Records Administration, 2012, roll 333; "California Death Index, 1940–1997," database, *Family Search* (https://familysearch.org/ark:/61903/1:1:VGTG-H1K: 26 November 2014), Gertrude J Polk, 02 Mar 1970; Department of Public Health Services, Sacramento; "Obituaries: Miss Gertrude Polk," *Vidette-Messenger* (March 7, 1970), p. 6.

101. "Indiana Marriages, 1811–2007," database with images, *Family Search* (https://familysearch.org/ark:/61903/1:1:KDHQ-TLP: 10 December 2017), H George Frank and Irene Lowenstine, 06 Oct 1915; citing Porter, Indiana, United States, Marriage Registration, Indiana Commission on Public Records, Indianapolis; FHL microfilm 005014499; "One O'Clock Luncheon," *Lake County Times* (September 16, 1915), p. 5; "Social News: Hammond Lady Attends," *Lake County Times* (October 1, 1915), p. 8.

102. Frank Bros. advertisement, *Waterloo Courier* (April 14, 1920), p. 16.

103. "United States Census, 1920," database with images, *Family Search* (https://familysearch.org/ark:/61903/1:1:MF4C-NPD: accessed 20 April 2020), Marie Windle in household of W G Windle, Jr, Valparaiso Ward 2, Porter, Indiana, United States; citing ED 142, sheet 3B, line 90, family 84, NARA microfilm publication T625 (Washington, D.C.: National Archives and Records Administration, 1992), roll 460; FHL microfilm 1,820,460; "Fire Levels Windle Residence," *Vidette-Messenger* (December 25, 1950), p. 1; "Loss in Two Blazes Set at $25,000," *Vidette-Messenger* (December 27, 1950), p. 1; "Begin to Excavate for New Nazarene Parsonage," *Vidette-Messenger* (April 22, 1952), p. 3.

104. "United States Census, 1900," database with images, *Family Search* (https://familysearch.org/ark:/61903/1:1:M9MG-BHC: accessed 20 April

2020), Marie Timmons in household of George Timmons, Center Township Valparaiso city Ward 4, Porter, Indiana, United States; citing enumeration district (ED) 84, sheet 10A, family 245, NARA microfilm publication T623 (Washington, D.C.: National Archives and Records Administration, 1972); FHL microfilm 1,240,398.

105. "Indiana Marriages, 1811–2007," database with images, *Family Search* (https://familysearch.org/ark:/61903/1:1:KDH7-7NV: 10 December 2017), William G Windle and Marie L Timmons, 20 Aug 1918; citing Porter, Indiana, United States, Marriage Registration, Indiana Commission on Public Records, Indianapolis; FHL microfilm 005014500; "United States World War II Draft Registration Cards, 1942," database with images, *Family Search* (https://familysearch.org/ark:/61903/1:1:-X5N4-QZZ: 13 March 2020), William Garland Windle Junior, 1942; citing NARA microfilm publication M1936, M1937, M1939, M1951, M1962, M1964, M1986, M2090, and M2097 (Washington, D.C.: National Archives and Records Administration, n.d.); "Local Grocer Dies at Noon; Ill 6 Months," *Vidette-Messenger* (December 14, 1942), p. 1; "Windle Services Will Be Thursday," *Vidette-Messenger* (December 16, 1942), p. 6.

106. "United States Census, 1930," database with images, *Family Search* (https://familysearch.org/ark:/61903/1:1:X4B7-RX7: accessed 20 April 2020), Garland W Windle, Valparaiso, Porter, Indiana, United States; citing enumeration district (ED) ED 5, sheet 6B, line 93, family 153, NARA microfilm publication T626 (Washington, D.C.: National Archives and Records Administration, 2002), roll 622; FHL microfilm 2,340,357; "Preserving Historic Valparaiso: Carriage Barn Ages Into Old Home with Character," *Vidette-Messenger* (September 4, 1987), p. 1.

107. "Mrs. Windle Found Dead in Illinois," *Vidette-Messenger* (October 25, 1958), p. 1; "Mrs. Windle's Rites," *Vidette-Messenger* (October 27, 1958), p. 6.

108. "Mandel Lowenstine to Build Washington Street Mansion for His Valparaiso Residence," *Vidette-Messenger* (April 5, 1928), p. 1; zillow.com.

109. "United States Census, 1920," database with images, *Family Search* (https://familysearch.org/ark:/61903/1:1:MJS5-4FH: accessed 22 April 2020), Daisy Temple in household of John D Gates, Chicago Ward 6, Cook (Chicago), Illinois, United States; citing ED 341, sheet 11A, line 35, family 183, NARA microfilm publication T625 (Washington, D.C.: National Archives and Records Administration, 1992), roll 310; FHL microfilm 1,820,310; "Illinois, Cook County Marriages, 1871–1920," database, *Family Search* (https://familysearch.org/ark:/61903/1:1:Q21J-6RM6: 28 November 2018), Mandel Lowenstine and Daisy Temple, 02 Jan 1922; citing Marriage, Cook, Illinois, United States, citing Cook County Clerk. Cook County Courthouse, Chicago; FHL microfilm 101941438.

110. "United States Census, 1900," database with images, *Family Search* (https://familysearch.org/ark:/61903/1:1:MSHW-TXC: accessed 22 April

2020), Daisy Temple in household of James Temple, Sparta Precinct (excl. Sparta), Randolph, Illinois, United States; citing enumeration district (ED) 76, sheet 3A, family 51, NARA microfilm publication T623 (Washington, D.C.: National Archives and Records Administration, 1972); FHL microfilm 1,240,338.

111. "United States Census, 1930," database with images, *Family Search* (https://familysearch.org/ark:/61903/1:1:X4BQ-VPN: accessed 30 May 2020), Daisy Lowenstein in household of Mandel Lowenstein, Valparaiso, Porter, Indiana, United States; citing enumeration district (ED) ED 5, sheet 7A, line 47, family 168, NARA microfilm publication T626 (Washington, D.C.: National Archives and Records Administration, 2002), roll 622; FHL microfilm 2,340,357; "United States Census, 1940," database with images, *Family Search* (https://familysearch.org/ark:/61903/1:1:V1YL-YMD: 16 November 2019), Daisy W Lowenstein in household of Wadel Lowenstein, Ward 2, Valparaiso, Center Township, Porter, Indiana, United States; citing enumeration district (ED) 64–5, sheet 61B, line 66, family, Sixteenth Census of the United States, 1940, NARA digital publication T627. Records of the Bureau of the Census, 1790–2007, RG 29. Washington, D.C.: National Archives and Records Administration, 2012, roll 1086.

112. "United States Census, 1940," database with images, *Family Search* (https://familysearch.org/ark:/61903/1:1:V1YG-3ZP: 16 November 2019), Walter E Brownell, Ward 2, Valparaiso, Center Township, Porter, Indiana, United States; citing enumeration district (ED) 64–5, sheet 61B, line 46, family, Sixteenth Census of the United States, 1940, NARA digital publication T627. Records of the Bureau of the Census, 1790–2007, RG 29. Washington, D.C.: National Archives and Records Administration, 2012, roll 1086; zillow.com.

113. "United States Census, 1910," database with images, *Family Search* (https://familysearch.org/ark:/61903/1:1:MKP6-1P2: accessed 18 April 2020), Floy Binyon in household of C W Binyon, Center, Lake, Indiana, United States; citing enumeration district (ED) ED 40, sheet 12B, family 154, NARA microfilm publication T624 (Washington, D.C.: National Archives and Records Administration, 1982), roll 362; FHL microfilm 1,374,375; "Obituary Mrs. Walter Brownell," *Vidette-Messenger* (June 11, 1975), p. 22.

114. "Illinois, Cook County Marriages, 1871–1920," database, *Family Search* (https://familysearch.org/ark:/61903/1:1:N7CL-R8V: 10 March 2018), Walter Ezra Brownell and Floy Gladys Binyon, 18 Sep 1912; "Lowell," *Lake County Times* (September 18, 1912), p. 6; "Former Joliet Boy Becomes a Benedict," *Joliet Evening Herald-News* (September 19, 1912), p. 4.

115. "Obituaries: Walter E. Brownell, 83," *Vidette-Messenger* (October 24, 1974), p. 14.

116. "Obituaries: Walter E. Brownell," p. 14.

117. Previously no. 14 and no. 22 W. Jefferson St. See *Valparaiso City Directory 1885–86*, p. 32; *Valparaiso City Directory 1893*, n.pag.;

*Bumstead's Valparaiso City and Porter County Directory 1902*, p. 54; "Obituaries: Mrs. Bartholomew," *Vidette-Messenger* (July 17, 1972), p. 8; "United States Census, 1900," database with images, *Family Search* (https://familysearch.org/ark:/61903/1:1:-M9MG-BYD: accessed 21 April 2020), Louise Bannister in household of Alfred Bannister, Center Township Valparaiso city Ward 3, Porter, Indiana, United States; citing enumeration district (ED) 83, sheet 2B, family 54, NARA microfilm publication T623 (Washington, D.C.: National Archives and Records Administration, 1972); FHL microfilm 1,240,398; "United States Census, 1910," database with images, *Family Search* (https://familysearch.org/ark:/61903/1:1:MK5D-X84: accessed 21 April 2020), Louise Bannister in household of Alfred Bannister, Center, Porter, Indiana, United States; citing enumeration district (ED) ED 140, sheet 1A, family 14, NARA microfilm publication T624 (Washington, D.C.: National Archives and Records Administration, 1982), roll 374; FHL microfilm 1,374,387.

118. *Valparaiso City Directory 1885–86*, p. 110; *Bumstead's Valparaiso City and Porter County Directory 1902*, p. 132; "Death Takes Former Local Businessman: Alfred Banister Succumbs Tuesday at Hospital Here," *Vidette-Messenger* (May 18, 1949), p. 1.

119. "Anniversary Dinner Tri Kappa Enjoyed Last Evening," *Vidette-Messenger* (February 7, 1928,), p. 3; "Obituaries: Mrs. Bartholomew," p. 8.

120. "Indiana Marriages, 1811–2007," database with images, *Family Search* (https://familysearch.org/ark:/61903/1:1:KDHQ-Y5J: 10 December 2017), Charles Leroy Bartholomew and Cora Louise Banister, 17 Oct 1912; citing Porter, Indiana, United States, Marriage Registration, Indiana Commission on Public Records, Indianapolis; FHL microfilm 005014499.

121. "Former Mayor Succumbs: Rites to Be Held Wednesday," *Vidette-Messenger* (December 19, 1960), p. 1. *A Biographical History of Porter County, Indiana* says it was the Chicago College of Dental Surgery in 1909 (http://www.inportercounty.org/Data/Biographies/Bartholomew73.html).

122. "United States Census, 1930," database with images, *Family Search* (https://familysearch.org/ark:/61903/1:1:X4B7-M1N: accessed 21 April 2020), C Leroy Bartholomew, Valparaiso, Porter, Indiana, United States; citing enumeration district (ED) ED 6, sheet 2A, line 7, family 28, NARA microfilm publication T626 (Washington, D.C.: National Archives and Records Administration, 2002), roll 622; FHL microfilm 2,340,357; "United States Census, 1940," database with images, *Family Search* (https://familysearch.org/ark:/61903/1:1:V1YL-YPZ: 16 November 2019), Charles Leroy Bartholem, Ward 3, Valparaiso, Center Township, Porter, Indiana, United States; citing enumeration district (ED) 64-6, sheet 3B, line 41, family 54, Sixteenth Census of the United States, 1940, NARA digital publication T627. Records of the Bureau of the Census, 1790–2007, RG 29. Washington, D.C.: National Archives and Records Administration, 2012, roll 1086.

123. "Obituaries: Mrs. Bartholomew," p. 8.

124. "United States Census, 1900," database with images, *Family Search* (https://familysearch.org/ark:/61903/1:1:M9MP-M43: accessed 30 May 2020), Ada M Roessler in household of John E Roessler, Center Township Valparaiso city Ward 1, Porter, Indiana, United States; citing enumeration district (ED) 81, sheet 2A, family 41, NARA microfilm publication T623 (Washington, D.C.: National Archives and Records Administration, 1972); FHL microfilm 1,240,398; "United States Census, 1910," database with images, *Family Search* (https://familysearch.org/ark:/61903/1:1:MK5D-FT3: accessed 19 April 2020), Ada Roessler in household of John Roessler, Center, Porter, Indiana, United States; citing enumeration district (ED) ED 138, sheet 15B, family 373, NARA microfilm publication T624 (Washington, D.C.: National Archives and Records Administration, 1982), roll 374; FHL microfilm 1,374,387.

125. "Mrs. Joseph Bartholomew," *Vidette-Messenger* (September 11, 1979), p. 3.

126. "J.E. Roessler, Ex-President of VU, Dies," *Vidette-Messenger* (March 14, 1941), p. 1; "Dr. J.E. Roessler Succumbs at 81," *Indianapolis Star* (March 15, 1941), p. 20.

127. "Former VU Teacher Dies," *Vidette-Messenger* (February 1, 1946), p. 1.

128. "Beulah Bondi, Noted for Screen Characterizations, Studies Unusual Types."

129. "Indiana Notes," *Muncie Morning Star* (May 1, 1906), p. 9.

130. "Mrs. Joseph Bartholomew," p. 3; http://www.inportercounty.org/Data/Biographies/Bartholomew75.html.

131. "Indiana Marriages, 1811–2007," database with images, *Family Search* (https://familysearch.org/ark:/61903/1:1:KDHQ-K5W: 10 December 2017), Joseph S Bartholomew and Ada May Roessler, 01 Jun 1911; citing Porter, Indiana, United States, Marriage Registration, Indiana Commission on Public Records, Indianapolis; FHL microfilm 005014499; "Joe Bartholomew Wed," *Lake County Times* (June 5, 1911), p. 2.

132. "United States World War I Draft Registration Cards, 1917–1918," database with images, *Family Search* (https://familysearch.org/ark:/61903/1:1:KZ25-P52: 25 August 2019), Joseph Spencer Bartholomew, 1917–1918; "United States World War II Draft Registration Cards, 1942," database with images, *Family Search* (https://familysearch.org/ark:/61903/1:1:X5FD-X46: 13 March 2020), Joseph Spencer Bartholomew, 1942; citing NARA microfilm publication M1936, M1937, M1939, M1951, M1962, M1964, M1986, M2090, and M2097 (Washington, D.C.: National Archives and Records Administration, n.d.); "Joseph Bartholomew," *Hammond Times* (March 28, 1947), p. 6.

133. "Indiana Deaths," *Indianapolis News* (August 1, 1904), p. 3; "Sad Death," *New Philadelphia Daily Times* (August 1, 1904), p. 2.

134. "United States World War I Draft Registration Cards, 1917–1918," Joseph Spencer Bartholomew; "United States Census, 1920," database with images, *Family Search* (https://familysearch.org/ark:/61903/1:1:MF4C-6ZS: accessed 30 May

2020), Ada Bartholmu in household of Joseph Bartholmu, Center, Porter, Indiana, United States; citing ED 140, sheet 1B, line 59, family 18, NARA microfilm publication T625 (Washington, D.C.: National Archives and Records Administration, 1992), roll 460; FHL microfilm 1,820,460; "United States Census, 1930," database with images, *Family Search* (https://familysearch.org/ark:/61903/1:1:-X4B7-HZQ: accessed 19 April 2020), Ada Bartholomew in household of Joseph S Bartholomew, Valparaiso, Porter, Indiana, United States; citing enumeration district (ED) ED 3, sheet 2A, line 36, family 42, NARA microfilm publication T626 (Washington, D.C.: National Archives and Records Administration, 2002), roll 622; FHL microfilm 2,340,357; "United States Census, 1940," database with images, *Family Search* (https://familysearch.org/ark:/61903/1:1:V1YL-T26: 16 November 2019), Ada Bartholomew in household of Joseph S Bartholomew, Ward 1, Valparaiso, Center Township, Porter, Indiana, United States; citing enumeration district (ED) 64–3, sheet 62A, line 29, family 97, Sixteenth Census of the United States, 1940, NARA digital publication T627. Records of the Bureau of the Census, 1790–2007, RG 29. Washington, D.C.: National Archives and Records Administration, 2012, roll 1086.

135. "New York, New York Passenger and Crew Lists, 1909, 1925–1957," database with images, *Family Search* (https://familysearch.org/ark:/61903/1:1:-2HH1-FWH: 15 March 2018), Ada R Bartholomew, 1955; citing Immigration, New York City, New York, United States, NARA microfilm publication T715 (Washington, D.C.: National Archives and Records Administration, n.d.); "Mrs. Joseph Bartholomew," p. 3.

136. "Industrialist Dies After 2 Month Illness," *Vidette-Messenger* (January 3, 1956), p. 1; "Illinois, Cook County Deaths, 1878–1994," database, *Family Search* (https://familysearch.org/ark:/61903/1:1:-Q2MJ-9YX5: 18 March 2018), Daisy Lowenstine, 15 Dec 1977; citing Chicago, Cook, Illinois, United States, source reference; record number, Cook County Courthouse, Chicago; FHL microfilm.

137. "Some Fifty Cent Dinners," *Emporia Gazette* (April 20, 1910), p. 6 reprints Eva Bondy's suggested menu, which had originally been submitted to a contest in the *Chicago Tribune*; Irene Bell Dickson, "The Civic Secretary," *Vidette-Messenger* (February 1, 1932), p. 5.

138. Eva Marble Bondy, "Bide a Wee," *Sunday Inter Ocean* (July 5, 1896), p. 38.

139. Bondy, *Worldkins*, p. 7.

140. "Valparaiso's Woman's Club Outstanding Institution," *Vidette-Messenger* (August 18, 1936), p. 14; "Beulah Bondi Here to Present Her Mother's Book of Poems," *Vidette-Messenger* (November 1, 1962), p. 5; Bondy, *Worldkins*, p. 119.

141. Bondy, *Worldkins*, p. 119.

142. "Franchise League Notes," *Indianapolis Star* (December 12, 1915), p. 43.

143. Bondy, *Worldkins*, p. 120.

144. "The Stroller," "Beulah Bondi Always Proud of Valparaiso," *Vidette-Messenger*

(December 18, 1958), p. 1; Bondy, *Worldkins*, p. 120.

145. "United States Census, 1900," Eva Bandy in household of Aldolph O Bandy.

146. "Woman's Clubs: Plans and Programs," *Vidette-Messenger* (May 5, 1943), p. 2.

147. "Mrs. Williams Hostess to Members Magazine Club, Monday Afternoon," *Vidette-Messenger* (June 13, 1928), p. 3.

148. "Woman's Club: Plans and Programs," *Vidette-Messenger* (December 7, 1932), p. 3.

149. Marion Kelley, "Beulah Bondi Back After 15 Years," *Philadelphia Inquirer* (October 22, 1950), p. 27.

150. Frank A. Aversano, "Dear Beulah: Reflection on the Long and Distinguished Career of Beulah Bondi," *American Classic Screen* 3.4 (March-April 1979), p. 34.

151. Black, "Who's News with Cobey Black," p. 13.

152. Nancy Anderson, "Beulah Bondi: A Vigorous Actress in Her 70s," *Cincinnati Enquirer* (April 16, 1972), p. 6F; reprinted in a slightly longer version as "Can't Stay Away," *Appleton Post-Crescent* (June 4, 1972), p. 3.

153. Aversano, "Dear Beulah," p. 34.

154. "The Stroller," "Beulah Bondi Always Proud," p. 1, 6.

155. Black, "Who's News with Cobey Black," p. 13.

156. Lane, "Beulah Accents the Positive," p. 5.

157. I base this description on a postcard entitled "Grand Opera House and Ex-Proprietor L.D. Bondy," https://www.flickr.com/photos/shookphotos/4181365622.

158. "L.D. Bondy Dies at Age 84," p. 1.

159. Rollie Bernhart, "Editor of 70 Years Ago Crammed Fact, Humor into Weekly Publication," *Vidette-Messenger* (July 12, 1963), p. 6.

160. "L.D. Bondy Dies at Age 84," p. 2.

161. "Twenty Years Ago: August 16, 1918," *Vidette-Messenger* (August 16, 1938), p. 4.

162. "Well, But What Rachel Say?," *Lake County Times* (July 27, 1916), p. 2.

163. "L.D. Bondy Dies at Age 84," p. 2.

164. "L.D. Bondy Dies at Age 84," p. 2.

165. "Hold Rites for Louis D. Bondy," *Vidette-Messenger* (July 15, 1937), p. 4.

166. This account of Bondi's stage debut has been based on John Parker, *Who's Who in the Theatre: A Biographical Record of the Contemporary Stage*, 7th ed. (London: Pitman, 1933), p. 281; Rollie Bernhart, "When Opportunity Knocks, Gay Nineties Group Scores," *Vidette-Messenger* (December 29, 1956, p. 1); Mannies, "Beulah's Debut 47 Pages Long," p. 1; Anderson, "Beulah Bondi: A Vigorous Actress in Her 70s," p. 6F; and Aversano, "Dear Beulah," p. 34.

167. BBP 1.30.

168. Mannies, "Beulah's Debut 47 Pages Long," p. 1.

169. An article in connection with Bondi's 1945 visit to the school, the first visit since her graduation, claims she was there for four years, graduating

in 1907. See "Miss Bondi is Week-End Guest at Mount Carroll," *Freeport Journal Standard* (July 31, 1945), p. 8. The earliest source I have found to claim she attended 1905-7 is "Three Women Will Receive Awards at Shimer College," *Freeport Journal-Standard* (May 10, 1967), p. 6.

170. Advertisement, *Chicago Tribune* (July 16, 1906), p. 9.

171. "Ladies' Dormitory Burned to Ground," *Freeport Journal-Standard* (February 9, 1906), p. 4.

172. Some of the earliest sources that mention her attending this school are Harriet Parsons, "Peeping Through Keyhole at Beulah Bondi," *Pittsburgh Sun-Telegraph* (January 30, 1938), p. 13; "Beulah Bondi Stars in 'Remember the Night' at Premiere Tonight, Saturday," *Vidette-Messenger* (May 10, 1940), p. 6; and Louis J. Allemann, *Beulah Bondi Bulletin* (August 26, 1940), n.pag.

173. http://www.psnm.qc.ca/psnm/histoire/.

174. Bessie N. Parks, findagrave.com, which also contains a brief death notice from an unnamed newspaper.

175. Beulah Bondi to Abram and Eva Bondy, Thursday [March 15, 1906] (BBP 3.5). Dating from the fact that Bondi mentions that St. Patrick's Day is on Saturday.

176. Beulah Bondi to Abram and Eva Bondy, Sunday [April 1906] (BBP 3.5). Bondi mentions her account of expenses in March and that Easter is approaching.

177. Bondi to Abram and Eva Bondy, Thursday [March 15, 1906] (BBP 3.5).

178. Beulah Bondi to Eva Bondy, Thursday [March-April 1906] (BBP 3.5).

179. The earliest of these sources, contemporaneous with the event, is "Valparaiso News," *Lake County Times* (June 14, 1907), p. 6.

180. "Frances Shimer College Invites Actress to Be Speaker at Homecoming," *Freeport Journal-Standard* (April 15, 1949), p. 6.

181. Harold Heffernan, "Cupid and Career Don't Mix, Says Bondi," *Indianapolis Star* (October 28, 1956), p. 13.

182. Black, "Who's News with Cobey Black," p. 13.

183. Burkett, "Beulah Bondi Wows Shimer," p. 3A.

184. See, for example, "Alumnae of Shimer to Meet for Party," *Los Angeles Times* (April 21, 1946), p. 2.

185. "Girl Graduates Make Own Gowns," *Chicago Tribune* (June 23, 1909), p. 8. There is no question that this is Bondi. All her standard bios claim that she graduated from Hyde Park High School, including Parker, *Who's Who in the Theatre*, p. 281, which does not list any of her other schools or her university degrees

186. Burkett, "Beulah Bondi Wows Shimer," p. 3A.

187. "The Rascal Pat," *Vernal Express* (March 8, 1912), p. 2.

188. "Willcox Academy," *Vernal Express* (May 24, 1912), p. 1. A similar item appeared in the paper on May 31.

189. "Young Bondy Vaudeville," *Vernal Express* (June 28, 1912), p. 1; *Vernal Express* (April 29, 1965), p. 11; Doris Karren Burton, "Pages from the Past: History of Orpheus Hall or Imperial Hall," *Vernal Express* (June 29, 1983), p. 19.

190. "Sun Dance Opera," *Vernal Express* (February 14, 1913), p. 1; "Sun Dance Opera," *Vernal Express* (February 21, 1913), p. 1; "Sun Dance Opera Was Big Success," *Vernal Express* (February 28, 1913), p. 1, 4; "Local and Personal," *Vernal Express* (April 4, 1913), p. 7.

191. "Local and Personal," *Vernal Express* (January 24, 1913), p. 5.

192. "Ute Indians Take Part in War Dance," *Vernal Express* (January 24, 1913), p. 6.

193. "Indian Girl Writes Opera," *El Paso Herald* (December 27, 1913), p. 31.

194. "Ute Indians Take Part in War Dance," p. 6.

195. "Sun Dance Opera Was Big Success," p. 1, 4. The weekly paper did not have sufficient space to review the play fully on February 21.

196. "United States Census, 1910," database with images, *Family Search* (https://familysearch.org/ark:/61903/1:1:M561-TK9: accessed 8 May 2020), Ashley Bartlett, Provo Ward 6, Utah, Utah, United States; citing enumeration district (ED) ED 195, sheet 4B, family 68, NARA microfilm publication T624 (Washington, D.C.: National Archives and Records Administration, 1982), roll 1610; FHL microfilm 1,375,623; "United States Census, 1940," database with images, *Family Search* (https://familysearch.org/ark:/61903/1:1:VT4H-4JP: 19 August 2019), Ashley Bartlett, Vernal, Election Precinct 3 South Vernal, Uintah, Utah, United States; citing enumeration district (ED) 24–3, sheet 2B, line 63, family 37, Sixteenth Census of the United States, 1940, NARA digital publication T627. Records of the Bureau of the Census, 1790–2007, RG 29. Washington, D.C.: National Archives and Records Administration, 2012, roll 4218; "Resident Attains 94th Milestone," *Vernal Express* (May 2, 1974), p. 20; "Ashley Bartlett," *Salt Lake Tribune* (December 12, 1979), p. D7.

197. "Sun Dance Opera Was Big Success," p. 1, 4.

198. "Indian Girl Writes Opera on Sioux Life," *Miami News* (July 5, 1913), p. 4.

199. "Sun Dance Opera Was Big Success," p. 1, 4.

200. "Recital at Uintah Academy," *Vernal Express* (May 23, 1913), p. 1.

201. "Three Songs," *Vernal Express* (March 19, 1915), p. 3.

202. "Utah, Birth Certificates, 1903–1914," database with images, *Family Search* (https://familysearch.org/ark:/61903/1:1:QL3W-9M96: 10 March 2018), Edythe Mary Neal, 18 Jan 1909; citing Vernal, Uintah, Utah, United States; citing p., ref. ID #, Utah State Archives, Salt Lake City; Family Search digital folder 004245234; "United States Census, 1910," database with images, *Family Search* (https://familysearch.org/ark:/61903/1:1:M5X8-6MP: accessed 5 May 2020), Edith C Neal in household of Charles Neal, Vernal, Uintah, Utah, United States; citing enumeration district (ED) ED 179, sheet 2B, family 42, NARA microfilm publication

T624 (Washington, D.C.: National Archives and Records Administration, 1982), roll 1609; FHL microfilm 1,375,622; "Charles J. Neal," *Salt Lake Tribune* (April 13, 1977), p. 21.

203. "Society," *Vernal Express* (July 12, 1945), p. 5; "Society Today: Brides Hold Spotlight," *Salt Lake Tribune* (June 19, 1946), p. 15; "Edith Neal Curtright," *Salt Lake Tribune* (August 3, 1996), p. D6; "United States Social Security Death Index," database, *Family Search* (https://familysearch.org/ark:/61903/1:1:JLBK-Y2V: 20 May 2014), Edythe N Curtright, 30 Jul 1996; citing U.S. Social Security Administration, *Death Master File*, database (Alexandria, Virginia: National Technical Information Service, ongoing).

204. "Claxton Speaker for Valpo Exercises," *Lake County Times* (August 7, 1914), p. 7.

205. Allemann, *Beulah Bondi Bulletin* (August 26, 1940); "Beulah Bondi in Visit Here," *Vidette-Messenger* (April 8, 1976), p. 1; Burkett, "Beulah Bondi Wows Shimer," p. 3; "Six to Receive Honorary Degrees from VU," *Vidette-Messenger* (April 21, 1978), p. 3.

206. Advertisement, *Chicago Tribune* (August 16, 1914), p. 13.

207. "Kappa Kaps Have Annual Luncheon," *Lake County Times* (February 19, 1917), p. 3.

208. "Tri Kappa Marks 100 Years," *Munster Times* (March 27, 2003), p. B5.

209. "Anniversary Dinner Iota Chapter Tri Kappa," *Vidette-Messenger* (February 7, 1928), p. 3.

210. "Tri Kappa Marks 100 Years," p. B5.

211. "Sorority Luncheon a Success," *Lake County Times* (February 22, 1915), p. 5; "Kappa Kaps Have Annual Luncheon," p. 3; "Tri Kappa's Sixteenth Annual Luncheon," *Lake County Times* (February 25, 1918), p. 5.

212. "Kappa Convention Opens," *Indianapolis News* (April 15, 1921), p. 25.

213. "'American Citizen' Tonight," *Valparaiso Evening Messenger* (June 30, 1914), p. 1.

214. BBP 1.32.

215. "Plays Old Ladies: Beulah Bondi of 'One of the Family' Is Still in Her 20s, However," *Boston Herald* (October 24, 1926) (NYPL); Kelley, "Beulah Bondi Back After 15 Years," p. 27; Aversano, "Dear Beulah," p. 34 (ellipsis in original).

216. Kelley, "Beulah Bondi Back After 15 Years," p. 27.

217. Aversano, "Dear Beulah," pp. 34–35.

218. Charles Witbeck, "Keynotes: 'Lincoln' Series Offers Sarah Bush Vignette," *Allentown Morning Call* (January 6, 1976), p. 24. There is a longer version of this anecdote, which also involves the character actress Louise Closser Hale, in Aversano, "Dear Beulah," pp. 34–35. As it happened, Hale was also in Bondi's debut play on Broadway.

219. "Massachusetts, Boston Passenger Lists, 1891–1943," database with images, *Family Search* (https://familysearch.org/ark:/61903/1:1:QV9W-1L7F: 13 March 2018), Frederick Maurice Browne, 1910; citing Immigration, Boston, Suffolk, Massachusetts, United States, NARA microfilm publication T843 (Washington, D.C.: National Archives

and Records Administration, n.d.); FHL microfilm 1,404,283; Maurice Browne, *Too Late to Lament: An Autobiography* (London: Victor Gollancz, 1955), p. 107.

220. Browne, *Too Late to Lament*, p. 116.

221. Browne, p. 124.

222. Browne, p. 111.

223. Adelaide Stiles, "It's All in the Trunk: Visiting Actress, Beulah Bondi, Tells Interesting Story of Rise to Fame," *Fort Lauderdale News* (May 6, 1953), p. 6B.

224. "United States Census, 1920," database with images, *Family Search* (https://familysearch.org/ark:/61903/1:1:MJ39-ZDB: accessed 10 May 2020), May D Kelso in household of Hugh A Kelso, Chicago Ward 3, Cook (Chicago), Illinois, United States; citing ED 170, sheet 2B, line 71, family 41, NARA microfilm publication T625 (Washington, D.C.: National Archives and Records Administration, 1992), roll 313; FHL microfilm 1,820,313; "Illinois, Cook County Deaths, 1878–1994," database, *Family Search* (https://familysearch.org/ark:/61903/1:1:Q2MK-VLS1: 18 March 2018), Mary Kelso, 10 Jul 1938; citing Chicago, Cook, Illinois, United States, source reference, record number, Cook County Courthouse, Chicago; FHL microfilm; Browne, *Too Late to Lament*, p. 145.

225. Kelley, "Beulah Bondi Back After 15 Years," p. 27; Aversano, "Dear Beulah," p. 35. According to an information leaflet about the school, they were accepting 12 students (BBP 3.1).

226. Maurice Browne to Beulah Bondi, October 16, 1916 (BBP 3.1).

227. Little Theatre School leaflet, undated (BBP 3.1).

228. Aversano, "Dear Beulah," p. 35.

229. Little Theatre School leaflet.

230. Aversano, "Dear Beulah," p. 35; Black, "Who's News with Cobey Black," p. 13.

231. Browne, *Too Late to Lament*, p. 209.

232. "Little Theatre Near End?," *Chicago Tribune* (December 12, 1916), p. 2.

233. Browne, *Too Late to Lament*, p. 129, 133.

234. Aversano, "Dear Beulah," p. 35.

235. Little Theatre School leaflet.

236. Aversano, "Dear Beulah," p. 35.

237. Browne, *Too Late to Lament*, p. 118.

238. "Fifteen Years Ago: December 26, 1916," *Vidette-Messenger* (December 16, 1931), p. 5.

239. *Cranford* program, undated (BBP 3.11).

240. *Cranford* program.

241. Kelley, "Beulah Bondi Back After 15 Years," p. 27.

242. Black, "Who's News with Cobey Black," p. 13.

243. Browne, *Too Late to Lament*, p. 115.

244. Anon., "Mr. Browne's Disciples in 'Cranford,'" *Chicago Evening Post* (December 28, 1916) (BBP 1.11).

245. "Fifteen Years Ago: February 3, 1917," *Vidette-Messenger* (February 3, 1932), p. 5.

246. See *Deirdre of the Sorrows* flyer, February 4, 1917 (BBP 1.12).

247. "Little Theater Goes on Rocks of

Bankruptcy," *Chicago Tribune* (February 24, 1917), p. 13; "Chicago Little Theater Broke: Debts of Maurice Browne Enterprise $15,000—Assets Dubious," *St. Louis Post-Dispatch* (February 24, 1917), p. 1.

248. Browne, *Too Late to Lament*, p. 211.

249. "Little Theater Company Revived," *Chicago Tribune* (June 28, 1917), p. 10; Browne, *Too Late to Lament*, p. 209.

250. Browne, *Too Late to Lament*, p. 369.

251. *Medea* program, November 28 and December 5, 1917 (BBP 1.34).

252. "Woe Once More Treads Stage of Little Theater," *Chicago Tribune* (December 2, 1917), p. 11.

## Chapter 2

1. Bondi quoted in Steve Hoffman, "Bondi, 83; 60 Years of Grandmothers," *Cincinnati Enquirer* (January 9, 1976), p. B5.

2. There has been some uncertainty about the year of Walker's birth, but it is clear from the 1880 U.S. Census and his death certificate, that he was born in 1880. See "United States Census, 1880," database with images, *Family Search* (https://familysearch.org/ark:/61903/1:1:M8SG-XV4: 16 July 2017), Stuart A Walker in household of David Openheimer, Portsmouth, Scioto, Ohio, United States; citing enumeration district ED 171, sheet 184A, NARA microfilm publication T9 (Washington, D.C.: National Archives and Records Administration, n.d.), FHL microfilm 1,255,064; "California, County Birth and Death Records, 1800–1994," database with images, *Family Search* (https://familysearch.org/ark:/61903/1:1:QGJ9-P9PG: 22 October 2019), Stuart Walker, 1941.

3. "Stuart Walker, 53, Producer Is Dead," *New York Times* (March 14, 1941), p. 21. The quotation is from "Best Plays Are Assured," *Cincinnati Enquirer* (June 20, 1929), p. 9.

4. JoAnn Yeoman, *Dream Dealer: Stuart Walker and the American Theater* (Scottsdale, AZ: Star Cloud Press, 2007), p. 32.

5. "Best Plays Are Assured," p. 9.

6. Robin Coons, "Hollywood News by Coons," *Richmond Palladium-Item* (February 9, 1940), p. 8.

7. "Backstage: Beulah Bondi Specialized in the Grandma Type Role," *Philadelphia Inquirer* (October 22, 1950), p. 25.

8. Young, *Reel Characters*, p. 57.

9. This account is based on Stiles, "It's All in the Trunk," p. 6B.

10. "In the Local Theaters," *Indianapolis Star* (May 6, 1919), p. 8.

11. M.J.B., "Theaters," *Indianapolis Star* (June 3, 1919), p. 8.

12. M.J.B., p. 8.

13. "Aldrich Bowker Dies, 72; Native of Ashby," *Fitchburg Sentinel* (March 25, 1947), p. 1, 6; "California Death Index, 1940–1997," database, *Family Search* (https://familysearch.org/ark:/61903/1:1:-VPCG-MGG: 26 November 2014), Aldrich Bowker,

21 Mar 1947; Department of Public Health Services, Sacramento; Alfred Aldrich Bowker, findagrave.com; imdb.com.

14. Yeoman, *Dream Dealer*, p. 38, 39.

15. Marguerite Tazelaar, "Beulah Bondi Likes to Look Old," unidentified clipping [1937] (NYPL).

16. See photograph in "Week's News of Plays and Players," *Indianapolis News* (June 21, 1919), p. 7.

17. Rudolf Besier, *Don* (New York: Duffield, 1910), p. 19.

18. Besier, p. 17.

19. "Plays and Players," *Indianapolis News* (July 8, 1919), p. 3.

20. "In the Local Theaters," *Indianapolis Star* (July 8, 1919), p. 13.

21. "Notes of the Stage," *Indianapolis Star* (August 1, 1919), p. 3.

22. Alice L. Tildesley, "You Don't Need Good Looks," *Honolulu Advertiser* (December 4, 1932), p. 32.

23. R.G.T., "Theaters," *Indianapolis Star* (July 29, 1919), p. 12; "Plays and Players," *Indianapolis News* (July 29, 1919), p. 13.

24. "Plays and Players," *Indianapolis News* (July 31, 1919), p. 6.

25. "Notes of the Stage," p. 3.

26. "Theaters," *Indianapolis Star* (June 16, 1919), p. 7.

27. "Plays and Players," p. 6.

28. "Notes of the Stage," p. 3.

29. C.S.K., "Theaters," *Indianapolis Star* (August 5, 1919), p. 11.

30. P.G. Wodehouse, *Piccadilly Jim* (London: Herbert Jenkins, n.d.), p. 36.

31. "Plays and Players," *Indianapolis News* (August 26, 1919), p. 8.

32. "'Piccadilly Jim' Proves Mixture of Fun and Thrills," *Wilkes-Barre Times Leader* (December 2, 1919), p. 19; "'Piccadilly Jim' Clever Young Man," *Hartford Courant* (December 19, 1919), p. 10; "Gregory Kelly in Grown Up Role," *Wilmington News Journal* (December 5, 1919), p. 6.

33. "Notes of the Stage," *Indianapolis News* (August 29, 1919), p. 6.

34. "Notes of the Stage," *Indianapolis Star* (August 30, 1919), p. 14.

35. "Society," *Indianapolis Star* (August 26, 1919), p. 7.

36. "Mulling Over the Walker Stock Season," *Indianapolis News* (August 30, 1919), p. 4.

37. Mary Cooke, "Character Actress Bondi Likes Her Role in Life," *Honolulu Advertiser* (May 26, 1961), p. 25.

38. Mannies, "Beulah's Debut 47 Pages Long," p. 1.

39. Aversano, "Dear Beulah," p. 35.

40. Tazelaar, "Beulah Bondi Likes to Look Old."

41. Cooke, "Character Actress Bondi Likes Her Role in Life," p. 25.

42. "United States Census, 1920," database with images, *Family Search* (https://familysearch.org/ark:/61903/1:1:MF4C-WVG: accessed 12 October 2019), A O Bondy, Valparaiso Ward 2, Porter,

Indiana, United States; citing ED 142, sheet 3A, line 50, family 71, NARA microfilm publication T625 (Washington, D.C.: National Archives and Records Administration, 1992), roll 460; FHL microfilm 1,820,460.

43. "United States Census, 1920," database with images, *Family Search* (https://familysearch.org/ark:/61903/1:1:MF4C-NPL: accessed 12 October 2019), Beulah Bondy, Valparaiso Ward 2, Porter, Indiana, United States; citing ED 142, sheet 3B, line 99, family 71, NARA microfilm publication T625 (Washington, D.C.: National Archives and Records Administration, 1992), roll 460; FHL microfilm 1,820,460.

44. "United States Census, 1920," database with images, *Family Search* (https://familysearch.org/ark:/61903/1:1:MJT6-NVS: accessed 12 October 2019), Beulah Bondy, Brooklyn Assembly District 5, Kings, New York, United States; citing ED 271, sheet 12A, line 27, family , NARA microfilm publication T625 (Washington, D.C.: National Archives and Records Administration, 1992), roll 1151; FHL microfilm 1,821,151.

45. R.G. Tucker, "English's—The Kelly Premiere," *Indianapolis Star* (April 12, 1921), p. 14.

46. "English's—'A Tailor-Made Man,'" *Indianapolis Star* (May 3, 1921), p. 11.

47. "Ten Year Ago: April 29, 1921," *Vidette-Messenger* (April 29, 1931), p. 2; "Dinner Program Marks 25th Year for Sphinx Club," *Vidette-Messenger* (February 17, 1945), p. 4.

48. "A New Acquisition at Toledo Theater," *Toledo Blade* (December 24, 1921) (NYPL).

49. John Corbin, "Drama," *New York Times* (December 27, 1918), p. 9.

50. Rachel Crothers, *Mary the Third. "Old Lady 31." A Little Journey: Three Plays by Rachel Crothers* (New York: Brentano's, 1923), p. 273, 285.

51. V.K.R., "Two New Players Given Enthusiastic Welcome," *Toledo Blade* (January 3, 1922) (NYPL).

52. W.S.G., "Cincinnati Theaters and Parks," *Cincinnati Enquirer* (May 15, 1922), p. 2.

53. "'The Saving Grace' with Cyril Maude," *New York Times* (October 1, 1918), p. 11.

54. "'The Saving Grace' with Cyril Maude," p. 11.

55. C. Haddon Chambers, *The Saving Grace* (New York: Brentano's, 1915), p. 166, 169.

56. G.M.W., *The Boomerang* review, *Toledo Blade* (September 19, 1922) (NYPL).

57. "Miss Illington in a Strong, New Play," *New York Times* (December 6, 1911), p. 13.

58. V.K.R., "Intense Drama at Toledo," *Toledo Blade* (February 28, 1922) (NYPL).

59. Charles Kenyon, *Kindling* (New York: Samuel French, 1914), p. 41.

60. W.S.G., "Cincinnati Theaters and Parks," *Cincinnati Enquirer* (July 3, 1922), p. 7.

61. "'The Saving Grace' with Cyril Maude," p. 11; "'Passers-by Who Have Come to Stay," *New York Times* (September 15, 1911), p. 9.

62. "'Passers-by Who Have Come to Stay," p. 9.

63. W.S.G., "Cincinnati Theaters and Parks," *Cincinnati Enquirer* (July 17, 1922), p. 5.

64. C.R.A., "Cincinnati Theaters and Parks," *Cincinnati Enquirer* (August 14, 1922), p. 3.

65. "'The Lottery Man' Not a Long Chance," *New York Times* (December 7, 1909), p. 7.

66. G.M.W., "A Real Rip-Roaring Farce Is The Lottery Man," *Toledo Blade* (January 10, 1922) (NYPL).

67. W. Somerset Maugham, *The Collected Plays of W. Somerset Maugham: Vol. II* (London: William Heinemann, 1931), p. 313.

68. Maugham, p. 315.

69. W.S.G., "Cincinnati Theaters and Parks," *Cincinnati Enquirer* (May 22, 1922), p. 11.

70. W.S.G., p. 11; "He's the Original 'Bad Boy,'" *Baltimore Sun* (March 16, 1924), p. 4.

71. W.S.G., "Cincinnati Theaters and Parks," *Cincinnati Enquirer* (May 29, 1922), p. 7.

72. "The New Play," *Brooklyn Times Union* (August 3, 1920), p. 3.

73. Alice Duer Miller and Robert Milton, *The Charm School* (London: Samuel French, 1922), p. 70.

74. See, for example, Alexander Woollcott, "The Play," *New York Times* (August 3, 1920), p. 12.

75. J.R. "The Charm School," *Cincinnati Enquirer* (August 28, 1922), p. 7.

76. Burns Mantle, ed., *The Best Plays of 1919–20* (Boston: Small, Maynard, 1920), p. 215, 216.

77. Rachel Barton Butler, "Mamma's Affair," *The Best Plays of 1919–20* (Boston: Small, Maynard, 1920), p. 242.

78. W.S. G., "Cincinnati Theaters and Parks," *Cincinnati Enquirer* (June 12, 1922), p. 7.

79. W.S.G., "Cincinnati Theaters and Parks," *Cincinnati Enquirer* (July 10, 1922), p. 5.

80. "Glittering Farce, Smartly Played," *New York Times* (November 1, 1916), p. 9.

81. "Glittering Farce," p. 9.

82. "Walker Underline," *Cincinnati Enquirer* (July 2, 1922), p. 2.

83. Alexander Woollcott, "The Play," *New York Times* (November 13, 1919), p. 11.

84. W.S.G., "Cincinnati Theaters and Parks," *Cincinnati Enquirer* (July 31, 1922), p. 3.

85. G.M.W., "Merry Play in Toledo Theater," *Toledo Blade* (October 10, 1922) (NYPL).

86. *Come Seven* advertisement, *Cincinnati Enquirer* (June 10, 1922), p. 4.

87. "Theaters and Parks," *Cincinnati Enquirer* (June 4, 1922), p. 2.

88. "'Come Seven!' Is Amusing Novelty," *New York Times* (July 20, 1920), p. 10.

89. W.S.G., "Cincinnati Theaters and Parks," *Cincinnati Enquirer* (June 5, 1922), p. 2.

90. "Kentucky Random Notes," *Cincinnati Enquirer* (July 25, 1937), p. 7.

91. Frances Howe McSurely to Beulah Bondi, January 12, 1949 (BBP 3.3); "United States Census, 1920," database with images, *Family Search* (https://familysearch.org/ark:/61903/1:1:MDYL-HRB: accessed 28 May 2020), Francis M Howe in household of Walter L Howe, Cincinnati Ward 3, Hamilton, Ohio, United States; citing ED 61, sheet 12A, line 38, family , NARA microfilm publication T625

(Washington, D.C.: National Archives and Records Administration, 1992), roll 1389; FHL microfilm 1,821,389.

92. "Foyer Gossip," *Cincinnati Enquirer* (September 3, 1922), p. 7.

93. G.M.W., *The Boomerang* review, *Toledo Blade* (September 19, 1922) (NYPL).

94. G.M.W., "Toledo Theater Players Give Truly Artistic Performance," *Toledo Blade* (September 26, 1922) (NYPL).

95. Alexander Woollcott, "The Play," *New York Times* (October 29, 1919), p. 11.

96. *Buddies* review, *Toledo Blade* (November 7, 1922) (NYPL).

97. See two clippings (BBP 1.15).

98. "Betrothal Scene Gets Laughs in 'Too Many Cooks,'" *Toledo Blade* (October 19, 1922) (NYPL); G.M.W., "Charming Broadway Player Heads Cast in 'Back Pay,'" *Toledo Blade* (October 31, 1922) (NYPL).

99. W.S.G. "Cincinnati Theaters and Parks," *Cincinnati Enquirer* (June 19, 1922), p. 5.

100. "Boyle," "Falling Airplane Is Only One of Real Thrills in 'The Broken Wing,'" *New York Daily News* (December 1, 1920), p. 7; "'The Broken Wing' Proves a New Thriller," *El Paso Herald* (December 18, 1920), p. 6.

101. "Drama Brevities," *Cincinnati Enquirer* (April 15, 1923), p. 3.

102. William Smith Goldenburg, "On Stage and Screen: Captain Applejack," *Cincinnati Enquirer* (June 19, 1923), p. 2.

103. Nunnally Johnson, "The New Plays," *Brooklyn Daily Eagle* (September 20, 1922), p. 8.

104. G.M.W., *It's a Boy!* review, *Toledo Blade* (February 6, 1923) (NYPL).

105. "The Comedy of a Good Young Man," *New York Times* (August 20, 1918), p. 7.

106. William Smith Goldenburg, "Amusements: 'A Very Good Young Man,'" *Cincinnati Enquirer* (July 3, 1923), p. 6.

107. Goldenburg, p. 6.

108. "New Walker Player," *Cincinnati Enquirer* (July 8, 1923), p. 2.

109. "The Theater," *Indianapolis Star* (July 10, 1923), p. 5.

110. "Plays and Players," *Indianapolis News* (July 10, 1923), p. 7.

111. "The Theater," *Indianapolis Star* (July 17, 1923), p. 5.

112. "Plays and Players," *Indianapolis News* (July 17, 1923), p. 7; William Smith Goldenburg, "Amusements: 'Spite Corner,'" *Cincinnati Enquirer* (July 24, 1923), p. 7.

113. Robert G. Tucker, "The Theater," *Indianapolis Star* (July 31, 1923), p. 5.

114. Frank Craven, *The First Year: A Comic Tragedy of Married Life* (New York: Samuel French, 1921), p. 47, 48, 49, 54.

115. "'First Year' Is Joyous," *New York Times* (October 21, 1920), p. 11.

116. "Plays and Players," *Indianapolis News* (August 7, 1923), p. 7.

117. William Smith Goldenburg, "Amusements: 'The Dover Road,'" *Cincinnati Enquirer* (August 14, 1923), p. 9.

118. Milne quoted in Goldenburg, "Amusements: 'The Dover Road,'" p. 9.

119. Alexander Woollcott, "The Play: Several Cheers for Mr. Milne," *New York Times* (December 24, 1921), p. 7.

120. Goldenburg, "Amusements: 'The Dover Road,'" p. 9.

121. Robert G. Tucker, "The Theater," *Indianapolis Star* (August 28, 1923), p. 5.

122. Carl B. Adams, "Amusements: 'Two Kisses,'" *Cincinnati Enquirer* (August 21, 1923), p. 6.

123. Mary Rose Bradford to Rita Halle Kleeman, January 29, 1949, enclosed with Rita Halle Kleeman to Beulah Bondi, February 1, 1949 (BBP 3.3).

124. "Doesn't Want Ingenue Roles," *Boston Herald* (October 17, 1926), n.pag.

125. "Doesn't Want Ingenue Roles."

126. Equity contract for *The Naked Man* dated November 13, 1923 (BBP 1.40).

127. "Plays of the Week," *Baltimore Sun* (December 9, 1923), p. 1.

128. "Next Week Offers Variety," *Baltimore Sun* (December 2, 1923), p. 2.

129. "Stage-News," *Chicago Tribune* (December 9, 1923), p. 3.

130. G.E.K., "'The Naked Man' Lyceum Offering," *Baltimore Evening Sun* (December 11, 1923), p. 14.

131. T.M.C. "Possibilities Are Seen in Boyd Fantasy," *Baltimore Sun* (December 16, 1923), p. 1.

132. "'The Naked Man' Is Well Worth While," *Hartford Courant* (December 18, 1923), p. 24.

133. "'The Naked Man' Is Well Worth While," p. 24.

134. T.M.C. "'The Naked Man' Opens for Week at Lyceum Theater," *Baltimore Sun* (December 11, 1923), p. 9; G.E.K., "'The Naked Man' Lyceum Offering," p. 14; T.M.C. "Possibilities Are Seen in Boyd Fantasy," *Baltimore Sun* (December 16, 1923), p. 1.

135. G.E.K., "'The Naked Man' Lyceum Offering," p. 14.

136. "Eddinger Star in Fantastic Play," *Hartford Courant* (December 9, 1923), p. 2C; "The Naked Man," *Brooklyn Daily Eagle* (December 9, 1923), p. E9.

137. "More or Less in the Broadway Spotlight: The Dual Miss Bondi," *New York Times* (March 27, 1927), p. 4; "The Talk of Hollywood," *Baltimore Evening Sun* (January 11, 1944), p. 12; "Beulah Bondi Sees Miami at Long Last," *Miami News* (January 11, 1946), n.pag; "Beulah Bondi Dead at 92," p. 1.

138. John Springer, "Beulah Bondi: Her Career Is Proof that 'Character Work' Is Also an Art," *Films in Review* (May 1963), p. 283; Brown, *Actors Talk*, p. 153; Young, *Reel Characters*, p. 57.

139. William Smith Goldenburg, "Amusements: 'Kempy,'" *Cincinnati Enquirer* (May 27, 1924), p. 4.

140. L.H.B., "Rinehart Drama is Presented by Stuart Walker Co.," *Baltimore Sun* (March 11, 1924), p. 9.

141. William Smith Goldenburg, "On Stage and Screen: 'The Hero,'" *Cincinnati Enquirer* (August 19, 1924), p. 6.

142. William Smith Goldenburg, "Amusements: 'The Goldfish,'" *Cincinnati Enquirer* (July 15, 1924), p. 2.

143. William Smith Goldenburg, "Amusements: 'Icebound,'" *Cincinnati Enquirer* (July 1, 1924), p. 7.

144. D.H.K., "'The Storm Bird' Is Presented by Walker Players," *Baltimore Sun* (March 25, 1924), p. 9; William Smith Goldenburg, "Cincinnati Theaters and Parks," *Cincinnati Enquirer* (June 24, 1924), p. 5; William Smith Goldenburg, "Amusements: 'Lady Windermere's Fan,'" *Cincinnati Enquirer* (September 23, 1924), p. 4.

145. James Muir, "Highly Ingenious Comedy," *Dayton Daily News* (July 29, 1924), p. 1; L.E.D., "Walker Actors Present Latest Nugent Comedy," *Dayton Herald* (July 29, 1924), p. 6.

146. William Smith Goldenburg, "Amusements: Stuart Walker Players," *Cincinnati Enquirer* (June 17, 1924), p. 5.

147. Carl B. Adams, "Amusements: 'The Proud Princess,'" *Cincinnati Enquirer* (August 7, 1928), p. 7.

148. M.E.L, "Repertory Co. Makes Bow in 'The Proud Princess,'" *Baltimore Evening Sun* (February 12, 1924), p. 18; William Smith Goldenburg, "Amusements: 'The Proud Princess,'" *Cincinnati Enquirer* (May 6, 1924), p. 5; Len G. Shaw, "The Theater," *Detroit Free Press* (December 8, 1924), p. 6.

149. T.M.C., "Stuart Walker's Company Makes Debut at Academy," *Baltimore Sun* (February 12, 1924), p. 9; William Smith Goldenburg, "Amusements: 'The Proud Princess,'" *Cincinnati Enquirer* (May 6, 1924), p. 5; William Smith Goldenburg, "On Stage and Screen,'" *Cincinnati Enquirer* (November 18, 1924), p. 5.

150. Stuart Walker to Beulah Bondi, December 15, 1924 (BBP 3.4).

## *Chapter 3*

1. Bondi quoted in "Doesn't Want Ingenue Roles."

2. "'Wild Birds' in N.Y.," *San Francisco Examiner* (April 26, 1925), p. 6E.

3. "Who's Who in 'One of the Family,'" *Bridgewater Courier-News* (October 23, 1925), p. 11.

4. Parker, ed., *Who's Who in the Theatre*, p. 281.

5. Gleason was still in the role on April 19. On April 21, her son James Gleason was slated to attend a special matinee performance. See "Theatrical Notes," *Brooklyn Daily Eagle* (April 16, 1925), p. 8 and "Notes," *Brooklyn Times Union* (April 19, 1925), p. 18.

6. Burns Mantle, ed., *The Best Plays of 1924–1925* (Boston: Small, Maynard), p. 385, 609.

7. Stark Young, "The Play," *New York Times* (April 10, 1925), p. 16.

8. "Theaters: 'Wild Birds' by Cherry Lane Players," *Brooklyn Standard Union* (April 10, 1925), p. 6.

9. "No Hodoo on Broadway's Easter Plays," *Reading Times* (April 17, 1925), p. 15; Burns Mantle, "'Wild Birds' Tragedy of the Lone Pa-rarie," *New York Daily News* (April 11, 1925), p. 20; Brett Page,

"Broadway," *Birmingham News* (April 19, 1925), p. 13; Charles Belmont Davis, "Author Defends 'Wild Birds,'" *South Bend Tribune* (May 3, 1925), p. 22.

10. Alexander Woollcott, "'Ten Best' 1924–25 Plays of New York Season Win Tags," *Spokesman-Review* (May 31, 1925), p. 2.

11. Dan Totheroh, "Wild Birds," *The Best Plays of 1924–1925*, ed. Burns Mantle (Boston: Small, Maynard), pp. 384–417.

12. "The Quill Pushers," *Cincinnati Enquirer* (April 19, 1925), p. 13.

13. Equity stock contract dated April 25, 1925 (BBP 1.16).

14. Young, *Reel Characters*, p. 59.

15. *One of the Family* advertisement, *Bridgeport Telegram* (October 16, 1925), p. 18; *One of the Family* advertisement, *Bridgewater Courier-News* (October 16, 1925), p. 3.

16. T.H.R, "The New Plays," *Brooklyn Times Union* (December 23, 1925), p. 28; "'One of the Family' Good Hokum Show," *Brooklyn Daily Eagle* (December 23, 1925), p. 7; "'One of the Family' at 49th Street Theatre," *Brooklyn Standard Union* (December 23, 1925), p. 7; J. Brooks Atkinson, "The Play," *New York Times* (December 23, 1925), p. 22.

17. ibdb.com.

18. Kenneth Webb, *One of the Family: A Comedy in Three Acts* (New York and London: D. Appleton, 1926), p. 2, 18, 30.

19. "The Theater," *Indianapolis Star* (April 14, 1926), p. 7; "Stuart Walker Returns to Indianapolis," *Greenfield Daily Reporter* (April 28, 1926), p. 7.

20. John Tuerk to Beulah Bondi, August 21, 1926 (BBP 3.4).

21. "'One of the Family' Pleases at Majestic," *Brooklyn Standard Union* (September 7, 1926), p. 4.

22. "'One of the Family' Pleases," p. 4; "'One of the Family' at Teller's Shubert," *Brooklyn Citizen* (September 28, 1926), p. 5; "'One of the Family' at the Wilbur," *Boston Globe* (October 5, 1926), p. 22; "Doesn't Want Ingenue Roles."

23. J.H.B., "Grant Mitchell Stars in Comedy at Auditorium," *Baltimore Sun* (November 16, 1926), p. 13.

24. See Lesley Ferris, "Kit and Guth: A Lavender Marriage on Broadway," *Passing Performances: Queer Reading of Leading Players in American Theater History*, ed. Robert A. Schanke and Kim Marra (Ann Arbor: U of Michigan P, 1998), pp. 197–220.

25. Aversano, "Dear Beulah," p. 36.

26. Lucille Leimert, "Confidentially," *Los Angeles Times* (June 10, 1947), p. 5.

27. Barrett H. Clark in *The Drama*, quoted in Anthony Slide, ed., *Selected Theatre Criticism: Volume 2, 1920–1930* (Metuchen, NJ: Scarecrow Press, 1985), p. 188.

28. J. Brooks Atkinson, "The Play," *New York Times* (January 27, 1927), p. 13.

29. J. Brooks Atkinson, p. 13; Burns Mantle, "'Saturday's Children at Booth," *New York Daily News* (January 27, 1927), p. 33; Rowland Field, "The New Plays," *Brooklyn Times Union* (January 27, 1927), p. 13.

30. Percy Hammond, "The Theaters," *New York Herald Tribune* (March 27, 1927) (NYPL); Bushnell Dimond, "A Glimpse of the New Plays and Pictures in New York," *Muncie Star Press* (April 10, 1927), p. 16.

31. C.F.F., "Mariners," *Boston Times Union* (March 29, 1927), p. 11.

32. "'My Golden Girl' at the Shubert," *Boston Globe* (September 6, 1927), p. 17. Bondi's given name is misspelled "Beaulah." See also "Beulah Bondi Completes Long Run at Booth Theatre," *Vidette-Messenger* (September 1, 1927), p. 3.

33. "Hope Denies Rift in 'My Princess'; Operetta Stays," *New York Daily News* (October 22, 1927), p. 21.

34. "Pauline Lord Records Her Joy at Being Fired Before the Premiere," *New York Herald Tribune* (January 15, 1933) (NYPL).

35. "Dorothy Donnelly, Dramatist, Dies," *New York Times* (January 4, 1928), p. 25.

36. *Saturday's Children* advertisement, *Chicago Tribune* (October 23, 1927), p. 2.

37. *Vidette-Messenger* (November 7, 1927), p. 2.

38. Elmer Rice and Philip Barry, *Cock Robin: A Play in Three Acts* (New York: Samuel French, 1929), p. 31, 143, 164.

39. J. Brooks Atkinson, "The Play," *New York Times* (January 13, 1928), p. 26; Burns Mantle, "'Cock Robin' Killing Comedy," *New York Daily News* (January 13, 1928), p. 45; Ray Harper, "The Premiere," *Brooklyn Citizen* (January 13, 1928), p. 7; Arthur Pollock, "Plays and Things," *Brooklyn Daily Eagle* (January 15, 1928), p. 2E.

40. Rowland Field, "The New Play: 'Cock Robin,'" *Brooklyn Times Union* (January 13, 1928), p. 3A.

41. "Locals," *Vidette-Messenger* (May 1, 1928), p. 3.

42. Beulah Bondy, passport dated March 23, 1928 (BPP 2.24).

43. "New York, New York Passenger and Crew Lists, 1909, 1925–1957," database with images, *Family Search* (https://familysearch.org/ark:/61903/1:1:-246B-6XG: 12 March 2018), Beulah Bondi, 1928; citing Immigration, New York, New York, United States, NARA microfilm publication T715 (Washington, D.C.: National Archives and Records Administration, n.d.).

44. William Smith Goldenburg, "Amusements: 'Kempy,'" *Cincinnati Enquirer* (August 21, 1928), p. 11.

45. William Smith Goldenburg, "Stuart Walker Players," *Cincinnati Enquirer* (August 26, 1928), p. 14.

46. "Delightful Comedy Seen at the Lyceum," *Brooklyn Daily Eagle* (September 6, 1914), p. 6.

47. See, for example, "Twenty Years Ago in Cincinnati," *Cincinnati Enquirer* (September 17, 1936), p. 6.

48. Carl B. Adams, "Theaters and Parks" *Cincinnati Enquirer* (August 14, 1928), p. 14.

49. Anthony Slide, ed., *Selected Theatre Criticism: Volume 2, 1920–1930* (Metuchen, NJ: Scarecrow Press, 1985), p. 18.

50. Philip Dunning and George Abbott, *Broadway* (New York: French, 1956), p. 35.

51. Dunning and Abbott, p. 2. Italics in original.

52. William Smith Goldenburg, "Amusements: 'Broadway,'" *Cincinnati Enquirer* (September 4, 1928), p. 7.

53. "Cerebral Hemorrhage Fatal to Enquirer Drama Critic," *Cincinnati Enquirer* (September 5, 1930), p. 1.

54. Elmer Rice, *Minority Report: An Autobiography* (London: Heineman, 1963), p. 236.

55. J. Brooks Atkinson, "The Play," *New York Times* (January 11, 1929), p. 20.

56. Edwin Schallert, "'Street Scene' Great Realism," *Los Angeles Times* (April 11, 1931), p. 7; Robert C. Benchley, *Life* (February 1, 1929), p. 23, reprinted in Anthony Slide, ed., *Selected Theatre Criticism: Volume 2, 1920–1930*, p. 209.

57. Elmer Rice, *3 Plays* (New York: Hill and Wang, 1965), p. 152.

58. Rice, p. 119.

59. "Beulah Bondi, Noted for Screen Characterizations, Studies Unusual Types."

60. "Beulah Bondi Creates Role," *Newark Advocate and American Tribune* (November 7, 1931), p. 5.

61. Rice, *Minority Report*, p. 244.

62. Young, *Reel Characters*, pp. 59–60.

63. My account in the last four paragraphs is based on Rice, *Minority Report*, pp. 243–51, 257.

64. J. Brooks Atkinson, "The Play," *New York Times* (January 11, 1929), p. 20; Benchley, *Life*, p. 23; Rowland Field, "The New Play," *Brooklyn Times Union* (January 11, 1929), p. 10; Richard Dana Skinner, *The Commonweal* 9.12 (January 23, 1929), pp. 348–49, reprinted in Anthony Slide, ed., *Selected Theatre Criticism: Volume 2, 1920–1930*, pp. 209–12; Burns Mantle, ed., *The Best Plays of 1928–29* (New York: Dodd, Mead, 1929), p. 26.

65. J. Brooks Atkinson, "The Play," *New York Times* (January 11, 1929), p. 20; Burns Mantle, "'Street Scene' Is Photographic," *New York Daily News* (January 11, 1929), p. 47; Rowland Field, "The New Play," *Brooklyn Times Union* (January 11, 1929), p. 10; Percy Hammond quoted in "Miss Bondi in Broadway Hit," *Vidette-Messenger* (January 25, 1929), p. 4.

66. John Anderson quoted in "Miss Bondi in Broadway Hit," p. 4; Gilbert Gabriel, "Critic Discovers Several Laughs Along Broadway," *Indianapolis Star* (March 17, 1929), p. 3.

67. E.P., "The Premiere: 'Street Scene,'" *Brooklyn Citizen* (January 11, 1929), p. 14; Walter Winchell quoted in "Miss Bondi in Broadway Hit," *Vidette-Messenger* (January 25, 1929), p. 4; Walter Winchell, "Winchell on Broadway," *Akron Beacon Journal* (December 3, 1929), p. 23.

68. James J. Geller, "Side Walks of New York," *Des Moines Register* (June 1, 1930), p. 2.

69. "'Street Scene' Ends Run; Given 600 Times," *Brooklyn Daily Eagle* (May 24, 1930), p. 11; Rowland Field, "Both Sides of the Curtain," *Brooklyn Times Union* (May 25, 1930), p. 2B; Burns Mantle,

ed., "Statistical Summary," *The Best Plays of 1929–30* (New York: Dodd, Mead, 1969), p. 551; Field, "Both Sides of the Curtain," p. 2B.

70. Richard Lockridge, "The Players Offer: 'Milestones' by Arnold Bennett and 'The Father of the Wilderness,'" *New York Sun* (June 3, 1930), p. 22; J. Brooks Atkinson, "The Players Revive 'Milestones' Ably," *New York Times* (June 3, 1930), p. 27; Burns Mantle, "Players' Revival of 'Milestones' and 'Little Father,'" *New York Daily News* (June 3, 1930), p. 35.

71. Henry Stillman to Beulah Bondi, April 11, 1930 (BBP 3.3).

72. Mantle, "Players' Revival of 'Milestones' and 'Little Father,'" p. 35; Atkinson, "The Players Revive," p. 27.

73. "Hatcher Hughes and a Pupil Have a Play for Harris," *New York Daily News* (February 8, 1930), p. 65.

74. I.B., "'Street Scene': Elmer Rice's Play in London," *London Guardian* (September 10, 1930), p. 13; Ivor Brown, "'Street Scene' by Elmer Rice," *London Observer* (September 14, 1930), p. 15.

75. "Social Brief," *Berkshire Eagle* (September 8, 1930), p. 4.

76. Elmer Rice to Beulah Bondi, September 19, 1930 (BBP 3.3).

77. Rice, *Minority Report*, p. 271.

78. "Guest Stars and Old Favorites Will Be Seen in Walker Casts," *Cincinnati Enquirer* (October 5, 1930), p. 2.

79. "Amusements," *Cincinnati Enquirer* (October 23, 1930), p. 10.

80. *Rebound* advertisement, *Cincinnati Enquirer* (October 20, 1930), p. 13.

81. "Amusements," p. 10.

82. George A. Leighton, "Amusements: 'The Stand-by,'" *Cincinnati Enquirer* (October 28, 1930), p. 17.

83. "Local Brevities," *Vidette-Messenger* (October 27, 1930), p. 3; Leighton, "Amusements: 'The Stand-by,'" p. 17.

84. "Plans for Season Disclosed; New Plays Listed by Walker," *Cincinnati Enquirer* (November 2, 1930), p. 2.

85. Stuart Walker to Beulah Bondi, December 3, 1930 (BBP 3.4).

86. *Those We Love* advertisement, *Cincinnati Enquirer* (November 9, 1930), p. 2.

87. Carl B. Adams, "Amusements: 'Those We Love,'" *Cincinnati Enquirer* (November 4, 1930), p. 7.

88. George S. Kaufman et al., *Kaufman & Co.: Broadway Comedies* (New York: Library of America, 2004), p. 14, 16, 22.

89. George A. Leighton, "Amusements: 'The Royal Family,'" *Cincinnati Enquirer* (November 11, 1930), p. 8.

90. "Beulah Bondi Gets Praise," *Vidette-Messenger* (November 17, 1930), p. 4.

91. Walker to Bondi, December 3, 1930.

## Chapter 4

1. Bondi quoted in James Watters and Horst P. Horst, *Return Engagement: Faces to Remember Then and Now* (New York: Clarkson N. Potter, 1984), p. 117.

2. Muriel Babcock, "'Street Scene' Players Named," *Los Angeles Times* (March 26, 1931), p. 11.

3. "Pulitzer Prize Winner Arrives to Direct Play," *Los Angeles Times* (March 23, 1931), p. 10; "Rehearsals Started on Rice Drama," *Los Angeles Times* (March 27, 1931), p. 11; *Street Scene* advertisement, *Los Angeles Times* (April 5, 1931), p. 13; "Vivid Play Due Tomorrow," *Los Angeles Times* (April 8, 1931), p. 9.

4. Edwin Schallert, "'Street Scene' Great Realism," *Los Angeles Times* (April 11, 1931), p. 7.

5. "Play Reactions Revealed," *Los Angeles Times* (May 11, 1931), p. 7.

6. "Beulah Bondi Creates Role," *Newark Advocate and American Tribune* (November 7, 1931), p. 5; Aversano, "Dear Beulah," p. 36.

7. Carlton Miles, "Carlton Miles Recalls Late Robert Edeson's Visits to Minneapolis," *Minneapolis Star* (April 1, 1931), p. 11.

8. Miles, p. 11; Irene Thirer, "Sylvia Sidney in 'Street Scene,'" *New York Daily News* (June 2, 1931), p. 42.

9. Brown, *Actors Talk*, p. 154.

10. "Stage Struck," *Modern Screen* [1937] (NYPL).

11. Thirer, "Sylvia Sidney in 'Street Scene,'" p. 42; "'Street Scene' Cast at Work," *San Bernardino County Sun* (July 5, 1931), p. 6.

12. "Goldwyn Finishing Elmer Rice Drama as Fourth on List," *Brooklyn Standard Union* (July 22, 1931), p. 11; Kate Cameron, "Milestone Voted Best Director," *New York Daily News* (July 30, 1931), p. 34; Edwin Schallert, "King Vidor Shows Fine Style in 'Street Scene,'" *Los Angeles Times* (August 13, 1931), p. 11; Florabel Muir, "Royalty Given Private Peak at 'Street Scene,'" *New York Daily News* (August 13, 1931), p. 32; George Shaffer, "'Street Scene' Preview Puts Stars in 'Arrowsmith': Beulah Bondi Is Signed Up," *Detroit Free Press* (August 17, 1931), p. 8; Eileen Percy, "In Hollywood," *Brooklyn Standard Union* (August 21, 1931), p. 11.

13. The film in question was *The Champ* at MGM and the role was that of Jackie Cooper's mother, which ultimately was played by Irene Rich. Bondi opted to do *Arrowsmith* for Sam Goldwyn, which was produced at roughly the same time as *The Champ*. Bondi describes King Vidor in the letter as "a joy to work with and the best in the director line here."

14. Beulah Bondi to Abram and Eva Bondy, Monday [July 1931] (BBP 3.5).

15. E.P., "Reel Reviews," *Brooklyn Citizen* (August 27, 1931), p. 12; Mordaunt Hall, "The Screen: When Murder Is Done," *New York Times* (August 27, 1931), p. 22.

16. E.P., "Reel Reviews," p. 12.

17. My account of the premiere is based on "'Street Scene' Tonight," *New York Times* (August

26, 1931), p. 15; Martin Dickstein, "The Screen," *Brooklyn Daily Eagle* (August 27, 1931), p. 19; Irene Thirer, "'Street Scene' a Vidor Triumph," *New York Daily News* (August 27, 1931), p. 34; and E.P., "Reel Reviews," p. 12.

18. "Local Brevities," *Vidette-Messenger* (September 3, 1931), p. 3.

19. E.P., "Reel Reviews," p. 12.

20. "What's Doing at the Theatres," *Reading Times* (September 18, 1931), p. 13.

21. Len G. Shaw, *Street Scene* film review, *Detroit Free Press* (September 4, 1931), p. 19.

22. Rice, *Minority Report*, p. 276.

23. Frank Miller, "*Street Scene*," tcm.com.

24. Mollie Merrick, "Street Scene Made Into Splendid Talkie," *Lincoln Evening Journal* (August 13, 1931), p. 5; Harold W. Cohen, "The New Films," *Pittsburgh Post-Gazette* (September 12, 1931), p. 11; Philip K. Scheuer, "Prize Play as Film Gratifies," *Los Angeles Times* (September 4, 1931), p. 13; Whitney Williams, "'Street Scene' Finely Enacted and Directed Drama," *Los Angeles Times* (September 6, 1931), p. 3; Walter Winchell, "On Broadway," *Scranton Republican* (September 3, 1931), p. 4; Sue Bernardine, "'Street Scene' Vivid Drama of Tenement Life," *San Bernardino County Sun* (September 10, 1931), p. 10; Corbin Patrick, "Vidor Again Rings Bell with Fine Film of 'Street Scene,'" *Indianapolis Star* (September 21, 1931), p. 3; Harold W. Cohen, "The New Films," *Pittsburgh Post-Gazette* (September 12, 1931), p. 11.

25. Mordaunt Hall, "The Screen: When Murder Is Done," *New York Times* (August 27, 1931), p. 22; Martin Dickstein, "The Screen," p. 19; Martin Dickstein, "Slow Motion," *Brooklyn Daily Eagle* (August 30, 1931), p. 10B.

26. "Cimarron Selected as Best Film of 1931 by Nation's Leading Critics," *Moline Dispatch* (January 16, 1932), p. 9.

27. Mollie Merrick, "Street Scene Made Into Splendid Talkie," *Lincoln Evening Journal* (August 13, 1931), p. 5; Thirer, "'Street Scene' a Vidor Triumph," p. 34; "Amusements," *Cincinnati Inquirer* (September 28, 1931), p. 5; "At the Local Theaters," *Des Moines Tribune* (October 5, 1931), p. 11.

28. Jimmy Starr, "'Street Scene' Brought to Screen with Startling Realism," *Pittsburgh Post-Gazette* (August 22, 1931), p. 9; "'Street Scene' Powerful and Factual Drama," *Salt Lake Telegram* (November 5, 1931), p. 9; Harold W. Cohen, "The New Films," *Pittsburgh Post-Gazette* (September 12, 1931), p. 11.

29. Merrick, "Street Scene Made Into Splendid Talkie," p. 5; Boyd Martin, "Piping the Plays," *Louisville Courier Journal* (September 19, 1931), p. 10; Aversano, "Dear Beulah," p. 37.

30. Shaffer, "'Street Scene' Preview Puts Stars in 'Arrowsmith,'" p. 8.

31. Sinclair Lewis, *Arrowsmith* (New York: Grosset and Dunlap, 1925), p. 100, 145.

32. Shaffer, "'Street Scene' Preview Puts Stars in 'Arrowsmith,'" p. 8.

33. *Tampa Times* (September 5, 1931), p. 6.

34. Felicia Feaster, "Arrowsmith (1931)," tcm.com.

35. Kenneth Barrow, *Helen Hayes: First Lady of the American Theatre* (Garden City, NY: Doubleday, 1985), p. 103.

36. Young, *Reel Characters*, p. 60; Kleiner, "Looking Back on a Charmed Life"; Brown, *Actors Talk*, pp. 154–55.

37. Aversano, "Dear Beulah," pp. 36–37; Brown, *Actors Talk*, pp. 154–55.

38. Potempa, "The Beloved Mother," p. 63. On the advantages of freelancing, see also Marjory Adams, "Career Forces Beulah Bondi to Alter Plans," *Boston Globe* (June 13, 1940), p. 13.

39. Green, "Beulah Bondi Back on Screen at 80," p. 21.

40. Brown, *Actors Talk*, p. 155.

41. *New York Daily News* (November 24, 1931), p. 39; *New York Daily News* (November 30, 1931), p. 33.

42. Theatre Notes," *New York Daily News* (January 4, 1932), p. 29; "Miss Lord's New Play," *Brooklyn Daily Eagle* (January 4, 1932), p. 19.

43. "Pauline Lord Stars in 'Distant Drums,'" *Brooklyn Times Union* (January 10, 1932), p. 8A; "'Drums' Deferred," *Brooklyn Daily Eagle* (January 11, 1932), p. 11; "'Brief Moment' Closes Saturday," *New York Daily News* (January 12, 1931), p. 41; Burns Mantle, ed., *The Best Plays of 1931–1932* (New York: Dodd, Mead, 1932), p. 11.

44. "Pauline Lord Back," *Pittsburgh Press* (December 2, 1931), p. 20; "Pauline Lord Cast in 'Distant Drums,'" p. 20.

45. Rowland Field, "The New Play," *Brooklyn Times Union* (January 19, 1932), p. 8.

46. Edwin C. Stein, "The Stage: The Pioneers Roll into the Belasco with Covered Wagons and Pauline Lord," *Brooklyn Standard Union* (January 19, 1932), p. 11; J. Brooks Atkinson, "Distant Drums," *New York Times* (January 30, 1932), p. 1; Edgar Price, "This Side of the Footlights," *Brooklyn Citizen* (January 23, 1932), p. 8.

47. Burns Mantle, *Distant Drums* review, *New York Daily News* (January 19, 1932), p. 37; Burns Mantle, "Actors Stronger Than Their Plays," *Chicago Tribune* (January 31, 1932), p. 8; Robert F. Sisk, "New Play by Totheroh Seems to Miss," *Baltimore Sun* (January 24, 1932), p. 1; Gilbert Swan, "Critic Calls Awarders' Attention to Pioneer Drama, 'Distant Drums,'" *Newark Advocate* (January 30, 1932), p. 12.

48. *Distant Drums* advertisement, *Brooklyn Daily Eagle* (February 19, 1932), p. 20; ibdb.com.

49. Mantle, ed., *The Best Plays of 1931–1932*, p. 11.

50. Martin Dickstein, "The Screen: Beulah Bondi Signed for 'Rain,'" *Brooklyn Daily Eagle* (May 5, 1932), p. 20.

51. "Local Brevities," *Vidette-Messenger* (April 18, 1932), p. 3; "Local Brevities," *Vidette-Messenger* (April 19, 1932), p. 3; "Beulah Bondi Enroute West, in New Talkie," *Vidette-Messenger* (May 5, 1932), p. 4.

52. Robin Coons, "Hollywood Sights and Sounds," *Indianapolis News* (October 3, 1932), p. 2.

53. Coons, p. 2.

54. Edwin Schallert, "Magic Isle Again Used to Depict Tropic Life," *Los Angeles Times* (June 18, 1932), p. 13, 19.

55. "Star of 'Rain' to Be on Hand for Premiere," *Los Angeles Times* (August 30, 1932), p. 6; tcm.com.

56. Mollie Merrick, "Hollywood in Person," *Los Angeles Times* (September 10, 1932), p. 7.

57. "Friends Fail to Recognize Beulah Bondi," *Los Angeles Times* (September 25, 1932), p. 17.

58. Edwin Schallert, "Studio Begins Revising Rain," *Los Angeles Times* (September 16, 1932), p. 18.

59. imdb.com, tcm.com.

60. Mordaunt Hall, "Sadie Thompson Again," *New York Times* (October 13, 1932), p. 22.

61. Merrick, "Hollywood in Person," p. 7.

62. "'Rain' Disappoints at the Stanley," *Philadelphia Inquirer* (October 23, 1932), p. 15; *Rain* review, *Davenport Daily Times* (November 21, 1932), p. 16; Mary Margaret Therese, "Galaxy," *Lafayette Journal and Courier* (November 26, 1932), p. 4; *Rain* review, *Harrisburg Sunday Courier* (November 27, 1932), p. 4.

63. "Beulah Bondi Plays Second Screen Role," *Los Angeles Times* (September 16, 1932), p. 11.

64. "Two Stars Engaged for Coming Plays," *New York Times* (September 23, 1932), p. 22.

65. "Walter Connolly Assigned to Role," *New York Times* (September 26, 1932), p. 18; "Theatre Notes," *New York Daily News* (September 28, 1932), p. 39.

66. "Theatre Notes," *New York Daily News* (October 11, 1932), p. 65; "Laugh Parade to be Seen at Ford's," *Baltimore Sun* (October 9, 1932), p. 8; *The Late Christopher Bean* advertisement, *New York Daily News* (October 31, 1932), p. 31.

67. Parker, *Who's Who in the Theatre*, p. 281.

68. Burns Mantle, ed., *The Best Plays of 1932–1933* (New York: Dodd, Mead, 1933), p. 238.

69. Rowland Field, "The New Play," *Brooklyn Times Union* (November 1, 1932), p. 4.

70. Arthur Pollock, "The Theatres," *Brooklyn Daily Eagle* (November 1, 1932), p. 13.

71. Burns Mantle, "'Late Christopher Bean' Happy Comedy," *New York Daily News* (November 1, 1932), p. 39; Brooks Atkinson, "The Play," *New York Times* (November 1, 1932), p. 24.

72. Field, "The New Play," p. 4; D.K., "Pauline Lord Seen in Comedy at Ford's Theatre," *Baltimore Sun* (October 25, 1932), p. 9; Gilbert Kanour, "French Comedy Seen at Ford's," *Baltimore Evening Sun* (October 25, 1932), p. 8; Ralph W. Carey, "Among the New York Theatres," *Hartford Courant* (November 13, 1932), p. 14; Pollock, "The Theatres," p. 13; Alvin J. Kayton, "The Premiere," *Brooklyn Citizen* (November 1, 1932), p. 14; Mantle, ed., *The Best Plays of 1932–1933*, p. 238.

73. *The Late Christopher Bean* advertisement, *New York Daily News* (April 29, 1923), p. 25; ibdb.com.

74. Burns Mantle, "Playwright Anderson Wins the Prize," *New York Daily News* (May 7, 1933), p. 50C; Mantle, ed., *The Best Plays of 1932–1933*, p. 238.

75. Louella O. Parsons, "Hays Bans Name Set for Mae West Movie," *Fresno Bee-Republican* (April 14, 1933), p. 2.

76. Wood Soanes, "Curtain Calls," *Oakland Tribune* (May 5, 1933), p. 28; tcm.com.

77. "Gable with Hopkins," *Los Angeles Times* (April 14, 1933), p. 7.

78. *The Stranger's Return* review, *New York Times* (July 28, 1933), p. 18.

79. Louella O. Parsons, "Sounding the Films," *Camden Courier-Post* (June 24, 1933), p. 6; Edwin Schallert, "New Actor May Play 'Barker,'" *Los Angeles Times* (June 26, 1933), p. 8.

80. Axel Nissen, *Mothers, Mammies and Old Maids: Twenty-Five Character Actresses of Golden Age Hollywood* (Jefferson, NC: McFarland, 2012), p. 99.

81. Boyd Martin, "Piping the Plays," *Louisville Courier-Journal* (July 22, 1933), p. 13; *The Stranger's Return* review, *Salt Lake Telegram* (July 27, 1933), p. 13; *The Stranger's Return* review, *Baltimore Sun* (July 29, 1933), p. 6; Harold W. Cohen, "The New Films," *Pittsburgh Post-Gazette* (July 29, 1933), p. 9; "Beulah Bondi in New Film Role," *Dayton Daily News* (June 9, 1933), p. 16.

82. *The Stranger's Return* advertisement, *Vidette-Messenger* (September 2, 1933), p. 8; *The Stranger's Return* advertisement, *Vidette-Messenger* (September 5, 1933), p. 8.

83. Corbin Patrick, "Marie Dressler, Lionel Barrymore to Co-Star in Film," *Indianapolis Star* (February 9, 1933), p. 14.

84. Wood Soanes, "Curtain Calls," *Oakland Tribune* (June 14, 1933), p. 18; Jimmy Starr, "Strolling Along Hollywood's Gossipy Corners," *Pittsburgh Post-Gazette* (June 17, 1933), p. 9.

85. Axel Nissen, *Actresses of a Certain Character: Forty Familiar Hollywood Faces from the Thirties to the Fifties* (Jefferson, NC: McFarland, 2006), p. 181.

86. "Film Fan Fare," *Cincinnati Enquirer* (July 23, 1933), p. 4; "Stage and Screen," *Minneapolis Star* (July 27, 1933), p. 10; Wanda Hale, "Henry B. Warner Joins Cast for Christopher Bean," *New York Daily News* (August 7, 1933), p. 28.

87. Edwin Schallert, "Elissa Landi and Fox Part by Mutual Agreement," *Los Angeles Times* (July 7, 1933), p. 11; "Barrymore-Dressler Picture Is Started," *San Francisco Examiner* (July 26, 1933), p. 12.

88. imdb.com, tcm.com.

89. Mordaunt Hall, "The Screen," *New York Times* (November 25, 1933), p. 10; John Wood, "Film Play Tailored for Stars," *Los Angeles Times* (December 1, 1933), p. 11; Martin Dickstein, "The Screen," *Brooklyn Daily Eagle* (November 25, 1933), p. 9.

90. Florence Fisher Parry, "On with the Show: Wherein 'The Late Christopher Bean' Is Changed from High Comedy to a Marie Dressler Starring Vehicle," *Pittsburgh Press* (November 25, 1933), p. 6.

91. Parry, p. 6.

92. Robin Coons, "Sights and Sounds," *Abilene Reporter-News* (November 24, 1933), p. 4; Edward E. Gloss, "Marie Steals Movie at Loew's," *Akron Beacon*

Journal (November 25, 1933), p. 2; "Miss Dressler Here in Film You Can't Miss," *Jefferson City Sunday News and Tribune* (November 26, 1933), p. 11; Wood, "Film Play Tailored for Stars," p. 11; "Seen and Heard at the Theaters," *Honolulu Star-Bulletin* (March 1, 1934), p. 14.

93. Erskine Johnson, "In Hollywood," *Dunkirk Evening Observer* (January 3, 1947), p. 14. There is a slightly different version of the story in Young, *Reel Characters*, p. 61.

94. *Two Alone* review, *Paducah Sun-Democrat* (March 2, 1934), p. 12; Wood Soanes, "Curtain Calls," *Oakland Tribune* (November 8, 1933), p. 11; Wanda Hale, "Gala Premiere for Paul Muni Picture," *New York Daily News* (October 24, 1933), p. 42; "Notes" to *Two Alone*, tcm.com.

95. Gilbert Kanour, "For Film Fans," *Baltimore Evening Sun* (February 26, 1934), p. 14.

96. Kate Cameron, "Baby LeRoy in Cast of 'Alice in Wonderland,'" *New York Daily News* (October 19, 1933), p. 48.

97. tcm.com.

98. Lloyd S. Thompson, *Two Alone* review, *San Francisco Examiner* (March 26, 1934), p. 10; Martin Dickstein, "The Screen," *Brooklyn Daily Eagle* (April 7, 1934), p. 13.

99. Louella Parsons, "Louella Parsons Hollywood Column," *Dayton Herald* (December 21, 1933), p. 13; Louella O. Parsons, "The Christmas Spirit Hits Hollywood's Heart, Homes," *Philadelphia Inquirer* (December 24, 1933), p. 8; "Screen Gossip," *Dayton Daily News* (February 4, 1934), p. 7; imdb.com, tcm.com.

100. Harold W. Cohen, "The New Films," *Pittsburg Post-Gazette* (April 9, 1934), p. 8.

101. *Greenwood Commonwealth* (August 8, 1934), p. 5.

102. imdb.com, tcm.com.

103. Martin Dickstein, "The Screen," *Brooklyn Daily Eagle* (April 30, 1934), p. 11; Bentley B. Stegner, *Finishing School* review, *Cincinnati Enquirer* (May 12, 1934), p. 9; T.H.C., "At the Call Theatre," *Kossuth County Advance* (May 31, 1934), p. 6; *Finishing School* review, *Hammond Times* (August 15, 1934), p. 8.

104. Susan Doll, "Finishing School," tcm.com.

105. "Miss Bondi Cast," *Los Angeles Times* (July 6, 1934), p. 13. See also Jerry Hoffman, "Writers," *Cincinnati Enquirer* (July 1, 1934), p. 3.

106. *Los Angeles Times* (August 5, 1934), p. 5.

107. "Local Brevities," *Vidette-Messenger* (October 5, 1934), p. 2.

108. "Local Scrappings," *Pittsburgh Post-Gazette* (November 28, 1934), p. 14.

109. "New Greta Garbo Film at Capitol Saturday," *Salt Lake Tribune* (December 1, 1934), p. 21; *The Painted Veil* review, *Boston Globe* (November 30, 1934), p. 41; "Movies—Greta Garbo in 'Painted Veil' at Century," *Baltimore Sun* (December 2, 1934), p. 6.

110. Nissen, *Mother, Mammies and Old Maids*, pp. 106–9.

111. André Sennwald, *The Good Fairy* review, *New York Times* (February 1, 1935), p. 18.

112. Breen is quoted in the "Notes" to *The Good Fairy*, tcm.com.

113. Sennwald, *The Good Fairy* review.

114. Edna R. Lawson, *The Good Fairy* review, *Honolulu Advertiser* (August 19, 1935), p. 3.

115. "Gahagan, Douglas, King in New Plays," *New York Daily News* (November 12, 1934), p. 41.

116. *Brooklyn Daily Eagle* (November 20, 1934), p. 6.

117. "News of the Stage," *Brooklyn Daily Eagle* (December 12, 1934), p. 11.

118. Seagoing Play for Burr; 'Mother Load' and 'Old Love' Go into Rehearsal," *New York Daily News* (November 26, 1934), p. 41; *Mother Lode* advertisement, *New York Daily News* (December 16, 1934), p. 101.

119. Rowland Field, "The New Play," *Brooklyn Times Union* (December 24, 1934), p. 6.

120. Brooks Atkinson "The Play," *New York Times* (December 24, 1934), p. 16; Michael March, "The Premiere," *Brooklyn Citizen* (December 24, 1934), p. 16; Field, "The New Play," p. 6; Burns Mantle, "'Mother Lode' Drama of Early West," *New York Daily News* (December 24, 1934), p. 23.

121. *Brooklyn Times Union* (December 28, 1934), p. 4A; ibdb.com.

122. "Local Brevities," *Vidette-Messenger* (December 22, 1934), p. 2.

123. "Local Brevities," *Vidette-Messenger* (June 13, 1935), p. 2.

124. "Local Brevities," *Vidette-Messenger* (August 2, 1932), p. 3.

125. tcm.com.

126. "Human Interest Rules in Film at the Victory," *Salt Lake Tribune* (February 15, 1936), p. 4.

127. "A.O. Bondy Is Dead at 79," p. 1.

128. Abram O. Bondy, Louis D. Bondy, findagrave.com.

129. Beulah Bondi to Eva Bondy, September 12, 1935 (BBP 3.6).

130. "Local Brevities," *Vidette-Messenger* (September 19, 1935), p. 2; "Local Brevities," *Vidette-Messenger* (November 21, 1935), p. 2.

131. *The Invisible Ray* review, *Baltimore Sun* (December 30, 1935), p. 6.

132. tcm.com.

## Chapter 5

1. Bondi quoted in Harold Heffernan, "Urges Actors to Shun Stardom," *Indianapolis Star* (February 14, 1940), p. 13.

2. "Beulah Bondi Has Craving for More Sympathetic Roles," *Lansing State Journal* (July 29, 1939), p. 3.

3. tcm.com.

4. "Local Brevities," *Vidette-Messenger* (November 21, 1935), p. 2.

5. Frank S. Nugent, "'Trail of the Lonesome Pine,' the First Outdoor Film in Technicolor, at the Paramount," *New York Times* (February 20, 1936), p. 23.

6. Edward E. Gloss, "Three Good Pictures

Brighten Prospects for Akron Film Fans," *Akron Beacon Journal* (April 25, 1936), p. 6.

7. Miriam Bell, "For Your Amusement," *Miami News* (February 22, 1936), p. 6; T.H.C., "Call and Junior Notes," *Kossuth County Advance* (April 30, 1936), p. 4; Herman J. Bernfield, *The Trail of the Lonesome Pine* review, *Cincinnati Enquirer* (April 19, 1936), p. 3; *The Trail of the Lonesome Pine* review, *Petaluma Argus-Courier* (April 11, 1936), p. 2; Florence Fisher Parry, "On with the Show," *Pittsburgh Press* (April 18, 1936), p. 6.

8. "Notice of Administration No. 752," *Vidette-Messenger* (December 12, 1935), p. 6; "Local Brevities," *Vidette-Messenger* (December 27, 1935), p. 2.

9. "Local Brevities," *Vidette-Messenger* (July 11, 1936), p. 2.

10. She is referred to as Mrs. J.H. Ressler in her father's obituary. See "Captain W. Cary, Old Time Lake Skipper, Is Dead," *Benton Harbor News-Palladium* (June 21, 1933), p. 9.

11. tcm.com.

12. "Sunset Las Palmas Studios," https://en.wikipedia.org/wiki/Sunset_Las_Palmas_Studios.

13. It was a shame that Hamilton and Bondi did not have any scenes together in what was their only mutual feature film. They could have compared notes off set about their experiences as kindergarten teachers. More than 20 years later, Hamilton would play Demetria Riffle to Bondi's Granny Northrup in a TV version of *On Borrowed Time*.

14. *The Moon's Our Home* reviews, *Cincinnati Enquirer* (May 2, 1936), p. 6; and *Chicago Tribune* (May 5, 1936), p. 14.

15. Ed Sikov, *Screwball: Hollywood's Madcap Romantic Comedies* (New York: Crown, 1989), p. 48, 222, 227, 231.

16. *The Case Against Mrs. Ames* reviews, *Salt Lake Telegram* (May 25, 1936), p. 7; *Detroit Free Press* (May 17, 1936), p. 13; and *Louisville Courier-Journal* (May 16, 1936), p. 12.

17. Rains played Mr. Brink in the 1957 TV version of *On Borrowed Time*.

18. Clarke Wales, "Reviews of the New Films," *Detroit Free Press* (September 6, 1936), p. 13; Kaspar Monahan, "The Show Shops," *Pittsburgh Press* (September 14, 1936), p. 20; Louella O. Parsons, "Letter from Hollywood," *Philadelphia Inquirer* (October 21, 1936), p. 20.

19. Howard Thompson, *James Stewart* (New York: Pyramid, 1974), p. 18.

20. Potempa, "The Beloved Mother," p. 67.

21. imdb.com, tcm.com.

22. imdb.com, tcm.com.

23. Marge Petsche, "Women Here and There," *Santa Cruz Sentinel* (September 27, 1936), p. 4; "Notes" to *Maid of Salem*, tcm.com.

24. "Drama, Humor, Romance in Capitol Film," *Salt Lake Tribune* (February 20, 1937), p. 13.

25. Edwin Schallert, "Beulah Bondi Paramount Find," *Los Angeles Times* (November 21, 1936), p. 8.

26. Green, "Beulah Bondi Back on Screen at 80," p. 21. See also Kleiner, "Looking Back on a Charmed Life."

27. Jeremy Arnold, "Make Way for Tomorrow," tcm.com.

28. McCarey's response to seeing *Death of a Salesman* was that he had "put that story on the screen 11 years ago with Victor Moore and Beulah Bondi." See Hedda Hopper, "'Honeymoon for One' Will Star MacRae," *Los Angeles Times* (June 27, 1949), p. 6.

29. Eddie Cohen, "For Your Amusement," *Miami News* (June 17, 1937), p. 6.

30. Harry Haller, "Films: Victor Moore, Beulah Bondi; The Coronation," *Baltimore Sun* (July 4, 1937), p. 8.

31. C.A. Lejeune, "Films of the Week, *London Observer* (June 27, 1937), p. 16.

32. Betty Kern, "Real Photodrama," *Dayton Herald* (June 19, 1937), p. 7.

33. B.R. Crisler, unidentified, undated clipping (NYPL).

34. "The Movie Lots Beg to Report," *Pittsburgh Post-Gazette* (June 23, 1936), p. 10.

35. "'Years Are So Long' Bought for Pictures," *Lansing State Journal* (July 7, 1936), p. 19.

36. Wood Soanes, "Curtain Calls," *Oakland Tribune* (July 1, 1936), p. 19.

37. Louella O. Parsons, "Letter from Hollywood," *Philadelphia Inquirer* (October 21, 1936), p. 20.

38. Louella O. Parsons, "Hot from Hollywood," *Princeton Clarion-News* (November 16, 1936), p. 3.

39. Sheilah Graham, "Comedian Turns to 'Tear-Jerker,'" *Spokane Spokesman-Review* (November 18, 1936), p. 5. See also "Beulah Bondi Paramount Find," *Los Angeles Times* (November 21, 1936), p. 8.

40. Idwal Jones, "Life Begins at Any Time—in Hollywood: The Amazing Change of Victor Moore from Comic to Tragedian," *Rochester Democrat and Chronicle* (April 25, 1937), p. 14.

41. Harriet Parsons, "Hollywood Letter," *Philadelphia Inquirer* (November 27, 1936), p. 16.

42. "Movies," *La Crosse Tribune* (August 12, 1936), p. 11.

43. "Writer Returns," *Los Angeles Times* (December 18, 1936), p. 10.

44. *Harrisburg Telegraph* (December 23, 1936), p. 15.

45. *Catalogue of Copyright Entries: Part 1, Group 3 Dramatic Compositions and Motion Pictures—Vol. 8 for 1935 Nos. 1–12* (Washington: United States Government Printing Office, 1936), p. 284.

46. "Leo MCarey to Direct 'Years Are So Long,'" *Brooklyn Daily Eagle* (August 3, 1936), p. 9.

47. Lloyd Pantages, "I Cover Hollywood," *San Francisco Examiner* (December 8, 1936), p. 22; "Notes" to *Make Way for Tomorrow*, tcm.com.

48. "'Make Way for Tomorrow' Now at the Paramount Theater," *Munster Times* (July 13, 1937), p. 11.

49. "Paramount Borrows 2 Feature Players," *Oakland Tribune* (December 20, 1936), p. 5.

50. Louella O. Parsons, "Three Stars Selected

for 'Kid Galahad,'" *Cedar Rapids Gazette* (December 23, 1936), p. 8.

51. Louella O. Parsons, "Irene Dunne Is Signed for New Kern Musical," *Cedar Rapids Gazette* (December 25, 1936), p. 15.

52. Harold W. Cohen, "The Drama Desk," *Pittsburgh Post-Gazette* (January 7, 1937), p. 13.

53. Edwin Schallert, "The Pageant of the Film World," *Los Angeles Times* (April 8, 1937), p. 15.

54. Louella O. Parsons, "Gene Fowler Completes Story for Eddie Cantor," *San Francisco Examiner* (January 8, 1937), p. 12. See also Louella O. Parson, "Has Ambitious Plans to Film 'Hippodrome,'" *Cedar Rapids Gazette* (January 20, 1937), p. 8.

55. Louella O. Parsons, "Lane Sisters Have Leads in 'Varsity Show,'" *Cedars Rapids Gazette* (April 15, 1936), p. 20.

56. Nissen, *Mothers, Mammies and Old Maids*, p. 140.

57. Hubbard Keavy, "Production Notes," *Indianapolis Star* (January 17, 1936), p. 1. Modern sources suggest production on the film began January 11, 1937 (imdb.com, tcm.com).

58. Ruth White, "'Married' 50 Years—Then They Were Introduced!," *Eugene Guard* (April 11, 1937), p. 26.

59. "Huge Set Used for Musical," *Los Angeles Times* (March 4, 1937), p. 15.

60. Read Kendall, "Around and About in Hollywood," *Los Angeles Times* (March 4, 1937), p. 15.

61. "Broadway Farer," *Hartford Courant* (March 14, 1937), p. 6.

62. "Much Comment," *San Francisco Examiner* (April 16, 1937), p. 18.

63. Thirer, "Beulah Bondi Sees Herself on Screen at Criterion"; B.R. Crisler.

64. B.R. Crisler.

65. White, "'Married' 50 Years," p. 26.

66. D.W.C., "Approaching Screen," *Baltimore Sun* (May 2, 1937), p. 7; Len G. Shaw, "Rich in Sentiment, Picture Is One of Best in Long Time," *Detroit Free Press* (June 4, 1937), p. 10; Cohen, "For Your Amusement," p. 6; Grace Kingsley, "Homely Film Highlight at Orpheum," *Los Angeles Times* (August 26, 1937), p. 8; H.M. Levy, "'Make Way for Tomorrow' Is Surprise Film of Year," *Oakland Tribune* (August 30, 1937), p. 8; Kaspar Monahan, "'The Best Ten,'" *Pittsburgh Press* (December 19, 1937), p. 6.

67. Frank S. Nugent, "The Screen," *New York Times* (May 10, 1937), p. 23; Mark Hellinger, "'Best' of 1937," *Rochester Democrat and Chronicle* (December 26, 1939), p. 15E.

68. See, for example, Elizabeth Kendall, *The Runaway Bride: Hollywood Romantic Comedy of the 1930s* (New York: Alfred A. Knopf, 1990), p. 193; Arnold, "Make Way for Tomorrow."

69. Levy, "'Make Way for Tomorrow Is Surprise Film of Year," p. 8.

70. "Epics of Land and Sea Head Month's Best Film List," *Quad-City Times* (September 5, 1937), p. 18.

71. Monahan, "'The Best Ten,'" p. 6.

72. "The Ten Best Films," *Tampa Times* (January 5, 1938), p. 6.

73. Mollie Merrick, "Mollie Merrick Makes Her New Year Wishes for Film People," *Detroit Free Press* (January 3, 1947), p. 14.

74. Keavy, "Production Notes," p. 1.

75. George Shaffer, "Cagney Ready to Start Work on New Movie," *Chicago Tribune* (January 16, 1937), p. 20.

76. Philip K. Scheuer, "'Bit' Player Boom Hits Industry: Character Actors at Premium," *Los Angeles Times* (February 14, 1937), p. 1, 3.

77. "Film Academy Announces Nominations for Awards," *Los Angeles Times* (February 8, 1937), p. 1.

78. "Beulah Bondi Paid $53,958 During 1937," *Vidette-Messenger* (April 8, 1939), p. 1.

79. "Film Salaries Top Nation's List of Incomes for 1937," *Los Angeles Times* (April 8, 1939), p. 4.

80. "Movie Colony in Victorville for Week-End," *San Bernardino County Sun* (March 23, 1937), p. 12; Hedda Hopper, "Hedda Hopper's Hollywood," *Los Angeles Times* (January 4, 1940), p. 12.

81. Hedda Hopper, "Fashion Show or Honeymoon," *Miami News* (May 18, 1955), p. 11B.

82. "Fiesta Date Is Set by Church," *San Bernardino County Sun* (September 4, 1937), p. 12; "Flood Benefit Show Planned," *San Bernardino County Sun* (March 23, 1938), p. 15; Hopper, "Hedda Hopper's Hollywood," p. 12; "Ginger Rogers Enjoying Rest in Victorville," *San Bernardino County Sun* (November 5, 1942), p. 13.

83. Bob Balzer, "Confidentially," *Los Angeles Times* (August 4, 1946), p. 5.

84. See "Hollywood Brevities," *Valley Morning Star* (April 11, 1937), p. 22; "Actress Has Summer Home on Desert," *Los Angeles Times* (April 25, 1937), p. 3; "Tattletale," *Los Angeles Times* (December 1, 1940), p. 7.

85. Hopper, "Fashion Show or Honeymoon," p. 11B; "Pioneer Guest Rancher Dies," *San Bernardino County Sun* (January 4, 1954), p. 11 and 13.

86. "L.D. Bondy Dies at Age 84," p. 1.

87. "L.D. Bondy Dies at Age 84," p. 2; "Hold Rites for Louis D. Bondy," p. 4; Louis D. Bondy, findagrave.com.

88. See, for example, "Hoosier Uncle Wills Beulah Bondi $30,000," *Indianapolis News* (July 17, 1937), p. 11.

89. See, for example, "Uncle of Actress Dies," *Logansport Pharos-Tribune* (July 13, 1937), p. 3 and "Film Star's Uncle Dies," *Indianapolis News* (July 13, 1937), p. 8.

90. Harriet Parsons, "Korda Latest Producer to Accept Color," *Pittsburgh Post-Gazette* (July 16, 1937), p. 10. There is no indication that she or her mother attended in the *Vidette-Messenger* news item about the funeral cited above.

91. "May Robson to Play Aunt Polly," *Los Angeles Times* (August 12, 1937), p. 10.

92. Young, *Reel Characters*, pp. 62–63.

93. Springer, "Beulah Bondi," p. 285.

94. "Cecil B. DeMille Blasts Censorship," *Lubbock Evening Journal* (January 23, 1956), p. 7; "Stars Fete DeMille," *Minneapolis Star Tribune* (January 28, 1956), p. 3.

95. tcm.com.

96. Edward E. Gloss, "'Of Human Hearts' Is Good Movie," *Akron Beacon Journal* (February 12, 1938), p. 3; *Of Human Hearts* review, *Manchester Guardian* (August 16, 1938), p. 11; Frank S. Nugent, "The Screen," *New York Times* (February 18, 1938), p. 23.

97. Eddie Cohen, "For Your Amusement," *Miami News* (February 10, 1938), p. 5.

98. tcm.com.

99. "'Of Human Hearts,' Historical Novel of Civil War Days Opens Wednesday," *Shamokin News-Dispatch* (March 22, 1938), p. 9.

100. *Harrisburg Sunday Courier* (October 24, 1937), p. 10.

101. "Hollywood Day by Day," *Santa Rosa Press Democrat* (October 30, 1937), p. 6; "Hollywood Day by Day," *Santa Rosa Press Democrat* (October 31, 1937), p. 11.

102. D.F.C., "'Of Human Hearts' Be Given World Premiere Here Today," *Greenville News* (February 7, 1938), p. 6; Cohen, "For Your Amusement," p. 5; Robin Coons, "In Hollywood," *Chillicothe Gazette* (February 17, 1938), p. 13.

103. *Of Human Hearts* review, *Indianapolis News* (April 9, 1938), p. 2; "'Of Human Hearts' Preview Held by Carolina Theater," *Daily Tar Heel* (February 15, 1938), p. 4; *Of Human Hearts* review, *Manchester Guardian*, p. 11.

104. Hedda Hopper, "Hedda Hopper's Hollywood," *Los Angeles Times* (April 21, 1940), p. 3.

105. Sikov, *Screwball*, p. 231.

106. Louella O. Parsons, "Warner Brothers Will Star Errol Flynn as Robin Hood," *San Francisco Examiner* (May 1, 1937), p. 17; Edwin Schallert, "Illness Costs Stewart Lead," *Los Angeles Times* (May 1, 1937), p. 27; "Flashes on the Screen," *New York Times* (September 19, 1937), p. 4; Edwin Schallert, "'Vivacious Lady' Troupe Disbands," *Los Angeles Times* (May 18, 1937), p. 25.

107. Edwin Schallert, "Ellison Set for Two Annually at RKO," *Los Angeles Times* (December 6, 1937), p. 10.

108. "News of the Screen," *New York Times* (December 20, 1937), p. 23.

109. "Beulah Bondi Signs for Ginger's Film," *Sioux-Falls Argus-Leader* (January 1, 1938), p. 16.

110. Harrison Carroll, "Behind the Scenes in Hollywood," *Massilon Evening Independent* (February 4, 1938), p. 4.

111. Mae Tinee, "Ginger Rogers a Star Without Astaire in Film," *Chicago Tribune* (May 22, 1938), p. 4; "The Screen in Review," *New York Times* (June 3, 1938), p. 17.

112. tcm.com.

113. Billy Gilbert, "In Hollywood," *Lancaster Eagle-Gazette* (June 27, 1938), p. 6. See also Harrison Carroll, "Behind the Scenes in Hollywood," *Vineland Daily Journal* (July 7, 1938), p. 5.

114. "Knitting Banned on Set," *Sioux Falls Argus-Leader* (July 19, 1938), p. 8.

115. June Provines, "Front Views and Profiles," *Chicago Times* (October 14, 1938), p. 24.

116. "'Sisters' Playing on Ritz Program," *San Bernardino County Sun* (October 23, 1938), p. 12; "Sisters' Careers Paralleled in Feature at Waikiki," *Honolulu Advertiser* (January 8, 1939), p. 3.

117. Frank Aversano, "Beulah Bondi: Part II," *American Classic Screen* 3.5 (May/June 1979), p. 36.

118. "Beulah Bondi Plays Robson Role," *Los Angeles Times* (August 29, 1937), p. 8; tcm.com.

119. "Broken Arm of Actress Costs Producer $60,000," *Harrisburg Evening News* (August 30, 1938), p. 1.

120. "Broken Arm of Actress," p. 1.

121. Harrison Carroll, "Behind the Scenes in Hollywood," *Massilon Evening Independent* (September 21, 1938), p. 4.

122. Hedda Hopper, "Hedda Hopper's Hollywood," *Cincinnati Enquirer* (September 30, 1938), p. 8.

123. Unidentified, undated clipping (NYPL).

124. Frank Miller, "They Made Me a Criminal," tcm.com.

125. "May Robson Returns to 'Criminal' Feature," *Los Angeles Times* (December 20, 1938), p. 13; "Long Time to Make a Criminal," *Jackson Sun* (February 5, 1939), p. 4.

126. Unidentified, undated clipping.

127. Unidentified, undated clipping.

128. May Robson to Beulah Bondi, September 19, 1938 (BBP 3.3).

129. "Beulah Bondi in Valparaiso for Short Visit," *Vidette-Messenger* (October 10, 1938), p. 1; "Lights of New York" *Decatur Daily Review* (November 11, 1938), p. 10.

130. *Des Moines Register* (October 30, 1938), p. 3.

131. Hedda Hopper, "Hedda Hopper's Hollywood," *Los Angeles Times* (May 5, 1939), p. 12.

132. "Notes" to *On Borrowed Time*, tcm.com.

133. Young, *Reel Characters*, p. 60.

134. "Pageant of the Film World," *Los Angeles Times* (April 1, 1939), p. 9; imdb.com, tcm.com.

135. "Beulah Bondi Performs with Bevies of Watsons," *Detroit Free Press* (May 13, 1939), p. 8.

136. "Movieland Jottings and Castings," *Los Angeles Times* (May 8, 1939), p. 14; tcm.com.

137. "'On Borrowed Time' Shown as Feature at Karlton," *Philadelphia Inquirer* (July 15, 1939), p. 24; E.B. Radcliffe, "Between Hollywood and Broadway," *Cincinnati Enquirer* (July 15, 1939), p. 20; "'On Borrowed Time' Praised in East," *Los Angeles Times* (July 17, 1939), p. 11; "'On Borrowed Time Rates with Best of Season," *Nebraska State Journal* (July 23, 1939), p. 7; *On Borrowed Time* review, *Warren Times Mirror* (August 4, 1939), p. 2.

138. "Movieland Jottings and Castings," *Los Angeles Times* (May 8, 1939), p. 14.

139. tcm.com.

140. Hedda Hopper, "Hedda Hopper's Hollywood," *Cincinnati Enquirer* (June 8, 1939), p. 11.

141. Boyd Martin, "Old Timers Bear Load," *Louisville Courier-Journal* (July 2, 1939), p. 20.

142. "Beulah Bondi Has Craving for More Sympathetic Roles," p. 3.

143. imdb.com, tcm.com.

144. Jean Craig, "Movie Memos," *Hammond Times* (April 23, 1939), p. 9.

145. Hedda Hopper, "Hedda Hopper's Hollywood," *Los Angeles Times* (May 23, 1939), p. 12.

146. Potempa, "The Beloved Mother," p. 62.

147. More than 20 years later, when his career as a film director was over, Leisen would direct Bondi in an episode of *Wagon Train* called "The Prairie Story."

148. "Screen," *Hanover Evening Sun* (July 29, 1939), p. 4; imdb.com, tcm.com.

149. Charles Tranberg, *Fred MacMurray: A Biography* (Albany, GA: BearManor Media, 2007), p. 72; Victoria Wilson, *A Life of Barbara Stanwyck: Steel-True, 1907–1940* (New York: Simon and Schuster, 2013), p. 821; imdb.com, tcm.com.

150. Wilson, p. 821.

151. Wilson, p. 821.

152. "Movies and Amusements," *St. Louis Star and Times* (July 25, 1939), p. 9.

153. Harold W. Cohen, "Hollywood," *Pittsburgh Post-Gazette* (August 22, 1939), p. 20.

154. This is Victoria Wilson's paraphrase of Bondi's letter to Ella Smith dated August 17, 1972 in Wilson, *A Life of Barbara Stanwyck*, p. 813.

155. Corbin Patrick, "New Film Set in Indiana," *Indianapolis Star* (January 20, 1940), p. 10.

156. "Beulah Bondi Stars in 'Remember the Night,'" *Vidette-Messenger* (May 10, 1940), p. 6.

157. Susan King, "Classic Hollywood: O 'Night' Divine," *Los Angeles Times* (December 24, 2009), p. 75.

158. Harold Heffernan, "The Grapes of Wrath," *St. Louis Post-Dispatch* (August 6, 1939), p. 1H.

159. Sheilah Graham, "Hollywood Today," *Scranton Times-Tribune* (August 10, 1939), p. 17.

160. Aversano, "Dear Beulah," p. 37.

161. Darryl F. Zanuck to Beulah Bondi, September 7, 1939 (BBP 3.4).

162. Philip K. Scheuer, "Dorris Bowdon to Play Rosasharn in 'Grapes,'" *Los Angeles Times* (September 11, 1939), p. 8.

163. Young, *Reel Characters*, p. 65.

164. Scott Eyman, *Print the Legend: The Life and Times of John Ford* (Baltimore: Johns Hopkins University Press, 2000), p. 216.

165. Young, *Reel Characters*, p. 63.

166. Heffernan, "Urges Actors to Shun Stardom," p. 13.

167. Irene Thirer, "Beulah Bondi, Character Veteran of 35 Pictures" [1940] (NYPL).

168. Brown, *Actors Talk*, p. 156.

## *Chapter 6*

1. Bondi quoted in Witbeck, "Keynotes: 'Lincoln' Series Offers Sarah Bush Vignette," p. 24.

2. Hedda Hopper, "Hedda Hopper's Hollywood," *Cincinnati Enquirer* (January 2, 1940), p. 6; Harold W. Cohen, "The Drama Desk," *Pittsburgh Post-Gazette* (January 2, 1940), p. 15. See also Edwin Schallert, "Kibbee, Erwin Join Cast of 'Our Town,'" *Los Angeles Times* (January 10, 1940), p. 13;

and "Three Character Actors Are Signed for 'Our Town,'" *Tampa Tribune* (January 28, 1940), p. 12. These articles indicate that Gene Lockhart was originally slated to play Dr. Gibbs, before the role finally went to Thomas Mitchell.

3. "Colorful Back-Stage Activities Highlight Filming of 'Our Town,'" *Greenwood Index-Journal* (September 29, 1940), p. 3; Harold Heffernan, "Beulah Bondi Also Takes Anti-Stardom Stance," *Detroit News* (February 15, 1940), n.pag.

4. Mayme Ober Peak, "The Front in Hollywood," *Boston Globe* (May 17, 1940), p. 30.

5. "New Films Reviewed," *Boston Globe* (May 24, 1940), p. 24.

6. Hedda Hopper, "Hedda Hopper's Hollywood," *Cincinnati Enquirer* (February 2, 1940), p. 6.

7. "Colorful Back-Stage Activities," p. 3; Alexander Kahn, "Bainter Can't Sing Anymore," *Passaic Herald-News* (March 7, 1940), p. 24.

8. "Ashes of Philip Wood to Be Brought Here," *Boston Globe* (March 6, 1940), p. 6.

9. Wilder's letter quoted in Robin Coons, "'Our Town' Moves Stage to Screen with Real Improvement," *Sioux Falls Argus-Leader* (May 14, 1940), p 14, probably from the pressbook.

10. Peak, "The Front in Hollywood," p. 30.

11. Bosley Crowther, "The Screen," *New York Times* (June 14, 1940), p. 25; Wood Soanes, "'Our Town' Is Candidate for Best 10," *Oakland Tribune* (August 23, 1940), p. 30; Coons, "'Our Town' Moves Stage to Screen," p 14.

12. Thornton Wilder to Beulah Bondi, May 6, 1940 (BBP 3.4).

13. "United States Census, 1940," database with images, *Family Search* (https://familysearch.org/ark:/61903/1:1:K9HG-SBH: 27 July 2019), Beulah Bondi, Councilmanic District 1, Los Angeles, Los Angeles Township, Los Angeles, California, United States; citing enumeration district (ED) 60–1321, sheet 1A, line 19, family 8, Sixteenth Census of the United States, 1940, NARA digital publication T627. Records of the Bureau of the Census, 1790–2007, RG 29. Washington, D.C.: National Archives and Records Administration, 2012, roll 377.

14. Louis J. Allemann, *Beulah Bondi Bulletin* (November 30, 1940), n.pag.

15. See, for example, Brian Cady, "The Captain Is a Lady," tcm.com.

16. Hedda Hopper, "Hedda Hopper's Hollywood," *Los Angeles Times* (May 8, 1940), p. 27.

17. catalog.afi.com.

18. Prunella Hall, "Screen Gossip" [1940] (NYPL).

19. "Court Hears Arguments in Estate Case," *Vidette-Messenger* (May 11, 1940), p. 1.

20. "Court Hears Arguments," p. 1.

21. "Beulah Bondi Stars in 'Remember the Night' at Premier Tonight, Saturday," *Vidette-Messenger* (May 10, 1940), p. 6.

22. "United States Census, 1900," database with images, *Family Search* (https://familysearch.org/ark:/61903/1:1:M346-TP9: accessed 25 August 2019), Mark Rockwell in household of Worden C

Rockwell, Lathrop Township Hopbottom borough, Susquehanna, Pennsylvania, United States; citing enumeration district (ED) 95, sheet 1B, family 14, NARA microfilm publication T623 (Washington, D.C.: National Archives and Records Administration, 1972); FHL microfilm 1,241,489; "Indiana Marriages, 1811–2007," database with images, *Family Search* (https://familysearch.org/ark:/61903/1:1:-KDHQ-Y17: 10 December 2017), Mark B Rockwell and Wilmina Hesser, 17 Sep 1913; citing Porter, Indiana, United States, Marriage Registration, Indiana Commission on Public Records, Indianapolis; FHL microfilm 005014499; "United States Census, 1940," database with images, *Family Search* (https:// familysearch.org/ark:/61903/1:1:V1YL-GY1: 20 August 2019), Mark B Rockwell, Ward 1, Valparaiso, Center Township, Porter, Indiana, United States; citing enumeration district (ED) 64–3, sheet 5B, line 74, family 113, Sixteenth Census of the United States, 1940, NARA digital publication T627. Records of the Bureau of the Census, 1790–2007, RG 29. Washington, D.C.: National Archives and Records Administration, 2012, roll 1086; "Former Judge Rockwell Dies," *Vidette-Messenger* (February 16, 1946), p. 1, 2.

23. "Judge Rules on Will of Louis Bondy," *Vidette-Messenger* (November 30, 1940), p. 1.

24. "Judge Rules," p. 1.

25. Mark B. Rockwell, "United States Census, 1940."

26. "Bondy Heirs File Motion for Retrial," *Vidette-Messenger* (December 30, 1940), p. 2.

27. "Judge Rules," p. 1.

28. "Request for New Trial Withdrawn," *Vidette-Messenger* (January 4, 1941), p. 2.

29. "Former Judge Rockwell Dies," *Vidette-Messenger* (February 16, 1946), p. 1, 2; Mark B. Rockwell, findagrave.com.

30. See, for example, "'Our Town' on KFAB," *Nebraska State Journal* (May 5, 1940), p. 7 and "Radio News and Reviews," *Montreal Gazette* (May 6, 1940), p. 2.

31. This account is based on "Premiere: Crowds at Hotel Halt Traffic as Guests Leave for Theatre," *Boston Globe* (May 24, 1940), p. 25.

32. Louella O. Parsons, "Studio Buys Rights to 'Fight for Life,'" *Philadelphia Inquirer* (May 24, 1940), p. 13.

33. Allemann, *Beulah Bondi Bulletin* (August 26, 1940); "F.P. Murphy Dead in New Hampshire," *New York Times* (December 20, 1958), p. 2.

34. This account is based on Marjory Adams, "Career Forces Beulah Bondi to Alter Plans," p. 13.

35. This account is based on "Screen Star Flies to Miami to Attend Brother's Wedding," *Miami News* (June 4, 1940), p. 5 and "Former Local Man Is Wed in Florida," *Vidette-Messenger* (June 14, 1940), p. 2.

36. Allemann, *Beulah Bondi Bulletin* (August 26, 1940).

37. Louis J. Allemann to Beulah Bondi, June 12, 1940 (BBP 3.1); "Today's Fair Program," *New York Daily News* (June 13, 1940), p. 53; "Mayors of

Tomorrow's Town," *New York Daily News* (June 27, 1940), p. 49B.

38. Walter Winchell, "Walter Winchell's On Broadway," *Dayton Herald* (June 19, 1940), p. 20.

39. Paul Walker, "Reviews and Previews," *Harrisburg Telegraph* (July 2, 1940), p. 3; see also Louis J. Allemann to Beulah Bondi, various dates 1940 (BBP 3.1).

40. Louis J. Allemann to Beulah Bondi, August 24, 1940 (BPP 3.1).

41. Louis J. Allemann to Beulah Bondi, September 11, 1940 (BPP 3.1).

42. Allemann to Bondi, September 11, 1940.

43. This account is based on Edwin Schallert, "Movieland Jottings and Castings," *Los Angeles Times* (July 9, 1940), p. 13; "Mohawk Festival Opens Tuesday," *Berkshire Eagle* (July 13, 1940), p. 3.

44. "The Week's Programs in the Theatres," *Berkshire Eagle* (July 20, 1940), p. 3. See also Charles Coburn to Beulah Bondi, July 29, 1940 (BBP 3.1).

45. "United States Census, 1940," database with images, *Family Search* (https://familysearch.org/ ark:/61903/1:1:KWYM-V87: 28 July 2019), Maida Butler in household of Albert Butler, Ward 5, Chicago, Chicago City, Cook, Illinois, United States; citing enumeration district (ED) 103–284, sheet 13A, line 5, family 339, Sixteenth Census of the United States, 1940, NARA digital publication T627. Records of the Bureau of the Census, 1790–2007, RG 29. Washington, D.C.: National Archives and Records Administration, 2012, roll 929.

46. This account is based on "Beulah Bondi Pays Visit to Friends Here," *Vidette-Messenger* (August 1, 1940), p. 2 and "Bondi Feted in Valparaiso," *South Bend Tribune* (August 2, 1940), p. 8.

47. "Curtain Falls for Playwright," *Los Angeles Times* (March 14, 1941), p. 16: "History," *The Shepherd of the Hills*, catalog.afi.com.

48. Harold W. Cohen, "The Drama Desk," *Pittsburgh Post-Gazette* (July 9, 1940), p. 8.

49. "California, County Birth and Death Records, 1800–1994," database with images, *Family Search* (https://familysearch.org/ark:/61903/1:1:-QGJ9-P9PG: 22 October 2019), Stuart Walker, 1941.

50. Harold V. Cohen, "The New Films," *Pittsburgh Post-Gazette* (July 19, 1941), p. 19.

51. Edward E. Gloss, "On with the Show: Story of Hills Is Impressive in Technicolor," *Akron Beacon Journal* (July 26, 1941), p. 8; Edna B. Lawson, "At the Theaters: 'Shepherd of Hills Plays at Hawaii," *Honolulu Advertiser* (November 17, 1941), p. 6; T.S., "The Screen in Review," *New York Times* (July 31, 1941), p. 13.

52. Harold W. Cohen, "The Drama Desk," *Pittsburgh Post-Gazette* (December 2, 1940), p. 27.

53. Boyd Martin, "Films Opening Here Friday Give Prospects of Best Entertainment Recently," *Louisville Courier-Journal* (April 24, 1941), p. 2.

54. "Stage Struck," *Modern Screen* [1937] (NYPL).

55. Vernon Scott, "Beulah Bondi: She's Never Acted Her Age," *Redlands Daily Facts* (December 26, 1975), p. B6.

56. Bosley Crowther, "The Screen in Review,"

New York Times (May 23, 1941), p. 25; Edna B. Lawson, "Grant, Miss Dunne Shine at Waikiki," *Honolulu Advertiser* (September 28, 1941), p. 3.

57. "Tattletale," *Los Angeles Times* (December 1, 1940), p. 7; "Mickey Rooney in the Radio Theater," *Belvedere Daily Republican* (December 23, 1940), p. 5; Ed Sullivan, "Little Old New York," *Pittsburgh Post-Gazette* (December 26, 1940), p. 20; Burdette Jay, "In Hollywood," *Santa Rosa Press Democrat* (December 28, 1940), p. 6.

58. "Final Chapter Written in Club Debt Thursday," *Vidette-Messenger* (December 1, 1939), p. 2.

59. "District Clubs Endorse Mrs. Oscar A. Ahlgren for Indiana President," *Munster Times* (October 18, 1940), p. 16.

60. "California, County Birth and Death Records, 1800–1994," database with images, *Family Search* (https://familysearch.org/ark:/61903/1:1:-QP4D-1B3D: 22 August 2018), Eva Marble Bondy, 1941.

61. "Local Brevities," *Vidette-Messenger* (June 2, 1941), p. 2.

62. Eva Marble Bondy, "California, County Birth and Death Records, 1800–1994"; "Mrs. E. Bondy Dies in West," *Vidette-Messenger* (June 9, 1941), p. 1.

63. Eva Marble Bondy, "California, County Birth and Death Records, 1800–1994"; "Obituary: Mrs. Eva Marble Bondy," *Los Angeles Times* (June 11, 1941), p. 16 (with death notice); "Mrs. E. Bondy Dies in West," p. 1. The chapel building is still there at the corner of Calvert St., but is now a law office.

64. Bondy, *Worldkins*, p. 124.

65. "Woman's Clubs: Plans and Programs," *Vidette-Messenger* (June 21, 1941), p. 2.

66. Bertram R. Marks to Beulah Bondi, September 29, 1941 (BBP 3.3) was sent to this address.

67. The first record of her living here is a voter registration from 1942 (movielanddirectory.com) and a news item in the *Los Angeles Times* for October 6, 1942, stating that she was hosting a luncheon for the League for Crippled Children at this address.

68. Ben Irvin Butler, "Walter Winchell: Gustatory Habits of the Stars," *Alabama Journal* (August 19, 1942), p. 4.

69. Bessie M. Gant, "Beulah Bondi, Character Actress, Gives You Her Recipe for 'Bean Soup,'" *Pittsburgh Courier* (February 6, 1943), p. 11.

70. Hunter, *Tab Hunter Confidential*, pp. 97–98.

71. Aversano, "Dear Beulah," p. 34.

72. Paul Walker, "Review and Previews," *Harrisburg Telegraph* (July 16, 1941), p. 12.

73. I profiled Watson in Nissen, *Actresses of a Certain Character*, pp. 202–8.

74. Edwin Schallert, "Reel Notes Reeled Off Briefly," *Los Angeles Times* (June 11, 1942), p. 14; catalog.afi.com.

75. Bosley Crowther, "The Screen," *New York Times* (August 28, 1943), p. 15.

76. Lillian Hellman, *Six Plays by Lillian Hellman* (New York: Vintage, 1979), p. 241, 245.

77. Crowther, "The Screen," p. 15; Edwin Schallert, "'Watch on the Rhine,' Dynamic Prewar Opus," *Los Angeles Times* (September 16, 1943), p.

14; Mildred Martin, "Watch on the Rhine Opens on Boyd Screen," *Philadelphia Inquirer* (August 27, 1943), p. 17; Kaspar Monahan, "Show Shops: 'Watch on the Rhine' a Stirring Picture," *Pittsburgh Press* (September 3, 1943), p. 26; Len G. Shaw, "Anti-Fascist Drama in Striking Presentation," *Detroit Free Press* (October 16, 1943), p. 10.

78. Bosley Crowther, "The Screen," *New York Times* (April 15, 1943), p. 20.

79. Katherine von Blon, "Brentwood Groups Scores with Three One-Act Plays," *Los Angeles Times* (June 3, 1943), p. 16.

80. Katherine von Blon, "Many Varieties of Humor Regale Brentwood Guests," *Los Angeles Times* (July 26, 1943), p. 11; "Beulah Bondi Play Selected," *Los Angeles Times* (August 9, 1943), p. 16.

81. Edwin Schallert, "Maternal Movie Roles Become Astor Routine," *Los Angeles Times* (July 5, 1943), p. 17; catalog.afi.com.

82. "'Our Hearts Were Young and Gay' at State Theatre," *McComb Daily Journal* (December 13, 1944), p. 3.

83. I profiled Kruger in Nissen, *Mothers, Mammies and Old Maids*, pp. 131–38.

84. catalog.afi.com.

85. A.W., *Our Hearts Were Young and Gay* review, *New York Times* (October 12, 1944), p. 24.

86. Joseph Cummings Chase to Beulah Bondi, August 5, 1942 (BBP 3.1).

87. Hedda Hopper, "Looking at Hollywood," *Los Angeles Times* (October 1, 1943), p. 14.

88. Hedda Hopper, "Hedda Hopper's Hollywood," *Honolulu Advertiser* (February 14, 1944), p. 6. See also "Beulah Bondi Keeping Busy," *Vidette-Messenger* (January 22, 1945), p. 5.

89. Avery B. Weaver, "Film Star Beulah Bondi Re-Visits City," *Vidette-Messenger* (July 24, 1945), p. 1.

90. Advertisement, *Los Angeles Times* (August 10, 1943), p. 3.

91. "Women's Activities: Today," *Los Angeles Times* (October 6, 1942), p. 5.

92. Margaret McKay, "Fashion Scene," *McKinney Courier-Gazette* (May 14, 1943), p. 4; "Beulah Bondi Keeping Busy," p. 5.

93. "I Love a Soldier," *Sydney Morning Herald* (July 2, 1945), p. 5.

94. Bosley Crowther, "The Screen," *New York Times* (November 2, 1944), p. 22; Kaspar Monahan, "Show Shops: Paulette and Sonny Romancing Again," *Pittsburgh Press* (August 26, 1944), p. 6; "'I Love a Soldier' Showing at the Paramount," *Jackson Sun* (September 3, 1944), p. 11; Edwin Schallert, "Tufts, Goddard Enliven Romantic Comedy of War," *Los Angeles Times* (October 13, 1944), p. 11.

95. catalog.afi.com.

96. Bosley Crowther, "The Screen: Lip-Reading in Film," *New York Times* (November 23, 1944), p. 38.

97. catalog.afi.com.

98. See Philip K. Scheuer, "Lusty Movie Made from 'Hairy Ape,' O'Neill Play," *Los Angeles Times* (August 18, 1944), p. 11; *She's a Soldier Too* advertisement, *Akron Beacon Journal* (September

23, 1944), p. 7; and "At the Theatres," *Lancaster Eagle-Gazette* (December 26, 1944), p. 9.

99. Vernon Scott, "Murder Is His Business, Pays Off in Boxoffice," *Sandusky Register* (November 4, 1964), p. 30.

100. catalog.afi.com.

101. Lorraine LoBianco, "The Very Thought of You," tcm.com.

102. T.M.P., *The Very Thought of You* review, *New York Times* (November 18, 1944), p. 16.

103. T.M.P., p 16; Tom Birks, "'Very Thought of You' Amiable in Penn," *Pittsburgh Sun-Telegraph* (December 8, 1944), p. 26; Corbin Patrick, "Defends War Brides," *Indianapolis Star* (December 7, 1944), p. 16; "Paramount Offers Service Morale Story with Appeal to Family," *Jackson Sun* (January 14, 1945), p. 11; George L. David, "Century's 'Very Thought of You' Warmly Human, Finely Acted," *Rochester Democrat and Chronicle* (January 11, 1945), p. 8.

104. "Mrs. Sure, Former U.W. Regent, Dies," p. 1; "Former Regent, Mrs. Sure, Dies," p. 2; "Obituary: Dr. Julius Hilton Sure," *Wisconsin Jewish Chronicle* (August 27, 1943), p. 3; Leola Hirschman Sure, Julius H. Sure, findagrave.com.

105. "Two Regents Are Named by Blaine," p. 1.

106. "Obituary: Dr. Julius Hilton Sure," p. 3.

107. This account based on "Bequests Willed to Jewish Institutions," *Wisconsin Jewish Chronicle* (May 26, 1944), p. 5; Rose E. Hirschman, findagrave.com.

108. "New Films Reviewed," *Sydney Morning Herald* (June 3, 1946), p. 5.

109. Hedda Hopper, "Looking at Hollywood," *Los Angeles Times* (September 7, 1944), p. 9; catalog.afi.com.

110. catalog.afi.com.

111. Robert H. Allen, "'Southerner' Exceptional as Sharecropper Picture," *Cincinnati Enquirer* (October 18, 1945), p. 17; Betty French, "On with the Show: 'The Southerner' Great Document," *Akron Beacon Journal* (August 24, 1945), p. 12; *The Southerner* review, *Quad-City Times* (December 2, 1945), p. 33; Dorothy Raymer, "Show Time," *Miami News* (December 12, 1945), p. 6B; Tom Birks, "'Southerner Soil Drama in Penn," *Pittsburgh Sun-Telegraph* (December 21, 1945), p. 16.

112. "New Films Reviewed," p. 5; Donald Kirkley, "Two New Photoplays on Downtown Screens," *Baltimore Sun* (August 25, 1945), p. 8; Edwin Schallert, "Rural Hardships Well Shown in 'Southerner,'" *Los Angeles Times* (October 4, 1945), p. 9; A.W., "The Screen," *New York Times* (August 27, 1945), p. 22 (this review is erroneously attributed to Bosley Crowther on the Turner Classic Movies website); Kaspar Monahan, "Show Shops: Penn's 'Southerner' Drama of the Soil," *Pittsburgh Press* (December 21, 1945), p. 28.

113. catalog.afi.com.

114. "MacArthur Makes History and a Movie," *Macon Chronicle-Herald* (December 7, 1944), p. 6.

115. Weaver, "Film Star Beulah Bondi Re-Visits City," p. 1.

116. "Character Research," *Brooklyn Daily Eagle* (November 27, 1932), p. E1.

117. catalog.afi.com.

118. Edwin Schallert, "Ireland of Stage Wins Stellar Role in Film," *Los Angeles Times* (November 11, 1944), p. 13.

119. Boyd Martin, "Bataan Story at Rialto Based on Raw History," *Louisville Courier-Journal* (July 6, 1945), p. 4; Donald Kirkley, "'Back to Bataan,'" *Baltimore Sun* (August 3, 1945), p. 12; "Orpheum Review: 'Back to Bataan,'" *Davenport Daily Times* (August 3, 1945), p. 11; Jane Corby, "Screen," *Brooklyn Daily Eagle* (October 8, 1945), p. 13; Crosby Day, "Classic Movies: A Stirring Salute to the Heroes of War," *Orlando Sentinel* (July 8, 2001), p. 17; Bill Diehl, "Bataan Film Is Vivid Story of Guerilla Help," *Newark Advocate* (July 9, 1945), p. 7; Harold V. Cohen, "The New Film," *Pittsburgh Post-Gazette* (August 20, 1945), p. 20; "Bataan Drama Shown at Fox," *Arizona Republic* (July 22, 1945), p. 6; Bosley Crowther, "The Screen: More Heroics," *New York Times* (September 13, 1945), p. 26.

## Chapter 7

1. Bondi quoted in John Archibald, "TV Comment," *St. Louis Post-Dispatch* (January 6, 1976), p. 34.

2. "Illinois, Cook County Deaths, 1878–1994," database, *Family Search* (https://familysearch.org/ark:/61903/1:1:Q2MD-KXG1: 18 March 2018), Maida Searles Butler, 03 May 1943; citing Chicago, Cook, Illinois, United States, source reference, record number, Cook County Courthouse, Chicago; FHL microfilm; Maida S. Butler, findagrave.com.

3. Avery B. Weaver, "Film Star Beulah Bondi Re-Visits City; Hints Her Next Role in Theater," p. 1.

4. "Miss Bondi is Week-End Guest at Mt. Carroll," *Freeport Journal-Standard* (July 31, 1945), p. 8.

5. "Guests at Hazelwood for the Weekend," *Dixon Evening Telegraph* (July 31, 1945), p. 5.

6. "Breakfast Role Set for Bonita," *Brooklyn Daily Eagle* (August 13, 1945), p. 5.

7. This account is based on information from "Tom Breneman, Radio Star, Dies Suddenly," *Los Angeles Times* (April 29, 1948), p. 1; "Tom Breneman, 48, Radio Leader, Dies," *New York Times* (April 29, 1948), p. 23; "Breneman Dies Suddenly: Heart Attack Fatal to Radio Performer," *San Francisco Examiner* (April 29, 1948), p. 3; and John Dunning, *On the Air: The Encyclopedia of Old-Time Radio* (New York: Oxford University Press, 1998), pp. 112–14. The final quote is from "Breneman Dies Suddenly," p. 3.

8. "Summing Up the Cinema," *Harrisburg Evening News* (May 16, 1946), p. 28; "The New Films," *Indianapolis News* (May 24, 1946), p. 12; "Breneman in 'Breakfast' at the Stanton," *Philadelphia Inquirer* (June 20, 1946), p. 26; John L. Scott, "'Breakfast' Enjoyed at Music Halls," *Los Angeles Times* (March 15, 1946), p. 7.

9. Bob Thomas, "'War Is Over' in Hollywood," *Decatur Daily* (November 1, 1945), p. 5.

10. Wood Soanes, "Kenny Polio Fight Comes to

Screen," *Oakland Tribune* (December 11, 1946), p. 16.

11. Harrison Carroll, "Hollywood Behind the Scenes," *Santa Rosa Press Democrat* (December 1, 1945), p. 12.

12. Harrison Carroll, "Behind the Scenes in Hollywood," *Wilkes-Barre Record* (January 1, 1946), p. 13.

13. "Beulah Bondi Sees Miami at Long Last," *Miami News* (January 11, 1945), p. 1B.

14. "Star Beulah Bondi" at Lincoln Theater," *Miami News* (February 8, 1946), p. 16-A.

15. "Character Actress Visits at Beach," *Fort Myers News-Press* (February 13, 1946), p. 7.

16. Louella O. Parsons, "Gary Cooper to Lead in New DeMille Epic," *San Francisco Examiner* (March 5, 1946), p. 9. See also Hedda Hopper, "Looking at Hollywood," *Los Angeles Times* (April 15, 1946), p. 7.

17. "Stewart Scores in Comeback," *Binghamton Press and Sun-Bulletin* (January 31, 1947), p. 18.

18. Edwin Schallert, "Stone 'Sleeper' Film; Korda Signs Falstaff," *Los Angeles Times* (May 14, 1946), p. 3; catalog.afi.com.

19. "Disney Premiere Here to Be Hollywood Style," *Indianapolis Star* (January 7, 1949), p. 21; "History," *So Dear to My Heart*, catalog.afi.com.

20. Hedda Hopper, "Davis, Wyman Wanted for 'Serenade' Leads," *Los Angeles Times* (January 7, 1949), p. 12.

21. "Known as Bicycling," *Pittsburgh Post-Gazette* (August 29, 1946), p. 15.

22. "Amusements," *Warren Times Mirror* (May 12, 1949), p. 2.

23. Mae Tinee, "Beulah Bondi Engaging Off Screen or On," *Chicago Tribune* (February 13, 1949), p. 17.

24. "So Dear to My Heart," tcm.com.

25. Hopper, "Davis, Wyman Wanted," p. 12.

26. Myles Standish, "The New Films," *St. Louis Post-Dispatch* (April 8, 1949), p. 2F.

27. Edwin Schallert, "'On Borrowed Time' Stage Event of Marked, Quality," *Los Angeles Times* (November 6, 1946), p. 6.

28. Hedda Hopper, "Looking at Hollywood," *Los Angeles Times* (November 8, 1946), p. 7.

29. Virginia MacPherson, "No Place Too Dangerous for Movie Fans," *Muncie Star Press* (September 25, 1946), p. 4.

30. catalog.afi.com.

31. "Double Feature at Palace," *Lancaster Eagle-Gazette* (September 24, 1947), p. 13.

32. catalog.afi.com.

33. Hedda Hopper, "Hollywood," *New York Daily News* (March 13, 1947), p. 66.

34. "Beulah Bondi Here to See Islands Herself," *Honolulu Star-Bulletin* (March 27, 1947), p. 9.

35. Lucille Leimert, "Confidentially," *Los Angeles Times* (April 1, 1947), p. 5.

36. "Mrs. Eaton is Hostess," *Honolulu Advertiser* (March 30, 1947), p. 1; "Valley Island News Notes," *Honolulu Star-Bulletin* (April 15, 1947), p. 14.

37. "In Brief: Volcano House Guests," *Hawaii Tribune-Herald* (April 23, 1947), p. 1; "Beulah Bondi

to Mainland," *Honolulu Advertiser* (May 18, 1947), p. 2.

38. Hedda Hopper, "Looking at Hollywood," *Los Angeles Times* (May 8, 1947), p. 3.

39. Peggy Hickock, "Beulah Bondi Describes Work Involved in Picture Production," *Honolulu Star-Bulletin* (April 19, 1947), p. 2; "Beulah Bondi Is Honor Guest," *Honolulu Star-Bulletin* (May 10, 1947), p. 12.

40. "Beulah Bondi to Mainland," p. 2.

41. catalog.afi.com.

42. Nissen, *Actresses of a Certain Character*, p. 47.

43. Edwin Schallert, "Beulah Bondi to Portray Mean Banker," *Los Angeles Times* (October 3, 1947), p. 9.

44. Philip K. Scheuer, "Fitzgerald Undertakes 'Sisters' Rescue," *Los Angeles Times* (May 7, 1948), p. 18; Leonard Mendlowitz, "Veronica and Joan Sisters," *Pittsburgh Sun-Telegraph* (April 23, 1948), p. 25.

45. Harold Heffernan, "Movie Chatter Confusion in Hollywood," *St. Louis Post-Dispatch* (December 14, 1947) n.pag.

46. "Studio Briefs," *Los Angeles Times* (July 6, 1948), p. 22.

47. "Eve Arden in La Jolla Play," *Los Angeles Times* (July 8, 1948), p. 23.

48. Robert Emmet Sherwood, "The Road to Rome," *The Best Plays of 1926–27*, ed. Burns Mantle (New York: Dodd, Mead, 1927), p. 154.

49. Harold V. Cohen, "The Drama Desk," *Pittsburgh Post-Gazette* (July 31, 1948), p. 5. See also Sheilah Graham, "Producer Gets Big Top Fever," *Tampa Times* (September 9, 1949), p. 5.

50. Philip K. Scheuer, "Pair Ask Public to Do Own Talent Scouting," *Los Angeles Times* (August 18, 1948), p. 16; catalog.afi.com.

51. catalog.afi.com.

52. Bosley Crowther, "'The Life of Riley,' with Bendix in the Title Role," *New York Times* (April 18, 1949), p. 18.

53. Hopper, "Davis, Wyman Wanted," p. 12.

54. Tinee, "Beulah Bondi Engaging," p. 17.

55. "Radio Highlights: Beulah Bondi Stars in Porter Novelette," *Indianapolis Star* (August 17, 1948), p. 17; "Tonight's Radio Aces," *Wisconsin State Journal* (August 20, 1948), p. 6; "Radio Programs," *Hanover Evening Sun* (January 29, 1949), p. 9.

56. Tinee, "Beulah Bondi Engaging," p. 17.

57. Jack Quigg, "Hobby Mart Sells Actors' Handiwork," *Indianapolis Star* (January 2, 1949), p. 13; "Actors Hobby Market Going Out of Business," *Decatur Herald* (June 29, 1950), p. 13.

58. "Chicago Party," *Dixon Telegraph* (January 27, 1949), p. 4.

59. This account is based on "Local Brevities," *Vidette-Messenger* (January 27, 1949), p. 2; Tinee, "Beulah Bondi Engaging," p. 17.

60. Hedda Hopper, "Metro Planning Air Shows for Its Stars," *Los Angeles Times* (September 2, 1949), p. 12.

61. Harold V. Cohen, "The Drama Desk," *Pittsburgh Post-Gazette* (November 18, 1949), p. 22.

62. Edwin Schallert, "Greer Garson Gives Go-Ahead on 'Europa,'" *Los Angeles Times* (October 20, 1949), p. 11.

63. catalog.afi.com; David Sterritt, "The Baron of Arizona," tcm.com.

64. Hedda Hopper, "Preminger to Direct Andrews, Gene Tierney," *Los Angeles Times* (November 14, 1949), p. 6.

65. Edwin Schallert, "Grayson-Lanza Film Claims Opera Expert," *Los Angeles Times* (December 13, 1949), p. 11.

66. "Recall Beulah Bondi for Role in 'Furies,'" *Lansing State Journal* (January 6, 1950), p. 20.

## *Chapter 8*

1. Burkett, "Beulah Bondi Wows Shimer," p. 3A.

2. Mike Connolly, "Mike Connolly in Hollywood," *Pittsburgh Post-Gazette* (May 26, 1962), p. 5.

3. Dick Kleiner, "Looking Back on a Charmed Life."

4. Hedda Hopper, "Drama: Patricia Neal Will Play Publisher Role," *Los Angeles Times* (Aug. 24, 1950), p. 6.

5. Louella Parsons, "Louella Parsons in Hollywood," *Camden Courier-Post* (September 23, 1950), p. 13.

6. John Chapman, "'Hilda Crane' Is a Good Sex Drama," *New York Daily News* (November 3, 1950), p. 15C.

7. "Stage Lure: Casting Play Tough Time for Producer," *Philadelphia Inquirer* (October 15, 1950), p. 29, 32.

8. Mark Barron, "On Broadway," *Central New Jersey Home News* (November 30, 1950), p. 8.

9. Louis Shaeffer, "Curtain Time: 'Hilda Crane' Gripping Drama of Confused Modern Woman," *Brooklyn Daily Eagle* (November 2, 1950), p. 4.

10. Donald Kirkley, "Broadway Notes," *Baltimore Sun* (November 1, 1950), p. 12.

11. Shaeffer, "Curtain Time," p. 4.

12. Samson Raphaelson, "'Hilda Crane'—Symbol of the Modern Woman," *New York Times* (October 29, 1959), p. 97.

13. Samson Raphaelson, *Hilda Crane* (New York: Random House, 1951), p. 4, 6.

14. Jack Gaver, "'Hilda Crane' Gives Jessica Tandy New Psychotic Role Like 'Streetcar,'" *Terre Haute Star* (November 3, 1950), p. 13.

15. I profiled Varden in Nissen, *Mothers, Mammies and Old Maids*, pp. 176–83 and discuss her performance in *Hilda Crane* at length.

16. Brooks Atkinson, "At the Theatre," *New York Times* (November 2, 1950), p. 38.

17. Gaver, "'Hilda Crane,'" p. 13.

18. Henry T. Murdock, "'Hilda Crane' Given Metropolitan Premiere at Locust," *Philadelphia Inquirer* (October 17, 1950), p. 35; Gaver, "'Hilda Crane,'" p. 13; Louis Shaeffer, "Curtain Time: Samson Raphaelson's 'Hilda Crane' an Unhappy Report on Modern Woman," *Brooklyn Daily Eagle* (November 12, 1950), p. 29.

19. Gaver, "'Hilda Crane,'" p. 13; Linton Martin, "The Call Boy's Chat: Jessica Tandy Impressive in New and Notable Drama," *Philadelphia Inquirer* (October 22, 1950), p. 25; Shaeffer, "Curtain Time," p. 4.

20. Mark Barron, "Broadway: Beulah Bondi Superb in 'Hilda Crane,'" *Elmira Star-Gazette* (December 31, 1950), p. 9.

21. A.W. "The Screen: Five Newcomers Arrive Here," *New York Times* (February 2, 1952), p. 11.

22. Hedda Hopper, "Subversive Results Detected in Pictures," *Los Angeles Times* (May 21, 1951), p. 8.

23. catalog.afi.com.

24. Edwin Schallert, "Lady with Millions Has Love Grief," *Los Angeles Times* (August 29, 1953), p. 10.

25. Theresa Loeb Cone, "Victor Moore, Critics' Council Award Winner, Reminisces on Stage Career," *Oakland Tribune* (January 12, 1953), p. 12; Leonard Lyons, "The Lyons Den," *Pittsburgh Post-Gazette* (April 14, 1953), p. 23.

26. Hedda Hopper, "Drama: Ben Hecht Directing Daughter, 8, in Film," *Los Angeles Times* (August 23, 1951), p. 8.

27. Harold V. Cohen, "The Drama Desk," *Pittsburgh Post-Gazette* (September 17, 1951), p. 26.

28. Theresa Loeb Cone, "'Borrowed Time' Revived Again at S.F. Theater," *Oakland Tribune* (December 30, 1952), p. 7.

29. Theresa Loeb Cone, "Victor Moore, Critics' Council Award Winner, Reminisces on Stage Career," *Oakland Tribune* (January 12, 1953), p. 12; Lyons, "The Lyons Den," p. 23.

30. Cyrus Durgin, "The Stage: 'On Borrowed Time' Splendidly Revived," *Boston Globe* (January 23, 1953), p. 6.

31. Walter F. Kerr, "The Theaters: 'On Borrowed Time,'" *New York Herald Tribune* [Feb. 10, 1953] (NYPL).

32. John Chapman, "Victor Moore Caps His Career as 'Gramps' in 'On Borrowed Time,'" *New York Daily News* (February 11, 1953), p. 73.

33. Jack Geiger, "Curtain Time," *Sandusky Register* (February 12, 1953), p. 8.

34. Brooks Atkinson, "First Night at the Theatre," *New York Times* (February 11, 1953), p. 34.

35. "Victor Moore, 86, Comedian, Is Dead," *New York Times* (July 24, 1962), p. 27.

36. "Beulah Bondi to Recreate Granny Role," *Provo Daily Herald* (November 10, 1957), p. 28.

37. Jack O'Brian, "On the Air: Vet Ed Wynn Gives Superb Performance," *Anderson Daily Bulletin* (November 18, 1957), p. 14; Donald Kirkley, "Look and Listen with Donald Kirkley," *Baltimore Sun* (November 19, 1957), p. 16.

38. "Beulah Bondi Back in 'Borrowed Time,'" *Oakland Tribune* (January 14, 1953), p. 31.

39. See Jean Thomas to Beulah Bondi, May 9, 1929 (BBP 3.4).

40. Estelle Culmer, "For Women: Flowers, Not Theater, Dominated Conversation," *Fort Lauderdale News* (June 10, 1957), p. 2B; Hedda Hopper, "Acapulco Setting for Zugsmith Film," *Los Angeles Times*

(June 27, 1957), p. 8; "The Cove Players to Attend Show Saturday Night as Audience," *San Rafael Daily Independent Journal* (July 19, 1957), p. 15.

41. Charlotte Buchen, "'Traipsin' Woman' Is Here," *Arizona Republic* (August 10, 1957), p. 18.

42. John Chapman, "A Great Drama Returns," *New York Daily News* (August 18, 1957), p. 8.

43. Hubbard Keavy, "Director Shoots Color Film but Only in Black and White," *Oakland Tribune* (July 17, 1954), p. 4D; "Black White Top Color Film," *Miami News* (July 18, 195), p. 14D.

44. Mae Tinee, "Colors Used in New Way to Point Up Plot," *Chicago Tribune* (July 25, 1954), p. 9.

45. Philip K. Scheuer, "Wellman's New Color Film to Stress Black and White," *Los Angeles Times* (July 25, 1954), p. 4.

46. Bosley Crowther, "The Screen in Review," *New York Times* (December 2, 1954), p. 38.

47. "Behind the Scenes in Hollywood," *Pottsville Republican and Herald* (June 1, 1954), p. 7; "Paradise Valley Is Movie Setting," *Spokane Chronicle* (June 18, 1954), p. 7; Hunter, *Tab Hunter Confidential*, p. 96, 97; catalog.afi.com.

48. "Ron Burton Says," *Akron Beacon Journal* (August 24, 1954), p. 16.

49. Aversano, "Beulah Bondi: Part II," p. 32. There's a slightly different version of this story in Brown, *Actor's Talk*, p. 152.

50. Hunter, *Tab Hunter Confidential*, pp. 97–98.

51. "Bondi Tops Glamor Girls," *Pittsburgh Press* (November 25, 1954), p. 23.

52. R.H. Gardner, "Of Stage and Screen: It's Realism Plus Horror," *Baltimore Sun* (November 20, 1954), p. 8.

53. Gilbert Kanour, "On the Screen," *Baltimore Evening Sun* (November 20, 1954), p. 9; Theresa Loeb Cone, "'Track of Cat' Portrays Some Eccentric Folk," *Oakland Tribune* (November 25, 1954), p. 61.

54. Mildred Martin, "'Track of the Cat,' Combination Drama, Makes Debut on Screen at Mastbaum," *Philadelphia Inquirer* (November 26, 1954), p. 15.

55. Edwin Schallert, "Dual Film Bill Yields Fair Values," *Los Angeles Times* (November 25, 1954), p. 4; Lillian Blackstone, "'Track of the Cat,' Has Unusual Photography," *St. Petersburg Times* (January 7, 1955), p. 8.

56. Crowther, "The Screen in Review," p. 38.

57. Nissen, *Actresses of a Certain Character*, p. 48.

58. Hedda Hopper, "Hollywood," *Hartford Courant* (April 25, 1950), p. 8.

59. Heffernan, "Cupid and Career Don't Mix, Says Bondi," p. 13.

60. BBP 2.24.

61. As evidenced by the visas and stamps of arrival and departure in her passport (BBP 2.24).

62. Beulah's Bondi's passport, p. 4, 14, 18 (BBP 2.24); "New York, New York Passenger and Crew Lists, 1909, 1925–1957," database with images, *Family Search* (https://familysearch.org/ark:/61903/1:1:-2HCG-P4X: 16 March 2018), Beulah Bondy, 1955; citing Immigration, New York City, New York, United States, NARA microfilm publication T715

(Washington, D.C.: National Archives and Records Administration, n.d.).

63. Louella Parsons, "Keeping Up with Hollywood," *Cumberland News* (April 12, 1955), p. 4.

64. John Farrow to Beulah Bondi, April 26, 1956 (BBP 3.2); Edith Gwynn, "Hollywood," *Pottstown Mercury* (February 23, 1956), p. 4; catalog.afi.com.

65. "Long Beach Goes South of Border Via Hollywood: Filmland Uses Airport as Scenery for Movie," *Long Beach Independent* (March 8, 1956), p. 5.

66. "Back to California," *Louisville Courier-Journal* (March 7, 1956), p 3.

67. Bosley Crowther, "Screen: Crash Landing," *New York Times* (September 8, 1956), p. 20.

68. "160 Actors Start 'Lady and Prowler,'" *Abilene Reporter-News* (September 16, 1956), p. 1.

69. Nissen, *Actresses of a Certain Character*, p. 48.

70. "Beulah Bondi Inks RKO Pact," *Oakland Tribune* (September 6, 1956), p. 21; "Beulah Bondi Fills In," *Louisville Courier-Journal* (September 7, 1956), p. 18.

71. Hedda Hopper, "Diana Dors to Star with Robert Mitchum," *Los Angeles Times* (September 29, 1956), p. 12.

72. H.H.T., "Screen: 'Unholy Wife,'" *New York Times* (March 7, 1958), p. 17.

73. "Jackie Coogan Gets a Joe E. Lewis Role," *Fremont News-Messenger* (October 13, 1956), p. 4.

74. "Noted Actress," *Honolulu Advertiser* (April 16, 1957), p. A8.

75. "Beulah Bondi…," *Honolulu Advertiser* (March 29, 1957), p. A10.

76. "United States Census, 1900," database with images, *Family Search* (https://familysearch.org/ark:/61903/1:1:M95M-NM3: accessed 27 February 2020), Juanita M Juda in household of Maun Juda, Winchester Township, Riverside, California, United States; citing enumeration district (ED) 223, sheet 2B, family 47, NARA microfilm publication T623 (Washington, D.C.: National Archives and Records Administration, 1972); FHL microfilm 1,240,097; "United States Census, 1910," database with images, *Family Search* (https://familysearch.org/ark:/61903/1:1:MVG1-H56: accessed 27 February 2020), Frediraka Judy in household of Martin Judy, Mendocino, Sonoma, California, United States; citing enumeration district (ED) ED 146, sheet 7A, family 174, NARA microfilm publication T624 (Washington, D.C.: National Archives and Records Administration, 1982), roll 109; FHL microfilm 1,374,122; "M. Judy, Former Methodist Minister Here, Passes Away," *Albany Evening Herald* (December 22, 1924), p. 4.

77. Unless otherwise indicated, biographical information in this paragraph is from "Heart Attack Is Fatal to GOP Leader," *Honolulu Advertiser* (April 4, 1947), p. 1, 5; Mary Verploegen, "The Smart Woman: Joie de Vivre Pervades All Facets of Artist's Life," *Honolulu Star-Bulletin* (October 11, 1958), p. 15. The quote is from "Artist Juanita Vitousek Dies at 98," *Honolulu Advertiser* (August 8, 1988), p. A7.

78. Besides Bondi's 1957 passport (BBP 2.24),

sources on this trip are: "Artist to Africa," *Honolulu Advertiser* (January 26, 1958), p. D2; "Roaming the Globe Over," *Honolulu Star-Bulletin* (February 1, 1958), p. 11, 13; Mary Verploegen, "People and Parties," *Honolulu Star-Bulletin* (February 14, 1958), p. 21; Mary Verploegen, "People and Parties: Capetown to North Cape," *Honolulu Star-Bulletin* (July 31, 1958), p. 41.

79. Louella O. Parsons, "Louella's Movie-Go-'Round," *Albuquerque Journal* (September 22, 1958), p. 15.

80. Frank Miller, "The Big Fisherman (1959)," tcm.com.

81. Henry Ward, "'Big Fisherman' Powerful Drama of Biblical Times," *Pittsburgh Press* (October 9, 1959), p. 12; A.H. Weiler, "A Dedicated Story of the Man Simon—Called Peter," *New York Times* (August 6, 1959), p. 18; Helen Wallace Younge, "Hollywood Raz-Ma-Tazz Messes Up Message of 'The Big Fisherman,'" *Arizona Daily Star* (January 16, 1960), p. 4.

82. Hedda Hopper, "Polly Dropping Song Bit for Drama Role," *Los Angeles Times* (February 24, 1959), p. 24.

83. Frank Miller, "A Summer Place (1959)," tcm.com; catalog.afi.com.

84. Helen Bower, "Star Gazing: Moral Confusion," *Detroit Free Press* (November 18, 1959), p. 34.

85. Springer, "Beulah Bondi," p. 284.

86. Howard Thompson, *A Summer Place* review, *New York Times* (October 23, 1959), p. 24; R.H. Gardner, "Of Stage and Screen: 'A Hollywood Sex Horror,'" *Baltimore Sun* (November 20, 1959), p. 17.

87. Hopper, "Acapulco Setting," p. 8.

88. "Dr. Raymond Marble Bondy," *Fort Lauderdale News* (August 1, 1959), p. 8A; "Death of Dr. R. Bondy Former Resident, Told," *Vidette-Messenger* (August 4, 1959), p. 2.

89. Howard Thompson, "Tammy Tell Me True," *New York Times* (July 27, 1961), p. 23.

90. Hedda Hopper, "Hollywood," *New York Daily News* (January 2, 1961), p. 46; Philip K. Scheuer, "Judy Garland Back in 'Judgement' Role," *Los Angeles Times* (January 13, 1961), p. 7; "Filmland Events: Miss Moore Signed for U-I's 'Tammy,'" *Los Angeles Times* (January 19, 1961), p. 9.

91. Philip K. Scheuer, "Sequel to Tammy Mixture as Before," *Los Angeles Times* (July 27, 1961), p. 7; Jack Anderson, "'Tammy' Is Folksy as All Get-Out," *Oakland Tribune* (August 10, 1961), 52D.

92. Mary Verploegen, "People and Parties: Summer Exodus Begins at School's End," *Honolulu Star-Bulletin* (May 22, 1961), p. 17; "Steve," "Party Line," *Honolulu Advertiser* (June 1, 1961), p. 35.

93. Sheilah Graham, "Hollywood Today," *Paterson News* (May 22, 1961), p. 21.

94. Harold Heffernan, "Film 'Tax Refugees' Look to H'wood Again," *Philadelphia Daily News* (January 5, 1962), p. 40.

95. Rob Nixon, "The Wonderful World of the Brothers Grimm," tcm.com.

96. Bosley Crowther, "Screen: 'Wonderful World of the Brothers Grimm,'" *New York Times* (August 8, 1962), p. 35.

97. Bosstick, "Beulah Bondi Here to Present Her Mother's Book of Poems," p. 5.

98. Burkett, "Beulah Bondi Wows Shimer," p. 3A.

99. "Video Films Shot Fast and Cheap," *Akron Beacon Journal* (May 1, 1949), p. 5B; Tim Brooks and Earle Marsh, *The Complete Directory of Prime Time Network and Cable TV Shows 1946-Present* (New York: Ballantine, 2003), p. 1345.

100. "Television," *Detroit Free Press* (November 12, 1950), p. 6B; Brooks and Marsh, *The Complete Directory of Prime Time Network and Cable TV Shows*, p. 1068.

101. "Friday Television," *Los Angeles Times* (December 1, 1950), p. 26. See also "Major Variety Show at 11:00 Thursday Night," *St. Louis Post-Dispatch* (November 12, 1950), p. 5G.

102. Hedda Hopper, "Looking at Hollywood," *Honolulu Advertiser* (August 14, 1952), p. 10.

103. "TV Highlights for Week in Western North Carolina," *Asheville Citizen-Times* (December 8, 1957), p. 4D; "Stars in Drama," *Lubbock Avalanche-Journal* (December 8, 1957), p. 3.

104. Brooks and Marsh, *The Complete Directory of Prime Time Network and Cable TV Shows*, p. 942.

105. Harry Harris, "Screening TV: 'Tomorrow' Interesting in Its Fashion," *Philadelphia Inquirer* (March 8, 1960), p. 32; Ogden White, "On Television," *Des Moines Register* (March 8, 1960), p. 13; B.L., "What's On?," *New York Daily News* (March 9, 1960), p. 69; Jim Gilmore, "Bright Spots on TV's Gray Screen," *Columbus Republic* (March 12, 1960), p. 13.

106. "Matriarch Scorns Her Son's Widow," *Biddeford-Saco Journal* (December 23, 1961), p. 16; TV Guide, *Los Angeles Times* (November 25, 1962), p. 23.

107. "New Drama Series, 'Front Row Center,' Bows Today," *Opelousas Daily World* (January 8, 1956), p. 5.

108. "Sunday TV Picks," *Council Bluffs Nonpareil* (September 9, 1956), p. 5B; "Tonight's Playbill," *Rochester Democrat and Chronicle* (September 9, 1956), p. 6F; "Unhappy Role," *Allentown Morning Call* (September 15, 1956), p. 12.

109. Betty Jenkins, "Television and Radio," *Dover Daily Reporter* (January 24, 1957), p. 12.

110. "The Onlooker," "As We See It," *Binghamton Press and Sun-Bulletin* (January 27, 1957), p. 7D.

111. "Excellent Cast in Play of Week," *Ottawa Journal* (April 15, 1961), p. 2.

112. Jimmy Johnson, "Jimmy Stewart on 'Murder,'" *San Bernardino County Sun* (March 13, 1973), p. A16.

113. Green, "Beulah Bondi Back on Screen at 80," p. 21. Bondi mistakenly claims here that they had not seen each other in 25 years, but they had done an episode of *General Electric Theatre* together in 1957. It was 25 years since they did their last film together, *It's a Wonderful Life*, which was produced in 1946.

114. Hoffman, "Bondi, 83, 60 Years of Grandmothers," p. B5.

115. "Radio Television: Down South," *Rock Island Argus* (October 31, 1953), p. 12.

116. Brooks and Marsh, *The Complete Directory of Prime Time Network and Cable TV Shows*, p. 761.

117. "Late New Briefs: Beulah Bondi Stars," *Catholic Advance* (January 14, 1955), p. 4; Margaret Buhrman, "The Open Mike," *Kokomo Tribune* (January 20, 1955), p. 19; Ralph Schroeder, "Radio Chatter: Jack Bailey to Be Family Theater Host Tonight," *Janesville Daily Gazette* (January 22, 1955), p. 8.

118. Pat Hinton, "Footlight Highlights," *Altoona Mirror* (February 9, 1957), p. 7.

119. "Tonight's Previews," *Orlando Evening Star* (December 30, 1960), p. 5A.

120. TV Guide, *Miami Herald* (January 29, 1961), p. 13.

121. "Sally's Parents Split," *Charleston Sunday Gazette-Mail* (February 10, 1974), p. 12.

122. "Excellent Cast Is 'Climax' Feature," *Coshocton Tribune* (January 21, 1956), p. 5; "Handkerchief Veils Fate of Youngster," *Jefferson City Post-Tribune* (January 26, 1956), p. 16.

123. TV Guide, *Los Angeles Times* (January 8, 1961), p. 23.

124. Hedda Hopper, "Ernie Has Made It," *Detroit Free Press* (May 13, 1965), p. 15A.

125. John Archibald, "TV Comment," *St. Louis Post-Dispatch* (January 6, 1976), p. 34.

126. Witbeck, "Keynotes: 'Lincoln' Series Offers Sarah Bush Vignette," p. 24; Richard K. Shull, "At 83, Still a Character," *Indianapolis News* (January 7, 1976), p. 17; Hoffman, "Bondi, 83, 60 Years of Grandmothers," p. B5.

127. Shull, "At 83, Still a Character," p. 17.

128. Shull, p. 17; Hoffman, "Bondi, 83, 60 Years of Grandmothers," p. B5.

129. Burkett, "Beulah Bondi Wows Shimer," p. 3A; Mannies, "Beulah's Debut 47 Pages Long," p. 1; Lane, "Beulah Accents the Positive," p. 5.

130. Shull, "At 83, Still a Character," p. 17.

131. "Six to Receive Honorary Degrees from VU," *Vidette-Messenger* (April 21, 1978), p. 3; "'Be Free' to Face Career, Post-College Challenges," *Vidette-Messenger* (May 22, 1978), p. 1. See also Richard Lee to Beulah Bondi, May 1, 1978 (BBP 3.3).

132. "Mrs. Joseph Bartholomew," p. 3; "Mrs. Bartholomew," *Indianapolis Star* (September 11, 1979), p. 26; "Mrs. Bartholomew," *Indianapolis News* (September 11, 1979), p. 26; Ada Roessler Bartholomew, findagrave.com.

133. Dale Pollock, "AFI Salutes Jimmy Stewart—A Most 'Fortunate Fella,'" *Los Angeles Times* (March 1, 1980), p. 41.

134. Hoffman, "Bondi, 83, 60 Years of Grandmothers," p. B5.

135. Hoffman, p. B5. See also Kleiner, "Looking Back on a Charmed Life."

136. Green, "Beulah Bondi Back on Screen at 80," p. 21.

137. Shirley Eder, "TV Show Looks for a Male '10,'" *Philadelphia Daily News* (September 19, 1980), p. 37.

138. Watters and Horst, *Return Engagement*, p. 116.

139. Ted Thackrey, Jr., "Actress Beulah Bondi Dies at 92: Spent 50-Year Film Career Playing Elderly Women," *Los Angeles Times* (January 12, 1981), p. 3, 14.

140. "Beulah Bondi Rites Planned," *Los Angeles Times* (January 13, 1981), p. 13; "Memorial for Beulah Bondi Attended by 200," *San Bernardino County Sun* (January 16, 1981), p. B11.

# Bibliography

Aversano, Frank. "Beulah Bondi: Part II," *American Classic Screen* 3.5 (May/June 1979): 32–36.

Aversano, Frank A. "Dear Beulah: Reflection on the Long and Distinguished Career of Beulah Bondi." *American Classic Screen* 3.4 (March–April 1979): 33–37.

Barrow, Kenneth. *Helen Hayes: First Lady of the American Theatre.* Garden City, NY: Doubleday, 1985.

Besier, Rudolf. *Don.* New York: Duffield, 1910.

Brooks, Tim, and Earle Marsh. *The Complete Directory of Prime Time Network and Cable TV Shows 1946-Present.* New York: Ballantine, 2003.

Brown, Dennis. *Actors Talk: Profiles and Stories from the Acting Trade.* New York: Limelight Editions, 1999.

*Bumstead's Valparaiso City and Porter County Directory 1902.* Chicago: Bumstead, 1902.

*Bumstead's Valparaiso City Directory 1905.* Chicago: Bumstead, 1905.

*Catalogue of Copyright Entries: Part 1, Group 3 Dramatic Compositions and Motion Pictures—Vol. 8 for 1935 Nos. 1–12.* Washington: United States Government Printing Office, 1936.

Chambers, C. Haddon. *The Saving Grace.* New York: Brentano's, 1919.

Craven, Frank. *The First Year: A Comic Tragedy of Married Life.* New York: Samuel French, 1921.

Crothers, Rachel. *Mary the Third. "Old Lady 31." A Little Journey: Three Plays by Rachel Crothers.* New York: Brentano's, 1923.

Dunning, John. *On the Air: The Encyclopedia of Old-Time Radio.* New York: Oxford University Press, 1998.

Dunning, Philip, and George Abbott. *Broadway.* New York: French, 1956.

Eyman, Scott. *Print the Legend: The Life and Times of John Ford.* Baltimore: Johns Hopkins University Press, 2000.

Ferris, Lesley. "Kit and Guth: A Lavender Marriage on Broadway." *Passing Performances: Queer Reading of Leading Players in American Theater History.* Ed. Robert A. Schanke and Kim Marra. Ann Arbor: U of Michigan P, 1998. 197–220.

Hellman, Lillian. *Six Plays by Lillian Hellman.* New York: Vintage, 1979.

Kaufman, George S., et al. *Kaufman & Co.: Broadway Comedies.* New York: Library of America, 2004.

Kendall, Elizabeth. *The Runaway Bride: Hollywood Romantic Comedy of the 1930s.* New York: Alfred A. Knopf, 1990.

Kenyon, Charles. *Kindling.* New York: Samuel French, 1914.

Lamparski, Richard. *Whatever Became of...?* 8th Series. New York: Crown, 1982.

Lewis, Sinclair. *Arrowsmith.* New York: Grosset and Dunlap, 1925.

Mantle, Burns, ed. *The Best Plays of 1919–20.* Boston: Small, Maynard, 1920.

_____, ed. *The Best Plays of 1924–1925.* Boston: Small, Maynard.

_____, ed. *The Best Plays of 1928–1929.* New York: Dodd, Mead, 1929.

_____, ed. *The Best Plays of 1929–1930.* New York: Dodd, Mead, 1969.

_____, ed. *The Best Plays of 1931–1932.* New York: Dodd, Mead, 1932.

_____, ed. *The Best Plays of 1932–1933.* New York: Dodd, Mead, 1933.

Maugham, W. Somerset. *The Collected Plays of W. Somerset Maugham: Vol. II.* London: William Heinemann, 1931.

Miller, Alice Duer, and Robert Milton. *The Charm School.* London: Samuel French, 1922.

Nissen, Axel. *Actresses of a Certain Character: Forty Familiar Hollywood Faces from the Thirties to the Fifties.* Jefferson, NC: McFarland, 2006.

_____. *Mothers, Mammies and Old Maids: Twenty-Five Character Actresses of Golden Age Hollywood.* Jefferson, NC: McFarland, 2012.

Parker, John. *Who's Who in the Theatre: A Biographical Record of the Contemporary Stage.* 7th ed. London: Pitman, 1933.

Potempa, Phil. "The Beloved Mother: Beulah Bondi." In *It's a Wonderful Life: A Memory Book* by Stephen Cox. Nashville, TN: Cumberland House, 2003. 62–67.

Raphaelson, Samson. *Hilda Crane.* New York: Random House, 1951.

Rice, Elmer. *Minority Report: An Autobiography.* London: Heineman, 1963.

_____. *3 Plays.* New York: Hill and Wang, 1965.

Rice, Elmer, and Philip Barry. *Cock Robin: A Play in Three Acts.* New York: Samuel French, 1929.

Sherwood, Robert Emmet. "The Road to Rome." *The Best Plays of 1926–27*. Ed. Burns Mantle. New York: Dodd, Mead, 1927. 153–92.

Sikov, Ed. *Screwball: Hollywood's Madcap Romantic Comedies*. New York: Crown, 1989.

Slide, Anthony, ed. *Selected Theatre Criticism: Volume 2, 1920–1930*. Metuchen, NJ: Scarecrow Press, 1985.

Springer, John. "Beulah Bondi: Her Career Is Proof that 'Character Work' Is Also an Art." *Films in Review* (May 1963): 282–91.

Thompson, Howard. *James Stewart*. New York: Pyramid, 1974.

Totheroh, Dan. "Wild Birds." *The Best Plays of 1924–1925*. Ed. Burns Mantle. Boston: Small, Maynard. 384–417.

Tranberg, Charles. *Fred MacMurray: A Biography*. Albany, GA: BearManor Media, 2007.

*Valparaiso City Directory 1885–86*. Valparaiso, IN: Talcott and Tevis, 1885.

*Valparaiso City Directory 1893*. Chicago: Kraft and Radcliffe, 1893.

Watters, James, and Horst P. Horst. *Return Engagement: Faces to Remember Then and Now*. New York: Clarkson N. Potter, 1984.

Webb, Kenneth. *One of the Family: A Comedy in Three Acts*. New York and London: D. Appleton, 1926.

Wilson, Victoria. *A Life of Barbara Stanwyck: Steel-True, 1907–1940*. New York: Simon & Schuster, 2013.

Wodehouse, P.G. *Piccadilly Jim*. London: Herbert Jenkins, n.d.

Yeoman, JoAnn. *Dream Dealer: Stuart Walker and the American Theater*. Scottsdale, AZ: Star Cloud Press, 2007.

Young, Jordan R. *Reel Characters: Great Movie Character Actors*. Beverly Hills, CA: Moonstone Press, n.d.

# Index

Numbers in **_bold italics_** indicate pages with illustrations

**237**